WORLD SOCCER RECORDS

This edition published in 2014

Copyright © Carlton Books Limited 2014

Carlton Books Limited
20 Mortimer Street
London W1T 3JW

A CIP catalogue record for this book is
available from the British Library

10 9 8 7 6 5 4 3 2 1

ISBN: 978-1-78097-575-7

Editor: Martin Corteel
Designers: Darren Jordan, Luke Griffin &
Katie Baxendale
Picture research: Paul Langan
Production: Rachel Burgess

Printed in Dubai

Right: Germany captain Philipp
Lahm raises the FIFA World
Cup after his team's 1-0 extra-
time defeat of Argentina in the
2014 Final at Rio de Janeiro's
Maracana Stadium.

Next pages (left to right): Top:
Manuel Neuer (Germany), Arjen
Robben (Netherlands): Middle:
Cristiano Ronaldo (Portugal),
Paul Pogba (France), Thomas
Muller (Germany); Bottom: James
Rodriguez (Colombia), Neymar
(Brazil), Lionel Messi (Argentina).

WORLD SOCCER RECORDS

SIXTH EDITION

KEIR RADNEDGE

CARLTON
BOOKS

CONTENTS

INTRODUCTION

WHEN Brazil and Croatia kicked off the FIFA World Cup finals in Sao Paulo on June 12, 2014, not even the most optimistic soccer fan expected the engrossing totality of the drama ahead.

Nothing cautious, nothing negative. Instead, day after day, game after game, the 32 contenders generated excitement and entertainment beyond anything previously seen at soccer's greatest showpiece.

The tournament produced a record 136 goals in the group stage and a record-equaling 171 across the entire 64 matches. These included 37 in the first four days, the most exciting start to the finals since 1958. Also the finals saw the lowest number of red cards (10) in 28 years and the fewest yellows (177) since 1990.

Not all the records were happy ones. Hosts Brazil suffered the worst defeat in its history by 7-1 in the semi-finals and it was small consolation that Germany, its conquerors, would become the first European winners of the FIFA World Cup in the Americas.

Yet the FIFA World Cup is merely the foreground of a great soccer landscape whose many aspects feature in this latest, sixth edition of *World Soccer Records*. Here are not only the FIFA World Cup finals but all of soccer's major international tournaments, for men and women, at senior and junior levels.

Much of the fascination and attraction of soccer is how a framework of individual brilliance contributes to the overall construction of a team. Hence the achievements of a Germany, an Argentina, a Netherlands, and a Brazil, are built on the individual contributions of a Gotze, a Messi, a Robben, and a Neymar.

The 2014 FIFA World Cup actually kicked off on June 15, 2011, at the Ato Boldon Stadium in Couva, Trinidad and Tobago. Belize beat Montserrat 5-2 in the first of 824 qualifying ties. Deon McCauley of Belize wrote his name into soccer history with the first goal of the entire tournament, in the 24th minute.

Not until seven minutes from the end of extra time in the very final match did Mario Gotze conjure up the magnificent winning strike. But an awful lot of soccer took place in between those two goals ... as these pages illustrate.

Keir Radnedge
London, July 2014

A spectacular fireworks display lights up the Rio de Janeiro skyline as the Maracana stadium and hosts Brazil bid a fond farewell to the 2014 FIFA World Cup finals, arguably the most exciting of the 20 tournaments to date.

PART 1:
FIFA ALL-TIME RECORDS
WORLD CUP

Germany, in Brazil, became the fourth country to win the FIFA World Cup at least four times, the same as Italy. However, Brazil remains the record-holder, with five victories, inspired by superstars from Pele and Garrincha to Ronaldo and Ronaldinho. Argentina and Uruguay (two each) are the other South American winners, with further past champions from Europe being England, France, and Spain (one apiece). Germany's 2014 glory was its first FIFA World Cup as Germany; the other three were as West Germany.

Four-star joy for Germany as its players show off the FIFA World Cup after winning the 2014 Final in Brazil, and thus earning the right to have four stars on its shirts—one for each FIFA World Cup won by the nation.

BALLON D'ORIBE

Mexico booked the final spot at the 2014 FIFA World Cup by beating Oceania representatives New Zealand 9-3 on aggregate in a two-legged play-off in November 2013. Caretaker coach Miguel Herrera—Mexico's fourth boss of the year—earned himself the job permanently by masterminding wins by 5-1 at home and 4-2 away. His squad relied purely on domestic-based players, meaning there were no European-based stars such as Villarreal's Giovani dos Santos or Manchester United's Javier Hernandez. The goalscoring hero was **Oribe Peralta**, who scored five goals in the two games, including the first three of the 4-2 victory in Wellington's Westpac Stadium.

T&T AT FULL STRETCH

Trinidad and Tobago share the record for the most games played to qualify for a FIFA World Cup finals. It played 20 in reaching the 2006 finals, beginning with 2-0 away and 4-0 home wins over the Dominican Republic in the preliminaries. T&T then finished second behind Mexico at the four-team first group stage to reach the six-team final group. After finishing fourth, it had to play off against Bahrain and won 2-1 on aggregate. Uruguay matched that figure in 2010, with 18 South America group matches and a two-legged play-off.

UAE IN A SQUEEZE

The **United Arab Emirates** reached the finals in 1990 by recording just one win and scoring only four goals in the Asian final round. It drew four of its five matches, but beat China 2-1 to qualify in second place, behind South Korea.

BIG BOS MAN

Bosnia and Herzegovina was the only first-time qualifier among the 32 nations at the 2014 FIFA World Cup. After losing to Portugal in play-offs for both the 2010 FIFA World Cup and the 2012 UEFA European Championship, it secured a place at the 2014 tournament by topping its qualification group, ahead of Greece on goal difference. Its coach since 2009 was Bosnian-born, and former Yugoslavia and Paris Saint-Germain midfielder, Safet Susic.

FIFA OPENS WORLD CUP TO THE WORLD

FIFA has enlarged the World Cup finals twice since 1978, to take account of the rising soccer nations of Africa and Asia. The rise in interest is reflected in the massive number of countries entering the competition, 204 for the 2014 event. Brazilian **João Havelange**, FIFA president from 1974 to 1998, enlarged the organization both to take advantage of commercial opportunities and to give smaller nations a chance. The number of teams in the finals was first increased from 16 to 24 for the 1982 finals in Spain, with an extra place given to both Africa and Asia, and a chance for a nation from Oceania to reach the finals. The number of finalists was further increased to 32 for the 1998 tournament in France.

TAKING AIM

The 2014 World Cup culminated in a final staged in Rio's Maracana Stadium. Some 203 countries initially entered the qualifying competition, two fewer than the record 205 tilting at South Africa in 2010. The Bahamas and Mauritius later withdrew from the 2014 qualifying competition, bringing the Brazil-bound contenders down to 201. The host nation, Brazil did not have to qualify and five other FIFA member states did not enter. Newly independent country South Sudan joined FIFA too late to compete, while four more nations opted not to take part this time: Bhutan, Brunei, Guam, and Mauritania.

ALL-TIME QUALIFICATIONS BY REGIONAL CONFEDERATION

1	Europe	231
2	South America	80
3	Africa	39
=	North/Central America & Caribbean	39
5	Asia	32
6	Oceania	4

THE FIRST SHOOT-OUT

The first penalty shoot-out in qualifying history came on January 9, 1977, when Tunisia beat Morocco 4-2 on spot-kicks after a 1-1 tie in Tunis. The first game, in Casablanca, had also finished 1-1. Tunisia went on to qualify for the finals.

SPANISH INVINCIBLES

Several countries have qualified for a FIFA World Cup without losing or even tying a single game. But the Spain team that cruised its way through to the 2010 tournament in South Africa was the first to do so while playing as many as 10 games. Qualifying for the same finals, but from a smaller group, the Netherlands won eight games out of eight. West Germany also went through eight games without dropping a point in reaching the 1982 FIFA World Cup in Spain, and Brazil won six out of six in qualifying for the 1970 competition—where Mario Zagallo's men won another six out of six on its way to lifting the trophy.

BAH HUMBUG

The Bahamas failed to qualify for Brazil despite winning all its games—or, rather, both of them. The CONCACAF country beat Turks and Caicos Islands 4-0 and then 6-0 in its first-round tie, but had to pull out of the competition because rebuilding work on its national arena, the Thomas A Robinson Stadium, was not completed in time for the second-round group games.

THE GROWTH OF THE QUALIFYING COMPETITION

This charts the number of countries entering qualifiers for the FIFA World Cup finals. Some withdrew before playing.

World Cup	Teams entering
Uruguay 1930	-
Italy 1934	32
France 1938	37
Brazil 1950	34
Switzerland 1954	45
Sweden 1958	55
Chile 1962	56
England 1966	74
Mexico 1970	75
West Germany 1974	99
Argentina 1978	107
Spain 1982	109
Mexico 1986	121
Italy 1990	116
USA 1994	147
France 1998	174
Japan/South Korea 2002	199
Germany 2006	198
South Africa 2010	205
Brazil 2014	203

BYERS MARKS IT

Three players shared the title of 11-goal top scorer in qualifiers for the 2014 FIFA World Cup: Dutch striker Robin van Persie and Uruguay's Luis Suarez, whose teams both qualified for Brazil, and Belize's **Deon McCaulay**. Antigua and Barbuda's Peter Byers was the only man to score two separate hat-tricks during the campaign, both against the US Virgin Islands.

THE FASTEST SUBSTITUTION

The quickest-ever substitution in the history of FIFA World Cup qualifiers came on December 30, 1980, when North Korea's Chon Byong Ju was substituted in the first minute of his country's home game against Japan.

KOSTADINOV STUNS FRANCE

On November 17, 1993, in the last game of the Group Six schedule, Bulgaria's Emil Kostadinov scored one of the most dramatic goals in qualifying history to deny France a place at the 1994 finals. France seemed to be cruising with the score at 1-1 in stoppage time, but Kostadinov earned Bulgaria a shock victory after David Ginola lost possession. The Bulgarians reached the semifinal of the tournament in the United States, losing 2-1 to Italy.

PALMER BEATS THE WHISTLE

Carl Erik Palmer's second goal in Sweden's 3-1 win over the Republic of Ireland in November 1949 was one of the most bizarre in FIFA World Cup qualifying history. Ireland's defenders stopped, having heard a whistle, while Palmer ran on and put the ball in the net. The goal stood, because the whistle had come from someone in the crowd, not the referee. The 19-year-old forward went on to complete a hat-trick.

BWALYA LEAVES IT LATE

Zambia's **Kalusha Bwalya** is the oldest player to have scored a match-winning goal in a FIFA World Cup qualifying match. The 41-year-old netted the only goal against Liberia on September 4, 2004, after coming on as a substitute. He had also scored in his first qualifier, 20 years earlier, in a 3-0 Zambia victory over Uganda.

AUSTRALIA'S INCREDIBLE GOAL SPREE

Australia set a FIFA World Cup qualifying record in 2001, one that is unlikely to be beaten, as the Socceroos scored 53 goals in the space of two days. The details:

April 9, 2001, Sydney: Australia 22, Tonga 0
Australia scorers: Scott Chipperfield 3, 83 mins; Damian Mori 13, 23, 40; John Aloisi 14, 24, 37, 45, 52, 63; **Kevin Muscat** (No. 2, right) 18, 30, 54, 58, 82; Tony Popovic 67; Tony Vidmar 74; David Zdrilic 78, 90; Archie Thompson 80; Con Boutsiania 87

April 11, 2001, Sydney: Australia 31, American Samoa 0
Australia scorers: Boutsiania 10, 50, 84 mins; Thompson 12, 23, 27, 29, 32, 37, 42, 45, 56, 60, 65, 68, 88; Zdrilic 13, 21, 25, 33, 58, 66, 78, 89; Vidmar 14, 80; Popovic 17, 19; Simon Colosimo 51, 81; Fausto De Amicis 55

THOMPSON SETS UNLIKELY MARK

Archie Thompson smashed Iran striker Karim Bagheri's record of seven goals in one FIFA World Cup qualifying game, as Australia thrashed American Samoa 31-0 on April 11, 2001, scoring 13 times. Team-mate David Zdrilic also beat Bagheri's total with eight goals. Australia had already broken Iran's team scoring record (a 19-0 win against Guam), two days earlier, after completing a 22-0 win over Tonga.

THE FASTEST GOAL

Davide Gualtieri, of minnow San Marino, recorded the fastest goal in FIFA World Cup qualifying history when he scored after just nine seconds against England on November 17, 1993. England went on to win 7-1 but still failed to qualify.

CRIS IS IT

The UEFA play-off between Portugal and Sweden was widely billed as Cristiano Ronaldo versus Zlatan Ibrahimovic. Neither player disappointed, and the pair were the only ones to get on the scoresheet. Portugal won 1-0 at home and then 3-2 away. Ibrahamovic's second-leg double was not enough, as two late goals from Ronaldo completed his second hat-trick of the campaign. His first international hat-trick had come in 15 minutes against Northern Ireland during the group stages, and it took him above Eusebio in Portugal's all-time scorers list. The second treble put him joint top with Pauleta.

REPEAT OFFENDERS

Three players were sent off twice during qualifiers for the 2014 FIFA World Cup: Bulgaria's Svetoslav Dyakov, Tanzania's Aggrey Morris, and Montenegro's Savo Pavicevic. A total of 100 red cards and 2,916 yellow cards were shown throughout the campaign, while 2,286 goals were scored, an average of 2.8 per game. The highest-scoring teams were Germany and New Caledonia (36 each), Argentina (35), the Netherlands (34), and England (31).

RECORD HAT-TRICK

Abdel Hamid Bassiouny of Egypt scored the fastest-ever hat-trick in qualifying history in its 8-2 win over Namibia on July, 13 2001. He netted three times in just 177 seconds between the 39th and 42nd minutes.

YOUNGEST AND OLDEST

The youngest player to appear in the FIFA World Cup qualifiers is Souleymane Mamam of Togo, who was 13 years and 310 days old when he played against Zambia on May 6, 2001. The oldest was MacDonald Taylor, aged 46 years and 180 days, when he played for the Virgin Islands against St Kitts and Nevis on February 18, 2004.

DAEI TOPS THE SCORERS

Iran's **Ali Daei** is the all-time top scorer in FIFA World Cup qualifiers. His nine goals in the 2006 qualifying campaign took his total to 30, nine ahead of the previous joint record-holder, Japan's Kazu Miura. Daei scored seven goals in the 1994 qualifiers, four in the 1998 preliminaries, and ten in 2002.

HORST THE FIRST TO GIVE WAY

The first player to be substituted during a FIFA World Cup qualifier was West Germany's **Horst Eckel**, when he was replaced by Richard Gottinger in its 3-0 victory over the short-lived protectorate of Saarland in October 1953. Eckel would go on to play on the right side of midfield in the team which beat Hungary in the 1954 FIFA World Cup final, while Gottinger's delayed appearance against Saarland was his first and last for his country. By the time of the 1958 FIFA World Cup qualifiers, Saarland had been integrated within West Germany.

UNITED STATES LEAVE IT LATE

The latest of all qualifying play-off games took place in Rome on May 24, 1934, when the United States beat Mexico 4-2 to clinch the last slot in the FIFA World Cup finals. Three days later, the Americans were knocked out 7-1 by host Italy in the first round of the tournament.

ITALY FORCED TO QUALIFY

Italy is the only host country which was required to qualify for its own tournament. The 1934 host nation beat Greece 4-0 to go through. FIFA decided that, for the 1938 finals, the champion and the host would qualify automatically. Things changed for the 2006 finals, since when only the host has been exempt from qualifying. South Africa, however, played in the second round of qualifying for 2010 FIFA World Cup, because it doubled up as a qualifying round for the 2010 Africa Cup of Nations.

TURKEY THROUGH ON LUCK OF THE DRAW

Turkey was the first team to qualify for the FIFA World Cup finals after the drawing of lots. Its play-off against Spain, in Rome on March 17, 1954, ended 2-2. Qualification was decided by a 14-year-old Roman boy, Luigi Franco Gemma. He was blindfolded to make the draw, and pulled out Turkey, at the expense of more-fancied Spain.

THE "SOCCER WAR"

War broke out between El Salvador and Honduras after El Salvador beat Honduras 3-2 in a play-off on June 26, 1969, to qualify for the 1970 FIFA World Cup finals. Tension had been running high between the neighbors over a border dispute and there had been rioting by fans at the game. On July 14, the Salvador army invaded Honduras.

FIRST-TIME QUALIFIERS

1930: Argentina, Belgium, Bolivia, Brazil, Chile, France, Mexico, Paraguay, Peru, Romania, USA, Uruguay, Yugoslavia

1934: Austria, Czechoslovakia, Egypt, Germany, Hungary, Italy, Netherlands, Spain, Sweden, Switzerland

1938: Cuba, Dutch East Indies, Norway, Poland

1950: England

1954: Scotland, South Korea, Turkey, West Germany

1958: Northern Ireland, Soviet Union, Wales

1962: Bulgaria, Colombia

1966: North Korea, Portugal

1970: El Salvador, Israel, Morocco

1974: Australia, East Germany, Haiti, Zaire

1978: Iran, Tunisia

1982: Algeria, Cameroon, Honduras, Kuwait, New Zealand

1986: Canada, Denmark, Iraq

1990: Costa Rica, Republic of Ireland, United Arab Emirates

1994: Greece, Nigeria, Russia, Saudi Arabia

1998: Croatia, Jamaica, Japan, South Africa, Yugoslavia

2002: China, Ecuador, Senegal, Slovenia

2006: Angola, Czech Republic, Ghana, Ivory Coast, Serbia and Montenegro, Togo, Trinidad and Tobago, Ukraine

2010: Serbia, Slovakia

2014: Bosnia and Herzegovina

PLAY-OFF YOU GO

For the fourth FIFA World Cup in a row, Uruguay reached the 2014 tournament via a play-off, this one an easy aggregate win over Jordan. It won the away leg 5-0, the fifth scored by **Edinson Cavani**—the biggest away win in the history of FIFA World Cup intercontinental play-offs—and eased through with a scoreless tie on home soil. Jordan, aiming for its first FIFA World Cup finals, played 20 qualifying games, including a 2-2 aggregate Asian play-off tie against Uzbekistan, which it won 9-8 on penalties.

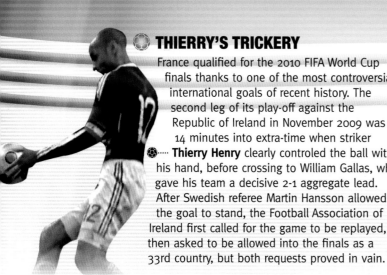

THIERRY'S TRICKERY

France qualified for the 2010 FIFA World Cup finals thanks to one of the most controversial international goals of recent history. The second leg of its play-off against the Republic of Ireland in November 2009 was 14 minutes into extra-time when striker **Thierry Henry** clearly controled the ball with his hand, before crossing to William Gallas, who gave his team a decisive 2-1 aggregate lead. After Swedish referee Martin Hansson allowed the goal to stand, the Football Association of Ireland first called for the game to be replayed, then asked to be allowed into the finals as a 33rd country, but both requests proved in vain.

NICE ONE, SON

The latest goal of 2014 FIFA World Cup qualifiers was **Son Heung-Min**'s winner for South Korea, six minutes into stoppage-time of its crucial March 2013 game against Qatar. The strike not only secured a 2-1 win, but also South Korea's qualification for the finals in Brazil.

GOING UNDERCOVER

The Kingdome in Seattle, Washington, hosted the first FIFA World Cup qualifier to be played indoors, when the US beat Canada 2-0 in October 1976. Just a few months earlier, the same venue had staged its first rock concert, by Paul McCartney's post-Beatles band Wings, and a religious rally featuring evangelist Billy Graham and country singer Johnny Cash. Canada gained revenge, by beating the US 3-0 in a play-off, hosted by Haiti, to reach the next stage of the CONCACAF qualifying round. But only Mexico went on to represent the Confederation at the 1978 FIFA World Cup in Argentina.

MAMADOU CAN DO

No European team had ever come from two goals down to win a FIFA World Cup play-off until November 2013, when France lost 2-0 in Ukraine but then won 3-0 in Paris thanks to a goal by striker Karim Benzema and a surprise double by center-back Mamadou Sakho, including a 72nd-minute winner.

NOT SO FASO

Burkina Faso lost its final qualifying play-off in the Africa section on away goals to Algeria, following a 3-2 victory at home and a 1-0 defeat away. It then tried to have Algeria disqualified, claiming that crucial goalscorer **Madjid Bougherra** was ineligible. Burkina Faso officials, hoping to reach its first FIFA World Cup, claimed he should have been suspended following two yellow cards in previous matches but FIFA ruled he had been booked only the once.

FIFA WORLD CUP TEAM RECORDS

EXTRA SPECIAL GERMANS

Germany, in beating Argentina 1-0 in the Maracana stadium in 2014, became the fifth team to win the FIFA World Cup Final in extra time, after Italy (1934), England (1966), Argentina (1978), and Spain (2010). In both 2010 and 2014, the Final had finished goalless after 90 minutes. Andres Iniesta, for Spain in 2010, and Mario Gozte, for Germany in Rio de Janeiro, both struck its lone winning goals in the second period of the additional 30 minutes. Extra time was not enough in 1994 and 2006, when Brazil and Italy, respectively, won on penalties.

CHAMPION 2014 FIFA World Cu

SHARING THE GOALS

France, in 1982, and winners Italy, in 2006, supplied the most individual goalscorers during a FIFA World Cup finals tournament, with ten. Germany's 17 goals were shared among seven players on its way to ultimate success in Brazil in 2014: Thomas Muller (five), Andre Schurrle (three), Mats Hummels (two), Miroslav Klose (two), Toni Kroos (two), Mario Gotze (two), and Mesut Ozil (one).

BRAZIL COLOR UP

Brazil's yellow shirts are famous around the world. But it wore **white shirts** at the first four FIFA World Cup finals. However, its 2-1 loss to Uruguay in the 1950 tournament's deciding Final Group game—when a tie would have given Brazil the Cup—was such a shock it switched to yellow. The Brazilian confederation insisted no further color change would follow the shock of the 7-1 semifinal defeat by Germany, and 3-0 third-place play-off loss to Holland in 2014.

COLOR CODE CONNECTION

Germany sought to engage with Brazilian fans by incorporating the colors of one of the country's most popular clubs, Flamengo, when *Die Nationalelf* wore red-and-black hoops as its second kit in the 2014 FIFA World Cup.

ITALY KEEP IT TIGHT

Italy set the record for the longest run without conceding a goal at the FIFA World Cup finals. It went five games without conceding at the 1990 finals, starting with its 1-0 group win over Austria. Goalkeeper Walter Zenga was not beaten until Claudio Caniggia scored Argentina's equalizer in the semifinal. Alas, the watertight defense did not bring Italy the glory it craved: Argentina reached the final by winning the penalty shoot-out 4-3.

TODAY EUROPE, TOMORROW THE WORLD

Spain's 2010 trophy-lifting coach **Vicente del Bosque** became only the second manager to have won both the FIFA World Cup and the UEFA Champions League or its previous incarnation, the European Champions' Cup. Marcello Lippi won the UEFA prize with Juventus in 1996, 10 years before his Italy team became world champions. Del Bosque won the UEFA Champions League twice with Real Madrid, in 2000 and 2002, though he was sacked in summer 2003 for "only" winning the Spanish league title the previous season.

SUPER EIGHT FOR 2014

The 2014 FIFA World Cup saw all eight group-winners win in the round-of-16 to reach the quarterfinal for the first time in the tournament's history. However there was an unwanted record, as well. Spain and 2010 Cup-winning skipper **Iker Casillas** exited in the first-round, meaning three of the last four FIFA World Cup winners have gone out in the following tournament's group stage (emulating France in 2002 and Italy in 2010). Only three countries have never exited at the first round group stage: Germany/West Germany, the Netherlands, and the Republic of Ireland.

MOST APPEARANCES IN THE FIFA WORLD CUP FINAL

1	Germany/West Germany	8
2	Brazil	7
3	Italy	6
4	Argentina	5
5	Netherlands	3
6	Czechoslovakia	2
=	France	2
=	Hungary	2
=	Uruguay	2
10	England	1
=	Spain	1
=	Sweden	1

BRAZIL PROFIT FROM RIMET'S VISION

Jules Rimet, president of FIFA 1921–54, was the driving force behind the first FIFA World Cup, in 1930. The tournament, in Uruguay, was not high-profile, with only 13 nations taking part. The long sea journey kept most European teams away, and only Belgium, France, Romania, and Yugoslavia, made the trip. Rimet's dream has been realized and the FIFA World Cup has grown enormously in popularity. Brazil has been the competition's most successful team, winning five times. The only FIFA World Cup finals ever-presents, Brazil has more wins (70) than any other country, though Germany (66 wins) has played more games: 106 to Brazil's 104. Germany and Italy are the most successful European nations, with four World Cup wins apiece. The original finalists, Uruguay and Argentina, are both two-time champions, though Argentina has also lost two Finals. England (1966) and France (1998) both won once as hosts. Spain failed as hosts in 1982, but won in South Africa in 2010.

WHY THE BRITISH TEAMS STAYED OUT

England and Scotland are considered the homelands of soccer, but neither country entered the FIFA World Cup until the qualifiers for the 1950 finals. The four British associations—England, Scotland, Wales, and Northern Ireland—resigned from FIFA in the 1920s over a row over broken-time (employment compensation) payments to amateurs. The British associations did not rejoin FIFA until 1946.

ONE-TIME WONDERS

Indonesia, then known as the Dutch East Indies, made one appearance in the FIFA World Cup finals, in the days when the tournament was a strictly knockout affair. On June 5, 1938, it lost 6-0 to Hungary in the first round, and has never qualified for the tournament since.

MOST APPEARANCES IN FIFA WORLD CUP FINALS TOURNAMENTS

1	Brazil	20
2	Germany/West Germany	18
=	Italy	18
4	Argentina	16
5	Mexico	15

FIFA WORLD CUP STOPS THE WORLD

The FIFA World Cup finals is the world's biggest single-sport event. Television was in its infancy when the first finals were held in 1930, and they have since become one of the most popular TV sporting events of all. The 2014 finals set ratings records around the world. In Germany, an all-time high of 41.89 million viewers (an 86.3 percent share) watched the victory over Argentina in the final. The global audience for the match was expected to top the 909 million who watched Spain beat the Netherlands in 2010. A further 12 million German fans were estimated to have watched the final in a public space back home. All manner of online records were set. Germany's 7-1 thrashing of Brazil in the semifinal generated a world sports record of 35 million tweets.

GOLDEN NARROWS

Before 2010, no country had won five consecutive FIFA World Cup matches by a one-goal margin, but **Arjen Robben** and the Netherlands and became the first, thanks to its 3-2 semifinal victory over Uruguay. Before then, the record belonged to Italy, which managed four single-goal wins in a row across the 1934 and 1938 FIFA World Cups. Spain's 1-0 defeat of the Dutch in the 2010 FIFA World Cup was also its fifth consecutive single-goal victory, and fourth in the knockout stages.

BRAZIL'S GOALS GLOOM

The 14 goals conceded by Brazil in the 2014 FIFA World Cup finals are the most ever conceded by the host nation. The overall record was 16 goals shipped by South Korea in Switzerland in 1954. In those finals, West Germany let in 14 but still won the tournament for the first time. It included eight in a group match against beaten finalists Hungary.

EVER RED

England's victory in 1966 was not just the only time it has won the FIFA World Cup, it also remains the only time the prize has been clinched by a team wearing red shirts in the final. Spain might have emulated England's fashion sense in 2010, but had to wear blue to avoid clashing with the Netherlands' bright orange. The team did, however, change back into its usual red to receive the trophy from FIFA president **Joseph S. Blatter**.

THE FEWEST GOALS CONCEDED

FIFA World Cup winners France (1998), Italy (2006), and Spain (2010) hold the record for the fewest goals conceded on its way to victory. All three conceded just two. Spain also hold the record for fewest goals scored by FIFA World Cup winners, netting just eight in 2010, below the 11 scored by Italy in 1938, England in 1966, or Brazil in 1994.

SPONSORS MAKE THE FINALS PAY

The Brazil 2014 FIFA World Cup was the most lucrative ever, with world soccer's governing body, FIFA, achieving a surplus of more than $2 billion. Two-thirds of FIFA World Cup revenues come from TV rights. This was the fifth finals played with 32 teams, the number going up from 24 for the France 1998 FIFA World Cup.

FEWEST GOALS CONCEDED IN ONE TOURNAMENT:
Switzerland: 0, 2006

MOST GOALS SCORED IN ONE TOURNAMENT
Hungary: 27, 1954

MOST WINS IN ONE TOURNAMENT
Brazil: 7, 2002

MOST GOALS SCORED IN ONE TOURNAMENT
Just Fontaine (France): 13, 1958

MOST CONSECUTIVE MATCHES SCORING A GOAL AT FIFA WORLD CUP FINALS

18	Brazil	1930–58
18	Germany	1934–58, 1986–98
17	Hungary	1934–62
16	Uruguay	1930–62
15	Brazil	1978–90
15	France	1978–86

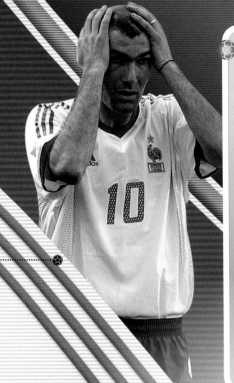

PERFORMANCES BY HOST NATION AT FIFA WORLD CUP FINALS

1930	Uruguay	Champions
1934	Italy	Champions
1938	France	Quarterfinals
1950	Brazil	Runners-up
1954	Switzerland	Quarterfinals
1958	Sweden	Runners-up
1962	Chile	Third place
1966	England	Champions
1970	Mexico	Quarterfinals
1974	West Germany	Champions
1978	Argentina	Champions
1982	Spain	Second round
1986	Mexico	Quarterfinals
1990	Italy	Third place
1994	United States	Second round
1998	France	Champions
2002	South Korea	Fourth place
	Japan	Second round
2006	Germany	Third place
2010	South Africa	First round
2014	Brazil	Fourth place

SAFE EUROPEAN HOME

Germany's 1-0 victory over Argentina in the 2014 FIFA World Cup final meant it became the first European nation to win the FIFA World Cup in any of the eight tournaments staged in North, Central or South America, going back to 1930. Spain, winners of the 2010 FIFA World Cup in South Africa, were the first European victors to achieve it outside its home continent.

HOLDERS CRASH OUT

France produced the worst performance by a defending FIFA World Cup winner in Japan and South Korea in 2002: it lost its opening game 1-0 to Senegal, tied 0-0 against Uruguay and was eliminated after losing 1-0 to Denmark. It was the first defending champion to be knocked out without scoring a goal. In 2010 Italy emulated France by exiting at the first-round stage, and without winning a game, nor even ever taking the lead. At least Italy did achieve two ties—and managed to score four goals. Italy opened with a 1-1 tie against Paraguay, needed a penalty to force another 1-1 tie against minnows New Zealand. But the team was on its way home after losing 3-2 to Slovakia.

THREE AND OUT

The Netherlands, coached by **Bert van Marwijk** in 2010, became the only country to have reached the final of three FIFA World Cups without managing to lift the trophy once. Its six victories en route to the 2010 final are also more than any other team has managed in one tournament without going on to claim the main prize.

BRAZIL LEAD THE WAY

Brazil scored the most victories in finals tournaments when it won all of its seven games in 2002. It began with a 2-1 group win over Turkey, and ended with a 2-0 final triumph over Germany. Brazil scored 18 goals in its unbeaten run and conceded on only four occasions.

HOME DISCOMFORT

South Africa became the first host nation to fail to reach the second round of a FIFA World Cup, when it staged the 2010 tournament. However, its first-round record of one win, one tie, and one defeat, was only inferior on goal difference to the opening three games played by hosts Spain, in 1982, and Team USA, in 1994, both of which reached the second round. Until Brazil were demolished 7-1 by Germany in 2014, Uruguay's 3–0 victory over South Africa in Pretoria on June 16, 2010, equaled the highest losing margin suffered by a FIFA World Cup host. Sweden, 5-2 to Brazil in the 1958 final, and Mexico, 4-1 to Italy in a 1970 quarterfinal, also lost by three goals.

FIFA WORLD CUP GOALSCORING

HOST WITH THE MOST

Brazil has scored more goals (nine) in the opening matches of the FIFA World Cup than any other nation, though its status as a two-time host, in 1950 and 2014, certainly helped. Between 1974 and 2002, the holders, rather than the hosts, also had the honor of kicking off proceedings. Brazil beat Mexico easily by 4-0 in the 1950 opener in the Maracana stadium, with goals from Jair, Baltazar, and Ademir (two). It defeated Scotland 2-1 in the opening game of France 1998 (Cesar Sampaio and Tom Boyd, own goal) and then Croatia, 3-1, in 2014, thanks to a double (one a penalty) from **Neymar,** and a third from Oscar. A Brazilian also netted the very first goal of the 2014 finals, as left-back Marcelo gave Croatia the lead with an own goal. Italy's total of eight goals in the opening game was mainly thanks to a 7-1 beating of the United States in 1934, and it tied 1-1 with Bulgaria in 1986.

HIGHEST SCORES

The highest-scoring game in the FIFA World Cup finals was the quarterfinal between Austria and Switzerland on June 26, 1954. Austria staged a remarkable comeback to win 7-5, with center-forward **Theodor Wagner** scoring a hat-trick, after trailing 3-0 in the 19th minute. Three other games have produced 11 goals:– Brazil's 6-5 win over Poland in the 1938 first round; Hungary's 8-3 win over West Germany in its 1954 group game; and the Hungarians' 10-1 rout of El Salvador at the group stage in 1982.

LOW-SCORING SPAIN

Spain won the 2010 FIFA World Cup despite scoring just eight goals in seven games on its way to the title, the fewest of any world champion. The previous record was goals, shared by Italy in 1934, England in 1966, and Brazil in 1994. Vicente del Bosque's Spain was also the first team to win by 1-0 in all four of its knockout matches. David Villa scored the decisive goal in two of those games.

GENEROUS OPPONENTS

Chile was the first team to benefit from an opponent's own goal at the FIFA World Cup. Mexico's Manuel Rosas put the ball into his own net during the Chileans' 3-0 win at the inaugural 1930 finals in Uruguay. France, Germany, and Italy share the record for receiving the most FIFA World Cup finals own goals, with four each. At the 2014 World Cup, France profited from two own goals, the first courtesy of Honduras goalkeeper Noel Valladares in a 3-0 group stage win; the second was by Nigeria's Joseph Yobo, to make it 2-0 in the second-round. Valladares's own goal—the ball struck him off a goal-post and thus denied Karim Benzema a hat-trick—was ratified by goal-line technology, in operation in the finals in Brazil for the first time.

ZERO TOLERANCE

Four is the most number of penalty shootouts in the knockout phases of the FIFA World Cup since the first one in 1982. A further 25 have been needed in the eight finals thereafter. The record of four came at Italy 1990, Germany 2006 and Brazil 2014, where 26 of 36 kicks succeeded. The most crucial failures came after the scoreless semifinal at Sao Paolo, when Argentina goalkeeper Sergio Romero saved from the Netherlands' Ron Vlaar and Wesley Sneijder.

THE FASTEST GOAL

Turkey's **Hakan Sukur** holds the record for the quickest goal scored in the FIFA World Cup finals. He netted after 11 seconds against South Korea in the 2002 third-place play-off. Turkey went on to win 3-2. The previous record was held by Vaclav Masek of Czechoslovakia, who struck after 15 seconds against Mexico in 1962.

BIGGEST FIFA WORLD CUP FINALS WINS

Hungary 10, El Salvador 1 (June 15, 1982)
Hungary 9, South Korea 0 (June 17, 1954)
Yugoslavia 9, Zaire 0 (June 18, 1974)
Sweden 8, Cuba 0 (June 12, 1938)
Uruguay 8, Bolivia 0 (July 2, 1950)
Germany 8, Saudi Arabia 0 (June 1, 2002)

MOST GOALS IN ONE FIFA WORLD CUP

Goals	Country	Year
27	**Hungary**	1954
25	**West Germany**	1954
23	**France**	1958
22	**Brazil**	1950
19	**Brazil**	1970

MOST GOALS IN FIFA WORLD CUP FINALS (MINIMUM 100)

1	**Germany/W Germany**	224
2	**Brazil**	221
3	**Argentina**	131
4	**Italy**	128
5	**France**	103

MOST AND LEAST

Mario Gotze's winner for Germany in the 2014 FIFA World Cup Final meant the tournament matched the record aggregate of 171 goals set at the 1998 finals in France, the first expanded to 32 teams and 64 games. The two finals shared a goals average of 2.67 per game. The record goals per match average is 5.38, set at the 1954 finals, when there were 140 goals in 26 games in Switzerland. The lowest average came at the 1990 FIFA World Cup in Italy, when the 52 games produced only 115 goals, an average of only 2.21.

YOUNGEST AND OLDEST

The youngest-ever scorer of a goal in FIFA World Cup finals history is **Pele.** He was 17 years and 239 days old when he notched Brazil's winner against Wales in the 1958 quarterfinal. Cameroon's **Roger Milla**, aged 42 years and 39 days, became the oldest scorer when he netted his country's only goal in a 6-1 defeat by Russia in 1994.

COLOMBIAN GOLD

James Rodriguez claimed the adidas Golden Boot prize as leading scorer at the 2014 FIFA World Cup in Brazil, the first Colombian winner. The AS Monaco forward's explosion was all the more of a surprise since Colombia had expected its goals to come from his club-mate Radamel Falcao, who missed the finals after a knee injury. Rodriguez scored in all five of his country's games, including a penalty in the 2-1 quarterfinal loss to Brazil and a volley in the second-round against Uruguay that was a contender for goal of the tournament. His six goals were one more than Germany's Thomas Muller and two more than Brazil's Neymar, Argentina's Lionel Messi and the Netherlands' Robin Van Persie.

KLOSE ENCOUNTERS

Eight players have scored at FIFA World Cups 12 years apart. The most notable was Miroslav Klose. The Polish-born center-forward opened with a hat-trick when Germany beat Saudi Arabia 8-0 in Japan in 2002, and scored a 16th goal in the 7-1 destruction of hosts Brazil in the 2014 semifinal. That established Klose as the finals' all-time record marksman with one more goal than Brazil's Ronaldo. The other seven men to have scored in FIFA World Cups 12 years apart are: Pele (Brazil), Uwe Seeler (West Germany), Diego Maradona (Argentina), Michael Laudrup (Denmark), Henrik Larsson (Sweden), Sami Al-Jaber (Saudi Arabia), and Cuauhtemoc Blanco (Mexico).

EUSEBIO THE STRIKE FORCE

Portugal's **Eusebio** was the striking star of the 1966 FIFA World Cup finals. Ironically, he would not be eligible to play for Portugal now. He was born in Mozambique, then a Portuguese colony, but now an independent country. He finished top scorer with nine goals, including two as Portugal eliminated champions Brazil and four as it beat North Korea 5-3 in the quarterfinal after trailing 3-0.

HEAD FOR FIGURES

When **Jermaine Jones** thundered home from 30 meters for the United States in its 2-2 tie with Portugal in a Group G clash at the 2014 FIFA World Cup, he registered the 2,300th goal of the finals. Mario Gotze's winning goal for Germany in the Final against Argentina lifted the overall tally to 2,379.

FIFA WORLD CUP FINALS TOP SCORERS

Maximum 16 teams in finals

Year	Venue	Top Scorer	Country	Goals
1930	Uruguay	Guillermo Stabile	Argentina	8
1934	Italy	Oldrich Nejedly	Czechoslovakia	5
1938	France	Leonidas	Brazil	7
1950	Brazil	Ademir	Brazil	9
1954	Switzerland	Sandor Kocsis	Hungary	11
1958	Sweden	Just Fontaine	France	13
1962	Chile	Garrincha	Brazil	4
		Vava	Brazil	
		Leonel Sanchez	Chile	
		Florian Albert	Hungary	
		Valentin Ivanov	Soviet Union	
		Drazen Jerkovic	Yugoslavia	
1966	England	Eusebio	Portugal	9
1970	Mexico	Gerd Muller	West Germany	10
1974	West Germany	Grzegorz Lato	Poland	7
1978	Argentina	Mario Kempes	Argentina	6

24 teams in finals

Year	Venue	Top Scorer	Country	Goals
1982	Spain	Paolo Rossi	Italy	6
1986	Mexico	Gary Lineker	England	6
1990	Italy	Salvatore Schillaci	Italy	6
1994	United States	Oleg Salenko	Russia	6
		Hristo Stoichkov	Bulgaria	6

32 teams in finals

Year	Venue	Top Scorer	Country	Goals
1998	France	Davor Suker	Croatia	6
2002	Korea/Japan	Ronaldo	Brazil	8
2006	Germany	Miroslav Klose	Germany	5
2010	South Africa	Thomas Muller*	Germany	5
		Diego Forlan	Uruguay	5
		Wesley Sneijder	Netherlands	5
		David Villa	Spain	5
2014	Brazil	James Rodriguez	Colombia	6

* = Won Golden Boot (had most assists)

KEMPES MAKES HIS MARK

Mario Kempes was Argentina's only foreign-based player in the host nation's squad at the 1978 finals. Twice top scorer in the Spanish league, Valencia's Kempes was crucial to Argentina's success. Coach Cesar Luis Menotti told him to shave off his moustache after he failed to score in the group games. Kempes then netted two against Peru, two more against Poland, and two decisive goals in the final against the Netherlands.

NO GUARANTEES FOR TOP SCORERS

Topping the FIFA World Cup finals scoring chart is a great honor for all strikers, but few have gained the ultimate prize and been leading scorer. Argentina's Guillermo Stabile started the luckless trend in 1930, topping the scoring charts but finishing up on the losing side in the final. The list of top scorers who have played in the winning side is small: Garrincha and Vava (joint top scorers in 1962), Mario Kempes (top scorer in 1978), Paolo Rossi (1982), and Ronaldo (2002). Gerd Muller, top scorer in 1970, gained his reward as West Germany's trophy winner four years later. Other top scorers, such as Sandor Kocsis, 1954, Just Fontaine, 1958, and Gary Lineker, 1986, have been disappointed in the final stages. Kocsis was the only other one to reach the final, but Hungary lost to West Germany. Four players finished tied on five goals at the 2010 FIFA World Cup and one, David Villa, collected a winner's medal, but the Golden Boot went to Germany's Thomas Muller.

STABILE MAKES AN IMPACT

Guillermo Stabile, top scorer in the 1930 FIFA World Cup finals, had never played for Argentina before the tournament. He made his debut—as a 25-year-old—against Mexico because first-choice Roberto Cherro had suffered a panic attack. He netted a hat-trick, then scored twice against both Chile and the United States as Argentina reached the final. He also scored one of his side's goals in the 4-2 defeat by Uruguay in the final.

SUPER SUBS

Germany's winner in the 2014 FIFA World Cup final was scored by **Mario Gotze,** and created by a pass from Andre Schurrle. It was the first time that both the assist and goal itself in a FIFA World Cup final had come from two substitutes. It was also the first winning goal scored by a substitute.

HURST MAKES HISTORY

England's **Geoff Hurst** remains the only player to score a hat-trick in a FIFA World Cup final when he netted three in the host nation's 4-2 victory over West Germany in 1966. Hurst headed England level after the Germans had taken an early lead, then scored the decisive third goal, in the first period of extra time, with a shot that bounced down off the crossbar and just over the goalline, according to the Soviet linesman. Hurst hit his third in the final minute. The British TV commentator Kenneth Wolstenholme described Hurst's strike famously with the words: "Some people are on the pitch ... They think it's all over ... It is now!"

THREE OUT OF 10

Only three players wearing the iconic No.10 shirt have won the FIFA World Cup finals Golden Boot: Argentina's Mario Kempes in 1978, England's Gary Lineker in 1986, and Colombia's six-goal James Rodriguez at Brazil 2014. Lionel Messi and Neymar, Argentina's and Brazil's No.10s, both scored four goals, one behind Germany's No.13, Thomas Muller.

ANDRES THE GIANT

Spain's hero in the 2010 FIFA World Cup final was **Andres Iniesta** (right), whose 116th-minute goal was also the latest trophy-winning strike in the tournament's history—excluding penalty shoot-outs.

FIFA WORLD CUP FINALS ALL-TIME LEADING GOALSCORERS

	Name	Country	Tournaments	Goals
1	Miroslav Klose	Germany	2002, 2006, 2010, 2014	16
2	Ronaldo	Brazil	1998, 2002, 2006	15
3	Gerd Muller	West Germany	1970, 1974	14
4	Just Fontaine	France	1958	13
5	Pele	Brazil	1958, 1962, 1966, 1970	12
6	Jurgen Klinsmann	Germany	1990, 1994, 1998	11
=	Sandor Kocsis	Hungary	1954	11
8	Gabriel Batistuta	Argentina	1994, 1998, 2002	10
=	Teofilo Cubillas	Peru	1970, 1978	10
=	Grzegorz Lato	Poland	1974, 1978, 1982	10
=	Gary Lineker	England	1986, 1990	10
=	Thomas Muller	Germany	2010, 2014	10
=	Helmut Rahn	West Germany	1954, 1958	10

THE BRADLEY BUNCH

Michael Bradley's late equalizer for the United States, in its Group C 2-2 tie with Slovenia in June 2010, made him the first person to score a FIFA World Cup goal for a team coached by his own father—in this case, Bob Bradley.

MESSI MISSING OUT

Argentina's captain **Lionel Messi** left the 2014 FIFA World Cup with a runners-up medal and the Golden Ball, awarded to the finals' best player. The winner, once chosen by a poll of journalists, was judged in Brazil by the technical study group. This comprises present and former coaches appointed by FIFA to monitor soccer trends. The last player to win both the award and the FIFA World Cup was Romario, back in 1994.

PELE SO UNLUCKY

Pele would surely have been the all-time FIFA World Cup top scorer but for injuries. He was sidelined early in the 1962 finals, and again four years later. He scored six goals in Brazil's 1958 triumph, including two in the 5-2 final victory over Sweden. He also netted Brazil's 100th FIFA World Cup goal as it beat Italy 4-1 in the 1970 final.

MULLER'S SCORING HABIT

West Germany's **Gerd Muller** had the knack of scoring in important games. He struck the winner against England in the 1970 quarterfinal and his two goals in extra-time against Italy almost carried his team to the final. Four years later, Muller's goal against Poland ensured that West Germany reached the final on home soil. Then he scored the winning goal against the Netherlands in the FIFA World Cup final. He also had a goal disallowed for offside—wrongly, as TV replays proved.

RONALDO SO CONSISTENT

Ronaldo was a consistent scorer in the three FIFA World Cup finals tournaments he played in. He netted four times in 1998, when Brazil was runner-up to France, eight as it won the 2002 tournament—including both goals in the final—and three more in 2006. He became the all-time top scorer when netting Brazil's opener in a 3-0 win over Ghana in the round-of-16 at Dortmund on June 27, 2006. As a teenager, Ronaldo had been a member of Brazil's FIFA World Cup winning squad in the United States in 1994, but did not play.

WHO SCORED THE FIRST HAT-TRICK?

For many years, Argentina's Guillermo Stabile was considered the first hat-trick scorer in the FIFA World Cup finals. He netted three in Argentina's 6-3 win over Mexico on July 19, 1930, but has since been superseded by Bert Patenaude of the United States. FIFA changed its records in November 2006, to acknowledge that Patenaude's treble two days earlier, in the Americans' 3-0 win over Paraguay, had been the tournament's first hat-trick.

KLINSMANN'S CONTRIBUTION

Jurgen Klinsmann has been one of the most influential personalities at the modern FIFA World Cup. He scored three goals when West Germany won the FIFA World Cup in 1990, and a further eight in 1994 and 1998. As team coach he then led Germany to third place in 2006, and the United States to the round-of-16 in 2014.

HIGH FIVES

Germany forwards **Thomas Muller**, in 2010 and 2014, and Miroslav Klose, in 2002 and 2006, are the only players to have scored five or more goals at back-to-back FIFA World Cup finals. Muller's 10 goals have come in only 13 matches, and he will be only 28 years old when the Russia 2018 FIFA World Cup kicks-off.

FIFA WORLD CUP APPEARANCES

Goalkeeper Gianluigi Buffon was in Italy's squad for his fifth FIFA World Cup in Brazil in 2014 and, after missing the victory over England, he captained the *Azzurri* in losses to Costa Rica and Uruguay. Buffon actually played in only four tournaments, however, having been an unused substitute in 1998. Two players have appeared in matches in five FIFA World Cups: Mexico's Antonio Carbajal (1950–66) and West Germany/Germany's Lothar Matthaus (1982–98).

YOUNGEST AND OLDEST

Northern Ireland's Norman Whiteside is the youngest player in FIFA World Cup finals history, being just 17 years and 41 days when he started against Yugoslavia in 1982. The oldest player to feature is Colombia goalkeeper Faryd Mondragon, as a late substitute in a 4-1 win over Japan, in 2014. Aged 43 years and three days, he outdid the 42 years and 39 days of Cameroon's Roger Milla.

THIS IS ENGLAND

England captain **Steven Gerrard** led the 110 players from the top-represented English Premier League at the 2014 FIFA World Cup. This was down seven on 2010. Celtic goalkeeper Fraser Forster was the England squad's only non-Premier League player. Belgium had 12 Premier League players and France 10. Chelsea sent 17 players, Manchester United 14, Liverpool 12, and champions Manchester City 10.

MOST APPEARANCES IN FIFA WORLD CUP FINALS

25	**Lothar Matthaus** (West Germany/Germany)
24	**Miroslav Klose** (Germany)
23	**Paolo Maldini** (Italy)
21	**Diego Maradona** (Argentina)
	Uwe Seeler (West Germany)
	Wladyslaw Zmuda (Poland)
20	**Cafu** (Brazil)
	Philipp Lahm (Germany)
	Grzegorz Lato (Poland)
	Bastian Schweinsteiger (Germany)

DOUBLE WINNERS

Players who have played on the winning team in two FIFA World Cup finals:

Giovanni Ferrari (Italy), 1934, 1938
Giuseppe Meazza (Italy), 1934, 1938
Pele (Brazil), 1958, 1970
Didi (Brazil), 1958, 1962
Djalma Santos (Brazil), 1958, 1962
Garrincha (Brazil), 1958, 1962
Gilmar (Brazil), 1958, 1962
Nilton Santos (Brazil), 1958, 1962
Vava (Brazil), 1958, 1962
Zagallo (Brazil), 1958, 1962
Zito (Brazil), 1958, 1962
Cafu (Brazil), 1994, 2002

THE "DOUBLE" CHAMPIONS

Franz Beckenbauer and Mario Zagallo are a unique duo. They have both won the FIFA World Cup as a player and a coach. Beckenbauer also had the distinction of captaining West Germany to victory on home soil in 1974. As coach, he steered it to the final in Mexico in 1986, and to victory over Argentina in Italy four years later. He was nicknamed "Der Kaiser" (The Emperor) both for his style and his achievements. Zagallo gained two winners' medals as a player. He was the left-winger in Brazil's triumphant march to the 1958 championship, before playing a deeper role in its 1962 victory. He took over from the controversial Joao Saldanha as Brazil coach three months before the 1970 finals and guided the team to victory in all six of its games, scoring 19 goals, and routing Italy 4-1 in the final. Zagallo later filled the role of the team's technical director when Brazil won the FIFA World Cup for a fourth time in 1994.

MOST FIFA WORLD CUP FINALS TOURNAMENTS

The following all played in at least four FIFA World Cup finals.

5 **Antonio Carbajal** (Mexico) 1950, 1954, 1958, 1962, 1966
Lothar Matthaus (W Germany/Germany) 1982, 1986, 1990, 1994, 1998
4 **Sami Al-Jaber** (Saudi Arabia) 1994, 1998, 2002, 2006
DaMarcus Beasley (United States) 2002, 2006, 2010, 2014
Giuseppe Bergomi (Italy) 1982, 1986, 1990, 1998
Gianluigi Buffon (Italy) 2002, 2006, 2010, 2014
Cafu (Brazil) 1994, 1998, 2002, 2006
Denis Caniza (Paraguay) 1998, 2002, 2006, 2010
Fabio Cannavaro (Italy) 1998, 2002, 2006, 2010
Iker Casillas (Spain) 2002, 2006, 2010, 2014
Samuel Eto'o (Cameroon) 1998, 2002, 2010, 2014
Thierry Henry (France) 1998, 2002, 2006, 2010
Miroslav Klose (Germany) 2002, 2006, 2010, 2014
Paolo Maldini (Italy) 1990, 1994, 1998, 2002
Diego Maradona (Argentina) 1982, 1986, 1990, 1994
Rafael Marquez (Mexico) 2002, 2006, 2010, 2014
Hong Myung-Bo (South Korea) 1990, 1994, 1998, 2002
Pele (Brazil) 1958, 1962, 1966, 1970
Gianni Rivera (Italy) 1962, 1966, 1970, 1974
Pedro Rocha (Uruguay) 1962, 1966, 1970, 1974
Djalma Santos (Brazil) 1954, 1958, 1962, 1966
Karl-Heinz Schnellinger (W. Germany) 1958, 1962, 1966, 1970
Enzo Scifo (Belgium) 1986, 1990, 1994, 1998
Uwe Seeler (West Germany) 1958, 1962, 1966, 1970
Rigobert Song (Cameroon) 1994, 1998, 2002, 2010
Franky van der Elst (Belgium) 1986, 1990, 1994, 1998
Xavi (Spain) 2002, 2006, 2010, 2014
Wladyslaw Zmuda (Poland) 1974, 1978, 1982, 1986
Andoni Zubizarreta (Spain) 1986, 1990, 1994, 1998

BAYERN BEAT

Seven of Germany's 2014 FIFA World Cup-winning squad came from champions Bayern Munich: Manuel Neuer, Philipp Lahm, Jerome Boateng, Bastian Schweinsteiger, Toni Kroos, Thomas Muller, and Mario Gotze. All started the final against Argentina, except for game-winner Gotze. Immediately after the final, the Bayern contingent was reduced when Kroos joined Real Madrid.

KHEDIRA'S DOUBLE PAIN

Sami Khedira was in a world of his own in Brazil in 2014 as he ended the season with a winner's medal from both the FIFA World Cup and the UEFA Champions League. First Khedira lined up in midfield as Spanish club Real Madrid scored a 4-1 extra-time win over neighbors Atletico in Europe's club season climax. He then joined up with Germany's World Cup squad in Brazil. Here he won a second medal, despite withdrawing from the final just before kick-off after aggravating a muscle injury in the warm-up. Khedira was the 10th player to clinch the World Cup/European Cup double.

SONG FAMILY GOES OFF KEY

In playing 17 minutes at the 2010 FIFA World Cup, Cameroon defender **Rigobert Song** became the first African to play in four finals tournaments, amounting to nine games, across 16 years and nine days. He featured in 1994, 1998, 2002, and 2010, and Cameroon failed to qualify in 2006. He, and Colombia's Faryd Mondragon, share the fourth-longest FIFA World Cup career-spans, bettered only by Mexicans Antonio Carbajal (spanning 16 years, 25 days) and Hugo Sanchez (16 years, 17 days), and West Germany/Germany's Lothar Matthaus (16 years, 14 days). On the down side, Song was sent off twice at World Cups and cousin Alex Song was dismissed at the 2014 finals for elbowing Mario Mandzukic in a 4-0 loss to Croatia. Thus, the Song family is responsible for three of Cameroon's eight FIFA World Cup finals red cards.

MOST FIFA WORLD CUP FINALS GAMES (BY POSITION)

Goalkeeper: Sepp Maier (West Germany, 18 matches) and Claudio Taffarel (Brazil, 18 matches)
Defense: Paolo Maldini (Italy, 23); Wladyslaw Zmuda (Poland, 21); Cafu (Brazil, 20); Philipp Lahm (Germany, 20)
Midfielders: Lothar Matthaus (W. Germany/Germany, 25); Bastian Schweinsteiger (Germany, 20)
Forwards: Miroslav Klose (Germany, 24); Diego Maradona (Argentina, 21); Uwe Seeler (West Germany, 21); Grzegorz Lato (Poland, 20)

PROSINECKI'S SCORING RECORD

Robert Prosinecki is the only player to have scored for different countries in FIFA World Cup finals tournaments. He netted for Yugoslavia in its 4-1 win over the United Arab Emirates in the 1990 tournament. Eight years later, following the break-up of the old Yugoslavia, he scored for Croatia in its 3-0 group-game win over Jamaica, and then netted the first goal in his team's 2-1 third-place play-off victory over the Netherlands.

QUICKEST SUBSTITUTIONS

The three fastest substitutions in the history of the FIFA World Cup finals have all come in the fourth minute. In each case the player substituted was so seriously injured that he took no further part in the tournament: Steve Hodge came on for Bryan Robson in England's 0-0 tie with Morocco in 1986; Giuseppe Bergomi replaced Alessandro Nesta in Italy's 2-1 win over Austria in 1998; and Peter Crouch subbed for Michael Owen in England's 2-2 tie with Sweden in 2006.

PRIZE PROBLEM

Winning the FIFA World Player of the Year award, or Ballon d'Or, has not proved a lucky omen for its proud bearers. The winner has never gone on to win the next World Cup. The 2014 FIFA World Cup was no different as **Cristiano Ronaldo**, 2013 FIFA World Player of the Year, and his Portugal team-mates went out in the group stage. His predecessor as Ballon d'Or-holder, Lionel Messi of Argentina, was on the losing side in the 2014 Final. Messi was also the incumbent going into the 2010 FIFA World Cup, but lost in the quarterfinal.

SIMUNIC'S THREE-CARD MATCH

Croatia's Josip Simunic shares (with Ray Richards of Australia in 1974) the record for collecting the most yellow cards in one game at the FIFA World Cup finals—three. He received three yellows against Australia in 2006 before he was sent off by English referee Graham Poll. When Poll showed Simunic his second yellow, he forgot he had already booked him.

LEADING CAPTAINS

Three players have each captained their teams in two FIFA World Cup finals: Diego Maradona of Argentina, Dunga of Brazil, and West Germany's Karl-Heinz Rummenigge. Maradona lifted the trophy in 1986, but was a loser four years later. Dunga was the winning skipper in 1994, but was on the losing side in 1998. Rummenigge was a loser on both occasions, in 1982 and 1986. Maradona has made the most appearances as captain at the FIFA World Cup finals, leading out Argentina 16 times between 1986 and 1994.

FIRST ELEVEN

In an age of squad numbers, **Brazil** may have pleased some traditionalists when fielding players wearing shirt numbers one to 11 in the starting line-ups for its first two games of the 2010 FIFA World Cup, against North Korea and the Ivory Coast. Kicking off for coach Dunga on each occasion were: 1 Julio Cesar, 2 Maicon, 3 Lucio, 4 Juan, 5 Felipe Melo, 6 Michel Bastos, 7 Elano, 8 Gilberto Silva, 9 Luis Fabiano, 10 Kaka, and 11 Robinho. **The Netherlands** managed a similar starting structure for not only its round-of-16 game against Slovakia, but the final against Spain: 1 Maarten Stekelenburg, 2 Gregory van der Wiel, 3 Johnny Heitinga, 4 Joris Mathijsen, 5 Giovanni van Bronckhorst, 6 Mark van Bommel, 7 Dirk Kuyt, 8 Nigel de Jong, 9 Robin van Persie, 10 Wesley Sneijder, and 11 Arjen Robben. Both Brazil and the Netherlands came close to the same feat when it met in a 2010 quarterfinal, though both featured a number 13: Brazil's Dani Alves, in place of 7 Elano, and the Netherlands' Andre Ooijer instead of 4 Joris Mathijsen (Elano and Mathijsen were unavailable through injury).

FASTEST RED CARDS IN THE FIFA WORLD CUP FINALS

1 min Jose Batista (Uruguay) v Scotland, 1986
8 min Giorgio Ferrini (Italy) v Chile, 1962
14 min Zeze Procopio (Brazil) v Czechoslovakia, 1938
19 min Mohammed Al Khlaiwi (Saudi Arabia) v France, 1998
Miguel Bossio (Uruguay) v Denmark, 1986
21 min Gianluca Pagliuca (Italy) v Rep of Ireland, 1994

FASTEST YELLOW CARDS IN THE FIFA WORLD CUP FINALS

1 min Sergei Gorlukovich (Russia) v Sweden, 1994
Giampiero Marini (Italy) v Poland, 1982
2 min Jesus Arellano (Mexico) v Italy, 2002
Henri Camara (Senegal) v Uruguay, 2002
Michael Emenalo (Nigeria) v Italy, 1994
Humberto Suazo (Chile) v Switzerland, 2010
Mark van Bommel (Netherlands) v Port., 2006

SUPER SUBS IMPOSE THEIR WILL

Substitutes scored more goals in the Brazil 2014 FIFA World Cup than in any previous finals. Mario Gotze's goal in the final was the 32nd by a substitute, extending the record from the previous mark of 24 set in 2006 in Germany. Substitutes, two of them, were first permitted for the 1970 finals in Mexico, and it went up to three from 1998. The 1998 FIFA World Cup finals also saw the fastest goal by a substitute. Denmark's **Ebbe Sand** scored 16 seconds after coming on against Nigeria.

YOUNGEST PLAYERS IN FIFA WORLD CUP FINAL
Pele (Brazil) – 17 years, 249 days, in 1958
Giuseppe Bergomi (Italy) – 18 years, 201 days, in 1982
Ruben Moran (Uruguay) – 19 years, 344 days, in 1950

OLDEST PLAYERS IN FIFA WORLD CUP FINAL
Dino Zoff (Italy) – 40 years, 133 days, in 1982
Gunnar Gren (Sweden) – 37 years, 241 days, in 1958
Jan Jongbloed (Netherlands) – 37 years, 212 days, in 1978
Nilton Santos (Brazil) – 37 years, 32 days, in 1962

PUZACH THE FIRST SUB
The first substitute in FIFA World Cup finals history was Anatoli Puzach of the Soviet Union. He replaced Viktor Serebrianikov at half-time of the Soviets' scoreless tie with hosts Mexico on May 31, 1970. The 1970 tournament was the first in which substitutes were allowed, with two permitted for each team. FIFA increased this to three per team for the 1998 finals.

FOUR AND OUT
The most players sent off in one FIFA World Cup finals game is four. Costinha and Deco of Portugal, and Khalid Boulahrouz and Giovanni van Bronckhorst of the Netherlands were sent off by Russian referee Valentin Ivanov in its round-of-16 game in Germany in 2006.

CANIGGIA SENT OFF, WHILE ON THE BENCH...
Claudio Caniggia of Argentina became the first player to be sent off from the substitutes' bench, during a game against Sweden in 2002. Caniggia was dismissed in first-half stoppage time for dissent towards UAE referee Ali Bujsaim. Caniggia carried on protesting after the referee warned him to keep quiet, so Bujsaim showed him a red card.

MALDINI'S MINUTES RECORD
Lothar Matthaus of West Germany/Germany has started the most FIFA World Cup finals matches—25. But Italy defender **Paolo Maldini** (left) has stayed on the field for longer, despite starting two games fewer. Maldini played for 2,220 minutes, Matthaus for 2,052. According to the stopwatch, the top four are completed by Uwe Seeler of West Germany, who played for 1,980 minutes, and Argentina's Diego Maradona, who played for 1,938.

GERMANY UNITED
Germany and West Germany are counted together in World Cup records because the Deutscher Fussball-Bund, founded in 1900, was the original governing body and the DFB was in charge of the national game before World War 2, during the East–West split, and post-reunification. German teams have won the FIFA World Cup four times and appeared in the final a record eight times. In 2014, match-deciding substitutes Andre Schurrle and Mario Gotze were the first players born in Germany since reunification to win the World Cup, while team-mate Toni Kroos was the only 2014 squad-member to have been born in what was East Germany. Kroos was also the first player from the former East Germany to win the World Cup.

UNBEATEN GOALKEEPERS IN THE FIFA WORLD CUP FINALS*

Walter Zenga (Italy)	517 minutes without conceding a goal, 1990
Peter Shilton (England)	502 minutes, 1986–90
Iker Casillas (Spain)	476 minutes, 2010–14
Sepp Maier (W Germany)	475 minutes, 1974–78
Gianluigi Buffon (Italy)	460 minutes, 2006
Emerson Leao (Brazil)	458 minutes, 1978
Gordon Banks (England)	442 minutes, 1966

* Pascal Zuberbuhler did not concede a goal in all 390 minutes played by Switzerland in the 2006 FIFA World Cup.

HAIL CESAR!

Brazil goalkeeper **Julio Cesar** wept with relief and joy after his penalty shoot-out defiance helped the 2014 FIFA World Cup host beat Chile in a round-of-16 tie in Belo Horizonte. Coach Luiz Felipe Scolari had kept faith with the 34-year-old, even though he had barely played for his English club Queens Park Rangers, and gone on loan to FC Toronto of the MLS. Cesar was blamed by many Brazilians for a mistake which led to defeat by Netherlands in a 2010 quarterfinal. In 2014, however, he saved Chile's first two spot-kicks and rocketed from scapegoat to national hero.

NOT THINKING OUTSIDE THE BOX

Italy's Gianluca Pagliuca was the first goalkeeper to be sent off at a FIFA World Cup match. He handled the ball outside his penalty area against Norway in 1994. Despite sacrificing playmaker Roberto Baggio for goalkeeper Luca Marchegiani, Italy still won 1-0.

ITALY'S ELDER STATESMEN

Dino Zoff became both the oldest player and oldest captain to win the FIFA World Cup when Italy lifted the trophy in Spain in 1982. He was 40 years 133 days old. A predecessor, as goalkeeper and captain of both Italy and Juventus, Gianpiero Combi, had led Italy to World Cup glory in 1934.

FIVE-STAR CARBAJAL

Antonio Carbajal, of Mexico, is one of only two men to have appeared at five FIFA World Cup finals—the other was Germany's versatile Lothar Matthaus. Carbajal, who played in 1950, 1954, 1958, 1962, and 1966, conceded a record 25 goals in his 11 FIFA World Cup finals appearances—the same number let in by Saudi Arabia's Mohamed Al-Deayea across ten games in 1994, 1998, and 2002. Al-Deayea was a member of the Saudi squad for the 2006 tournament but did not play.

ZERO TO HERO

One of the unlikeliest stars of the 2014 FIFA World Cup finals was Mexico goalkeeper **Guillermo Ochoa**. He had spent the previous three years in the European shadows at modest French Corsican club Ajaccio. He feared for his World Cup place when Ajaccio was relegated, but Mexico coach Miguel Herrera was unconcerned and Ochoa repaid him with a string of outstanding performances. Best of all was his brilliant defiance of hosts Brazil in a scoreless tie in the group phase. Ochoa, who ended the finals with 61 caps for Mexico, conceded just three goals in four games as Mexico lost 2-1 to two late Netherlands goals in the round-of-16.

NUMBER-ONE NUMBER ONES

The Lev Yashin Award was introduced in 1994 for the man voted best goalkeeper of the FIFA World Cup—though a goalkeeper was selected subsequently for an all-star team at the end of every tournament dating back to 1930. The all-star team was expanded from 11 to 23 players in 1998, allowing room for more than one goalkeeper, but returned to 11 players in 2010. Players who were picked for the all-star teams but missed out on the Lev Yashin Award were Paraguay's Jose Luis Chilavert in 1998, Turkey's Rustu Recber in 2002, and Germany's Jens Lehmann and Portugal's Ricardo in 2006. The first Lev Yashin Award was presented to Belgium's Michel Preud'homme, even though he only played four games, conceding four goals, at the 1994 competition, as his team was edged out 3-2 by Germany in the second round. Legendary Soviet goalkeeper Lev Yashin, after whom the trophy was named, played in the 1958, 1962 and 1966 FIFA World Cups, and was a member of his country's 1970 squad as third-choice keeper and assistant coach. Strangely, he was never chosen for a FIFA World Cup team of the tournament. From 2010, commercial priorities led to Yashin's name being dropped from the award and it was renamed the Golden Glove award.

OLIVER'S ARMS

Germany's **Oliver Kahn** is the only goalkeeper to have been voted FIFA's Player of the Tournament, winning the award at the 2002 FIFA World Cup, despite taking a share of the blame for Brazil's winning goals in the final.

RIGHT WAY FOR RICARDO

Spain's Ricardo Zamora became the first man to save a penalty in a FIFA World Cup finals match, stopping Valdemar de Brito's spot-kick for Brazil in 1934. Spain went on to win 3-1.

HOWARD'S WAY

Tim Howard wrote his name into the FIFA World Cup history books with his amazing performance in the United States' round-of-16 game with Belgium in 2014. Howard registered 16 superb saves in defying wave upon wave of Belgian attacks. This was the most saves ever recorded in a FIFA World Cup tie since the statistic was first introduced in 1966. It was not enough, however, as the United States lost a thriller of a match 2-1 after extra time.

LEADING FROM THE BACK

Iker Casillas became the third goalkeeper to captain his country to FIFA World Cup glory, when Spain became champions in South Africa in 2010. He emulated Italians Gianpiero Combi (in 1934) and Dino Zoff (1982). Casillas was also the first man to lift the trophy after his team had lost its opening match of the tournament.

UNLUCKY BREAK

Goalkeeper Frantisek Planicka broke his arm during Czechoslovakia's 1938 second-round game against Brazil, but played on, even though the game went to extra-time before ending in a 1-1 tie. Not surprisingly, given the extent of his injury, Planicka missed the replay two days later, which the Czechs lost 2-1, and the best goalkeeper of the 1938 FIFA World Cup never added to his tally of 73 caps.

PLAYERS VOTED BEST GOALKEEPER OF THE TOURNAMENT

Year	Player	Year	Player
1930	Enrique Ballestrero (Uruguay)	1978	Ubaldo Fillol (Argentina)
1934	Ricardo Zamora (Spain)	1982	Dino Zoff (Italy)
1938	Frantisek Planicka (Czechoslovakia)	1986	Harald Schumacher (West Germany)
1950	Roque Maspoli (Uruguay)	1990	Sergio Goycoechea (Argentina)
1954	Gyula Grosics (Hungary)	1994	Michel Preud'homme (Belgium)
1958	Harry Gregg (Northern Ireland)	1998	Fabien Barthez (France)
1962	Viliam Schrojf (Czechoslovakia)	2002	Oliver Kahn (Germany)
1966	Gordon Banks (England)	2006	Gianluigi Buffon (Italy)
1970	Ladislao Mazurkiewicz (Uruguay)	2010	Iker Casillas (Spain)
1974	Jan Tomaszewski (Poland)	2014	Manuel Neuer (Germany)

BATTERING RAMON

Argentina's 6-0 win over Peru at the 1978 FIFA World Cup aroused suspicion because the host nation needed to win by four goals to reach the final at the expense of arch-rivals Brazil—and Peruvian goalkeeper Ramon Quiroga had been born in Argentina. He insisted, though, that his saves prevented the defeat from being even more embarrassingly emphatic. Earlier in the same tournament, Quiroga had been booked for a foul on Grzegorz Lato after running into the Polish half of the field.

END TO END STUFF

When Miroslav Klose raced on to a long ball from German team-mate **Manuel Neuer** to score against England in its 2010 FIFA World Cup round-of-16 game, it made Neuer the first goalkeeper to directly set up a finals goal for 44 years. The last before then had been the Soviet Union's Anzor Kavazashvili, providing an assist for Valery Porkuyan's late winner against Chile in the 1966 group stage.

MORE AND MORA

Luis Ricardo Guevara Mora holds the unenviable record for most goals conceded in one FIFA World Cup finals game. The 20-year-old had to pick the ball out of the net ten times in El Salvador's thrashing by Hungary in 1982—and his team-mates managed only one goal in reply. In this game Mora also set a new record for being the youngest goalkeeper to play in a FIFA World Cup finals match.

TONY AWARD

United States goalkeeper **Tony Meola** left the national team after the 1994 FIFA World Cup because he wanted to switch sports and take up American football instead. He failed to make it in gridiron and returned to soccer, but did not play for his country again until 1999. He retired for a second time after reaching a century of international appearances and still holds the record for being the youngest FIFA World Cup captain, having worn the armband for the US's 5-1 defeat to Czechoslovakia in 1990, aged 21 years and 316 days.

SWEDISH STALEMATE

Gilmar and Colin McDonald were the two goalkeepers who made history at Ullevi Stadium, Gothenburg, Sweden, in the 1958 FIFA World Cup when first-round group rivals Brazil and England played to the first scoreless tie in the history of the finals.

KEEPING THE FAITH

Switzerland's **Diego Benaglio** was the only goalkeeper to register a shot at the 2014 FIFA World Cup in Brazil. With the Swiss losing 1-0 to Argentina in its round-of-16 game, at Sao Paulo, he charged upfield at a corner. The ball fell loose to him in the penalty area, but his effort on goal was blocked. Benaglio's Swiss predecessor, at the 2006 finals, was equally unlucky. Pascal Zuberbuhler managed to keep a clean sheet in all four Switzerland games at the FIFA World Cup, three in the group stage, and a scoreless tie with Ukraine in the round-of-16. The Swiss lost the resulting penalty shoot-out 3-0, even though Zuberbuhler saved Ukraine's first kick, taken by Andriy Shevchenko.

TOP GOALS

Year	Goals	Average
1930	70	(3.89 per match)
1934	70	(4.12 per match)
1938	84	(4.67 per match)
1950	88	(4 per match)
1954	140	(5.38 per match)
1958	126	(3.6 per match)
1962	89	(2.78 per match)
1966	89	(2.78 per match)
1970	95	(2.97 per match)
1974	97	(2.55 per match)
1978	102	(2.68 per match)
1982	146	(2.81 per match)
1986	132	(2.54 per match)
1990	115	(2.21 per match)
1994	141	(2.71 per match)
1998	171	(2.67 per match)
2002	161	(2.52 per match)
2006	147	(2.3 per match)
2010	145	(2.27 per match)
2014	171	(2.67 per match)
Total	2,379	(2.85 per match)

THE PETER PRINCIPLE

Peter Shilton became the oldest FIFA World Cup captain when he led England for its 1990 third-place play-off against host nation Italy. He was 40 years and 292 days old as he made his 125th and final appearance for his country, but his day was spoiled by a 2-1 defeat. He also made an error which gifted the opening goal to Italy's Roberto Baggio. Shilton, who was born in Leicester on September 18, 1949, also played for England at the 1982 and 1986 tournaments. He became captain in Mexico in 1986, after Bryan Robson was ruled out of the tournament by injury and Ray Wilkins by suspension, and featured in one of the FIFA World Cup's all-time memorable moments, when he was out-jumped by Argentina's Diego Maradona for the infamous "Hand of God" goal. Shilton jointly holds the record for most FIFA World Cup clean sheets, with ten, along with France's Fabien Barthez, who played at the 1998, 2002, and 2006 tournaments. Both men made 17 FIFA World Cup finals appearances.

TRADING PLACES

The first goalkeeper to be substituted at a FIFA World Cup was Romania's Stere Adamache, who was replaced by Rica Raducanu 27 minutes into a 3-2 defeat to Brazil in 1970. Romania were losing 2-0 at the time.

PLAYING THROUGH THE PAIN BARRIER

The first FIFA World Cup clean sheet was kept by Jimmy Douglas of the United States, in a 3-0 win over Belgium in 1930. He followed that up with another, as Paraguay was beaten by the same scoreline. But, in the semifinal, Argentina proved too good, winning 6-1. Unfortunately, Douglas injured his knee after only four minutes, but had to play on as it would be another 40 years before substitutes were permitted in the FIFA World Cup.

HOW GOING DUTCH PAYS OFF

Argentina's **Sergio Romero** will never be forgotten in the Netherlands, as he used the experience he had gained there to put the Dutchmen out of the 2014 FIFA World Cup. Romero had been brought to Europe in 2007—by Louis Van Gaal, when the Dutch master coach was boss of AZ Alkmaar. In 2011, Romero moved to Italy to play for Sampdoria. Then he fell out of favor with the Genoese club and was loaned to French club AS Monaco in August 2013. Romero was hardly a regular in Ligue 1 either, indeed he played only three league matches in the season leading up to the FIFA World Cup. However, he did remain the first-choice with Argentina coach Alejandro Sabella. Argentina won all its group games, and then Romero kept clean sheets in initial knockout victories over Switzerland and Belgium. When the semifinal went to penalties, Romero became a national hero, with match-winning saves from the Netherlands' Ron Vlaar and Wesley Sneijder. Romero said later he owed Van Gaal special thanks ... "for teaching me how to save penalties."

FIFA WORLD CUP MANAGERS

MANAGING SUCCESS

Germany provided the largest single contingent of coaches at the 2014 FIFA World Cup in Brazil. Most successful was *Die Nationalelf*'s boss, **Joachim Low**, who became, following the 1-0 final victory over Argentina, the fourth German coach to win the trophy after Sepp Herberger (1954), Helmut Schon (1974), and Franz Beckenbauer (1990). Low was appointed in 2006, having been assistant for two years. **Jurgen Klinsmann** (United States) and Ottmar Hitzfeld (Switzerland) both reached the round-of-16, but the group stage was the end of the line for Volker Finke (Cameroon) and Berlin-born Nico Kovac (Croatia).

YOUNG JUAN

Juan Jose Tramutola remains the youngest-ever FIFA World Cup coach, leading Argentina in the 1930 tournament at the age of 27 years and 267 days. Italian Cesare Maldini became the oldest in 2002, taking charge of Paraguay when aged 70 years and 131 days.

DREAM TO NIGHTMARE

Luiz Felipe Scolari quit as Brazil coach after the 2014 FIFA World Cup brought the worst defeat in its history, by 7-1 against Germany in the semifinal, and then a 3-0 defeat to the Netherlands in the third-place play-off. However, he did win the 2002 FIFA World Cup with Brazil, and went on, with Portugal in 2006, to set an individual record of 11 consecutive wins at the finals.

PUFF DADDIES

The coaches of the two teams contesting the 1978 FIFA World Cup final were such prolific smokers that an oversized ashtray was produced for Argentina's Cesar Luis Menotti and the Netherlands' Ernst Happel so they could share it on the touchline.

SOCCER SIX

Only one man has gone to six FIFA World Cups as coach: Brazilian **Carlos Alberto Parreira**, whose greatest moment came when he guided Brazil to the trophy for the fourth time in 1994. His second stint as Brazil coach was less successful—it fell in the quarterfinal in 2006. Parreira also led Kuwait (1982), the United Arab Emirates (1990), Saudi Arabia (1998), and hosts South Africa (2010) at the finals. He had stepped down as South Africa coach in April 2008, for family reasons, but returned late the following year. Parreira was once sacked midway through a FIFA World Cup. In 1998, he coached Saudi Arabia for the first two of its three first round games, losing to Denmark (1-0) and France (4-0), after which he was given his pink slip.

ELDEST STATESMAN OTTO

Otto Rehhagel became the oldest coach in FIFA World Cup history in South Africa in 2010. He was 71 years and 317 days old when his Greece team lost 2-0 to Argentina in its final group game. German Rehhagel had led Greece to its UEFA European Championship victory in 2004.

CRASHING BORA

Only one tournament behind record-holder Carlos Alberto Parreira, **Bora Milutinovic** has coached at five different FIFA World Cups, with a different country each time, two of them being host nations. As well as Mexico in 1986 and the United States in 1994, he led Costa Rica in 1990, Nigeria in 1998, and China in 2002. He reached the knockout stages every time, except in 2002, when China failed to score even a single goal.

DIVIDED LOYALTIES

No coach has won the FIFA World Cup in charge of a foreign team, but several have faced their homeland. These include Jurgen Klinsmann, who played for Germany when it won the Cup in 1990, and then coached the team to third-place in 2006. He was German boss 2004–06 and, having already made his home in California, was appointed United States coach in 2011. In the 2014 FIFA World Cup, "Klinsi" and the US lost 1-0 in a group match to Germany, now led by his former assistant Joachim Low, whom he had appointed in 2004. Other coaches who faced their native land include Brazilian Didi (with Peru in 1970), Frenchman Bruno Metsu (with Senegal in 2002), and Swede Sven-Goran Eriksson (with England in 2002 and 2006).

FIFA WORLD CUP– WINNING COACHES

1930	Alberto Suppici
1934	Vittorio Pozzo
1938	Vittorio Pozzo
1950	Juan Lopez
1954	Sepp Herberger
1958	Vicente Feola
1962	Aymore Moreira
1966	Alf Ramsey
1970	Mario Zagallo
1974	Helmut Schon
1978	Cesar Luis Menotti
1982	Enzo Bearzot
1986	Carlos Bilardo
1990	Franz Beckenbauer
1994	Carlos Alberto Parreira
1998	Aime Jacquet
2002	Luiz Felipe Scolari
2006	Marcello Lippi
2010	Vicente del Bosque
2014	Joachim Low

SCHON SHINES

West Germany's **Helmut Schon** was coach for more FIFA World Cup games than any other man – 25, across the 1966, 1970, 1974, and 1978 tournaments. He has also won the most games as a coach, 16 in all, including the 1974 final against the Netherlands. The 1974 tournament was third time lucky for Schon. He had taken West Germany to second place in 1966, and to third in 1970. Before taking charge of the national side, Schon had worked as an assistant to Sepp Herberger, coach of West Germany's 1954 FIFA World Cup-winning team, while also coach of the then-independent Saarland regional team. Dog-lover Schon, born in Dresden on September 15, 1915, scored 17 goals in 16 internationals for Germany between 1937 and 1941. He succeeded Herberger in 1964, and spent 14 years as national coach. Schon was the first coach to win the FIFA World Cup (1974) and UEFA European Championship (1972).

FIFA DISCIPLINE
WORLD CUP

FIFA BITES BACK

Uruguay's **Luis Suarez** incurred a record instant FIFA sanction after biting Italy's Giorgio Chiellini during Uruguay's 1-0 win in the 2014 World Cup, a result that put it, and not the *Azzurri*, into the second round. Suarez missed the subsequent 2-0 defeat by Colombia, because he had been banned from all soccer for four months, from international competition for nine games, and fined 100,000 Swiss francs. It was not the first time Suarez had been in trouble at the FIFA World Cup finals: he was banned for one game at the 2010 finals after being red-carded for handball on the goal-line in the quarterfinal against Ghana.

REPEAT OFFENDERS

France's **Zinedine Zidane** and Brazil's **Cafu** are both FIFA World Cup winners, and both notched up a record six FIFA World Cup cards. Cafu did not receive any red cards, but Zidane was sent off twice. Most infamously, Zidane was dismissed for headbutting Italy's Marco Materazzi during extra-time of the 2006 final in Berlin, in what he had already announced would be the last game of his legendary career. He had also been sent off during a first-round game against Saudi Arabia in 1998, but returned from suspension in time to help France win the trophy with a sensational two-goal performance in the final. The only other man to have been sent off twice at two different FIFA World Cups is Cameroon's Rigobert Song. When dismissed against Brazil in 1994, he became the FIFA World Cup's youngest red card offender—aged just 17 years and 358 days. He saw red for the second time against Chile in 1998.

NOT LEADING BY EXAMPLE

The first man to be sent off at a FIFA World Cup was Peru's Placido Galindo, at the first tournament in 1930 during a 3-1 defeat to Romania. Chilean referee Alberto Warnken dismissed the Peruvian captain for fighting.

ARGIE BARGEY

Argentina defender Pedro Monzon became the first player sent off in a World Cup final when he was dismissed in 1990 for a foul on West Germany's Jurgen Klinsmann. Monzon had been on the pitch only 20 minutes after coming on as a half-time substitute. Three minutes from full-time, Mexican referee Edgardo Codesal reduced Argentina to nine men when he red-carded Gustavo Dezotti following a skirmish with Jurgen Kohler. Marcel Desailly of France, in 1998, is the only member of a winning team to be sent off in a World Cup final.

CARDS CLOSE TO CHEST

Only one group in FIFA World Cup finals history has featured no bookings at all: Group 4 in 1970, featuring West Germany, Peru, Bulgaria, and Morocco. In contrast, the 2006 FIFA World Cup in Germany was the worst for both red and yellow cards, with 28 dismissals and 345 bookings in 64 games.

FIFA WORLD CUP RED CARDS, BY TOURNAMENT

Year	Red Cards
1930	1
1934	1
1938	4
1950	0
1954	3
1958	3
1962	6
1966	5
1970	0
1974	5
1978	3
1982	5
1986	8
1990	16
1994	15
1998	22
2002	17
2006	28
2010	17
2014	10

FINAL COUNT

England's Howard Webb set a record with one red card and 14 yellow in the 2010 FIFA World Cup final between Spain and Netherlands. The previous 18 finals had featured 40 bookings and three dismissals between them. Webb's card total of 15 was nine more than the six shown by Brazil's Romualdo Arppi Filho in the 1986 final between Argentina (four) and Germany (two). Italy's Nicola Rizzoli showed four yellow cards (two each) when the same teams met in the 2014 FIFA World Cup final.

SOLE CHANCE OF GLORY

India withdrew from the 1950 FIFA World Cup because some of its players wanted to play barefoot, but FIFA insisted all players must wear soccer boots. India has not qualified for the tournament since.

BREAKING COVER

Zaire defender Mwepu Llunga was booked for running out of the wall and kicking the ball away as Brazil prepared to take a free-kick, at the 1974 FIFA World Cup. Romanian referee Nicolae Rainea ignored Llunga's pleas of innocence.

GOOD SON, BAD SON

Cameroon's Andre Kana-Biyik served two suspensions during the 1990 FIFA World Cup. The first came after he was sent off in the opening match against Argentina—six minutes before his brother Francois Omam-Biyik scored the only goal. His second ban came after yellow cards in the final group game against Russia and in the second-round defeat of Colombia.

YELLOW MELO'S RED MIST

Felipe Melo's red card for stamping on Arjen Robben, in Brazil's 2010 FIFA World Cup quarterfinal defeat to the Netherlands, meant Brazil has had more players sent off in FIFA World Cup history (11) than any other team, one more than Argentina. Melo's dismissal came a few days after Kaka had seen red in a first-round victory over the Ivory Coast. Melo could also have gone down as the first player ever to score an own goal and be sent off in the same FIFA World Cup gamr, but the first Dutch goal was later officially awarded to its own playmaker Wesley Sneijder.

ALL'S FAIR

FIFA World Cup organizers hailed a vast improvement in fair play at the 2014 finals in Brazil. The total of 10 red cards was the lowest since eight in Mexico in 1986 and the tally of 177 yellow cards the fewest since 165 in Italy in 1990 (when the finals had 24 teams and 52 games). The first dismissal in the group stage was Uruguay's Maxi Pereira,w against Costa Rica, but the earliest in a game was Portugal defender **Pepe**, for a headbutt on Germany's Thomas Muller in the 37th minute of its clash in Salvador. FIFA referee's chief Massimo Busacca also put a sharp reduction in injuries down to greater discipline among players.

THREE LIONS' THREE REDS

Ray Wilkins, David Beckham, and Wayne Rooney are the only three England players to have been sent off at the FIFA World Cup. Wilkins was dismissed for a second yellow card in a group game against Morocco in 1986; Beckham incurred a straight red in the second round against Argentina in 1998; and Rooney also received a straight red against Portugal in the 2006 quarterfinal. All three matches ended in ties, but England lost penalty shoot-outs to Argentina and Portugal.

YEARS OF EXPERIENCE

Spain's Juan Gardeazabal Garay remains the youngest referee at a FIFA World Cup, being just 24 years and 193 days old when he took charge at the 1958 tournament in Sweden. He also officiated in 1962 and 1966. Englishman **George Reader** is not only the oldest man to have refereed a FIFA World Cup final—he was 56 years and 236 days old when he took charge of the decisive final group game between Brazil and Uruguay in 1950—but also the oldest referee at any FIFA World Cup. He died on July 13, 1978, 48 years to the day after the very first FIFA World Cup fixture.

THE ITALIAN JOB

Nicola Rizzoli had designs on refereeing the FIFA World Cup final ever since he was promoted to the FIFA international list in 2007. Rizzoli, an architect away from the world's soccer fields, had made such high-speed progress that he was refereeing in Italy's Serie A at the age of 30. He was named in FIFA's world elite group in the spring of 2013 and, two months later, refereed the UEFA Champions League final. He was in the middle for four matches at the 2014 FIFA World Cup, and became the third Italian to referee the Final.

BAKU OF THE NET

The official who signaled that Geoff Hurst's controversial extra-time goal for England in the 1966 FIFA World Cup final had crossed the line is often wrongly described as a Russian linesman. In fact, Tofik Bakhramov was from Azerbaijan, so he was officially a Soviet Union linesman. The Azeri national soccer stadium, in the capital Baku, is now named after him.

DOUBLE DUTY

Only two men have refereed a FIFA World Cup final and a UEFA European Championship final. Italian Sergio Gonella officiated at the 1978 World Cup final between Argentina and the Netherlands, two years after overseeing the European Championship final between West Germany and Czechoslovakia. Swiss official Gottfried Dienst took control of the 1966 FIFA World Cup final, between England and West Germany, and the tied 1968 UEFA European Championship final, between Italy and Yugoslavia. Spain's Jose Maria Ortiz de Mendibil was awarded the replay.

FRENCH CONNECTION

Frenchman **Georges Capdeville**, in charge for Italy's win over Hungary in 1938, is the only man to referee the final in a FIFA World Cup hosted by his own country.

FIFA WORLD CUP FINAL REFEREES

1930	Jean Langenus (Belgium)
1934	Ivan Eklind (Sweden)
1938	Georges Capdeville (France)
1950	George Reader (England)
1954	William Ling (England)
1958	Maurice Guigue (France)
1962	Nikolay Latyshev (USSR)
1966	Gottfried Dienst (Switzerland)
1970	Rudi Glockner (West Germany)
1974	Jack Taylor (England)
1978	Sergio Gonella (Italy)
1982	Arnaldo Cezar Coelho (Brazil)
1986	Romualdo Arppi Filho (Brazil)
1990	Edgardo Codesal (Mexico)
1994	Sandor Puhl (Hungary)
1998	Said Belqola (Morocco)
2002	Pierluigi Collina (Italy)
2006	Horacio Elizondo (Argentina)
2010	Howard Webb (England)
2014	Nicola Rizzoli (Italy)

COUPE DU MONDE 1938

WORLDWIDE WEBB

Former Yorkshire policeman **Howard Webb** became the fourth Englishman to referee a
FIFA World Cup final, when he was chosen for the 2010 showdown between Spain and
the Netherlands. He had earlier controled two group games and the round-of-16
contest between Spain and Chile. The honor came less than two months after he had
refereed the UEFA Champions League final, between Inter Milan and Bayern Munich,
making him the first man to be in charge of both FIFA World Cup and UEFA European
Cup final games in the same summer. Webb also became the first FIFA World Cup
debutant ref to be given the final. At just three days short of his 39th birthday,
Webb was also the youngest FIFA World Cup final referee since Frenchman Georges
Capdeville, who took charge of the 1938 final aged 38 years and 232 days. Webb
also refereed two games at the 2014 FIFA World Cup finals in Brazil.

PROLIFIC OFFICIALS

Ravshan Irmatov, from Uzbekistan, became the most experienced
FIFA World Cup referee of all time at the 2014 finals. He totaled a record
nine games after controling five in 2010 and four in Brazil. Irmatov,
whose father had also been a top referee in the former Soviet Union,
became a FIFA official when only 26 in 2003. Four times he was voted
best referee in Asia and he controled the final of the FIFA Club World
Cup in both 2008 and 2011. His FIFA World Cup debut was in South
Africa in 2010 when, despite being the youngest official present, he
was awarded the opening game, between host nation South Africa and
Mexico. In Brazil, Irmatov was the subject of controversy after he took
no action against Netherlands goalkeeper Tim Krul as he confronted
all of Costa Rica's penalty-takers during the shootout to decide the
quarterfinal—which the Netherlands won, thanks to Krul's two
saves. Irmatov's multi-match campaign saw him break the
previous record of eight games officiated, by Frenchman Joel Quiniou,
Mexico's Benito Archundia, and Uruguay's Jorge Larrionda.

TIME, GENTLEMEN

Welsh referee Clive Thomas disallowed what would have
potentially been a winning goal by Brazil against Sweden
in the 1978 FIFA World Cup. Thomas said he had blown the
final whistle seconds before Zico headed in from a corner,
and the game ended in a 1-1 tie. In contrast, Israeli referee
Abraham Klein had to blow the final whistle several times
when England played Brazil at the 1970 FIFA World Cup in
Guadalajara, but none of the players appeared to hear him.

NOW YOU SEE IT ...

Referees were given two supporting aids at the 2014 FIFA
World Cup. One was goal-line technology, approved two
years earlier by the law-making International Board. The
other was a vanishing spray used by referees to "fix"
defensive walls in their place at free-kicks. The spray,
which faded after half a minute, had been developed by
Brazilian inventor Heine Allemagne. Already used widely
in Latin America and FIFA junior tournaments, it impressed
European referees by helping quell dissent at free-kicks.

RED CARD CARTER

Mexican referee **Arturo Brizio Carter** sent off more players
at FIFA World Cups than any other official. He showed
seven red cards in his six games at the 1994 and 1998
finals. "Victims" included Italy's Gianfranco Zola, Argentina's
Ariel Ortega, and France's Zinedine Zidane.

CAPACITY PLANNING

If current plans are realized and every seat is occupied, the attendances at the final of each of the next two FIFA World Cups will significantly exceed the 74,738 who attended the Maracana in Rio de Janeiro for the 2014 climax. Projected capacity for the redeveloped Luzhniki in Moscow, which will stage the 2018 FIFA World Cup final, is 81,000 while 86,250 is the maximum estimated for the **Lusail** Iconic Stadium in Qatar in 2022. The smallest proposed capacities at the next two World Cups are 43,702 at the Rostov-on-Don stadium in 2018, and then 43,520 at the Qatar University Stadium in Doha in 2022. FIFA regulations insist on a minimum capacity for a finals venue of 40,000.

TWO'S COMPANY, 300'S A CROWD

The 300 people who were recorded as watching Romania beat Peru 3-1 in 1930 formed the FIFA World Cup finals' smallest attendance, with plenty of room for maneuver inside the Estadio Pocitos in Montevideo. A day earlier, ten times as many people are thought to have been there to watch France's 4-1 win over Mexico.

BONANZA IN BRAZIL

The 2014 FIFA World Cup in Brazil was watched by a total of 3,429,873 spectators, across the 64 matches in 12 different stadia—the second highest aggregate attendance in the tournament's history, behind only the United States in 1994. The average attendance was 53,592 which meant a 98.4 percent capacity. That was a significant improvement on 2010 FIFA World Cup, when the attendance average was 49,670 with "only" 92.9 percent of the seats in South Africa being filled.

CITY SLICKER

The capacity of **Soccer City**, venue for the first FIFA World Cup final in Africa, was 84,490. This followed a total redevelopment of the original Johannesburg stadium, which had held a maximum 78,000. The design of the new stadium was based on traditional African pottery and nicknamed "The Calabash." Soccer City was used for the opening game, one in the round-of-16, one quarterfinal, and the final itself.

GENDER EQUALITY

Only two stadiums have hosted the finals of the FIFA World Cup for both men and women. The **Rose Bowl**, in Pasadena, California, was the venue for the men's final in 1994—when Brazil beat Italy—and the women's showdown between the victorious US and China five years later. The 1999 final attracted a women's soccer world-record 90,185 fans. Sweden's Rasunda Stadium, near Stockholm, had to endure a much longer wait between the men's (1958) and women's (1995) finals. The fans at the Rose Bowl certainly got their money's worth, as both games ended as scoreless ties after 120 minutes, before being decided in penalty shootouts.

FIFA WORLD CUP FINAL ATTENDANCES

Year	Attendance	Stadium	City
1930	93,000	Estadio Centenario	Montevideo
1934	45,000	Stadio Nazionale del PNF	Rome
1938	60,000	Stade Olympique de Colombes	Paris
1950	173,850	Estadio do Maracana	Rio de Janeiro
1954	60,000	Wankdorfstadion	Berne
1958	51,800	Rasunda Fotbollstadion	Solna
1962	68,679	Estadio Nacional	Santiago
1966	98,000	Wembley Stadium	London
1970	107,412	Estadio Azteca	Mexico City
1974	75,200	Olympiastadion	Munich
1978	71,483	Estadio Monumental	Buenos Aires
1982	90,000	Estadio Santiago Bernabeu	Madrid
1986	114,600	Estadio Azteca	Mexico City
1990	73,603	Stadio Olimpico	Rome
1994	94,194	Rose Bowl	Pasadena
1998	80,000	Stade de France	Paris
2002	69,029	International Stadium	Yokohama
2006	69,000	Olympiastadion	Berlin
2010	84,490	Soccer City	Johannesburg
2014	74,738	Maracana	Rio de Janeiro

TOURNAMENT ATTENDANCES

Year	Total	Average
1930	434,500	24,139
1934	358,000	21,059
1938	376,000	20,889
1950	1,043,500	47,432
1954	889,500	34,212
1958	919,580	26,274
1962	899,074	28,096
1966	1,635,000	51,094
1970	1,603,975	50,124
1974	1,768,152	46,530
1978	1,546,151	40,688
1982	2,109,723	40,572
1986	2,393,331	46,026
1990	2,516,348	48,391
1994	3,587,538	68,991
1998	2,785,100	43,517
2002	2,705,197	42,269
2006	3,359,439	52,491
2010	3,178,856	49,670
2014	3,429,873	53,592
TOTAL	34,538,837	44,903

FAN FESTS FIND FAVOR

City center "Fan Fests," including giant television screens, food service, and entertainment provision, proved more popular than ever at the 2014 FIFA World Cup in Brazil. Several of the 12 city authorities had been reluctant, initially, to put in the work. But their efforts were rewarded with more than five million fans visiting the sites across Brazil. This was a major improvement on the total of 2.6 million across South Africa in 2010 and the initial fan fests in Germany in 2006. Not surprisingly, the liveliest party venue in 2014 was the fan fest on **Copacabana** beach in Rio de Janeiro.

ABSENT FRIENDS

Only 2,823 spectators turned up at the Rasunda Stadium in Stockholm to see Wales play Hungary in a first-round play-off match during the 1958 FIFA World Cup. More than 15,000 had attended the first game between the two teams, but boycotted the replay in tribute to executed Hungarian uprising leader Imre Nagy.

MORBID MARACANA

The largest attendance for a FIFA World Cup match was at Rio de Janeiro's Maracana for the last game of the 1950 tournament. However, no one sure exactly how many were there. The final tally was officially given as 173,850, though some estimates suggest as many as 210,000 witnessed the host country's traumatic defeat. Tensions were so high at the final whistle, winning Uruguay captain Obdulio Varela was not awarded the trophy in the traditional manner, but had it surreptitiously nudged into his hands. FIFA president Jules Rimet described the crowd's overwhelming silence as "morbid, almost too difficult to bear." Uruguay's triumphant players barricaded themselves inside their locker room for several hours, before they judged it safe enough to emerge. At least, in 1950, Brazil made it to the final game at the Maracana. In the 2014 FIFA World Cup, as the host nation, Brazil played in Sao Paulo once, and Fortaleza and Belo Horizonte twice each. But, after losing in the semifinal, Brazil made a second trip to Brasilia for the third-place play-off, instead of to Rio for the final.

FIFA WORLD CUP STADIUMS & HOSTS

BERLIN CALL

Despite later becoming the capital of a unified Germany, then-divided Berlin only hosted three group games at the 1974 FIFA World Cup in West Germany—the host nation's surprise loss to neighboring East Germany took place in Hamburg. An unexploded World War Two bomb was discovered beneath the seats at Berlin's Olympiastadion in 2002, by workers preparing the ground for the 2006 tournament. Germany, along with Brazil, had applied to host the tournament in 1942, before it was canceled due to the outbreak of World War Two.

TWIN PEAKS

Five stadiums hold the distinction of having staged both the final of a FIFA World Cup and the Olympic Games track and field events: Berlin's Olympiastadion (1936 Olympics, 2006 World Cup), Paris's Stade Colombes (1924 Olympics, 1938 World Cup), London's Wembley (1948 Olympics, 1966 World Cup), Rome's Stadio Olimpico (1960 Olympics, 1990 World Cup), and Munich's Olympiastadion (1972 Olympics, 1974 World Cup). The Estadio Azteca (Mexico City) and Rose Bowl (Pasadena) have both hosted World Cup finals as well as Olympic soccer finals.

OLYMPIC NAMES

The stadium hosting the opening game of the 1930 FIFA World Cup had stands named after great Uruguayan soccer triumphs: Colombes, in honor of the 1924 Paris Olympics venue; Amsterdam, after the site where that title was retained four years later; and Montevideo, even though it would be another fortnight before the home team clinched the first FIFA World Cup in its own capital city. ,

RIO'S MARIO

Most people know Brazil's largest stadium as the Maracana, named after the Rio neighborhood and a small nearby river. But, since the mid-1960s, the official title has been "Estadio Mario Filho" after the influential sports journalist and editor who campaigned for the stadium's construction on that site.

TERRITORIAL GAINS

History was made twice over when **FIFA** decided in December 2010 which countries would stage the 2018 and 2022 FIFA World Cups. The 2018 vote went in favor of Russia—ahead of Spain/Portugal, Belgium/Netherlands, and England—making it the first FIFA World Cup to be held in Eastern Europe. The tournament will then go to the Middle East for the first time in 2022, after Qatar emerged ahead of rival bids from the United States, Japan, South Korea, and Australia.

MEXICAN SAVE

Mexico was not the original choice to host the 1986 FIFA World Cup, but it stepped in when Colombia withdrew in 1982, due to financial problems. Mexico held on to the staging rights despite suffering a devastating earthquake, in September 1985, that left approximately 10,000 people dead, but did not damage any of the stadiums. FIFA kept faith in Mexico, and the **Azteca Stadium** became the first venue to host the FIFA World Cup final twice. Mexico also became the first country to stage two FIFA World Cup tournaments. The Azteca, officially the "Estadio Guillermo Canedo"—named after a Mexican soccer official—was built in 1960, using 100,000 tonnes of concrete, four times as much as was needed to construct the old Wembley.

ARCHITECTS' PREROGATIVE

Distinctive and creative elements were added to the stadiums built especially for the 2010 FIFA World Cup in South Africa, including the giraffe-shaped towers at **Nelspruit's Mbombela stadium**, the 350-meter-long arch with its mobile viewing platform soaring above **Durban's main arena**, and the white "petals" shrouding the Nelson Mandela Bay stadium in Port Elizabeth.

UNSUCCESSFUL HOSTING BIDS

1930	Hungary, Italy, Netherlands, Spain, Sweden
1934	Sweden
1938	Argentina, Germany
1950	None
1954	None
1958	None
1962	Argentina, West Germany
1966	Spain, West Germany
1970	Argentina
1974	Spain
1978	Mexico
1982	West Germany
1986	Colombia*, Canada, USA
1990	England, Greece, USSR
1994	Brazil, Morocco
1998	Morocco, Switzerland
2002	Mexico
2006	Brazil, England, Morocco, South Africa
2010	Egypt, Libya/Tunisia, Morocco
2014	None
2018	England, Netherlands/Belgium, Spain/Portugal
2022	Australia, Japan, South Korea, USA

* Colombia won hosting rights for 1986 but later withdrew.

MORE MARACANA

No stadium other than the **Maracana** in Rio de Janeiro was considered for even a moment when it came to choosing the host venue for the 2014 FIFA World Cup in Brazil. On July 13, it duly became the second venue, after the Estadio Azteca in Mexico City, to host the FIFA World Cup final for the second time. Although the official attendance is now given as 173,850, it is thought that anything up to 210,000 may have jammed the Maracana for the 1950 final group game between Brazil and Uruguay. Several redevelopments saw capacity reduced to an all-seater capacity of around 75,000 by the time of the 2014 showpiece between Germany and Argentina. The latest facelift for Maracana, which is owned by the Rio de Janeiro state government, cost an estimated $500m. As one of the first stadiums to be ready, it hosted the final of the 2013 FIFA Confederations Cup "rehearsal" tournament. The Maracana will also stage the Opening and Closing Ceremonies of the Rio de Janeiro 2016 Olympic Games.

RATIONAL IN RUSSIA

Organizers of the 2018 FIFA World Cup in Russia plan to return to the "clusters" system of adjacent city venues to ease travel, accommodation, and logistical problems, thus reducing the costs for fans. Unlike Brazil 2014, one city—Moscow—will have two venues: the **Luzhniki** Olympic Stadium and Spartak Moscow's new home. The "clusters" concept was last used in the United States in 1994. Michel Platini, president of the France 1998 organizing committee, scrapped the idea to spread the top teams all around the country. FIFA wanted to reinstate the system for the 2014 finals in Brazil but local organizers refused.

HOSTS WITH THE MOST

No other single-hosted FIFA World Cup has used as many venues as the 14 spread across Spain in 1982. The 2002 tournament was played at 20 different venues, but ten of these were in Japan and ten in co-host country South Korea.

FIFA WORLD CUP PENALTIES

FIFA WORLD CUP PENALTY SHOOT-OUTS

Year	Round	120-minute Score	Winners	Shoot-out Score
1982	Semifinal	West Germany 3 France 3	West Germany	5-4
1986	Quarterfinal	West Germany 0 Mexico 0	West Germany	4-1
1986	Quarterfinal	France 1 Brazil 1	France	4-3
1986	Quarterfinal	Belgium 1 Spain 1	Belgium	5-4
1990	Second round	Republic of Ireland 0 Romania 0	Republic of Ireland	5-4
1990	Quarterfinal	Argentina 0 Yugoslavia 0	Argentina	3-2
1990	Semifinal	Argentina 1 Italy 1	Argentina	4-3
1990	Semifinal	West Germany 1 England 1	West Germany	4-3
1994	Second round	Bulgaria 1 Mexico 1	Bulgaria	3-1
1994	Quarterfinal	Sweden 2 Romania 2	Sweden	5-4
1994	Final	Brazil 0 Italy 0	Brazil	3-2
1998	Second round	Argentina 2 England 2	Argentina	4-3
1998	Quarterfinal	France 0 Italy 0	France	4-3
1998	Semifinal	Brazil 1 Netherlands 1	Brazil	4-2
2002	Second round	Spain 1 Republic of Ireland 1	Spain	3-2
2002	Quarterfinal	South Korea 0 Spain 0	South Korea	5-3
2006	Second round	Ukraine 0 Switzerland 0	Ukraine	3-0
2006	Quarterfinal	Germany 1 Argentina 1	Germany	4-2
2006	Quarterfinal	Portugal 0 England 0	Portugal	3-1
2006	Final	Italy 1 France 1	Italy	5-3
2010	Second round	Paraguay 0 Japan 0	Paraguay	5-3
2010	Quarterfinal	Uruguay 1 Ghana 1	Uruguay	4-2
2014	Second round	Brazil 1 Chile 1	Brazil	3-2
2014	Second round	Costa Rica 1 Greece 1	Costa Rica	5-3
2014	Quarterfinal	Netherlands 0 Costa Rica 0	Netherlands	4-3
2014	Semifinal	Argentina 0 Netherlands 0	Argentina	4-2

BAGGIO OF DISHONOR

Pity poor **Roberto Baggio**: the Italian maestro stepped up in three FIFA World Cup penalty shoot-outs, more than any other player—and was a loser in every one. Most painfully, it was his shot over the bar that gifted Brazil the trophy at the end of the 1994 Final. But he had also ended on the losing team against Argentina in a 1990 semifinal and would do so again, against France in a 1998 quarterfinal. At least, in 1990 and 1998, his own attempts were successful.

FIRST IS BETTER

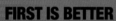

Nine penalty shoot-outs in a row were won by the team taking the first kick. The run started with South Korea's quarterfinal defeat of Spain in the 2002 FIFA World Cup and ended after Costa Rica's round-of-16 win over Greece in 2014. The Netherlands went second and still defeated Costa Rica in the 2014 quarterfinal, but then went first when losing the semifinal to Argentina.

WOE FOR ASAMOAH

Ghana striker **Asamoah Gyan** is the only player to have missed two penalties during match-time at FIFA World Cups. He hit the post with a spot-kick against the Czech Republic during a group game at the 2006 tournament, then struck a shot against the bar with the final kick of extra-time in Ghana's 2010 quarterfinal versus Uruguay. Had he scored then, Gyan would have given Ghana a 2–1 win—following Luis Suarez's goal-stopping handball on the goal-line—and a first African place in a FIFA World Cup semifinal. Despite such a traumatic miss, Gyan did then step up to take Ghana's first penalty in the shoot-out, again striking it high, but this time into the back of the net. His team still lost the shoout, 4–2.

FRENCH KICKS

The first penalty shoot-out at a FIFA World Cup finals came in the 1982 semifinal in Seville between West Germany and France, when French takers Didier Six and **Maxime Bossis** were the unfortunate players to miss. The same two countries met in the semifinal four years later—and West Germany again won, though in normal time, 2-0. The record for most shoot-outs is shared by the 1990, 2006, and 2014 tournaments, all with four. Both semifinals in 1990 went to penalties, while the 2006 final was the second to be settled that manner— Italy beating France 5-3 after David Trezeguet struck the crossbar.

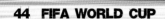

COSTA RICA'S KRUL FATE

Costa Rica enjoyed a thrilling ride at the 2014 FIFA World Cup. "Los Ticos" started by topping a first round "Group of Death," featuring three former world champions: Uruguay, Italy, and England. Coach Jorge Luis Pinto then saw his team earn a 1-1 tie with Greece in the round-of-16, before winning the shoot-out 5-3, to reach the quarterfinal for the first time. Heroes were goalkeeper Keylor Navas, in saving from Teo Gekas, and last-shot defender Michael Umaña. History appeared to be repeating itself when Costa Rica held Netherlands to a scoreless tie to earn another shoot-out. But this time it was foiled by Dutch coach Louis Van Gaal. He sent on reserve goalkeeper **Tim Krul** to replace the less-tall Jasper Cillessen in the last minute of extra time, as Van Gaal explained, "because he has a longer reach." Krul duly saved kicks from Bryan Ruiz and Umaña, and the Dutch won the shoot-out 4-3. Costa Rica was still welcomed home as heroes.

THREE IN ONE

Argentina's stand-in goalkeeper Sergio Goycochea set a tournament record by saving four shoot-out penalties in 1990, though West Germany's Harald Schumacher managed as many, across the 1982 and 1986 finals. Portugal's Ricardo achieved an unprecedented feat by keeping out three attempts in a single shoot-out, becoming an instant hero in his team's quarterfinal win over England in 2006.

PENALTY SHOOT-OUTS BY COUNTRY

5	Argentina (4 wins, 1 defeat)	1	Belgium (1 win)
4	Germany/West Germany (4 wins)	1	Bulgaria (1 win)
4	Brazil (3 wins, 1 defeat)	1	Paraguay (1 win)
4	France (2 wins, 2 defeats)	1	Portugal (1 win)
4	Italy (1 win, 3 defeats)	1	South Korea (1 win)
3	Netherlands (1 win, 2 defeats)	1	Sweden (1 win)
3	Spain (1 win, 2 defeats)	1	Ukraine (1 win)
3	England (3 defeats)	1	Uruguay (1 win)
2	Costa Rica (1 win, 1 defeat)	1	Yugoslavia (1 win)
2	Republic of Ireland (1 win, 1 defeat)	1	Chile (1 defeat)
2	Mexico (2 defeats)	1	Ghana (1 defeat)
2	Romania (2 defeats)	1	Greece (1 defeat)
		1	Japan (1 defeat)
		1	Switzerland (1 defeat)

GERMAN EFFICIENCY

Germany, or West Germany, has won all four of its FIFA World Cup penalty shoot-outs, more than any other team. Argentina also has four wins, but it lost one—to Germany in the 2006 quarterfinal. The German run began with a semifinal victory over France in 1982, when goalkeeper Harald Schumacher was the match-winner, despite being lucky to stay on the pitch for a vicious extra-time foul on France's Patrick Battiston. West Germany also reached the 1990 final thanks to its shoot-out expertize, this time proving superior to England—as it would do in the 1996 UEFA European Championship semifinal. In the 2006 quarterfinal, Germany's goalkeeper Jens Lehmann consulted a note predicting the direction Argentina's players were likely to shoot toward. The vital information was scribbled on a scrap of hotel notepaper by Germany's chief scout Urs Siegenthaler. The only German national team to lose a major tournament penalty shoot-out was the squad that contested the 1976 UEFA European Championship final against Czechoslovakia. It was West Germany's first shoot-out experience—and it learned a good lesson, as it has not lost a shoot-out since then.

THE PLAYERS WHO MISSED IN SHOOT-OUTS

Argentina: Diego Maradona (1990), Pedro Troglio (1990), Hernan Crespo (1998), Roberto Ayala (2006), Esteban Cambiasso (2006)
Brazil: Socrates (1986), Julio Cesar (1986), Marcio Santos (1994), Willian (2014), Hulk (2014)
Bulgaria: Krassimir Balakov (1994)
Chile: Mauricio Pinilla (2014), Alexis Sanchez (2014), Gonzalo Jara (2014)
Costa Rica: Bryan Ruiz (2014), Michael Umana (2014)
England: Stuart Pearce (1990), Chris Waddle (1990), Paul Ince (1998), David Batty (1998), Frank Lampard (2006), Steven Gerrard (2006), Jamie Carragher (2006)
France: Didier Six (1982), Maxime Bossis (1982), Michel Platini (1986), Bixente Lizarazu (1998), David Trezeguet (2006)
Germany/West Germany: Uli Stielike (1982)
Ghana: John Mensah (2010), Dominic Adiyiah (2010)
Greece: Theofanis Gekas (2014)
Italy: Roberto Donadoni (1990), Aldo Serena (1990), Franco Baresi (1994), Daniele Massaro (1994), Roberto Baggio (1994), Demetrio Albertini (1998), Luigi Di Biagio (1998)

Japan: Yuichi Komano (2010)
Mexico: Fernando Quirarte (1986), Raul Servin (1986), Alberto Garcia Aspe (1994), Marcelino Bernal (1994), Jorge Rodriguez (1994)
Netherlands: Phillip Cocu (1998), Ronald de Boer (1998), Ron Vlaar (2014), Wesley Sneijder (2014)
Portugal: Hugo Viana (2006), Petit (2006)
Republic of Ireland: Matt Holland (2002), David Connolly (2002), Kevin Kilbane (2002)
Romania: Daniel Timofte (1990), Dan Petrescu (1994), Miodrag Belodedici (1994)
Spain: Eloy (1986), Juanfran (2002), Juan Carlos Valeron (2002), Joaquin (2002)
Sweden: Hakan Mild (1994)
Switzerland: Marco Streller (2006), Tranquillo Barnetta (2006), Ricardo Cabanas (2006)
Ukraine: Andriy Shevchenko (2006)
Uruguay: Maximiliano Pereira (2010)
Yugoslavia: Dragan Stojkovic (1990), Dragoljub Brnovic (1990), Faruk Hadzibegic (1990)

PART 2:
THE COUNTRIES

SOME call it soccer, others say football, futbol or calcio or futebol, but go to virtually any country on earth and someone will be speaking about this sport by whatever label. Soccer—association football— knows no boundaries of race or politics or religion.

The structure is simple, helping ensure the sport's international success. At the head of the world soccer pyramid is FIFA, the world federation. Supporting FIFA's work are the six regional geographical confederations, representing Africa, Asia, Europe, Oceania, South America, plus the Caribbean, Central, and North America. Backing up the regions in turn are the national associations of 209 countries. FIFA, therefore, can boast more member countries than even the United Nations or the Olympic movement.

The countries are pivotal. They field the national teams which have built sporting history through their many and varied achievements in world-focused competitions such as the FIFA World Cup. But they also oversee the growth of soccer in their nations. from professional leagues to the sport at grass-roots level.

Representative teams from England and Scotland played out the first formal internationals in the late 19th century, thus laying the foundation for the four British home nations' unique independent status within a world soccer family almost without exception comprising nation states. The original British Home Championship was the first competition for national teams but its demise, as a result of a congested fixture list, has left the Copa America in South America as the oldest survivor—apart from the Olympic Games.

The trend-setting example of the Olympic Games in the 1920s led directly to the creation of the FIFA World Cup and its launch in 1930. Already South America had its own national team championship and all the other five FIFA regions followed in due course. The winners meet once every four years in the FIFA Confederations Cup which is the rehearsal event for the extravaganza, one year later, which is the FIFA World Cup itself—the ultimate celebration of the planet's favorite sport.

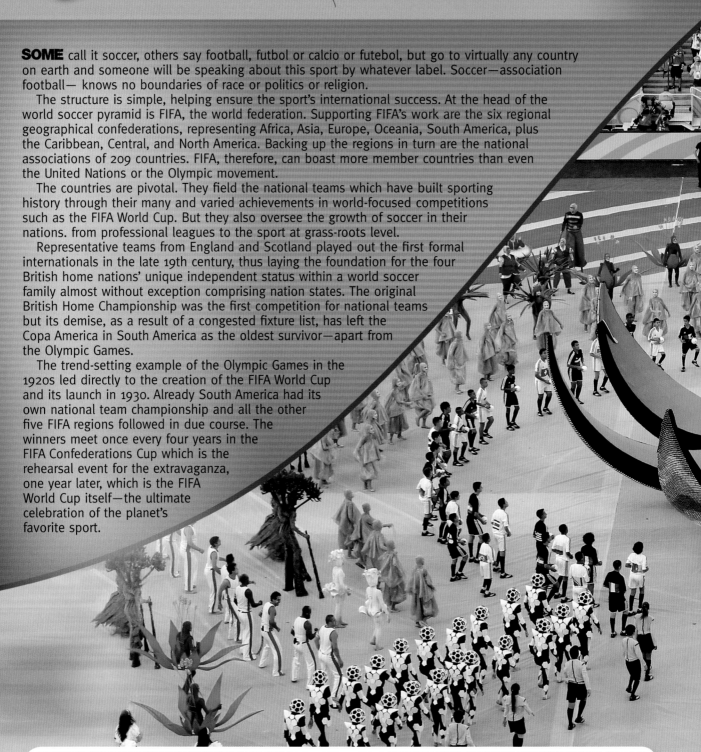

Jennifer Lopez, Pitbull, and Claudia Leitte raise the excitement levels in Sao Paulo in a colorful Opening Ceremony for the 2014 FIFA World Cup, ahead of Brazil's 3-1 win over Croatia in the opening game.

EUROPE

As soon as modern soccer's rules were written in England the game's growth was rapid, with enthusiasm spreading swiftly across Europe, the cradle of the sport. UEFA, the European soccer confederation, now boasts 54 member states, from tiny Andorra and Gibraltar to world giants, Spain, Germany, Italy, England, the Netherlands, and France. Soccer is played and followed with a fervent passion across the continent, not only at club but also at national levels. Germany's 2014 FIFA World Cup glory made it a record three straight wins for Europe.

German fans, in Brazil in 2014, celebrate their heroes' fourth FIFA World Cup victory—making history as Europe's first winners in eight stagings of the finals in the Americas.

ENGLAND

England is where soccer began; the country where the sport was first developed, which saw the creation of the game's first Football Association and the first organized league, and which now plays host to the richest domestic league in the world. But England has not had it all its own way on the international scene. Far from it. One solitary FIFA World Cup win apart, as the host in 1966, the Three Lions have found it hard to shake off the "underachievers" tag when it comes to major tournaments.

IF THE CAP FITS

England's players in the historic first game against Scotland all wore **cricket-style caps** while the Scots wore hoods. England's "fashion statement" prompted the use of the term "cap" to refer to any international appearance. The tradition of awarding a cap to British international players still survives today.

HAVE A BASH, ASH

Left-back **Ashley Cole** is one of only eight England soccer players to win 100 caps, but is the only outfield player to reach the mark without ever having scored a goal—next on the list is Gary Neville (85 caps). Cole overtook Kenny Sansom as England's most-capped full-back when he represented his country for the 87th time, against Denmark in February 2011, and made his 100th appearance against Brazil at Wembley in February 2013. Cole's 98th international, against Italy in the Euro 2012 quarterfinal, ended unhappily, as he missed England's final penalty in the shoot-out. But he did set another record that day: his 22nd finals game is the most by an England player. After 107 appearances, Cole announced his retirement from international soccer, having been omitted from England's 2014 FIFA World Cup squad. In the club game he boasts more FA Cup winner's medals than any other player, three with Arsenal and four with Chelsea.

RUNAWAY SUCCESS

England has scored double figures five times: it beat Ireland 13-0 in 1882 and 13-2 in 1899; thrashed Austria 11-1 in 1908, crushed Portugal 10-0 in Lisbon in 1947; and the United States 10-0 in 1964 in New York. The ten goals against the US were scored by Roger Hunt (four), Fred Pickering (three), Terry Paine (two,) and **Bobby Charlton**.

IN THE BEGINNING

The day it all began ... November 30, 1872, when England played its first official international game, against Scotland, at Hamilton Crescent, Partick. The result was a scoreless tie in front of a then massive crowd of 4,000, each of whom paid an admission fee of one shilling (5p). In fact, teams representing England and Scotland had played five times before, but most of the Scottish players had been based in England, and the games are now considered unofficial. England's team for the first official game was selected by Charles Alcock, the secretary of the Football Association. His one regret was that, because of injury, he could not pick himself to play. In contrast, the first rugby union international between England and Scotland had been played in 1871, but England's first Test cricket match was not played until March 1877, against Australia in Melbourne.

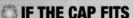

FIRST DEFEAT

Hungary's 6-3 win at Wembley in 1953 was the first time England had lost at home to continental opposition. Its first home defeat by non-British opposition came against the Republic of Ireland, a 2-0 reverse at Goodison Park, Liverpool, in 1949.

STEVIE G FORCE

Steven Gerrard won his 100th cap in a November 2012 exhibition against to Sweden. There would have been many more, but for a string of injuries. He scored at the 2006 and 2010 FIFA World Cups, and was the only England player named in the UEFA Euro 2012 "team of the tournament". His next international brought an unwanted record: a red card against Ukraine in September 2012 made him England's oldest player to be sent off.

ENGLAND'S BIGGEST WINS

1882	Ireland 0 England 13
1899	England 13 Ireland 2
1908	Austria 1 England 11
1964	United States 0 England 10
1947	Portugal 0 England 10
1982	England 9 Luxembourg 0
1960	Luxembourg 0 England 9
1895	England 9 Ireland 0
1927	Belgium 1 England 9
1896	Wales 1 England 9
1890	Ireland 1 England 9

ENGLAND'S BIGGEST DEFEATS

1954	Hungary 7 England 1
1878	Scotland 7 England 2
1881	England 1 Scotland 6
1958	Yugoslavia 5 England 0
1964	Brazil 5 England 1
1928	England 1 Scotland 5
1882	Scotland 5 England 1
1953	England 3 Hungary 6
1963	France 5 England 2
1931	France 5 England 2

WORST OF ALL WORLDS

England recorded its worst-ever performance at a FIFA World Cup finals in Brazil in 2014, when it finished bottom of Group D and was eliminated in the first round. It was the country's first exit at the first-round stage since Sweden 1958, and only the third time overall—the first occasion had been in 1950, the first time the finals had been in Brazil. Roy Hodgson's men managed just one point from its three group games, losing 2-1 to both Italy and Uruguay, before playing out a scoreless tie with surprise group-winners Costa Rica. Back in 1950 it did at least win one game, and lose two, while in 1958 it tied all three group games before losing a play-off to the Soviet Union. To add injury to insult in 2014, veteran physio Gary Lewin was suffered a dislocated ankle and was flown home early after slipping on a water bottle while celebrating **Daniel Sturridge's** equalizer against Italy.

NAUGHTY BOYS

Raheem Sterling's red card against Ecuador in June 2014 was the 15th for an England player in a full international, but only the second in an exhibition, after Trevor Cherry against Argentina in June 1977. Alan Mullery was England's first player to be dismissed, against Yugoslavia in June 1968 in the UEFA European Championship. David Beckham and Wayne Rooney have both been sent off twice, while Rob Green is the only England goalkeeper to be red-carded—in a FIFA World Cup qualifier against Ukraine in October 2009. **Paul Scholes** was the only England player to be sent off at the old Wembley Stadium, against Sweden in June 1999, before it was refurbished in the 2000s.

SENIOR MOMENT

Goalkeeper David James became the oldest player ever to make his FIFA World Cup finals debut, aged 39 years and 321 days, when he appeared for England at the 2010 competition in South Africa. He kept a clean sheet in a scoreless tie in Group C against Algeria.

HEAD FOR GOAL

Robust and commanding center-backs had the honor of scoring both the last England goal at the old Wembley stadium, closed down in 2000, and the first in the new version, which was finally opened in 2007. Tony Adams scored England's second in a 2-0 win over Ukraine in May 2000—Germany's Dietmar Hamann hit the only goal of the final international at the old Wembley, four months later—and captain John Terry headed his team ahead in the new stadium's showpiece June 2007 exhibition against Brazil, which ended 1-1. Terry shares the honor of scoring the most England goals (six) by a defender with 1966 FIFA World Cup winner **Jack Charlton**.

BLANKS OF ENGLAND

A scoreless tie against Algeria in Cape Town in June 2010 made England the first country to finish 10 different FIFA World Cup matches 0-0. Its first was against Brazil in 1958, while the tally also includes both second-round group games in 1982 against eventual runner-up West Germany and host nation Spain. England's 11th scoreless tie was in a first round game against Costa Rica in 2014.

THE LONG AND THE SHORT OF IT

At 6ft 7in, center-forward Peter Crouch is the tallest player ever to stretch above opposing defenses for England—while Fanny Walden, the Tottenham winger who won two caps in 1914 and 1922, was the shortest at 5ft 2in. Sheffield United goalkeeper Billy "Fatty" Foulke became the heaviest England player, at 252 pounds, when he played against Wales on March 29, 1897.

TEENAGE PROMISE

England left-back Luke Shaw was the youngest player to appear at the 2014 FIFA World Cup, at 18 years and 347 days old, when starting against Costa Rica on June 24. He was 36 days younger than US forward Julian Green. The youngest squad member at the tournament was Cameroon striker Fabrice Olinga, ten months Shaw's junior, but he did not play. England's youngest debutant is **Theo Walcott**, aged 17 years and 75 days old, against Hungary in May 2006. Michael Owen, at 18 years and 183 days, set the national record for the FIFA World Cup when a substitute against Tunisia in 1998.

WAITING FOR THE CALL

Four England internationals played at the 1966 FIFA World Cup yet missed out on the triumphant final against West Germany: Ian Callaghan, John Connelly, Jimmy Greaves, and Terry Paine. Liverpool winger Callaghan would then endure the longest wait between England appearances, when he went 11 years and 49 days between the 2-0 win over France at that 1966 tournament and his return to international action in a scoreless tie with Switzerland in September 1977. The game against the Swiss was his third—and penultimate —appearance for England.

FRANK'S A LOT

Frank Lampard has scored more penalties for England than any other player, successfully converting nine since his debut in October 2005, and he has also missed two. The prolific ex-West Ham United and Chelsea midfielder should have had another goal to add to his international tally, but his potential equalizer against Germany during the 2010 FIFA World Cup round-of-16 game was wrongly deemed not to have crossed the line—a catalyst for the eventual introduction of goal-line technology. Lampard became then-reigning European champion Chelsea's all-time leading scorer in May 2013 with his 203rd goal for the club, despite being a midfielder.

BECKHAM'S RECORD

David Beckham played for England for the 109th time when he appeared as a second-half substitute in the 4-0 win over Slovakia in an international exhibition game on March 28, 2009. That overtook the record number of England games for an outfield player, which had been set by Bobby Moore, England's 1966 FIFA World Cup-winning captain. Beckham, born on May 2, 1975, in Leytonstone, London, made his first appearance for his country on September 1, 1996, in a FIFA World Cup qualifier against Moldova. He was appointed full-time England captain in 2001 by then manager Sven-Goran Eriksson, and stepped down after England's quarterfinal defeat to Portugal at the 2006 FIFA World Cup. He ended his England career on 115 caps and hung up his boots in May 2013, at the age of 38, having just won the league in a fourth different country with French club Paris Saint-Germain. His 68 competitive games for England are also a national record. Also retiring from the game in summer 2013 was England's fourth highest scorer **Michael Owen**, who netted a stunning solo goal against Argentina at the 1998 FIFA World Cup— only for Beckham to be sent off in a 2-2 tie before England lost on penalties.

ALEXANDER THE LATE

The oldest player to make his debut for England remains Alexander Morten, who was 41 years and 114 days old when facing Scotland on March 8, 1873, in England's first home game, at The Oval in Kennington, London. He was also captain that day and is still the country's oldest-ever skipper.

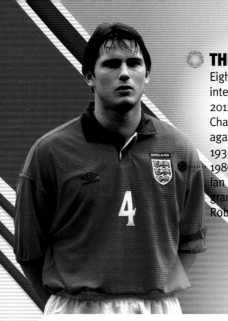

THE GOOD SONS

Eighteen-year-old winger Alex Oxlade-Chamberlain became the fifth son of a former England international to earn a cap for his country when he made his debut against Norway in May 2012—28 years after the last of his father Mark Chamberlain's eight appearances. Oxlade-Chamberlain became England's youngest scorer in a FIFA World Cup qualifier with his strike against San Marino in October 2013. The earlier pairings were George Eastham Snr (one cap, 1935) and George Eastham Jnr (19, 1963–66); Brian Clough (two, 1959) and Nigel Clough (14, 1989–93); Frank Lampard Snr (two, 1972–80) and **Frank Lampard Jnr** (106, 1999–date); and Ian Wright (33, 1991–98) and his adopted son Shaun Wright-Phillips (36, 2004–10). The only grandfather and grandson to play for England are Bill Jones, who won two caps in 1950, and Rob Jones, who won eight between 1992 and 1995.

GRAND OLD MAN

Stanley Matthews became England's oldest-ever player when he lined up at outside-right against Denmark on May 15, 1957, at the age of 42 years 104 days. That was 22 years and 229 days after his first appearance. Matthews was also England's oldest marksman. He was 41 years eight months old when he scored against Northern Ireland on October 10, 1956.

CAPTAIN SOLO

Claude Ashton, the Corinthians center-forward, set a record when he captained England on his only international appearance. This was a 0-0 tie against Northern Ireland in Belfast on October 24, 1925.

TOP SCORERS

1	Bobby Charlton	49
2	Gary Lineker	48
3	Jimmy Greaves	44
4	Michael Owen	40
=	Wayne Rooney	40
6	Tom Finney	30
=	Nat Lofthouse	30
=	Alan Shearer	30
9	Frank Lampard	29
=	Vivian Woodward	29

TOP CAPS

1	Peter Shilton	125
2	David Beckham	115
3	Steven Gerrard	114
4	Bobby Moore	108
5	Ashley Cole	107
6	Bobby Charlton	106
=	Frank Lampard	106
8	Billy Wright	105
9	Wayne Rooney	95
10	Bryan Robson	90

CAPTAINS COURAGEOUS

The international careers of Billy Wright and **Bobby Moore**, who both captained England a record 90 times, very nearly overlapped. Wright, from Wolves, played for England between 1946 and 1959, and Moore, from West Ham, between 1962 and 1973, including England's FIFA World Cup win in 1966.

SHARED RESPONSIBILITY

Substitutions meant the captain's armband passed between four different players during England's 2-1 exhibition win over Serbia and Montenegro on June 3, 2003. Regular captain David Beckham was missing, so Michael Owen led the team out, but was substituted at half-time. England's second-half skippers were Owen's then-Liverpool team-mates Emile Heskey and Jamie Carragher, and Manchester United's Philip Neville. The first time three different players have captained England in one FIFA World Cup finals match was against Morocco in 1986, when first-choice skipper Bryan Robson went off injured, his vice-captain Ray Wilkins was then sent off, and goalkeeper Peter Shilton took over leadership duties.

CAMEO ROLE

Tottenham Hotspur striker **Jermain Defoe** has come on as substitute for England more often than any other player in history, 34 times since his debut in March 2004. And, all of his first 17 starting appearances ended in him being replaced before the end of 90 minutes.

SEVEN UP

Roy Hodgson's England equaled a national record when it trounced San Marino 8-0 in a March 2013 FIFA World Cup qualifier: the seven different goalscorers were as many who found the net when England defeated Luxembourg 9-0 in December 1982. This time, though, thanks to an opening own goal by Alessandro Della Valle, only six of the scorers were Englishmen. Completing the rout were: Jermain Defoe, two goals, and one each from **Alex Oxlade-Chamberlain**, Ashley Young, Frank Lampard, Wayne Rooney, and Daniel Sturridge.

WAITING WAYNE

The 2-1 defeats to Italy and Uruguay in 2014 made it only the second time England had lost consecutive matches at a FIFA World Cup, having previously done so against the United States and Spain in 1950, also in Brazil. The Uruguay game did at least give **Wayne Rooney** his first FIFA World Cup goal, having failed to find the net at the 2006 and 2010 tournaments. The close-range strike took him to 40 international goals, level with former England and Manchester United team-mate Michael Owen.

COMING OVER HERE

Argentina was the first non-UK side to play at Wembley—England won 2-1 on May 9, 1951—while Ferenc Puskas and the "Magical Magyars" of Hungary were the first "foreign," or "continental," team to beat England on home soil, with its famous 6-3 victory at Wembley in 1953. This humiliation marked Alf Ramsey's last game as an England player. England first tasted defeat to a non-British Isles team when it lost 4-3 to Spain in Madrid on May 15, 1929. Two years later England gained its revenge with a 7-1 win at Highbury.

WRONG WAY!

Though the goal is sometimes credited to Scottish striker John Smith, it is believed that Edgar Field was the first England player to score an own goal, which was his fate as Scotland crushed England 6-1 at The Oval on March 12, 1881. By the time Field put the ball in his own net, Scotland already held a 4-1 lead. The full-back, who was an FA Cup winner and loser with Clapham Rovers, is in good company. Manchester United's Gary Neville scored two own goals on England duty.

ROLL UP, ROLL UP

The highest attendance for an England game was at Hampden Park, Glasdow, on April 17, 1937, when 149,547 saw Scotland win 3-1 in the British Home Championship. England's lowest crowd was in Bologna, Italy, when only 2,378 turned up to see San Marino score nine seconds into a FIFA World Cup qualifier in 1993. It did rally to win 7-1, but still failed to qualify for the 1994 FIFA World Cup.

FIRST AND FOREMOST

England's first official international was a 0-0 tie against Scotland in Glasgow on November 30, 1872, though England and Scotland had already played a number of unofficial representative matches against each other prior to that. Given that England's only opponents for four decades were the home nations, and only Scotland for the first seven years, it is not surprising that England's first win, loss, and tie, were all against its northern neighbor. After the scoreless first game, the second fixture, played at The Oval on March 8, 1873, proved a more exciting affair: England won 4-2 in a six-goal thriller. In its third game, back in Glasgow almost exactly a year later, Scotland evened things up with a 2-1 win. These fixtures completed the trio of first wins, losses and ties for the oldest participants in international soccer. The Football Association's 150-year anniversary celebrations in 2013 included a 2013 Wembley exhibition against Scotland, the first time the two sides were scheduled to meet since a two-leg play-off to qualify for Euro 2000 in October 1999. England won that game 2-1 on aggregate, after a 2-0 victory at Hampden Park and a 1-0 defeat at home.

ROY'S BOYS

After Fabio Capello faced criticism for his struggles with the English language, his successor **Roy Hodgson** could claim fluency in not only his mother tongue but also Swedish, Norwegian, Italian and German. Much-traveled Hodgson, a former Switzerland, Finland and Inter Milan coach, was appointed England boss just six weeks before the 2012 UEFA European Championship. His team topped its group, before losing to Italy in the quarterfinal on penalties. First-round victories came against Sweden—England's first competitive victory over it at the eighth attempt—and co-host Ukraine, the first time it had won against the host of a major tournament since beating Switzerland in the 1954 FIFA World Cup.

YOUR COUNTRY NEEDS YOU

The first England teams were selected from open trials of Englishmen who responded to the FA's adverts for players. It was only when these proved too popular and unwieldy that, in 1887, the FA decided that it would be better to manage the process through an International Selection Committee, which continued to pick the team until Sir Alf Ramsey's appointment in 1962.

MANAGERIAL ROLL OF HONOR

Walter Winterbottom	(1946–62)
Sir Alf Ramsey	(1962–74)
Joe Mercer	(1974)
Don Revie	(1974–77)
Ron Greenwood	(1977–82)
Bobby Robson	(1982–90)
Graham Taylor	(1990–93)
Terry Venables	(1994–96)
Glenn Hoddle	(1996–98)
Howard Wilkinson	(1999–2000)
Kevin Keegan	(1999–2000)
Peter Taylor	(November 2000)
Sven-Goran Eriksson	(2001–06)
Steve McClaren	(2006–07)
Fabio Capello	(2008–2012)
Stuart Pearce	(March 2012)
Roy Hodgson	(2012–)

THE ITALIAN JOB

Italian Fabio Capello became England's second foreign coach when he took over from Steve McClaren in January 2008 and led the country to the 2010 FIFA World Cup in South Africa. Capello already had happy memories of England's national stadium, Wembley, from his playing days – he scored the only goal for Italy there on November 14, 1973, giving it its first-ever away win against England. He steered England through qualifiers for the 2012 UEFA European Championship, but suddenly resigned in February 2012, in protest at the Football Association stripping John Terry of the captaincy.

WONDERFUL WALTER

Walter Winterbottom was the England national team's first full-time coach—and remains both the longest-serving (with 138 games in charge) and the youngest-ever England manager, aged just 33 when he took the job in 1946 (initially as a coach and then, from 1947, as manager). The former teacher and Manchester United player led England to four FIFA World Cups.

FRANCE

France, nicknamed "Les Bleus," is one of the most successful teams in the history of international soccer. It is one of only three countries to be World and European champion at the same time. It won the FIFA World Cup in 1998 as tournament host, routing Brazil 3-0 in the final. Two years later, it staged a sensational, last-gasp recovery to overhaul Italy in the Euro 2000 final. The French equalized in the fifth minute of stoppage time, then went on to win 2-1 on a golden goal. France had previously won the UEFA European Championship in 1984, beating Spain 2-0 in the final in Paris. It reached the 2006 FIFA World Cup final ,too, but lost to Italy in a penalty shoot-out. France also won the 2001 and 2003 FIFA Confederations Cup and took the Olympic Games soccer gold medal in 1984.

KOPA – FRANCE'S FIRST SUPERSTAR

Raymond Kopa (born on October 13, 1931) was France's first international superstar. Born into a family of Polish immigrants (the family name was Kopaszewski), he was instrumental in Reims's championship successes of the mid-1950s. He later joined Real Madrid and became the first French player to win a European Cup winner's medal. He was the playmaker for the France team which finished third in the 1958 FIFA World Cup finals. His performances for his country that year earned him the European Footballer of the Year award.

PLATINI'S GLITTERING CAREER

Michel Platini (born in Joeuf on June 21, 1955) has enjoyed a glittering career, rising from a youngster at Nancy, to become one of France's greatest-ever players, a hero in Italy, and now the president of UEFA. He was also joint organizing president (along with Fernand Sastre) of the 1998 FIFA World Cup finals in France. Platini was the grandson of an Italian immigrant who ran a café in Joeuf, Lorraine. He began with the local club, Nancy, before starring for Saint-Etienne, Juventus, and France. He was instrumental in France's progress to the 1982 FIFA World Cup semifinal, and was the undisputed star of the UEFA European Championship two years later, when France won the tournament on home soil.

BENZ MAKES AMENDS

Karim Benzema was the first French player to miss a penalty during a FIFA World Cup match—excluding shoot-outs. His effort, saved by Diego Benaglio, came in a Group E match against Switzerland at the 2014 tournament, was the tenth FIFA World Cup spot-kick awarded to France. He did atone for the failure by scoring France's fourth goal in its 5-2 victory. Benzema had struck twice in France's first game, a 3-0 defeat of Honduras, and was denied a hat-trick after his shot struck the far post and trickled over the goal-line, but it entered the goal only after rebounding off goalkeeper Noel Valladares, so was ruled an own goal. This was the first time in FIFA World Cup history that a goal was given thanks to goal-line technology, introduced for the 2014 finals. And Benzema was denied another goal in the Swiss game when Dutch referee Bjorn Kuipers blew the final whistle as he was in the act of smashing a long-range shot which ended up in the Swiss net. Benzema's three goals at the 2014 finals lifted him up to ninth place in France's all-time scoring table, above Jean Vincent, who had died at the age of 82 the previous October.

TO BE FRANCK

Franck Ribery has become one of modern-day France's most important and influential players. His displays off both wings helped it to reach the 2006 FIFA World Cup final as well as helping lift Bayern Munich to success in the 2013 UEFA Champions League. He is the first man to have been named Footballer of the Year in both France and Germany. Yet he was rejected as a teenager by French club Lille, with 1.7m-tall Ribery later claming it deemed him too short. Ribery was severely injured in a car crash as a two year old, leaving him with lifelong scars across the right side of his face. He finished third behind Cristiano Ronaldo and Lionel Messi for FIFA's annual Ballon d'Or award in December 2013. Ribery's luck turned the following summer when a back injury ruled him out of the 2014 FIFA World Cup.

KISSING COLLEAGUES

Marseille colleagues center-back **Laurent Blanc** and goalkeeper **Fabien Barthez** had a special ritual during France's run to the 1998 FIFA World Cup crown. Before each game, Blanc would kiss Barthez's shaven head, even when the veteran defender was suspended for the final. Blanc was on the winning team when France won the 2000 UEFA European Championship final, after which he announced his international retirement. He said at the time: "The French team has been my life and has led me to do things I shouldn't have. It has been my mistress—a beautiful mistress."

IT'S A SHAME ABOUT RAY

France's failure to win a game at the 2010 FIFA World Cup meant coach Raymond Domenech equaled, but failed to exceed, Michel Hidalgo's record of 41 victories in charge of the national team. Domenech did at least end his six-year reign having passed Euro 84-winning Hidalgo's total of games in the job. Domenech's final game, against South Africa, was his 79th as coach, four more than Hidalgo achieved. Domenech, a tough-tackling defender who was picked for France by Hidalgo, proved eccentric as national coach. He admitted partly judging players by their star signs and responded to being knocked out of the 2008 UEFA European Championship by proposing to his girlfriend on live television.

MICHEL PLATINI (league and national career)

Duration	Team	Appearances	Goals
1972–79	Nancy	181	98
1979–82	Saint-Etienne	104	58
1982–87	Juventus	147	68
1976–87	France	72	41

WRONG KIND OF STRIKERS

During France's disastrous 2010 FIFA World Cup campaign, the players went on strike, refusing to train two days before its final Group A match, in protest at striker Nicolas Anelka being sent home early for insulting coach Raymond Domenech. France finished bottom of the group after a scoreless tie with Uruguay and defeats to Mexico and hosts South Africa. The country's president Nicolas Sarkozy ordered an investigation into all that had gone wrong, while former French international defender Lilian Thuram called for captain **Patrice Evra** to be banned from playing for the team ever again. Despite serving a five-match international ban for his role in the unrest, Evra returned to the fold in 2011—albeit no longer as skipper—and was a starter for France at both the 2012 UEFA European Championship and the 2014 FIFA World Cup.

FRANCE AND FIFA

France were one of FIFA's founding members in 1904. Frenchman Robert Guerin became the first president of the governing body. Another Frenchman, Jules Rimet, was president from 1921 to 1954. He was the driving force behind the creation of the FIFA World Cup and the first version of soccer's most coveted trophy was named in his honor.

HENRY BENCHED

France's record scorer Thierry Henry missed out on an appearance in the 1998 FIFA World Cup final because of Marcel Desailly's red card. Henry was France's leading scorer in the competition, with three goals, and coach Aime Jacquet planned to use him as a substitute in the final. But Desailly's sending-off forced a re-think: Jacquet decided to reinforce the midfield, with Arsenal team-mate Patrick Vieira going on instead, so Henry spent the full 90 minutes of the final on the bench. But Henry does have the distinction of being the only Frenchman to play at four different FIFA World Cups (1998, 2002, 2006, and 2010). He passed Michel Platini's all-time goal-scoring record for France with a late double against Lithuania in October 2007.

TOP SCORERS

1	Thierry Henry	51
2	Michel Platini	41
3	David Trezeguet	34
4	Zinedine Zidane	31
5	Just Fontaine	30
=	Jean-Pierre Papin	30
7	Youri Djorkaeff	28
8	Sylvain Wiltord	26
9	Karim Benzema	24
10	Jean Vincent	22

UNITED FOR ABIDAL

Defender Eric Abidal, a key member of the French teams at the 2006 and 2010 FIFA World Cups, was enjoying his best form for Spanish club Barcelona when he was diagnosed with liver cancer in March 2011—but managed to recover in time for a surprise return to action by the season's end. Club rivalries were put aside when players from rivals Real Madrid wore T-shirts bearing the supportive message "Animo Abidal" after its UEFA Champions League game against Abidal's former club Olympique Lyonnais a few days later. Barcelona fans then applauded throughout the 22nd minute of its La Liga game against Getafe, in recognition of Abidal's shirt number. Remarkably, he was fit enough to return to action, as a substitute, in Barcelona's UEFA Champions League semifinal victory over Madrid in May 2011. Abidal started in the final and, although he was not the captain, the armband was given to him, so he could lift the cup after Barcelona's 3-1 win over Manchester United. Abidal came through further trauma in March 2012, when he was told he needed a liver transplant. Once more, he returned to action with Barcelona, taking the field again towards the end of the 2012–13 season.

TOP CAPS

1	Lilian Thuram	142
2	Thierry Henry	123
3	Marcel Desailly	116
4	Zinedine Zidane	108
5	Patrick Vieira	107
6	Didier Deschamps	103
7	Laurent Blanc	97
=	Bixente Lizarazu	97
9	Sylvain Wiltord	92
10	Fabien Barthez	87

DESCHAMPS THE LEADER

Compatriot Eric Cantona contemptuously dismissed him as a mere "water-carrier" in central midfield, but **Didier Deschamps** provided his infamous critic with the perfect riposte in becoming the most successful captain in French soccer history. He lifted both the 1998 FIFA World Cup and 2000 UEFA European Championship trophies as skipper and wore the captain's armband a record 55 times during his 103 internationals before retiring in July 2000. Deschamps succeeded Laurent Blanc as national coach after the 2012 UEFA European Championship. Deschamps' ten-match unbeaten run at FIFA World Cups, as a player and manager, came to an end in the 2014 quarterfinal as his team lost 1-0 to Germany. Until then he had enjoyed five wins and one tie on the pitch, and three wins and one tie in the dug-out.

BITTERSWEET FOR TREZEGUET

Striker David Trezeguet has bittersweet memories of France's clashes with Italy in major finals. He scored the "golden goal" to beat the Italians in extra-time in the Euro 2000 final but, six years later, he was the man who missed as France lost the FIFA World Cup final on penalties. Trezeguet's shot bounced off the bar and failed to cross the line.

PRESIDENTIAL PARDON

Imperious center-back Laurent Blanc was known as "Le President" during his playing days and went on to become national coach when he succeeded Raymond Domenech after the 2010 FIFA World Cup. He was unlucky to miss the 1998 FIFA World Cup final after being sent off in the semifinal for pushing Slaven Bilic in the face, though replays showed Bilic had over-reacted. Blanc did enjoy some redemption by being part of the French team that won the UEFA European Championship two years later. He became national coach 12 months after leading Bordeaux to the 2008–09 domestic championship, ending Olympique Lyonnais's run of seven league titles in a row.

ARMBAND FINALLY IN SAFE HANDS

After Patrick Evra lost the French captaincy for his role in its 2010 FIFA World Cup fiasco, new coach Laurent Blanc tried three captains before turning to goalkeeper **Hugo Lloris,** who was finally named as permanent skipper ahead of Euro 2012. He was the only man to play every single minute of France's qualifying campaign, and was an ever-present in the finals too. Overall, he kept seven clean sheets in France's 14 matches. Lloris remained captain throughout qualifying for the 2014 FIFA World Cup and at the tournament itself, in which he kept three clean sheets and conceded three goals in five games.

THE FULL SET

Five France stars have a full set of top international medals as FIFA World Cup, UEFA European Championship and UEFA Champions League winners: Didier Deschamps, Marcel Desailly, Christian Karembeu, Bixente Lizarazu, and Zinedine Zidane, all played for France's winning teams in 1998 and 2000. Desailly won the European Cup with Marseille in 1993, and with AC Milan the following year. Deschamps won with Marseille in 1993, and Juventus in 1996; Lizarazu did so with Bayern Munich in 2001; Karembeu with Real Madrid in 1998 and 2000; and Zidane with Real Madrid in 2002. While Karembeu ended the 1999–2000 season with UEFA Champions League and UEFA European Championship winners' medals, he was an unused substitute in both finals—making him the only player to have achieved that particular bittersweet double.

LILIAN IN THE PINK

Defender **Lilian Thuram** made his 142nd and final appearance for France in its defeat by Italy at Euro 2008. His international career had spanned nearly 14 years, since his debut against the Czech Republic on August 17, 1994. Thuram was born in Pointe a Pitre, Guadeloupe, on January 1, 1972. He played club soccer for Monaco, Parma, Juventus, and Barcelona before retiring in the summer of 2008, because of a heart problem. He was one of the stars of France's 1998 FIFA World Cup-winning side, and scored both goals in its semifinal victory over Croatia— the only international goals of his career. He gained another winner's medal at Euro 2000. He first retired from international soccer after Euro 2004, but was persuaded by coach Raymond Domenech to return for the 2006 FIFA World Cup campaign, and made his second appearance in a FIFA World Cup final. He broke Marcel Desailly's record of 116 caps in the group game against Togo.

ALBERT THE FIRST

Albert Batteux (1919–2003) was France's first national coach. Before his appointment in 1955, a selection committee had picked the team. Batteux was also the most successful coach in the history of French soccer. He combined managing France with his club job at Reims. His biggest achievement was guiding the national team to third place at the 1958 FIFA World Cup finals. The team's two big stars, Raymond Kopa and Just Fontaine, had both played under his charge at Reims.

REVEILLERE REMAINS

Anthony Reveillere is the only player to be picked by all of the last four France managers: Jacques Santini, Raymond Domenech, Laurent Blanc, and Didier Deschamps. However, the full-back has appeared only 19 times in the decade since his debut against Israel in October 2003.

OVAL BALL

The father of France's most capped goalkeeper, Fabien Barthez, was also a French international. Alain Barthez was a fine rugby union player who won one cap for France.

JACQUET'S TRIUMPH

Aime Jacquet, who guided France to FIFA World Cup glory in 1998, was one of its most controversial national coaches. He had been attacked for alleged defensive tactics, despite France's run to the semifinal of Euro 96, and a record of only three defeats in four years. A month before the 1998 finals, the sports daily newspaper *L'Equipe* claimed he was not capable of building a successful team!

NO TIME FOR FONTAINE

Former striker **Just Fontaine** spent the shortest-ever spell as coach of the France team. He took over on March 22, 1967, and left on June 3, after two defeats in exhibitions. More happily, he still holds the record for most goals at a single FIFA World Cup—13 across all six games he played at the 1958 tournament, including four in France's 6-3 victory over West Germany to finish third.

FRANCE MANAGERS

Albert Batteux	1955–62
Henri Guerin	1962–66
Jose Arribas/Jean Snella	1966
Just Fontaine	1967
Louis Dugauguez	1967–68
Georges Boulogne	1969–73
Stefan Kovacs	1973–75
Michel Hidalgo	1976–84
Henri Michel	1984–88
Michel Platini	1988–92
Gerard Houllier	1992–93
Aime Jacquet	1993–98
Roger Lemerre	1998–2002
Jacques Santini	2002–04
Raymond Domenech	2004–10
Laurent Blanc	2010–12
Didier Deschamps	2012–

JOLLY OLI DAY

France became the fifth country to score 100 FIFA World Cup goals, when **Olivier Giroud** scored the 17th-minute opener during a 5-2 win over .... Switzerland at Salvador in its 2014 first-round clash. The French thus joined Brazil, Germany (including West Germany), Argentina, and Italy on three-figure tallies. By the end of the 2014 FIFA World Cup, France, with 106 in total, was more than 20 goals behind fourth-placed Italy—which had slipped behind Argentina after a second consecutive poor showing— but a dozen clear of the sixth most prolific nation, Spain.

WINNING WITH YOUTH

In the early 1990s, France became the first European country to institute a national youth development programme. The best young players were picked to attend the national youth academy at Clairefontaine. Then they went on to the top clubs' academies throughout the nation. The scheme has produced a rich harvest of stars. FIFA World Cup winners Didier Deschamps, Marcel Desailly, and Christian Karembeu, started at Nantes. Lilian Thuram, Thierry Henry, Manu Petit, and David Trezeguet, began with Monaco and **Zinedine Zidane** and .... Patrick Vieira were graduates from Cannes.

BLINK AND YOU'LL MISS HIM

Unfortunate defender Franck Jurietti's international debut proved bittersweet, as it lasted just five seconds and he never won another cap. The Bordeaux full-back came on just before the final whistle of France's match against Cyprus in October 2005, amounting to an international career even shorter than fellow defender Bernard Boissier's two minutes against Portugal in April 1975.

PACKING THEM IN

A record home crowd of 80,051 people were inside the Stade de France, in Saint-Denis, to see France take a major step towards qualifying for the 2008 UEFA European Championship with a 2-0 defeat of Ukraine in June 2007. The goals were scored by Franck Ribery and Nicolas Anelka.

EARNING ITS STRIPES

France is the only country to play at a FIFA World Cup wearing another team's kit. In the 1978 tournament in Argentina, for a first-round match at Mar del Plata, *Les Bleus* were forced to wear the green and white stripes of a local club side, Atletico Kimberley, when it met Hungary. France brought its second, white, kit instead of its normal blue, while Hungary turned up in its second strip, also white. The quick-change did not seem to affect France, which won the game 3-1.

WHAM BAM THANK YOU SAM

Samir Nasri scored the winner to give France a 2-1 victory over Spain in the final of .... the UEFA European U-17 Championship on home soil in 2004, the only time France has lifted that trophy. It has also won the UEFA European U-19 Championship seven times, most recently in 2010 with another final triumph over Spain, and the UEFA European U-21 Championship once, in 1988, when Laurent Blanc was named player of the tournament. Midfielder Nasri is one of the successful graduates from that acclaimed "Generation '87" team that won in 2004, also featuring Jeremy Menez, Hatem Ben Arfa, and Karim Benzema. After behaving badly with the senior side at the 2010 FIFA World Cup and 2012 UEFA European Championship, Nasri was left out of Didier Deschamps' 2014 FIFA World Cup squad, despite having just played a key role in Manchester City winning the English league title. Nasri's girlfriend, Anara Atanes, loyally if divisively responded to his omission by posting a series of Twitter messages abusing Deschamps.

GERMANY

Germany's players are almost ever-presents in the closing stages of major tournaments, but its well-deserved 2014 FIFA World Cup triumph provided much joy and relief back home, as it ended an 18-year trophy drought. It was also the first FIFA World Cup triumph for the unified Germany, having been West Germany when becoming champions in 1954, 1974, and 1990. The Germans are also three-time UEFA European champions, 1972, 1980, and 1996, and in 1974 became the first country to hold the world and European titles simultaneously. Further glory always feels likely.

SHOOT–OUT SURE–SHOTS

Germany is famous for winning penalty shootouts, but it needed none when winning the 2014 FIFA World Cup. When it won its previous two titles, the 1990 FIFA World Cup and the 1996 UEFA European Championship, these both involved semifinal victories, on penalties, against England.

BELITTLE ITALY

Germany may now be England's bogey-team, but its misfortune against Italy goes on. It has never managed to beat the Italians in international tournament play, a sequence that reached eight games when Germany, with stars such as midfielder **Bastian Schweinsteiger** and goalkeeper Manuel Neuer, lost 2-1 in its 2012 UEFA European Championship semifinal. Perhaps the most dramatic contest was Italy's 4-3 victory, after extra-time, in the semifinal of the 1970 FIFA World Cup. Italy also reigned triumphant in the 2006 FIFA World Cup semifinal and the 1982 FIFA World Cup final. Germany can at least celebrate one recent success over its Italian rival—albeit at club level. Since 2011–12, Germany's Bundesliga has had four clubs eligible for each year's UEFA Champions League, gaining the extra place at the expense of Italy's Serie A. And first-round departees Italy watched enviously as Germany clinched the 2014 FIFA World Cup.

NO LOSS

Germany maintained its record of never losing its opening game at a UEFA European Championship by beating Portugal 1-0 at Euro 2012, thanks to a header by **Mario Gomez**. Its 4-2 quarterfinal victory over Greece that same summer set a new world record of 15 consecutive wins in competitive matches, one more than the best tallies set by both Spain and the Netherlands.

BOTH SIDES NOW

Eight players appeared for both the old East Germany and then Germany after reunification in October 1990.

Player	East Germany	Germany
Ulf Kirsten	49	51
Matthias Sammer	23	51
Andreas Thom	51	10
Thomas Doll	29	18
Dariusz Wosz	7	17
Olaf Marschall	4	13
Heiko Scholz	7	1
Dirk Schuster	4	3

EAST GERMANY –
TOP APPEARANCES AND GOALS

Appearances

1 **Joachim Streich** 98
2 Hans-Jurgen Dorner 96
3 Jurgen Croy 86
4 Konrad Weise 78
5 Eberhard Vogel 69

Goals

1 Joachim Streich 53
2 Eberhard Vogel 24
3 Hans-Jurgen Kreische 22
4 Rainer Ernst 20
5 Henning Frenzel 19

SAMBA SILENCED

Germany's 1-0 win over Argentina in 2014 came in its record eighth FIFA World Cup Final, this coming after it was the first team to reach four consecutive semifinals. But it may be that the 7-1 semifinal humiliation of Brazil will live longest in the memory—and the record books. Germany led 5-0 at half-time in what became the biggest FIFA World Cup semifinal win and the hosts' heaviest defeat. Other FIFA World Cup finals records include: Toni Kroos's two goals in 69 seconds were the fastest double and Germany was the first team to score four goals in six minutes. Also Thomas Muller's opening goal was Germany's 2,000th.

BERLIN ALL

Berlin will host the 2015 UEFA Champions League final, making it the second German city, after Munich, to have hosted the Olympic Games, FIFA World Cup final, and UEFA Champions League final. Berlin hosted the Olympic Games in 1936, and the 2006 FIFA World Cup final; Munich staged the Olympics in 1972, the FIFA World Cup final in 1974, and four European Cup finals.

HOTTEST SHOTS

Germany's 7-1 defeat of Brazil in the 2014 FIFA World Cup semifinal not only stunned the hosts, but also toppled it as the tournament's all-time top scorers. Germany's FIFA World Cup goals total is now 224, three more than Brazil. Stanislaus Kobierski scored Germany's first FIFA World Cup goal, in a 5-2 victory over Belgium in 1934. Germany became the first team to enjoy three four-goal sprees at one tournament, beating Australia 4-0, England 4-1, and Argentina 4-0 in 2010. The 2014 vintage got off to a flying start by crushing Portugal 4-0 in its opening match.

HISTORY MAN

East and West Germany met only once at senior national team level. That was on June 22, 1974, in the FIFA World Cup finals. Drawn in the same group, East Germany produced a shock 1-0 win in Hamburg, but both teams advanced. Jurgen Sparwasser, scorer of East Germany's winning goal, defected to West Germany in 1988—two years before the two countries reunified.

SCHNELL, SCHNELL

Lukas Podolski scored one of the fastest goals in international soccer history when he gave Germany the lead after just nine seconds in its May 2013 exhibition away to Ecuador. When Lars Bender added another shortly afterwards, it was the first time ever that Germany had scored twice in the opening four minutes of a game. Both Podolski and Bender had scored again by the time 24 minutes were on the clock. Germany went on to win the game 4-2.

GOLDEN WONDER

Germany became the first team to win a major title thanks to the now-discarded golden goal system when it beat the Czech Republic in the UEFA Euro 96 final at Wembley. **Oliver Bierhoff**'s equalizer forced extra-time after Patrik Berger scored a penalty for the Czechs. Bierhoff grabbed Germany's winner five minutes into extra-time to end the game and the championship.

MEIN BENDERS

You could have thought you were seeing double when manager Joachim Low made a double substitution, with 12 minutes remaining of Germany's 5-3 defeat to Switzerland in May 2012. His two new midfielders were twin brothers, **Lars** and **Sven Bender**. Born on April 27, 1989, they both began their careers with 1860 Munich before Lars (the elder by 12 minutes) moved to Bayer Leverkusen, and Sven joined Borussia Dortmund. Both were members of Germany's 2008 UEFA U-19 European Championship-winning team, but only Lars was selected for Euro 2012. They were were the second pair of twins to play for Germany, after Erwin and Helmut Kramers. Striker Erwin scored three goals in 15 games between 1972 and 1974, while full-back Helmut played eight times without scoring. Erwin was part of the 1972 UEFA European Championship-winning squad, but was overlooked for the 1974 FIFA World Cup-winning squad, a set-up that included Helmut.

"DER BOMBER"

Gerd Muller was the most prolific scorer of the modern era. Neither tall nor graceful, he was quick, strong, and had a predator's eye for the net. He also had the temperament to score decisive goals in big games, including the winner in the 1974 FIFA World Cup final, the winner in the semifinal against Poland, and two goals in West Germany's 1972 UEFA European Championship final victory over the USSR. He netted 68 goals in 62 appearances for West Germany, and remains the leading scorer in the Bundesliga and all-time record scorer for his club, Bayern Munich.

KING OTTO

Thomas Muller was the last man to score a hat-trick for Germany, in his country's opening game of the 2014 FIFA World Cup finals, a 4-0 victory over Portugal. Gerd Muller has more hat-tricks than any other German international—eight in all, four of which were four-goal hauls. But Otto Siffling remains the only player to score five in one game for Germany, during an 8-0 triumph over Denmark on May 16, 1937, in the Polish city of Wroclaw—then a German territory known as Breslau.

A LAHM CALL

Philipp Lahm surprised many when retiring from international soccer after the 2014 FIFA World Cup, at the age of only 30. He went out on a high, having just lifted the trophy as German captain at the end of his 113th appearance. Lahm had already made a mark in his two previous finals. He scored the opening goal of the 2006 FIFA World Cup, and played every minute of that tournament. Four years later, he became the youngest man to captain Germany at a FIFA World Cup, and the only action he missed was when given a well-earnest rest for the third-place play-off against Uruguay. In his youth, Lahm had been a ballboy at Bayern Munich, and he later captained the team to victory in the 2013 UEFA Champions League final.

DER KAISER

Franz Beckenbauer is widely regarded as the greatest player in German soccer history. He has also made a huge mark as a FIFA World Cup-winning coach, administrator and organizer. Beckenbauer (born on September 11, 1945) was a 20-year-old attacking wing-half when West Germany reached the 1966 FIFA World Cup final. He later defined the role of attacking sweeper, first in the 1970 FIFA World Cup finals, and then as West Germany won the 1972 UEFA European Championship and the 1974 FIFA World Cup. When West Germany needed a coach in the mid-1980s, it turned to Beckenbauer, despite his lack of experience. He delivered a FIFA World Cup final appearance in 1986, a Euro 88 semifinal, and 1990 FIFA World Cup triumph in his final game in charge. He later became president of Bayern Munich, the club he captained to three consecutive European Cup victories between 1974 and 1976. He also led Germany's successful bid for the 2006 FIFA World Cup finals, and headed the organizing committee. No wonder he is known as "Der Kaiser" ("the Emperor") for his enormous influence on German soccer.

MAGICAL MATTHAUS

Lothar Matthaus is Germany's most-capped player. He appeared in five FIFA World Cup finals, 1982, 1986, 1990, 1994, and 1998, a record for an outfield player. Versatile Matthaus could operate as a defensive midfielder, attacking midfielder, or sweeper. He was a FIFA World Cup winner in 1990, a finalist in 1982 and 1986, and a UEFA European Championship winner in 1980. His record 150 appearances—spread over a 20-year international career—were split 87 for West Germany and 63 for Germany. He also scored 23 goals, and was voted top player at the 1990 FIFA World Cup.

TOP CAPS
(West Germany & Germany)

1	Lothar Matthaus	150
2	Miroslav Klose	137
3	Lukas Podolski	116
4	Philipp Lahm	113
5	Jurgen Klinsmann	108
=	Bastian Schweinsteiger	108
7	Jurgen Kohler	105
8	Per Mertesacker	104
9	Franz Beckenbauer	103
10	Thomas Hassler	101

TOP SCORERS
(West Germany & Germany)

1	Miroslav Klose	71
2	Gerd Muller	68
3	Jurgen Klinsmann	47
=	Lukas Podolski	47
=	Rudi Voller	47
6	Karl-Heinz Rummenigge	45
7	Uwe Seeler	43
8	Michael Ballack	42
9	Oliver Bierhoff	37
10	Fritz Walter	33

KLOSE ENCOUNTERS

Miroslav Klose became the third player, after Uwe Seeler and Pele, to score in four FIFA World Cup finals. His first goal in Brazil, an equalizer against Ghana, put him alongside Ronaldo at the top of the all-time FIFA World Cup scoring charts. And it was against Ronaldo's Brazil that Klose moved ahead on his own, his 16th finals goal being a typically-opportunistic finish to give Germany a 2-0 semifinal lead. All 16 of Klose's FIFA World Cup goals came from inside the penalty area. He ended the 2014 FIFA World Cup not only with the scoring record and a winners' medal, but also on 24 appearances—behind only Italy's Lothar Matthaus (25)—and 17 wins, one ahead of previous record-holder Cafu, of Brazil. Klose retired from international soccer in August 2014 as Germany's all-time leading scorer, with 71 goals in 137 games. The national team never lost a game in which Klose scored.

GOLDEN GLOVES

Sepp Maier was at the heart of West Germany's triumphs of the early 1970s, including the 1972 UEFA European Championship and the 1974 FIFA World Cup. He remains West Germany's most-capped goalkeeper, winning 95 caps in an international career lasting from 1965 to 1979. He played his whole club career for Bayern Munich and helped it to win the European Cup three times. A car crash in 1979, in which he received life-threatening injuries, ended his playing days, but he went on to become a goalkeeping coach for both Germany and his old club.

YOUNGEST CENTURION LUKAS

Lukas Podolski became the youngest European player to reach 100 caps when, aged 27 years and 13 days old, he appeared in Germany's third first-round game of the 2012 UEFA European Championship, against Denmark. He marked the occasion by scoring the opener in a 2-1 win, his 44th international goal. Podolski was born in Gliwice in Poland, but opted to play for Germany—his family having emigrated there when he was two years old. He was voted best young player of the tournament when Germany hosted and finished third at the 2006 FIFA World Cup.

KHEDIRA CROCKED

Midfielder **Sami Khedira** was an injury doubt ahead of the 2014 FIFA World Cup but was among Germany's scorers and best players in its 7-1 semifinal rout of Brazil. His luck changed, though, moments before the Final, as he was injured in the warm-up and replaced by Christoph Kramer. Sadly, Kramer lasted only 31 minutes before a concussion forced him off. Kramer later admitted he could not remember any of the first half. Germany's triumph made Khedira the tenth player to win the FIFA World Cup and UEFA Champions League in the same season, having been part of Real Madrid's successful side a few weeks earlier.

KEEPING A LOW PROFILE

Joachim Low was, in 2014, the 19th coach to win the FIFA World Cup, but the first German coach to do so without having played for his country. After a respectable career as a midfielder for a number of clubs, including Freiburg, and coaching spells in Germany, Austria, and Turkey, Low was appointed as Jurgen Klinsmann's assistant in 2004, before taking the top job after the 2006 FIFA World Cup. He led Germany to the 2008 UEFA European Championship final and the semifinal of Euro 2012, as well as third-place at the 2010 FIFA World Cup. West Germany's 1954 FIFA World Cup-winning manager Sepp Herberger had won three caps as a player, 1974 boss Helmut Schon made 16 appearances, and 1990 coach Franz Beckenbauer won 103 caps and lifted the trophy as captain in 1974.

THE WORST OF STARTS

Goalkeeper Marc-Andre ter Stegen had an international debut to forget when Switzerland beat Germany 5-3 in a May 2012 exhibition. He became the first German goalkeeper to concede more than three goals on his debut for 58 years. The last to do so was Heinrich Kwiatowski, who was in goal when Hungary won 8-3 in West Germany's opening game of the 1954 FIFA World Cup. It was Kwiatowki's only appearance of the finals—he made only three further appearances—but he did still end up with a winners' medal when West Germany gained revenge on the Hungarians, 3-2 in the final. Despite ter Stegen's promise, Germany's current undisputed number one is 52-cap Manuel Neuer.

GERMANY'S MANAGERS

Otto Nerz	1928–36
Sepp Herberger	1936–64
Helmut Schon	1964–78
Jupp Derwall	1978–84
Franz Beckenbauer	1984–90
Berti Vogts	1990–98
Erich Ribbeck	1998–2000
Rudi Voller	2000–04
Jurgen Klinsmann	2004–06
Joachim Low	2006–

BONUS BATTLE

Helmut Schon's 1974 FIFA World Cup winners almost walked out before the finals started. Schon was prepared to send his squad home in a row over bonuses. A last-minute deal was brokered between Franz Beckenbauer and federation vice-president Hermann Neuberger. The vote among the squad went 11–11, but Beckenbauer persuaded the players to accept the DFB's offer. It was a great decision: it beat the Netherlands 2-1 in the final.

GOAL RUSH

Germany's biggest win was 16-0, against Russia in the 1912 Olympic Games, in Stockholm. Karlsruhe's Gottfried Fuchs scored ten of the goals, still a national team record.

NEW BOYS REUNION

Bayern Munich's **Mario Gotze** was the hero when Germany finally overcame Argentina's resistance in the 2014 FIFA World Cup final. His 113th-minute volley was the first winner scored by a substitute. It seemed apt that Germany's first FIFA World Cup triumph since the reunification of East and West Germany in 1990 was secured by Gotze, set up by Andre Schurrle. They had jointly become the first German soccer internationals born post-reunification, when making their debuts as 79th-minute substitutes against Sweden in November 2010.

SCHON IN SAARLAND

Helmut Schon is remembered as one of Germany's most successful coaches. He started his international coaching career with Saarland—now part of Germany—but which had been made a separate state (with a population of 970,000) after the country's post-war division. Saarland's greatest moment came in the 1954 FIFA World Cup qualifiers, when it beat Norway 3-2 in Oslo to top its qualifying group. It was eventually eliminated by Sepp Herberger's West Germany.

GERMANY'S BRONZE AGES

The 2010 FIFA World Cup third-place play-off between Germany and Uruguay was a rematch of the same game at the 1970 tournament, when West Germany won 1-0. The German team again took third place, 40 years later, thanks to a dramatic 3-2 victory in Port Elizabeth's Nelson Mandela Bay stadium. The result, secured by Sami Khedira's late goal, meant Germany had a record four third-place finishes at FIFA World Cups, having also come third in 1934 and 2006.

PRESSURE ON JULIAN

Julian Draxler became Germany's fifth-youngest player when he made his debut against Switzerland in May 2012, aged 18 years and 248 days old. Team-mate Mario Gotze is third on that list, having been 18 years and 166 days old when he made his first appearance, against Sweden in November 2010. Germany's youngest-ever player remains Oskar Ritter, who was 17 years and 254 days old when he made his debut, also against Sweden, in June 1925. Uwe Seeler was 90 days older when he debuted for West Germany against France in October 1954. Fourth on the list is Olaf Thon, who was 63 days older than Gotze when he made his first international appearance, against Malta, in December 1984.

SEPP'S SURPRISE

Sepp Herberger (1897–1977) was one of the most influential figures in Germany's soccer history. He was its longest-serving coach (28 years at the helm) and his legendary status was assured after West Germany surprised odds-on favorite Hungary to win the 1954 FIFA World Cup final. The result was credited with dragging the country out of a post-war slump. Herberger took charge in 1936 and led the team into the 1938 FIFA World Cup finals. During the war years he used his influence to try to keep his best players away from the heavy fighting. When organized soccer resumed in 1949, the federation decided to advertize for a national coach, but Herberger persuaded DFB chief Peco Bauwens to give him back his old job. He had a clause in his contract guaranteeing him a totally free hand in organization and selection policy. Among Herberger's favorite sayings was: "The ball is round and the match lasts 90 minutes. Everything else is just theory."

ITALY

Only Brazil (with five victories) can claim to have won the FIFA World Cup more times than Italy. The *Azzurri* became the first nation to retain the trophy (through back-to-back successes in 1934 and 1938), snatched a surprise win in Spain in 1982, and collected soccer's most coveted trophy for a fourth time in 2006, following a dramatic penalty shoot-out win over France. Add the 1968 UEFA European Championship success to the mix and few nations can boast a better record. The success story does not end there. Italian clubs have won the European Cup on 11 occasions, and the country's domestic league, Serie A, is considered among the strongest in the game. Italy is a true powerhouse of world soccer.

ROTTEN RETURN

Italy was knocked out of the FIFA World Cup in the first round in both 2010 and 2014—the first time it had done so in consecutive tournaments since 1962 and 1966. At least the modern players did not suffer the fate of those arriving home from England in 1966: it was pelted with rotten fruit after a dismal showing, most notable for a 1-0 defeat to minnows North Korea.

OFF THE SPOT

Only England has lost as many FIFA World Cup penalty shoot-outs as Italy—three apiece.  **Roberto Baggio**, nicknamed "The Divine Ponytail," was involved in all three of Italy's spot-kick defeats, in 1990, 1994, and 1998. Left-back Antonio Cabrini is the only man to have missed a penalty during normal time in a FIFA World Cup final—the score was 0-0 at the time but, fortunately for Cabrini, Italy went on to beat West Germany 3-1 in 1982.

THE IDES OF MARCH

Juventus midfielder Claudio Marchisio went from hero to villain at the 2014 FIFA World Cup. He opened Italy's account at the tournament with a fizzing long-range drive against England in Manaus, in what proved to be a 2-1 Italy win. This was his second goal in consecutive internationals – having managed just two goals in his previous 43 appearances for his country. But his tournament turned sour not only with a 1-0 defeat to Costa Rica in its second match, but another 1-0 defeat and a straight red card in its decisive final first-round fixture against Uruguay.

IN SAFE KEEPING

During World War Two, the Jules Rimet Trophy, the FIFA World Cup – won by Italy in 1938 – was hidden in a shoebox under the bed of soccer official Ottorino Barassi. He preferred to keep it there, rather than at its previous home – a bank in Rome. The trophy was handed back to FIFA, safe and untouched, only when the FIFA World Cup resumed in 1950.

BLUE BOYS

Internazionale full-back Davide Santon became Italy's second-youngest international of the post-war era when he played against Northern Ireland in a June 2009 exhibition, aged just 18 years and 155 days, and following just 20 first-team appearances for his club. Another Internazionale defender, the richly moustachioed Giuseppe Bergomi, was 42 days younger when he made his debut against East Germany in April 1982, just three months before helping Italy win the FIFA World Cup. Even more junior were Casale midfielder Luigi Barbesino, 18 years and 61 days old against Sweden in July 1912, and record-holder Renzo De Vecchi, an AC Milan defender who was aged just 16 years and 112 days when he lined up against Hungary in May 1910.

GLOVE CONQUERS ALL

Walter Zenga went 517 minutes without conceding a goal at the 1990 FIFA World Cup, an all-time tournament record. It was brought to an end by Argentina's Claudio Caniggia in the semifinal.

BOSSI DE ROSSI

Combative central midfielder **Daniele de Rossi** was roundly condemned when he was sent off for elbowing the United States' Brian McBride during Italy's second game of the 2006 FIFA World Cup. He returned from suspension in time to come on as a substitute in the final, which Italy won against France. Yet earlier that year, in March, he had won widespread praise for his honesty during a Serie A game for AS Roma against Messina. Roma was awarded a goal when he diverted the ball into the net using his hand, but De Rossi persuaded the referee to disallow his strike, and Roma still won 2-1. His international honors for Italy include a bronze medal at the 2004 Summer Olympics, not long before he made his international debut.

TOP DRAW

No team has tied more FIFA World Cup games than Italy. It took its tally to 21, with 1-1 ties against both Paraguay and New Zealand in Group F at the 2010 competition in South Africa. Its first tie, on May 31, 1934, had also been 1-1, against Spain in a quarterfinal game. Italy's Giuseppe Meazza scored the only goal of the replay, which took place the following day. On June 10, 1934, Italy won the World Cup for the first time after beating Czechoslovakia in the final.

TOURNAMENT SPECIALISTS

FIFA WORLD CUP: 18 appearances – winners 1934, 1938, 1982, 2006
UEFA EUROPEAN CHAMPIONSHIP: 8 appearances – winners 1968
FIRST INTERNATIONAL: Italy 6 France 2 (Milan, May 15, 1910)
BIGGEST WIN: Italy 9 USA 0 (Brentford, London, August 17, 1948 – Olympic Games)
BIGGEST DEFEAT: Hungary 7 Italy 1 (Budapest, April 6, 1924)

FLYING HIGH

Vittorio Pozzo is the only man to have won the FIFA World Cup twice as coach—both times with Italy, in 1934 and 1938 (only two players, Giuseppe Meazza and Giovanni Ferrari, were selected in both finals). Pozzo also led Italy to the Berlin 1936 Olympic Games gold medal. Born in Turin, on March 2, 1886, Pozzo learned to love soccer as a student in England, watching Manchester United. He returned home, reluctantly, when his family bought him a return ticket for his sister's wedding, but refused to let him leave Italy again. Pozzo fired up Italy ahead of the 1938 semifinal against by revealing that opponent Brazil had already booked its plane to Paris for the final. Duly motivated, Italy won the semifinal 2-1.

CHAMPS TO CHUMPS

Italy's dismal 2010 FIFA World Cup campaign was the worst in its history, despite going into the tournament as the defending world champion. Its two ties, and 3-2 defeat to Slovakia, meant it ended a FIFA World Cup without a win for the first time ever. Finishing bottom of its first-round group was also unprecedented. The poor showing must have left 2006 World Cup-winning coach **Marcello Lippi** regretting his decision to resume control in 2008. Immediately after the Slovakia match, which ended the defending champions' run, Lippi insisted the players should not be faulted and he should take all the blame. He had already announced his intention to resign after the finals.

ITALY'S NATIONAL COACHES

Vittorio Pozzo	1912, 1924
Augusto Rangone	1925–28
Carlo Carcano	1928–29
Vittorio Pozzo	1929–48
Ferruccio Novo	1949–50
Carlino Beretta	1952–53
Giuseppe Viani	1960
Giovanni Ferrari	1960–61
Giovanni Ferrari/Paolo Mazza	1962
Edmondo Fabbri	1962–66
Helenio Herrera/Ferruccio Valcareggi	1966–67
Ferruccio Valcareggi	1967–74
Fulvio Bernardini	1974–75
Enzo Bearzot	1975–86
Azeglio Vicini	1986–91
Arrigo Sacchi	1991–96
Cesare Maldini	1997–98
Dino Zoff	1998–2000
Giovanni Trapattoni	2000–04
Marcello Lippi	2004–06
Roberto Donadoni	2006–08
Marcello Lippi	2008–10
Cesare Prandelli	2010–14

COMEBACK KID

Paolo Rossi was the unlikely hero of Italy's 1982 FIFA World Cup triumph, winning the Golden Boot with six goals—including a memorable hat-trick against Brazil in the second round, and the first of Italy's three goals in its final win over West Germany. But he only just made it to the tournament at all, having completed a two-year ban for his alleged involvement in a betting scandal only six weeks before the start of the tournament.

HELPING HANDS

Goalkeeper Angelo Peruzzi was a 14-year-old ballboy at the 1984 European Cup final between Roma and Liverpool. He made 16 appearances for Roma before playing for Juventus, Internazionale and Lazio, as well as 31 times for Italy between 1995 and 2006.

ONCE BITTEN, TWICE SHY

Italy crashed out of the 2014 FIFA World Cup in Brazil in the first round, just as it had done in South Africa four years earlier. After beating England in Manaus, Italy lost 1-0 to surprise group winners Costa Rica—its first FIFA World Cup defeat to a Central American nation in eight meetings. It then lost a decisive final game against Uruguay by the same scoreline, thanks to a late goal by Diego Godin. The Italians were incensed, however, that Uruguay's striker Luis Suarez had not been dismissed a few minutes earlier for biting **Giorgio Chiellini** on the shoulder. The Italy vice-captain pulled down his shirt to show Mexican referee Marco Rodriguez the toothmarks left in his skin, but to no avail.

MISTER INTER, GIACINTO

No Internazionale player will ever wear the No.3 shirt after it was retired in tribute to the legendary full-back **Giacinto Facchetti**, following his death in 2006 at the age of 64. He spent his entire senior career at Inter, between 1960 and 1978, and later served as the club's technical director and president. In his playing days he helped pioneer the role of a full-back as a stampeding, attacking presence. He favored his right foot, despite advancing down the left side. He captained Italy 70 times, during his 94-cap international career and lifted the UEFA European Championship trophy in 1968.

TOP CAPS

1	Gianluigi Buffon	142
2	Fabio Cannavaro	136
3	Paolo Maldini	126
4	Andrea Pirlo	112
=	Dino Zoff	112
6	Gianluca Zambrotta	98
7	Daniele De Rossi	97
8	Giacinto Facchetti	94
9	Alessandro Del Piero	91
10	Franco Baresi	82

TOP SCORERS

1	Luigi Riva	35
2	Giuseppe Meazza	33
3	Silvio Piola	30
4	Roberto Baggio	27
=	Alessandro Del Piero	27
6	Alessandro Altobelli	25
=	Adolfo Baloncieri	25
=	Filippo Inzaghi	25
9	Francesco Graziani	23
=	Christian Vieri	23

ZOFF THE SCALE

Goalkeeper **Dino Zoff** set an international record by going 1,142 minutes without conceding a goal between September 1972 and June 1974. Zoff was Italy's captain when it won the 1982 FIFA World Cup—emulating the feat of another Juventus goalkeeper, Gianpiero Combi, who had been the victorious skipper in 1934. Zoff coached Italy to the final of the 2000 UEFA European Championship, which it lost 2-1 to France thanks to an extra-time "golden goal." He resigned a few days later, unhappy following the criticism leveled at him by Italy's then prime minister, Silvio Berlusconi.

SOMETIMES SUPER MARIO

Mario Balotelli is one of soccer's most explosive players—and not only because the fire brigade had to be called when fireworks were set off from the bathroom of his home the night before he scored in his club Manchester City's 6-1 trouncing of local rivals United. He marked his opening goal by revealing a T-shirt under his club kit bearing the question: "WHY ALWAYS ME?" His turbulent time in Manchester included a Premier League title but also a training-ground fight with manager Roberto Mancini and a reported $165,000 in parking fines. He was born in Palermo to Ghanaian parents, but health problems as a child prompted him to be adopted by an Italian couple when he was three, changing his name from Mario Barwuah to Mario Balotelli. He was given clearance to play for Italy when given citizenship at the age of 18 and was one of the country's star players at the 2012 UEFA European Championship. He scored his first three international goals—including a decisive double against Germany Germany in the semifinal. But his volatile nature brought him a red card in a 2014 FIFA World Cup qualifier against the Czech Republic in June 2013. As he was making his way off the field, he lashed out at water bottles and then a brick wall.

RIGHT CALL

Italy captain Giacinto Facchetti called correctly when its 1968 UEFA European Championship semifinal against the Soviet Union ended in a tie after extra-time—it was in the days before a penalty shoot-out—and had to be settled by the toss of a coin. The attacking left-back had luck on his side that time, and lifted the trophy after a 2-0 replay victory in the final against Yugoslavia. Facchetti, who also won the European Cup with Internazionale in 1964 and 1965, had an impressive scoring record for a defender, ending his career with 59 goals in 476 league appearances. He played on the left flank, even though he was a naturally right-footed player.

ROLLING RIVA

Italy's all-time top scorer is **Luigi "Gigi" Riva**, who scored 35 goals in 42 appearances for his country. One of his most important strikes was the opening goal in the 1968 UEFA European Championship final win over Yugoslavia. Despite his prolific form, after switching from left-winger to striker, he never played for one of Italy's traditional club giants. Instead, Riva, born in Leggiuno on November 7, 1944, spent his entire league career with unfashionable Sardinian club Cagliari, and at one point turned down a move to the mighty Juventus. His goals (21 of them) fired the club to its one and only league championship in 1970. Riva suffered his fair share of bad luck with injuries. He broke his left leg while playing for Italy in 1966, then his right leg in 1970, once more when he was away on international duty.

HAPPY CENTENARY

After captaining Italy to the 2006 FIFA World Cup title, **Fabio Cannavaro** was named FIFA World Player of the Year. Aged 33, he was the oldest winner of the prize, as well as the first defender. Cannavaro, born in Naples in 1973, played every minute of the 2006 tournament, and the final triumph against France was the ideal way to celebrate his 100th international appearance.

WHEN THE GOING GETS BUFF

Italy goalkeeper **Gianluigi Buffon** has not only been one of the finest modern-day goalkeepers in the world but has also even surpassed some of the achievements of legendary Italian predecessor Dino Zoff. Buffon emulated 1982 world champion Zoff by being part of Italy's 2006 FIFA World Cup-winning side—conceding only two goals during the tournament, one an own goal, and the other a penalty. Italy's progress to the 2012 UEFA European Championship final allowed him to play his 25th game at a finals for Italy, one more than Zoff, and behind only defenders Paolo Maldini (36) and Fabio Cannavaro (26). Italy's dismal first-round exit at the 2010 FIFA World Cup could be blamed at least more than a little on Buffon's back injury in the first half of its first game that ruled him out of the rest of the tournament. Unlike fellow veterans Cannavaro and Gennaro Gattuso, who retired from internationals after the finals, Buffon insisted he would go on and was rewarded with the captaincy by incoming coach Cesare Prandelli. Buffon became only the third player selected for five different FIFA World Cups when he made two appearances in Brazil in 2014, only missing the opening match against England due to a late ankle injury.

CLEAN SWEEP

Italian clubs won all three UEFA trophies in the 1989–90 season, a unique treble. AC Milan won the European Cup (beating Benfica 1-0 in the final), Juventus the UEFA Cup (beating Fiorentina 3-1), and Sampdoria the Cup-Winners' Cup (beating Anderlecht 2-0 in the final).

KEEPING IT IN THE FAMILY

Cesare and **Paolo Maldini** are the only father and son to have hoisted the European Cup as winning captains—both with AC Milan, and both for the first time in England. Cesare lifted the trophy after his team beat Benfica at Wembley, London, in 1963. Paolo repeated the feat 40 years later, when Milan defeated Juventus at Old Trafford, Manchester. Cesare was Italy coach and Paolo Italy captain at the 1998 FIFA World Cup, and they both featured at the 2002 tournament, though Cesare was in charge of Paraguay. The Maldini dynasty may not end there, as Paolo's son, Christian, is emerging through the youth ranks at Milan. If he makes it into the first team, Christian will be the only player allowed to wear Paolo's famous No. 3 jersey. Paolo retired as Italy's second most-capped player, but he never managed to win an international tournament. He played for Italy teams which finished third (1990) and runners-up (1994) at the FIFA World Cup, and runners-up in the UEFA European Championship (2000).

ITALY'S GREATEST PLAYERS
(as chosen by the Italian soccer association)

1 Giuseppe Meazza
2 Luigi Riva
3 Roberto Baggio
4 Paolo Maldini
5 Giacinto Facchetti
6 Sandro Mazzola
7 Giuseppe Bergomi
8 Valentino Mazzola

TRAVELING TRAPATTONI

Italian **Giovanni Trapattoni** has won domestic league titles as a coach in Italy, Germany, Portugal and Austria – with Juventus, Bayern Munich, Benfica and Salzburg. Only Portugal's Jose Mourinho has also coached teams in four different top countries to league title success. Trapattoni is the only manager to have won all three UEFA club competitions as well as the World Club Cup, all with the great Juventus sides of the 1980s.

PEERLESS PIRLO

Deep-lying playmaker **Andrea Pirlo** is one of the  finest passers of a soccer ball in the modern era. He was one of the stand-out performers when Italy won the 2006 FIFA World Cup, and the only player to win three man-of-the-match prizes at the 2012 UEFA European Championship. Perhaps his finest moment of Euro 2012 was the "Panenka" penalty he audaciously chipped down the center of the goal in Italy's quarterfinal shoot-out victory over England. Pirlo came to the tournament having gone through the Italian league season unbeaten, helping Juventus lift the Serie A title after joining it in 2011 from AC Milan on a free transfer.

MEDAL COLLECTORS

Giovanni Ferrari not only enjoys the status of having won both the 1934 and 1938 FIFA World Cups with Italy, he also shares the record for most Serie A titles, with eight triumphs. Five were with Juventus, two with Internazionale, and one with Bologna. He shares the record of eight league championship medals with Virginio Rosetta, twice with Pro Vercelli and six times with Juventus, and Giuseppe Furino, all with Juventus.

ITALIAN LEAGUE TITLES

Juventus	30	Lazio	2
Internazionale	18	Napoli	2
AC Milan	18	Cagliari	1
Genoa	9	Casale	1
Bologna	7	Hellas Verona	1
Pro Vercelli	7	Novese	1
Torino	7	Sampdoria	1
Roma	3	Spezia	1
Fiorentina	2		

GRAND OLD TEAM TO PLAY FOR

Every Italian FIFA World Cup squad has featured at least one Juventus player. The Turin team, known as the "Grand Old Lady" of Italian club soccer, was relegated a division in 2006 after being found guilty of match-fixing. As a result, it was forced to endure its first season outside the top division since the club's foundation in 1897. Juventus's 55 trophies are an Italian club record, following the three consecutive league title triumphs of 2012–14. In 1985, Juventus became the first team to have won the European, UEFA and Cup Winners' Cups.

PRANDELLI'S PLEDGE

Cesare Prandelli was in Africa during the 2010 FIFA World Cup tournament, before he succeeded Marcello Lippi as Italy coach. But the ex-Fiorentina boss went there not only to watch soccer; he and his daughter went to Zanzibar, Tanzania, to open a school in memory of his wife Manuela, who had died of cancer three years earlier. Prandelli's first competitive home game in charge of Italy was in Florence, and his new team crushed the Faroe Islands 5-0. The coach exceeded most expectations by leading Italy to the 2012 UEFA European Championship final. The defeat that day to Spain was Prandelli's first in 16 competitive matches in charge. Prandelli's son Nicolo, a fitness coach, became part of the national team's back-up staff in the build-up to Euro 2012.

BEEFING UP

The stadium shared by AC Milan and Internazionale is popularly known as the San Siro, after the district in which it is located. Its official title, however, is Stadio Giuseppe Meazza, named after the star inside-forward on the pitch and dance enthusiast off it who played for both clubs as well as Italy's 1934 and 1938 FIFA World Cup-winning sides. Meazza, born in Milan on August 23, 1910, was first spotted by an Inter scout while doing ball skills in the street with a ball made of rags. Hhe was so thin he had to be bulked up with plenty of steaks. His last goal for Italy was a penalty in the 1938 World Cup semifinal against Brazil. He did it while trying hold up his shorts, because the elastic had broken.

TRAGIC TORINO

Torino was Italy's most successful club when its first-team squad was wiped out in an air crash at Superga, above Turin, on May 4, 1949. The club has only won the Serie A title once since then, in the 1976–77 season. Among the victims was star forward Valentino Mazzola, who had gone along on the trip despite being ill. His son **Sandro Mazzola**, only six at the time of the disaster, went on to star in the Italy teams that won the 1968 UEFA European Championship and finished as FIFA World Cup beaten finalist two years later.

The walled banks of orange-shirted Netherlands fans may have become a regular feature at the world's major soccer tournaments, but that has not always been the case. It wasn't until the 1970s, with Johan Cruyff and his team's spectacular brand of "Total Football," that the country possessed a side worthy of the modern legend. It won the UEFA European Championship in 1988 and has regularly challenged for soccer's major honors.

NETHERLANDS COACHES (SINCE 1980)

Jan Zwartkruis	1978–81
Rob Baan	1981
Kees Rijvers	1981–84
Rinus Michels	1984–85
Leo Beenhakker	1985–86
Rinus Michels	1986–88
Thijs Libregts	1988–90
Nol de Ruiter	1990
Leo Beenhakker	1990
Rinus Michels	1990–92
Dick Advocaat	1992–95
Guus Hiddink	1995–98
Frank Rijkaard	1998–2000
Louis van Gaal	2000–02
Dick Advocaat	2002–04
Marco van Basten	2004–08
Bert van Marwijk	2008–12
Louis van Gaal	2012–14
Guus Hiddink	2014–

MICHELS THE MASTER

Rinus Michels (1928–2005) was named FIFA's Coach of the Century in 1999 for his achievements with the Netherlands and Ajax. The former Ajax and Netherlands striker took over the manager's job at his old club in 1965 and began creating a team that would dominate European soccer in the early 1970s. Michels built the team around Johan Cruyff—as he later did with the national side—and introduced the concept known as "Total Football." He moved to Barcelona after Ajax's 1971 European Cup victory, but he was called back to mastermind the Netherlands' 1974 FIFA World Cup bid. Nicknamed "The General," he was known as a disciplinarian who could impose order on the many different factions within the Dutch dressing room. Michels used that skill to great effect after taking over the national team again for its 1988 UEFA European Championship campaign. In the finals, the Dutch beat England and the Republic of Ireland to reach the last four, then knocked out hosts West Germany before beating the Soviet Union 2-0 in the final. Michels took charge for a third spell as coach when the Netherlands reached the semifinal of Euro 92. He retired straight after the tournament.

CRUYFF THE MAGICIAN

Johan Cruyff's soccer achievements have made him the most famous living Dutchman. Cruyff (born in Amsterdam on April 25, 1947) was the catalyst for the rise of both Ajax and the national team. As one Dutch paper wrote before the 1974 FIFA World Cup final: "Cruyff woke up the Netherlands and took us to a world-class level." His great opponent, Franz Beckenbauer, said: "He is the best player to have come from Europe." Cruyff joined Ajax as a ten-year-old, and made his league debut at 17. He led the club to eight championships and the European Cup three consecutive years 1971–73. He, and coach Rinus Michels, also developed the style of playing known as "Total Football", which became a trademark for club and country. Cruyff made his national debut, against Hungary, on September 7, 1966. He scored 33 goals in 48 appearances and was captain 33 times. He was named Player of the Tournament in the 1974 FIFA World Cup finals and was voted European Player of the Year three times.

THIS ONE GOES UP TO ELEVEN

The Netherlands' biggest-ever win was an 11-0 thrashing of San Marino in September 2011, during a UEFA European Championship qualifier in Eindhoven. Robin van Persie scored four, while there were doubles for **Wesley Sneijder** and Klaas-Jan Huntelaar, and one each for Dirk Kuyt, John Heitinga, and Georginio Wijnaldum, who made his international debut as an 86th-minute substitute, and scored within four minutes.

LOUIS LOUIS

Louis van Gaal returned for a second spell as Netherlands coach after the 2012 UEFA European Championship. He has enjoyed great success at clubs around Europe, winning the UEFA Champions League with Ajax, two La Liga titles with Barcelona, and the Bundesliga with Bayern Munich. After the 2014 FIFA World Cup, he took over as manager of Manchester United. The Dutch are no strangers to reappointing former coaches: Karel Kaufman, Friedrich Donenfeld, Leo Beenhakker, Dick Advocaat, and Rinus Michels all had more than one spell—and Michels had four. Van Gaal was succeeded by Guus Hiddink, his second spell, too, having been national coach 1995–98.

GOALS GALORE

Only four players have scored five goals in a game for the Netherlands: Jan Vos, as Finland were crushed 9-0 in July 1912; Leen Vente, in a 9-3 defeat of Belgium in March 1934; John Bosman, in an 8-0 home trouncing of Cyprus in October 1987; and Marco van Basten, in an 8-0 win in Malta in December 1990. Bosman scored three separate hat-tricks for the Dutch, as did Mannes Francken, Beb Bakhuys, and Faas Wilkes. Two of Wilkes' trebles were scored in 1946—the third came a full 13 years later.

ALL CHANGE FOR THE ORANJE

Ten of the 11 men who started the 2010 FIFA World Cup final were in the Dutch squad for a disastrous UEFA European Championship in 2012. It lost all three first-round games and missed the knock-out stages of a major tournament for the first time since failing to qualify for Euro 2004. Things improved dramatically at the 2014 FIFA World Cup as the Netherlands finished third, after losing the semifinal to Argentina in a penalty shoot-out. Only nine members of the 23-man Euro 2012 squad made it to Brazil 2014. The most memorable Dutch display in Brazil came in its opening game: avenging its 2010 FIFA World Cup final defeat by demolishing defending champion Spain 5-1 in Salvador. **Robin van Persie**'s fantastic diving header from the edge of the penalty area, that looped over goalkeeper Iker Casillas, was the highlight. Van Persie thus became the first Dutchman to score at three separate FIFA World Cups. The 2014 FIFA World Cup was the first one which the Netherlands ended with a win: a 3-0 third-place play-off defeat of hosts Brazil. This set another record as the Netherlands became the first country to beat Brazil in FIFA World Cup finals three times.

HERO HAPPEL

Ernst Happel is second only to Rinus Michels for his coaching achievements with Dutch teams. The former Austria defender made history by steering Feyenoord to the European Cup in 1970—the first Dutch club to win the trophy. He was drafted in to coach the Netherlands at the 1978 FIFA World Cup finals after guiding Belgian side Brugge to the European Cup final. In Johan Cruyff's absence, Happel drew the best from Ruud Krol, Johan Neeskens, and Arie Haan, as the Netherlands reached the final before losing in extra-time to Argentina in Buenos Aires.

VAN BASTEN'S TOURNAMENT

Marco van Basten was the hero of the Netherlands' 1988 UEFA European Championship success. He netted a hat-trick to see off England in a group game, scored a semifinal winner against West Germany, and then cracked a spectacular flying volley to clinch a 2-0 victory over the Soviet Union in the final. The Dutch forward also starred in Italy's Serie A with AC Milan, and was twice the league's top scorer before persistent ankle trouble ended his career prematurely.

HANGING AROUND

Sander Boschker waited a long time for his full introduction to international soccer, but he set two Dutch records when he finally came on, as a second-half substitute against Ghana in a June 2010 exhibition. At the age of 39 years and 256 days, he was not only the oldest Dutchman to win his first cap—but also the oldest Dutch international ever. That remains his only cap ... so far.

FLYING FEAR DENIED BERGKAMP MORE CAPS

Dennis Bergkamp would have won many more than 79 caps, but for his fear of flying. The legendary playmaker refused to board aircraft after the Netherlands squad had been involved in a bomb hoax incident during the 1994 FIFA World Cup in the United States. He missed away games for the Netherlands, and his clubs, unless he could reach the venue by road, rail or boat.

DIFFERENT SIDES OF SNEIJDER

Wesley Sneijder was hoping to achieve an unprecedented quintuple when his Netherlands team took on Spain in the 2010 FIFA World Cup final. He was trying to become the first player ever to win the FIFA World Cup in the same season as a domestic league and cup double, and the UEFA Champions League or European Cup—let alone adding the FIFA World Cup Golden Boot. Sneijder won the 2009–10 treble with his club, Internazionale, before only just missing out on the FIFA World Cup and the Golden Boot. Despite his FIFA World Cup final heartbreak, Sneijder did enjoy some romantic solace six days after defeat to Spain, when he married Dutch actress and TV presenter Yolanthe Cabau van Kasbergen.

VORM WELCOME

The Netherlands became the first country to use all 23 squad players at a FIFA World Cup, when substitute goalkeeper Michel Vorm replaced Jasper Cillessen during stoppage-time of the third-place play-off against Brazil. Cillessen set another record as the first goalkeeper to be substituted twice in one tournament. Earlier in the finals, Robin van Persie's suspension from its final first-round game against Chile meant the Dutch played without a single player named "van" for the first time since 1996, a run lasting 221 matches.

NEESKENS'S EARLY GOAL

The Netherlands took a first-minute lead in the 1974 World Cup final without a West German player having touched the ball. The Dutch built a move of 14 passes from the kick-off, and Johan Cruyff was tripped just inside the penalty area by Uli Hoeness. Johan Neeskens converted the first penalty in a World Cup final history ... but West Germany hit back to win 2-1.

KRUL TO BE KIND

Louis van Gaal pulled a masterstoke when he replaced goalkeeper Jasper Cillessen with **Tim Krul** in the 119th minute of the Netherlands' quarterfinal against Costa Rica in the 2014 FIFA World Cup. He reasoned that the Dutch stood a better chance of winning the resulting shoot-out with Krul between the sticks as he is two inches taller than Cillessen. Sure enough, Krul saved two penalties and the Dutch went through. Enforced substitutions during the semifinal against Argentina meant van Gaal could not repeat the trick and Cillessen could not emulate Krul's earlier heroics.

NETHERLANDS' DOUBLE LOSERS

Nine Netherlands players were on the losing side in both the 1974 (2-1 to West Germany) and 1978 (3-1 to Argentina) FIFA World Cup finals: Jan Jongbloed, Ruud Krol, Wim Jansen, Arie Haan, Johan Neeskens, Johnny Rep, and Rob Rensenbrink started both games; Wim Suurbier started in 1974, but was a substitute in 1978, and Rene van de Kerkhof was a substitute in 1974, before being in the starting line-up in 1978.

THE WINNING CAPTAIN

With his distinctive dreadlocks, Ruud Gullit cut a swathe through world soccer through the 1980s and 1990s. Twice a European Cup winner with AC Milan, and a former European Footballer of the Year, he will always be remembered fondly by the Dutch fans as being the first man in a Netherlands shirt to lift a major trophy, the 1988 UEFA European Championship.

NETHERLANDS' EURO STARS

Three Dutch players have won the European Footballer of the Year award: Johan Cruyff, **Ruud Gullit,** and Marco van Basten. Cruyff picked up the award in 1971, 1973 and 1974; Gullit was honored in 1987, and Van Basten was chosen in 1988, 1989 and 1992.

TOP SCORERS

1	Robin van Persie	47
2	Patrick Kluivert	40
3	Dennis Bergkamp	37
4	Klaas-Jan Huntelaar	35
=	Ruud van Nistelrooy	35
=	Faas Wilkes	35
7	Johan Cruyff	33
=	Abe Lenstra	33
9	Beb Bakhuys	28
10	Wesley Sneijder	27

DE BOER BOYS SET RECORD

Twins Frank and Ronald de Boer hold the record for the most games played by brothers together for the Netherlands. Frank won 112 caps, while Ronald won 67.

TOP CAPS

1	Edwin van der Sar	130
2	Frank de Boer	112
3	Rafael van der Vaart	109
4	Gio van Bronckhorst	106
5	Wesley Sneijder	105
6	Dirk Kuyt	103
7	Phillip Cocu	101
8	Robin van Persie	91
9	John Heitinga	87
=	Clarence Seedorf	87

WORK OF VAART

Rafael van der Vaart became the fifth player to make 100 appearances for the Netherlands, following Edwin van der Sar, Frank de Boer, Giovanni van Bronckhorst, and Philip Cocu. Yet, for a while, it looked as if van der Vaart might just miss out on the milestone: he ended the 2012 UEFA European Championship on 99 caps, and coach Bert van Marwijk said he may be left out of future squads. But Van Marwijk's departure, after Euro 2012, was a boost for van der Vaart, who made his 100th appearance in a 4-2 exhibition loss to Belgium in August 2012. Van der Vaart had marked his 99th cap with a stunning long-range goal against Portugal in the Netherlands' final first-round game at Euro 2012, and hit a post, in the 2-1 defeat that ended Dutch interest earlier than expected. Sadly, a calf injury ruled him out of the 2014 FIFA World Cup three days before Louis van Gaal announced his 23-man squad.

ALL-TIME LEADING SCORER

Patrick Kluivert made his Netherlands debut in 1994 and, in the following ten years, won 79 caps and scored a then national record 40 goals. That mark was beaten by Robin van Persie, who was Netherlands captain at the 2014 FIFA World Cup, while Kluivert watched on as Louis van Gaal's assistant coach.

EARLY DAYS

The Netherlands played its first international, against Belgium, in Brussels on April 30, 1905. Eddy de Neve scored all the goals in the Netherlands' 4-1 win. The Dutch and its Belgian neighbor have been arch-rivals ever since.

BLIND LEADING THE BLIND

Dutch defender **Danny Blind** won 42 caps between 1986 and 1996, and appeared at the FIFA World Cups of 1990 and 1994. He was also involved at the 2014 finals, this time as an assistant to coach Louis van Gaal. He thus got to see his son **Daley**—like Danny, a defender who plays his club soccer for Ajax Amsterdam—not only feature as a regular starter but score his first international goal, in the third-place play-off victory over Brazil. Danny Blind was appointed as Guus Hiddink's assistant for the 2016 UEFA European Championship qualifying campaign, with the promise of the top job at the end of that tournament.

SIXTH SENSE

Maarten Stekelenburg, Edwin van der Sar's successor as the Netherlands' first-choice goalkeeper, impressed many with his performances at the 2010 FIFA World Cup, conceding just six goals in seven games—two of them penalties. His rise is all the more startling because he is deaf in one ear. He also has the unenviable distinction of being the first Dutch international goalkeeper to be shown a red card. On September 6, 2008, in a 2-1 exhibition defeat against Australia in Eindhoven, he was sent off for fouling Josh Kennedy.

KOEMAN PEOPLE

The only man to both play for and manage all of Dutch domestic soccer's "big three" of Ajax Amsterdam, PSV Eindhoven, and Feyenoord, is Ronald Koeman. He won the UEFA European Cup twice, with PSV Eindhoven in 1988, and with Barcelona four years later—a game in which he scored the winning goal, a ferocious long-range free-kick. Despite largely playing in defence, he scored 14 goals in 78 games for the Netherlands. Elder brother Erwin played 31 times for the Netherlands, and their father Martin won one cap for his country in 1964. Both Ronald and Erwin were part of the Netherlands' 1988 UEFA European Championship-winning side.

MEMPHIS SWELL

Substitute Memphis Depay became the youngest FIFA World Cup goalscorer in Dutch history. He was 20 years and 125 days old when he scored in a 3-2 Group B win over Australia at Porto Alegre in 2014. He also scored against Chile, five days later, once again as a substitute. Depay was one of three nominees for the Best Young Player award, but lost out to France's Paul Pogba.

JETRO POWERED

Left-back **Jetro Willems** became the youngest player
in UEFA European Championship tournament history
when he started for the Netherlands against
Denmark in its opening Group B game in Kharkiv,
Ukraine, on June 9, 2012. He was 18 years and 71
days old, 44 days younger than Belgium's Enzo
Scifo had been at the 1984 finals. Willems is
the fourth-youngest player to be capped by the
Netherlands, with the record held by Jan van Breda
Kolff, who was 17 years and 74 days old when
making his debut against Belgium on April 2, 1911.
Van Breda Kolff's goal in a 3-1 win, the only one
of his 11-cap career, means he remains his country's
youngest scorer.

NETHERLANDS SO CLOSE

The Netherlands came within a post's width of winning the
1978 FIFA World Cup final. A Rob Rensenbrink shot bounced off
an upright in the last minute of normal time. It was 1-1 after 90
minutes and Argentina went on to win 3-1 in extra-time, shattering
Dutch final dreams for the second FIFA World Cup in a row.

PENALTY PLAGUE

Missed penalties have become a Dutch nightmare, causing its
downfall in several tournaments. The jinx started in the 1992
UEFA European Championship semifinal, when Denmark's
Peter Schmeichel won the shoot-out by saving from Marco van
Basten. The Netherlands lost a Euro 96 quarterfinal shoot-out
to France and, two years later, went down on penalties to Brazil
in a FIFA World Cup semifinal. Then as a co-host of Euro 2000,
the Dutch missed two penalties in normal time in the semifinal
against Italy, and another two in the shoot-out. There was
finally some shoot-out joy at the 2014 FIFA World Cup, when
Costa Rica was beaten in the quarterfinal, but it soon turned to
misery in the semifinal, when it lost to Argentina on penalties.

KEY PLAYER

Maintaining harmony has often been a tricky task for Dutch
coaches at major international tournaments, but Bert van
Marwijk managed to do so at the 2010 FIFA World Cup, despite
rumored tension between several of his star players. When
not conducting his team from the touchline, van Marwijk could
occasionally be found playing the piano in the lobby of the
squad's Johannesburg hotel.

VAN DER SAR TOPS THE LOT

Goalkeeper **Edwin van der Sar** (born in Voorhout on October 29, 1970)
is the Netherlands' most-capped player, having made 130 appearances
for the national team. He joined Ajax in 1990 and helped it to win the
European Cup five years later. He made his Netherlands debut on
June 7, 1995, against Belarus, and was first-choice keeper for 13 years.
He quit international soccer after the Netherlands' elimination at Euro
2008, but new coach Bert van Marwijk persuaded him to return briefly
after injuries to his successors, Maarten Stekelenburg and Henk Timmer.
Van der Sar has also won the UEFA Champions League with Manchester
United, as well as spending spells with Juventus and Fulham.

GOING DUTCH FULL-TIME

Professionalism was not introduced into
Dutch soccer until 1954. The Netherlands'
emergence as a major power came even
later, after Ajax and Feyenoord decided
to go full-time professional in the early
1960s. Until then, even stars such as Ajax
left-winger Piet Keizer—who worked for a
tailor—held down part-time jobs outside
of soccer.

DUTCH CLOGS

The Netherlands became the first team
to be shown as many as nine cards
during a single FIFA World Cup match
when it received eight yellows, including
a lenient one for Nigel de Jong's chest-
high challenge on Xabi Alonso, and a red
during the 2010 final against Spain. The
Netherlands were also involved in the FIFA
World Cup game with the most cards: its
second-round defeat to Portugal four years
earlier, when 20 cards were shown in
total – 16 yellows and four reds.

WHOLE LOTTA SCHAKEN

Feyenoord winger Ruben Schaken
netted the Netherlands' 1,500th
international goal to complete a
3-0 victory over Estonia in a FIFA
World Cup qualifier in March 2013.
It was his second goal in three
appearances for his country.

SPAIN

Spain is home to some of Europe's strongest clubs (boasting 14 European Cup/UEFA Champions League wins between them) and has produced some of soccer's biggest names. For years, however, the national team was considered the world game's biggest underachievers (*La Roja's* only success being the 1964 UEFA European Championship). Things changed in 2008, when Spain won the UEFA European Championship, its first international success for 44 years, and achieved its first-ever top position in the Coca-Cola/FIFA World Rankings. Even better came with victory in the 2010 FIFA World Cup, and an unprecedented third straight major trophy when the European crown was retained in 2012. But a disappointing first-round exit at the 2014 FIFA World Cup saw the run end.

"FALSE NINE"

Spain not only began and ended its Euro 2012 campaign against Italy, but also became the first team to win a UEFA European Championship fielding the same starting XI in the opening game and the final. Perhaps even more surprising was that Vicente del Bosque's men won the tournament so convincingly despite kicking off without an orthodox striker, preferring a 4-6-0 formation with midfielder **Cesc Fabregas** deployed as a "false nine."

DOUBLING UP

Spain's 2010 FIFA World Cup triumph made it the first country since West Germany in 1974 to lift the trophy as the reigning European champions. When France combined the two titles, it did it the other way around, by winning the 1998 FIFA World Cup and then the UEFA European Championship two years later. Yet no country had won three major tournaments in a row until Spain won Euro 2012, trouncing Italy 4-0 in the final. This also made Spain the first team to make a successful defense of its UEFA European Championship title. That scoreline was also the largest victory in a FIFA World Cup or UEFA European Championship final. The clean sheet in the final also stretched its run without conceding a goal in knockout games at major tournaments to 990 minutes.

THREE AND EASY

David Villa and Fernando Torres share Spain's record for most hat-tricks, with three. They even managed one apiece in the same game, the 10-0 crushing of Tahiti at the 2013 FIFA Confederations Cup. It was Spain's third-largest victory, behind only a 13-0 win over Bulgaria in 1933, and a 12-1 rout of Malta in 1983. Torres set another record at the 2009 FIFA Confederations Cup: the fastest ever hat-trick for Spain, all coming in the first 17 minutes of a 5-0 victory over New Zealand.

GROUNDS FOR APPEAL

No single country has provided more venues when hosting a FIFA World Cup finals than the 17 stadiums—in 14 cities—used by Spain in 1982. The 2002 tournament was played at 20 different venues but ten were in Japan and ten in South Korea. The 1982 competition was the first FIFA World Cup to be expanded from 16 to 24 teams. The final was played in Madrid's Estadio Santiago Bernabeu.

RIGHT SAID FRED

When Spain came back from 2-0 and then 3-2 down to win 4-3 in Madrid in May 1929, it became the first non-British team to beat England. Spain's victory, in the Estadio Metropolitano, came with the help of its English coach Fred Pentland, who had moved to Spain in 1920. He had most success with Athletic Bilbao, leading it to league and cup doubles in 1930 and 1931, and inflicting Barcelona's worst-ever defeat, a 12-1 rout in 1931.

NOT TOO SHABY XABI

Passmaster Xabi Alonso scored both goals as Spain beat France 2-0 in its 2012 UEFA European Championship quarterfinal, an ideal way for him to celebrate a day in which he became the fifth Spaniard, after Iker Casillas, Raul, Xavi, and Andoni Zubizarreta, to make 100 international appearances. The central midfielder's father, Periko Alonso, won 21 Spanish caps as well as three La Liga titles—two with Real Sociedad and one with Barcelona—though Xabi would later play for Barca's arch-rival Real Madrid. Xabi's brother Mikel, and half-brother Marcos, are both professional players, while another brother Jon is a referee.

NO DEFENSE

Spain went into the 2014 FIFA World Cup in Brazil aiming not only to retain its crown, but also to clinch a historic fourth consecutive international title, having also won the UEFA European Championship in 2008 and 2012. But Spain's defense of the FIFA World Cup was a disaster. It took the lead, through a **Xabi Alonso** penalty, in its opening game against the Netherlands, but lost the game 5-1: the heaviest FIFA World Cup finals defeat any reigning champion has suffered. A 2-0 defeat to Chile made it the first defending champion to be eliminated with one group game remaining. Spain gained a token of consolation with a 3-0 victory against Australia, but the early exit brought to an end the otherwise-glorious international careers of players such as Xavi and David Villa.

MAJOR TOURNAMENTS

FIFA WORLD CUP:
14 appearances – winners 2010

UEFA EUROPEAN CHAMPIONSHIP:
9 appearances – winners 1964, 2008, 2012

FIRST INTERNATIONAL:
Spain 1 Denmark 0 (Brussels, Belgium, August 28, 1920)

BIGGEST WIN:
Spain 13 Bulgaria 0 (Madrid, May 21, 1933)

BIGGEST DEFEAT:
Italy 7 Spain 1 (Amsterdam, Netherlands, June 4, 1928); England 7 Spain 1 (London, England, December 9, 1931)

RED ALERT

Spain refused to play in the first UEFA European Championship in 1960, in protest at having to travel to the Soviet Union, a Communist country. But it changed its minds four years later, not only hosting the tournament but also winning it—and by beating the visiting Soviets 2-1 in the final. Spain was captained by Fernando Olivella, and managed by Jose Villalonga, who had been the first coach to win the European Cup, with Real Madrid in 1956.

WISE HEAD, OLD SHOULDERS

In 2008, a month short of his 70th birthday, Spain's **Luis Aragones**, full name Luis Aragones Suarez, became the oldest coach to win the UEFA European Championship. A former center-forward and known only as "Luis" during his playing days, he won 11 caps for Spain. As coach, the "Wise Man of Hortaleza" won 38 games between 2004 and 2008, a national record since beaten by his successor Vicente Del Bosque. Aragones died from leukaemia on February 1, 2014, aged 75. Tributes were paid across soccer, but especially at his former club Atletico Madrid which, that same weekend, went top of La Liga for the first time since 1995–96—when Aragones was the coach. Atletico went on to win its first title since that season. The players also wore his name, embroidered in gold, inside the collars of their shirts during the 2014 UEFA Champions League final.

TORRES! TORRES!

As a child, **Fernando Torres** wanted to be a goalkeeper, but made the wise decision to become a striker instead. He has a penchant for scoring the only goal in the final of a tournament, doing so in the 2008 UEFA European Championship, for Spain against Germany in Vienna, having done the same in the Under-16 UEFA European Championship in 2001 and for the Under-19s the following year. Torres became the most expensive Spanish soccer player ever when Chelsea paid €58.5million to sign him from fellow English club Liverpool in January 2011. In 2012, Torres became the first player to score in the final of two different UEFA European Championships, when he came on as a substitute, and found the net against Italy. Torres's goal in Spain's 3-0 victory over Australia in June 2014 was his first at a FIFA World Cup finals since Germany 2006. He thus became the ninth Spanish player to have scored four FIFA World Cup goals.

TOP CAPS

1	Iker Casillas	156
2	Xavi Hernandez	133
3	Andoni Zubizarreta	126
4	Sergio Ramos	119
5	Xabi Alonso	114
6	Fernando Torres	110
7	Raul Gonzalez	102
8	Carles Puyol	100
=	Andres Iniesta	100
10	David Villa	97

TOP SCORERS

1	David Villa	59
2	Raul Gonzalez	44
3	Fernando Torres	38
4	Fernando Hierro	29
5	Fernando Morientes	27
6	Emilio Butragueno	26
7	Alfredo Di Stefano	23
8	Julio Salinas	22
9	Michel	21
10	David Silva	20
=	Telmo Zarra	20

HAPPY HERNANDEZ

Relentlessly precise passer **Xavi Hernandez** has proved himself a more than worthy heir to Pep Guardiola at the heart of the Barcelona and Spain midfields. As well as winning the UEFA Champions League with his club in 2006, 2009, and 2011, he was voted Player of the Tournament when Spain won the 2008 UEFA European Championship, starred as *La Roja* claimed the FIFA World Cup crown two years later, and retained its European crown in 2012. Xavi was third, behind club mate Lionel Messi, in the 2010 and 2011 FIFA Ballon d'Or voting. Yet he nearly left Barcelona for Italy's AC Milan when aged just 17. However, Xavi was not keen on the proposed move, and later expressed his relief at staying in Spain.

BEST CAS SCENARIO

Spain suffered a rare defeat when goalkeeper and captain Iker Casillas equaled the national record for most international appearances, in a 1-0 exhibition defeat to England in November 2011. *La Roja* then tied 2-2 with Costa Rica three days later when he broke the record. Seven months later, Casillas was lifting a third trophy in a row, at Euro 2012, and extending not just his international appearances record but several more. The 4-0 Euro 2012 final victory over Italy made him the first player to reach a century of international wins. It was also his 78th clean sheet for his country, more than any other goalkeeper has achieved—the closest challenger was the Netherlands' Edwin van der Sar, on 72. The pair also share the record for the most UEFA European Championship clean sheets—nine. Casillas went 821 minutes without conceding a goal for Spain, until Olivier Giroud scored for France in a FIFA World Cup qualifier in October 2012.

SAVING FOR A REINA DAY

Jose "Pepe" Reina finally saw action in the FIFA World Cup, at his third finals, when selected for Spain's 3-0 defeat of Australia in June 2014. He had been an unused squad member at both Germany 2006 and South Africa 2010. It was Reina's 34th appearance for Spain since making his debut in 2005. His father, Manuel Reina, also a goalkeeper, played in five internationals between 1969 and 1973.

VILLA FILLS HIS BOOTS

David Villa became Spain's all-time top scorer in FIFA World Cups with his first-round goal against Chile in 2010, his sixth overall across the 2006 and 2010 tournaments. Villa also became the first Spaniard to miss a penalty in a FIFA World Cup game, when he wasted the chance of a hat-trick against Honduras, also in 2010, by putting his spot-kick wide. Spain had scored its previous 14 FIFA World Cup penalties, not counting shoot-outs. Villa became Spain's all-time leading scorer with two goals against the Czech Republic in March 2011, but a broken leg ruled him out of the 2012 UEFA European Championship, thus missing out on adding to his Euro 2008 and 2010 FIFA World Cup winners' medals. Villa retired from international soccer as Spain departed the 2014 FIFA World Cup, signing off with a neat backheel goal against Australia, his 59th international strike in 97 appearances, and the first backheeled goal at a FIFA World Cup since Austria's Bruno Pezzey against Northern Ireland in 1982.

SERGING SERGIO

Sergio Ramos became the youngest-ever European player to reach 100 international caps, in March 2013, at the age of 26 years and 358 days—and marked the occasion by scoring the opening goal in a 1-1 tie with Finland. He claimed the record from Germany's Lukas Podolski, who had been 21 days older when he reached his century of caps. South Korea's Cha Bum-Kun, who was 24 years and 139 days old when he achieved the landmark, holds the global record. Ramos, who can play both at right-back or in central defence, was a member of the Spain team which won the 2008 and 2012 UEFA European Championships, as well as the 2010 FIFA World Cup. He held those trophies in safer hands than he had done when he raised the Spanish Copa del Rey, won by his club Real Madrid, during an open-top bus tour in April 2011: on that occasion, he dropped the cup from the upper deck and saw it crushed beneath the bus's wheels.

FIT FOR PURPOSE

Luis Suarez played through injury for Spain in the 1964 UEFA European Championship final. It was lucky for his team-mates, as he set up both goals in a 2-1 triumph. He was named European Footballer of the Year in 1960—the only Spanish-born player to win that prize, though Andres Iniesta did win a revamped award in 2012.

TRI-NATIONS

Ladislav Kubala played for not one, not two, but three different countries, but he never appeared in the finals of a major international tournament. Despite being born in Budapest on June 10, 1927, he made his international debut for Czechoslovakia in 1946, and won five more caps for the country of his parents' birth. He then appeared three times for his native Hungary, after moving back there in 1948. Kubala also played 19 games for Spain, after leaving Hungary as a refugee and securing a transfer to Barcelona in 1951.

VICTORY MARCH

Center-back Carlos Marchena became the first player to go 50 internationals in a row unbeaten, when he played in Spain's 3-2 victory over Saudi Arabia in May 2009—one more than Brazil's 1950s and 1960s winger Garrincha. Marchena was a member of Spain's successful 2010 FIFA World Cup squad, ending the tournament on 54 consecutive internationals without defeat. Marchena's 57-game unbeaten run came to an end when Argentina beat Spain 4-1 in September 2010.

TREASURE CHEST

The Spanish top division goalkeeper who concedes the fewest goals per game each season is awarded the Zamora Trophy. This is named after legendary keeper **Ricardo Zamora**, who played 46 times for Spain between 1920 and 1936, including the legendary 4-3 win over England in Madrid in 1929. Zamora was the first Spanish star to play for both Barcelona and Real Madrid. Later he was league title-winning coach of ... Atletico Madrid.

LUCKY JUAN

Only one player has failed to score in a FIFA World Cup penalty shoot-out with a spot-kick that would have won the game had it gone in: Spain's Juan Carlos Valeron, whose effort went wide against the Republic of Ireland in 2002. The shoot-out score was 2-1 in Spain's favor, with one Irish attempt remaining. Valeron missed Spain's fourth kick, but Gaizka Mendieta made no mistake to seal a 3-2 shoot-out win.

FAMILIAR FACES, UNFAMILIAR OUTCOME

Sixteen players from Spain's triumphant 2010 FIFA World Cup squad were picked for the 2014 tournament, and seven who played in the final started against the Netherlands in its opening game four years later—the Dutch had four. It was the first time that the two countries in a FIFA World Cup final played each other in the first-round of the next tournament. Spain's 5-1 defeat at the hands of the Dutch in Salvador was its heaviest in the FIFA World Cup since losing 6-1 to Brazil in 1950.

SPANISH LEAGUE CHAMPIONSHIPS

Real Madrid	32
Barcelona	22
Atletico Madrid	10
Athletic Bilbao	8
Valencia	6
Real Sociedad	2
Deportivo de la Coruna	1
Sevilla	1
Betis	1

THE RAUL THING

Raul Gonzalez Blanco—known as Raul—is not only Spain's second-most prolific scorer, with 44 goals from 102 games, but also holds the records for the most UEFA European Cup/ Champions League goals (71, including five for Schalke 04) and for the most goals for Real Madrid (323), having passed Alfredo di Stefano's tally of 309 in 2008–09. But despite his glittering career, he missed out on international glory for Spain: he was controversially left out of the 2008 UEFA European Championship-winning squad and was also overlooked for the FIFA World Cup two years later.

SUPER PED

Spanish winger **Pedro** is the only player to have scored in six separate official club tournaments in one calendar year, managing to hit the net for Barcelona in Spain's Primera Liga, Copa del Rey, and Super Cup in 2009, as well as the UEFA Champions League, UEFA European Super Cup, and FIFA Club World Cup. He was also in the starting line-up for the 2010 FIFA World Cup final—less than two years after being a member of the Barcelona reserve team in Spain's third division and needing new club coach Pep Guardiola's intervention to prevent him being sent home to Tenerife.

SEMI PRECIOUS

Center-back **Carles Puyol**'s thumping header not only gave Spain victory in its 2010 FIFA World Cup semifinal, it was also the country's first win over Germany in four FIFA World Cup matches. West Germany had won 2-1 in both 1966 and 1982, before a 1-1 tie at the 1994 tournament. But Spain's 1-0 win in 2010 was a repeat of its triumph over Germany in the UEFA European Championship final two years earlier. Puyol played his 100th and final international against Uruguay in February 2013, and retired from all forms of the game aged 36 in May 2014.

PERFECT PICHICHI

The annual award for top scorer in La Liga is called the "Pichichi"—the nickname of Rafael Moreno, a striker for Athletic Bilbao between 1911 and 1921. He scored 200 goals in 170 games for the club, and once in five matches for Spain. Pichichi, who often took the field wearing a large white cap, died suddenly in 1922, aged just 29.

CLUB SANDWICH

Spanish clubs have won the UEFA European Cup/Champions League 14 times, more than any other country. Italy and England are joint second, on 12 apiece. The 14 include victories in six of the 15 finals since the start of the 21st century, culminating in the first all-Spanish final in 2014, which Real Madrid won 4-1 against local rivals Atletico Madrid. This was Real's 10th European Cup—dubbed "La Decima" – and the first since 2002, having seen Barcelona win three times in the interim.

SPAIN'S PLAYERS IN EURO 2008/FIFA WORLD CUP 2010/EURO 2012 SQUADS

Iker Casillas*
Sergio Ramos*
Andres Iniesta*
Xabi Alonso*
Xavi Hernandez*
Cesc Fabregas*
Fernando Torres*
David Silva
Alvaro Arbeloa
Raul Albiol
Pepe Reina

*= appeared in all three finals.

TOP BOSS DEL BOSQUE

Vicente Del Bosque was an unused substitute during Ladislao Kubala's 68th and final match in charge of Spain in 1980. He was on Spain bench again when *La Roja* played Denmark in March 2013, but this time as coach, and for the 69th time, enabling him to surpass Kubala's record. Del Bosque won the 2010 FIFA World Cup and the 2012 UEFA European Championship as Spain coach, adding to the two UEFA Champions League titles he claimed as Real Madrid boss. He, and Italy's Marcelo Lippi, are the only men to have won both the UEFA Champions League, or European Cup, and the FIFA World Cup, but Del Bosque's UEFA Euro 2012 triumph gave him an unprecedented hat-trick. Another unmatched feat was his 13 victories in his first 13 games as Spain coach after he succeeded Luis Aragones in 2008.

FIFA FIRST

Real Madrid was the only Spanish club formally represented at FIFA's first meeting in Paris in 1904—though the club was then known simply as Madrid FC. Spanish clubs, such as Real Madrid and Real Betis, dropped the word "Real"—meaning "Royal"— from its names during the Second Spanish Republic, between 1931 and 1939.

BELGIUM

Belgium, nicknamed "The Red Devils," embarked on a golden period in the Eighties after eight decades spent on the fringes of international competition: first a runner-up finish at the 1980 UEFA European Championship, followed by a run to the semifinal of the 1986 FIFA World Cup. A new crop of elite European stars did, however, help Belgium to reach the 2014 FIFA World Cup quarterfinal—in its first finals appearance since 2002. There is clearly hope for many more impressive performances from Belgium in the next few years.

BELGIAN LEAGUE CHAMPIONSHIP WINS

33	Anderlecht
13	Club Brugge
11	Union Saint-Gilloise
10	Standard Liege
7	Beerschot
6	Racing de Bruxelles
5	RFC de Liege
5	Daring de Bruxelles
4	Antwerp
4	Mechelen
4	Lierse
3	Genk
3	Cercle Brugge
2	Beveren
1	Molenbeek

ERWIN–WIN SITUATION

Belgium caused a sensation in the opening game of the 1982 FIFA World Cup by defeating the reigning champion Argentina, 1-0, thanks to a 62nd-minute goal by striker **Erwin Vandenburgh** in Barcelona's Nou Camp stadium. The same opponent had its revenge, in the semifinal four years later, when two unanswered goals by Diego Maradona were enough to put Argentina into the 1986 FIFA World Cup final. Vandenburgh had also scored in Belgium's opening game of that tournament, a 2-1 Group B defeat to hosts Mexico.

SIXTH SENSE

By qualifying for the 2002 FIFA World Cup, Belgium became the first country to reach six successive FIFA World Cup finals without having been either the host or defending champion.

HE'S OUR GUY

Unquestionably Belgium's greatest coach—as well as its longest-serving—was **Guy Thys**. He led it to the final of the 1980 UEFA European Championship and, with a team featuring the likes of Enzo Scifo and Nico Claesen, the semifinal of the FIFA World Cup six years later. Thys spent 13 years in the job, from 1976 to 1989, then returned for a second spell just eight months after resigning. He stepped down again after coaching Belgium at the 1990 FIFA World Cup. During his playing days, in the 1940s and 1950s, he was a striker and won two caps for Belgium. He died at the age of 80 in August 2003.

DIVOCK'S DIVIDEND

Divock Origi was a late choice for Belgium's 2014 FIFA World Cup squad,  picked by coach Marc Wilmots to replace the injured Christian Benteke. He justified that faith with the only goal of Belgium's second game, in the 88th minute, against Russia, half an hour after coming on as a substitute. Aged 19 years and 65 days, he became Belgium's youngest FIFA World Cup goalscorer. Divock's father, Mike Origi, was an international for his native Kenya, but spent most of his career in Belgium, where Divock was born and raised. Belgium's oldest FIFA World Cup scorer remains center-back Leo Clijsters, who was 33 years and 250 days old when he headed the opener in a 3-1 win over Uruguay at Italia 90.

CUP CONSOLATIONS

Belgium lost in the second round of the 2002 FIFA World Cup, beaten 2-0 by eventual champion Brazil. But there was some solace as Belgium won the tournament's fair play prize, and it was complemented by coach Luiz Felipe Scolari, who said Belgium was Brazil's toughest opponent en route to lifting the trophy.

TRIUMPHS AND TRAGEDY

The largest football venue in Belgium is the 50,000-capacity **King Baudouin Stadium** in Brussels. It opened as the Jubilee Stadium on August 23, 1930, then took the name of Heysel in 1946. It was the scene of tragedy in 1985, when a wall collapsed and 39 fans died in disturbances while attending the European Cup final between Liverpool and Juventus. The stadium was rebuilt and given its current name in 1995. When Belgium and the Netherlands were co-hosts of the 2000 UEFA European Championship, the stadium staged the opening ceremony and first game, Belgium's 2-1 victory over Sweden. It is now used for Belgium's home internationals.

BARON RUN

The first man given honorary membership of world soccer's governing body FIFA was Baron Edouard de Laveleye. The Belgian was rewarded for persuading The Football Association in England to join FIFA in 1905, rather than remain independent. De Laveleye was the first chairman of the Belgian FA, founded in 1895, and stayed in the role for 29 years. He was also the founder, and first chairman, of the Belgian Olympic Committee, and successfully campaigned for Antwerp to stage the Games in 1920.

CLUB MATES

Belgium ended a 1964 exhibition game against neighbor and rival the Netherlands with a team entirely composed of Anderlecht players. Liege goalkeeper Guy Delhasse went off and was replaced by the Brussels club's Jean Trappeniers.

LONGEST–SERVING COACHES*

1. Guy Thys (1976–89, 1990–91)
2. William Maxwell (1910–13, 1920–28)
3. Constant Vanden Stock (1958–68)
4. Raymond Goethals (1968–76)
5. Bill Gormlie (1947–53)
6. Jack Butler (1935–40)
7. Paul Van Himst (1991–96)
8. Hector Goetinck (1930–34)
9. Aime Anthuenis (2002–05)
10. Rene Vandereycken (2006–09)

* Marc Wilmots, who took over in 2012, is contracted until 2018 which would take him to fifth on the list.

THE FOUR–MOST

A collection of players widely described as Belgium's "Golden Generation" helped the country achieve its finest run of victories at a FIFA World Cup when it won four consecutive games at the 2014 finals, all by a single goal. It defeated Algeria 2-1, Russia and South Korea both 1-0, in Group H, then downed the United States, 2-1 after extra-time in the round-of-16. The run ended when it lost 1-0 to Argentina in the quarterfinal. None of Belgium's six goals in Brazil were scored before the 70th minute of a game, and four were courtesy of substitutes. Marouane Fellaini and Dries Mertens (both against Algeria), Divock Origi (the 88th minute winner against Russia), and Romelu Lukaku (the second against the US) all found the net after coming off the bench, whereas **Jan Vertonghen** (to beat South Korea) and Kevin De Bruyne (the opener in the round-of-16) got on the scoresheet having started.

SWINE FEVER

Nicknamed "The Fighting Pig" and "The Bull from Dongelberg," **Marc Wilmots** has hogged more goals for Belgium than all but two compatriots, Paul van Himst and Bernard Voorhoof. His 28 goals in 70 internationals between 1990 and 2002 included a Belgian record five at FIFA World Cups. After retiring, he spent a short spell as an elected Belgian senator before becoming assistant coach for the national team in 2009. And, when Georges Leekens suddenly resigned as Belgium coach in 2012, Wilmots was promoted to the top job. He not only successfully qualified Belgium for the 2014 FIFA World Cup in Brazil, but also oversaw record runs of seven wins in a row and 14 consecutive games unbeaten.

SPECS APPEAL

Most soccer players with poor vision make do with contact lenses before going out to play, but Belgium captain Jef Jurion stood out in the late 1950s and early 1960s. He wore a pair of specially-made spectacles during matches.

VOORHOOF'S A JOLLY GOOD FELLOW

Belgium's scoring record is shared by Bernard Voorhoof and Paul van Himst, both on 30 goals, though Voorhoof's came in 61 games between 1928 and 1940, compared to van Himst's 81 games from 1960 to 1974. Voorhoof is one of only five players to feature at all three of the pre-Second World War FIFA World Cups, in 1930, 1934, and 1938. The others were Edmond Delfour and Etienne Mattler of France, Nicolae Kovacs of Romania, and Brazil's Patesko. Voorhoof's only FIFA World Cup goals were the two he scored in 1934. Van Himst went into management after retiring as a player in 1977, coaching Anderlecht when it won the UEFA Cup in 1983, and taking Belgium to the 1994 FIFA World Cup.

SAINT MICHEL

Belgium goalkeeper Michel Preud'homme was the first man to win the Lev Yashin Award for the best goalkeeper at a FIFA World Cup, when it was introduced in 1994. Preud'homme's four displays—conceding four goals—impressed the panel of judges even though Belgium was knocked out in the second round in the US. He was dubbed "Saint Michel" by supporters when playing for Portuguese club Benfica.

PRINCE FERNAND

Fernand Nisot was part of the Belgium team that won the soccer gold medal when Antwerp hosted the Olympic Games in 1920. He still holds the record for Belgium's youngest international, being just 16 years and 19 days old on his debut.

THE EDEN PROJECT

Dazzling playmaker **Eden Hazard** made himself one of the hottest properties in world soccer with his performances for French club Lille. In 2011, he became the youngest man to be named the country's player of the year, and retained the award 12 months later, just before joining the then-reigning European champion Chelsea. The London club also signed Hazard's brother Thorgan, two years Eden's junior, and a Belgium under-21 international. Eden Hazard, who has been compared to Belgian great **Enzo Scifo**, made his full international debut at the age of 17 years and 316 days, becoming the eighth-youngest player to represent Belgium at full international level. The brothers are the sons of not just one former soccer player but two. Their father, Thierry, played as a semi-professional, and mother Carine only retired from women's soccer when she was pregnant with Eden.

COURT RISE

Belgium's 1-0 loss against Argentina in its 2014 FIFA World Cup quarterfinal in Brasilia was goalkeeper **Thibaut Courtois**'s 22nd appearance for his country, but it was the first time the Red Devils had suffered defeat with him between the posts. The 22-year-old had made a last-minute save from Lionel Messi, however, which extended to nine games the Argentine's barren run against him. Courtois went into the tournament having just helped Atletico Madrid to win the Spanish league title and reach the UEFA Champions League final, before being recalled from a three-year loan by his parent club Chelsea. Courtois' international debut had come against France in November 2011, when he not only kept a clean sheet in a scoreless tie, but also became Belgium's youngest ever goalkeeper, aged 19 years and 188 days.

TOP CAPS

1	Jan Ceulemans	96
2	Timmy Simons	93
3	Eric Gerets	86
=	Franky van der Elst	86
5	Enzo Scifo	84
=	Daniel van Buyten	84
7	Paul van Himst	81
8	Bart Goor	78
9	Georges Grun	77
10	Lorenzo Staelens	70
=	Marc Wilmots	70

MOTHER'S BOY

Belgium's most-capped player, **Jan Ceulemans**, is unusual in having turned down a move to Italian giants AC Milan – and he did so on the advice of his mother. He opted to stay loyal to Club Brugge, where he spent most of his playing career, and became a national hero with his linchpin displays at three consecutive FIFA World Cups in 1982, 1986 and 1990. He scored three goals and was captain at Mexico 1986 as Belgium finished fourth. The Lier-born midfielder retired from international football after Belgium's second-round exit at the 1990 FIFA World Cup.

TOP SCORERS

1	Bernard Voorhoof	30
=	Paul van Himst	30
3	Marc Wilmots	29
4	Joseph Mermans	28
5	Robert De Veen	26
6	Wesley Sonck	24
7	Raymond Braine	23
=	Marc Degryse	23
9	Jan Ceulemans	22
10	Henri Coppens	21

KOMPANY MAN

Belgium's current captain **Vincent Kompany** has emerged as one of the most commanding center-backs in world soccer, and one of the most respected and articulate off the field. He combines his professional career with part-time business administration studies at Manchester Business School. He captained Manchester City to its first English league title for 44 years in 2011–12, and when it won it again in 2013–14. Kompany was recalled by his club, SV Hamburg of Germany, and was forced to miss the semifinal of the men's Beijing 2008 Olympic Games soccer tournament and, eithout him, Belgium lost 4-1 to Nigeria. Then, after losing 3-0 to Brazil in the third-place game, Belgium was denied a medal to add to the Olympic gold it won as hosts at Antwerp in 1920. Kompany was named Belgium's permanent captain in November 2011, replacing fellow centre-back Thomas Vermaelen.

BULGARIA

The glory days of the "golden generation" apart—when Bulgaria finished fourth at the 1994 FIFA World Cup in the United States, and sensationally beat defending champion Germany 2-1 in the quarterfinal—a consistent pattern emerges with Bulgarian soccer. Regular qualifiers for the game's major competitions, and the birthplace of some of the sport's biggest names (such as Hristo Stoichkov and Dimitar Berbatov), the country has too often failed to deliver on the big occasions and make its mark on world soccer.

TOP SCORERS

1	Dimitar Berbatov	48
=	Hristo Bonev	48
3	Hristo Stoichkov	37
4	Emil Kostadinov	26
5	Ivan Kolev	25
=	Petar Zhekov	25
7	Atanas Mihaylov	23
=	Nasko Sirakov	23
9	Dimitar Milanov	20
=	Martin Petrov	20

MAYOR WITH NO HAIR

Balding Yordan Letchkov headed the winning goal against the defending champion Germany in the 1994 FIFA World Cup quarterfinal in the United States. At the time, he played for German club Hamburg. He later became mayor of Sliven, the Bulgarian town where he was born in July 1967.

TEETHING TROUBLES

Martin Petrov suffered a terrible start to his international career, when he was sent off for two yellow cards just eight minutes into his debut as a substitute in a 2000 UEFA European Championship qualifier against England. He broke down in tears when leaving the field, but recovered from the experience to become one of his country's most-capped players. Petrov enjoyed spells with top clubs, such as Atletico Madrid in Spain and Manchester City in England. His 90 caps and 20 goals included Bulgaria's only strike at the 2004 UEFA European Championship, against Italy.

A NATION MOURNS

Bulgaria lost two of its most popular soccer talents when a June 1971 car crash claimed the lives of strikers Georgi Asparukhov (28) and Nikola Kotkov (32). Asparukhov scored 19 goals in 50 internationals, including Bulgaria's only goal of the 1966 FIFA World Cup finals in a 3-1 defeat to Hungary.

MOB RULES

Much-traveled Bulgaria center-forward **Dimitar Berbatov** claims to have learned English by watching the *Godfather* movies. Berbatov joined Manchester United from Tottenham in 2008 for a club and Bulgarian record fee of $49m. Before joining Spurs, he had been a member of the Bayer Leverkusen team which had narrowly missed out on a treble in 2002. It lost in the final of both the UEFA Champions League and the German cup, and finished runner-up in the German Bundesliga. Berbatov surprised and disappointed fans back home when he announced his international retirement, aged just 29, in May 2010, having scored a national-record 48 goals in his 78 appearances for Bulgaria. He briefly considered a return to the national team in 2012, but ultimately opted against the idea, saying that he wanted to "give chances to younger players." After joining Fulham in the summer of that year, he raised eyebrows during one game by revealing a T-shirt with the slogan: "Keep calm and pass me the ball."

STAN THE BURGER VAN MAN

Stiliyan Petrov, nicknamed "Stan" by fans of his English club Aston Villa, was applauded onto the field when he became Bulgaria's first outfield player to reach 100 caps, against Switzerland in March 2011. The midfielder and Bulgaria captain had been playing in Britain since 1999, having joined Scottish giants Celtic as a 20-year-old, but had to struggle against bouts of homesickness. He later revealed that his English only improved when he started working behind the counter of a Scottish friend's burger van. Petrov said: "Some of the customers used to stare, thinking: 'That looks like Stiliyan Petrov, but it can't be.' But soon I started to understand things better." Tributes from across soccer and around the world poured in for Petrov when, in March 2012, he revealed he had been diagnosed with acute leukaemia. After 19 minutes of every home game for the next couple of seasons, Villa fans stood and applauded for 60 seconds—19 being his squad number.

TOP OF THE POPS

Ivelin Popov has eight international goals to his name. Sofia-born Popov trained with Feyenoord as a 17-year-old, when Netherlands legend Ruud Gullit was the Dutch club's coach, before making his name with Bulgarian team Litex Lovech. He was club captain by the age of 21, and given the Bulgaria armband in 2012, aged 24. He was soon the skipper of both the national team, and Russian club Kuban Krasnador, which he joined in 2012.

PLAYING LUBO

Bulgaria's current coach is Lubo Penev, nephew of Dimitar Penev, who coached the country to its best-ever FIFA World Cup finish, fourth, in 1994. Lubo, a center-forward, missed that tournament after being diagnosed with testicular cancer, but recovered to play for his country at both the 1996 UEFA European Championship and 1998 FIFA World Cup.

ALL—ROUNDER ALEKSANDAR

Defender Aleksandar Shalamanov played for Bulgaria at the 1966 FIFA World Cup, six years after representing his country as an alpine skier at the Winter Olympics at Lake Placid. He also went to the 1964 Tokyo Summer Olympics, as an unused member of the volleyball squad. Shalamanov was voted Bulgaria's best sportsman in both 1967 and 1973.

HRISTO'S HISTORY

Hristo Stoichkov, born in Plovdiv, Bulgaria, on February 8, 1968, shared the 1994 FIFA World Cup Golden Boot, awarded to the tournament's top scorer, with Russia's Oleg Salenko. Both scored six times, though Stoichkov became the sole winner of that year's European Footballer of the Year award. Earlier in 1994, he had combined in attack with Brazil's Romario to help Barcelona to reach the final of the UEFA Champions League. Stoichkov was banned for one year, after a brawl earlier in his career, during the 1985 Bulgarian cup final between CSKA Sofia and Levski Sofia. Stoichkov won trophies with clubs in Bulgaria, Spain, Saudi Arabia, and the United States, before retiring as a player in 2003.

TOP CAPS

1	Stiliyan Petrov	106
2	Borislav Mikhailov	102
3	Hristo Bonev	96
4	Krasimir Balakov	92
5	Dimitar Penev	90
=	Martin Petrov	90
7	Radostin Kishishev	88
8	Hristo Stoichkov	83
9	Zlatko Yankov	80
10	Ayan Sadkov	79
=	Nasko Sirakov	79

HEAD BOY

Bulgaria's second most-capped player is **Borislav Mikhailov**, born in Sofia on February 12, 1963, who sometimes wore a wig while playing, and later had a hair transplant. After retiring in 2005, he was appointed president of the Bulgarian Football Union. His father Bisser was also a goalkeeper and Borislav's son, Nikolay, made his international debut in goal against Scotland in May 2006. All three have played for Levski Sofia.

CROATIA

Croatia's distinctive red-and-white checkered shirt has become one of the most recognized in world soccer—just ask England. Croatia broke English hearts not once but twice in the UEFA Euro 2008 qualifying tournament. First Croatia beat England 2-0 in Zagreb and then shocked it 3-2 at Wembley to secure qualification. Croatia's march to the quarterfinal at the 2008 UEFA European Championship was followed by failure to qualify for the 2010 FIFA World Cup, but it impressed again at Euro 2012, though it was edged out in the first round by Spain and Italy.

TOP SCORERS

1	Davor Suker	45
2	Eduardo da Silva	29
3	Darijo Srna	21
4	Ivica Olic	19
5	Niko Kranjcar	16
6	Mario Mandzukic	15
=	Goran Vlaovic	15
8	Niko Kovac	14
9	Mladen Petric	13
10	Zvonimir Boban	12
=	Ivan Klasnic	12

ROCK AND A HARD PLACE

Slaven Bilic and Igor Stimac were formidable central defensive partners as Croatia finished third at the 1998 FIFA World Cup. Bilic was more successful as national coach, taking Croatia to the 2008 and 2012 UEFA European Championships during his six-year reign. Stimac took over in 2012, but an underwhelming 2014 FIFA World Cup qualifying campaign saw him replaced by another former international, **Niko Kovac**, for the play-off against Iceland in November 2013, which it won 2-0 on aggregate. Croatia went out in the first round in Brazil. It took the lead in its opening game, against the host nation, but went on to lose 3-1.

LUKA LOOPY

Luka Modric scored the fastest penalty in UEFA European Championship history: his fourth-minute strike was the only goal of Croatia's first-round victory against co-hosts Austria at the 2008 tournament. But he would miss one of the spot-kicks as Croatia lost a shoot-out to Turkey in the quarterfinal. His much-loved status back home remains unaffected, though, as the diminutive playmaker is now widely seen as one of the world's most skilful midfielders. Modric spent four years with English club Tottenham Hotspur from 2008, before moving to Real Madrid in the summer of 2012. At Madrid, he won a UEFA Champions League medal in 2014.

HAPPY OPENINGS

Few national teams have been as successful in its infancy as Croatia. Formerly part of Yugoslavia, Croatia reached the quarterfinal in its very first senior competition (UEFA Euro 96) and finished third at the 1998 FIFA World Cup. Since becoming eligible to participate in 1993, Croatia qualified for every FIFA World Cup (except for 2010), and missed only one UEFA European Championship (in 2000). Croatia has scored four goals at all four of UEFA European Championships for which it qualified: in 1996, 2004, 2008, and 2012. Three of the goals at Euro 2012 came from **Mario Mandzukic**, the first after just two minutes and 38 seconds against the Republic of Ireland—the sixth fastest UEFA European Championship finals goal of all-time. Mandzukic was suspended for Croatia's opening game of the 2014 FIFA World Cup finals, but he scorde twice in the second game, a 4-0 defeat of Cameroon in Manaus.

SUPER SUKER

Striker Davor Suker won the Golden Boot as top scorer at the 1998 FIFA World Cup, scoring six goals in seven games as Croatia finished third. His strikes included the opening goal in Croatia's 2-1 semifinal defeat to eventual champion France, and the winner in a 2-1 triumph over the Netherlands in the third-place play-off. Suker, by far his country's leading scorer of all time, had hit three goals at the UEFA European Championship in 1996, including an audacious long-distance lob over Denmark goalkeeper Peter Schmeichel. Suker was named president of the Croatian Football Federation in July 2012.

TOP CAPS

1	Darijo Srna	116
2	Stipe Pletikosa	114
3	Josip Simunic	105
4	Dario Simic	100
5	Ivica Olic	95
6	Robert Kovac	84
7	Niko Kovac	83
8	Robert Jarni	81
=	Niko Kranjcar	81
10	Luka Modric	78

DEER DARIJO

Darijo Srna is Croatia's third top scorer of all time, despite playing many games as a right-back or wing-back. He has a tattoo on his calf in the shape of a deer, the Croatian word for which is "srna." He also has a tattoo on his chest: the name of his brother Igor, who has Down's syndrome and to whom he dedicates each goal he scores. Now Croatia's most capped player, Srna was one of three players to reach 100 appearances for their country against South Korea in February 2013. The other two were goalkeeper Stipe Pletikosa and defender Josip Simunic.

THE KIDNEYS ARE ALL RIGHT

Striker Ivan Klasnic returned to international duty with Croatia despite suffering kidney failure in early 2007. A first attempt at a transplant failed when his body rejected a kidney donated by his mother, but follow-up surgery—using a kidney from his father—proved successful. He recovered enough to play for Croatia again in March 2008 and represented his country in that summer's UEFA European Championship. He scored twice, including the winning goal against Poland.

DOUBLE IDENTITY

Robert Jarni and Robert Prosinecki share the rare distinction of playing for two different countries at different FIFA World Cup tournaments. They both represented Yugoslavia in Italy in 1990, then for newly independent Croatia eight years later in France. Full-back Jarni actually played for both Yugoslavia and Croatia in 1990, then only Yugoslavia in 1991, before switching back—permanently—to Croat colors in 1992 after the country officially joined UEFA and FIFA. He retired with 81 caps for Croatia, seven for Yugoslavia.

OLE, OLIC

Croatia's second game at the 2014 FIFA World Cup, a 4-0 trouncing of Cameroon, was doubly notable. It was the first time it had scored as many as four goals in a single FIFA World Cup finals match. It also saw striker Ivica Olic become the first player to score for Croatia at two separate FIFA World Cups, having previously found the net in 2002. His lengthy break between finals goals is matched only by Denmark's Michael Laudrup, who scored at the 1986 tournament and then had to wait until the 1998 finals to do so again.

MLAD ALL OVER

Mladen Petric is the only player to score four goals in one game for Croatia—a 7-0 trouncing of Andorra in October 2006. That equaled Croatia's record victory, having previously beaten Australia by the same scoreline in August 1998. **Davor Suker** scored a hat-trick that day, making him the only Croatian to complete two trebles—his first came in a 7-1 defeat of Estonia in September 1995.

CZECH REPUBLIC

The most successful of the former Eastern Bloc countries, as Czechoslovakia they finished as runner-up in the 1934 and 1962 FIFA World Cups, and shocked West Germany in a penalty shoot-out to win the 1976 UEFA European Championship. Playing as the Czech Republic since 1994, it lost—on a "golden goal"—in the UEFA Euro 96 final, and in the semifinal eight years later. Recent times have been tougher, and although one of Europe's stronger nations, the Czechs failed to qualify for the 2010 or 2014 FIFA World Cups, but was a UEFA Euro 2012 quarterfinalist.

EURO-VER AND OVER AND OVER AGAIN

Vladimir Smicer, now general manager of the Czech national team, is one of only seven players to score at three different UEFA European Championships, along with Germany's Jurgen Klinsmann, France's Thierry Henry, Portugal's Nuno Gomes, Helder Postiga, and Cristiano Ronaldo, and Sweden's Zlatan Ibrahimovic. Smicer struck at the finals in 1996, 2000 and 2004. Perhaps his other greatest achievement came in his final game for English club Liverpool, during which he scored as a second-half substitute as his team came back from 3-0 down to beat AC Milan in the 2005 UEFA Champions League final. Smicer's wife Pavlina is the daughter of former Czechoslovakia striker Ladislav Vizek, who won a soccer gold medal with his country at the 1980 Olympic Games, but was then sent off against France at the FIFA World Cup two years later.

CHIP WITH EVERYTHING

One of the most famous penalties ever taken was Antonin Panenka's decisive spot-kick for Czechoslovakia against West Germany in the final of the 1976 UEFA European Championship, giving the Czechs victory in the shoot-out. Despite the tension, and the responsibility resting on him, Panenka cheekily chipped the ball into the middle of the goal—as goalkeeper Sepp Maier dived to the side. That style of spot-kick is now widely known as a "Panenka," and has been replicated by the likes of France's Zinedine Zidane, in the 2006 FIFA World Cup final.

POPULAR KAREL

UEFA Euro 96 gave **Karel Poborsky** the perfect platform to take his career to new heights as he helped the Czech Republic reach the final, and then sealed a dream move to Manchester United. His lob against Portugal in the quarterfinals was rated as one of the finest opportunist goals in the tournament's history. His 118 appearances is a record for his country.

CECH CAP

Goalkeeper **Petr Cech** has worn a protective cap while playing ever since suffering a fractured skull during an English Premier League match in October 2006. He later added a chin protector after requiring a facial operation following a training accident. Cech was born as a triplet, along with sister Sarka and brother Michal, who sadly died of an infection at the age of two. Cech served notice of his talents when he was beaten by only one penalty in a shoot-out against France to decide the 2002 UEFA U-21 European Championship final, helping the Czechs to win the trophy. He has also earned winners' medals as Chelsea collected the 2012 UEFA Champions League (he was named man of the match in the penalty shoot-out win over Bayern at its Munich home) and 2013 UEFA Europa League. He celebrated his 100th appearance for the Czech Republic with a clean sheet in a 3-0 March 2013 victory over Armenia.

PASSING THE PUC

The final of the 1934 FIFA World Cup was the first to go into extra-time, with Czechoslovakia ultimately losing 2-1 to host nation Italy, despite taking a 76th-minute lead through Antonin Puc. Puc was Czechoslovakia/the Czech Republic's top international goalscorer when he retired in 1938. until he was passed, first by Jan Koller, 67 years later, and, latterly, by Milan Baros.

WALK–OUT

Belgium's 1920 victory in the Olympic Games was overshadowed when Czechoslovakia's players walked off the field after half an hour in protest at what they saw as biased refereeing. Czechoslovakia is thus the only team in Olympic Games soccer history of to have been disqualified.

SPEED DEMON

Milan Baros, second to Jan Koller in the Czech Republic's all-time goalscoring list, is the only Czech player to win the Golden Boot at a FIFA World Cup or a UEFA European Championship. He won the prize after scoring five goals at Euro 2004, when the Czechs lost to eventual winner Greece in the semifinal. Baros helped the Czech Republic win the 2002 UEFA European U-21 Championship in Switzerland. Three team-mates in the final also became full internationals: Petr Cech, Martin Jiranek, and Zdenek Grygera. Baros set a less impressive landmark in November 2007, when his Ferrari was caught traveling at 168 mph between Lyon and Geneva—the fastest speed ever recorded in France's Ain region. He was, inevitably, given a driving ban. He retired from international soccer in 2012, aged 30, after playing in his third Euro finals.

THE CANNON COLLECTS

Pavel Nedved's election as European Footballer of the Year in 2003 ended an impatient wait for fans in the Czech Republic, who had seen a string of outstanding players overlooked since Josef Masopust had been honored back in 1962. Masopust, a midfield general, had scored the opening goal in the 1962 FIFA World Cup final, but Brazil hit back to win 3-1 in the Chilean capital of Santiago. Years later, Masopust was remembered by Pele and nominated as one of his 125 greatest living soccer players. At club level, Masopust won eight Czechoslovak league titles with Dukla Prague, the army club. He was also the winner, in 1962, of the first Czech Golden Ball as domestic player of the year. It was another day and in another age. Masopust was presented with his award before the kick-off of a European Cup quarterfinal against Benfica—with a minimum of fuss. Years later, Masopust said: "Eusebio just shook hands with me, I put the trophy in my sports bag and went home on the tram."

TOP SCORERS

1	Jan Koller	55
2	Milan Baros	41
3	Vladimir Smicer	27
4	Pavel Kuka	22
=	Tomas Rosicky	22
6	Patrik Berger	18
=	Pavel Nedved	18
8	Vratislav Lokvenc	14
9	Marek Jankulovski	11
10	Michal Kadlec	8
=	Karel Poborsky	8

TOP CAPS

1	Karel Poborsky	118
2	Petr Cech	107
3	Tomas Rosicky	94
4	Milan Baros	93
5	Jan Koller	91
=	Pavel Nedved	91
7	Jaroslav Plasil	89
8	Vladimir Smicer	81
9	Marek Jankulovski	78
=	Tomas Ujfalusi	78

TEN OUT OF TEN

Giant striker **Jan Koller** is Czech soccer's all-time leading scorer with 55 goals in 91 appearances. Koller netted on his senior debut against Belgium, and struck ten goals in ten consecutive internationals. He scored six goals in each of the 2000, 2004, and 2008 UEFA European Championship qualifying campaigns. He began his career—as a goalkeeper—with Sparta Prague, but was converted into a goalscorer. Koller moved to Belgium, where he was top scorer with Lokeren, before grabbing 42 goals in two league title-winning campaigns with Anderlecht. Later, at Borussia Dortmund in Germany, he once went in goal after Jens Lehmann had been sent off and kept a clean sheet—having scored in the first half.

DENMARK

Denmark has been playing international soccer since 1908, but it was not until the mid-1980s that it became competitive at major tournaments. The country's crowning moment came in 1992 when, after being called up as a replacement just ten days before the start of the tournament, Denmark walked away with the UEFA European Championship crown, shocking defending world champion West Germany 2-0 in the final. It may not have been able to repeat that success, but it remains a significant player in world soccer.

GOLDEN GLOVES

Peter Schmeichel was rated as the world's best goalkeeper in the early 1990s, winning many club honors with Manchester United and, famously, the UEFA European Championship with his native Denmark. His son Kasper Schmeichel was a member of Denmark's squad at the 2012 UEFA European Championship. Kasper was called up after first-choice Thomas Sorensen suffered a back injury, though began and ended the tournament still waiting for his first cap.

LEADERSHIP STYLE

Morten Olsen captained Denmark at the 1986 FIFA World Cup and later became the first Dane to reach a century of caps, eventually stepping down from the national team with four goals in 102 international appearances between 1970 and 1989. After he retired from playing all soccer that year, he switched to coaching, first at club level with Brondby, FC Koln, and Ajax Amsterdam, before taking on the job as Danish national coach in 2000 and leading it to the 2002 and 2010 FIFA World Cups. Denmark's 2-1 loss against England in a February 2011 exhibition was his 116th international in charge, taking him past the previous record set between 1979 and 1990 by his former national team boss Sepp Piontek. Olsen planned to step down after the 2012 UEFA European Championship, but changed his mind and agreed a new deal extending his stay to the 2014 FIFA World Cup. Posters bearing Olsen's image can often be seen across Denmark—though these are advertizing hearing aids, approved by the manager who suffers from deafness.

TOP CAPS

1	Peter Schmeichel	129
2	Dennis Rommedahl	126
3	Jon Dahl Tomasson	112
4	Thomas Helveg	108
5	Michael Laudrup	104
6	Martin Jorgensen	102
=	Morten Olsen	102
8	Thomas Sorensen	101
9	Christian Poulsen	92
10	John Sivebaek	87

PENALTY REDEMPTION

Former Dundee, Celtic, and Brondby midfielder Morten Wieghorst is the only player to be sent off twice while playing for Denmark, but he has also received a special award for fair play. His first international red card came just three minutes after entering the field as a substitute, against South Africa in the 1998 FIFA World Cup. He was again dismissed after coming on as a substitute against Italy in the 2000 UEFA European Championship, though this time he managed all of 28 minutes of action —and scored a goal—in Denmark's 3-2 victory. The other side of his character was shown during a Carlsberg Cup game against Iran in February 2003, when he deliberately missed a penalty. The spot-kick had been awarded after Iranian defender, Jalal Kameli Mofrad, had picked the ball up, thinking—wrongly—that a whistle from the crowd was actually the referee blowing for half-time. The International Olympic Committee later presented Wieghorst with a special fair play prize for striking the spot-kick wide. The gesture became all the more sporting as Denmark went on to lose the game 1-0.

DANISH DYNAMITE

Denmark's 6-1 defeat of Uruguay in the 1986 FIFA World Cup first-round group stage in Neza, Mexico, ranks among the country's best performances. Sadly, its adventure was ended by Spain in the last 16, losing 5-1 after a horrendous back pass by Jesper Olsen had allowed Spain to open the scoring. The Danes had already been hampered by the loss of playmaker Frank Arsesen through suspension. He had been sent off during the final group game against eventual runner-up West Germany. The team, popularly known as "Danish Dynamite," was captained by future national coach Morten Olsen and led by Sepp Piontek, a German who became the Danish national team's first professional coach when appointed in 1979. Michael Laudrup, a star member of Denmark's classic mid-1980s team, described it as "Europe's answer to Brazil."

CHRISTIAN AID

Nimble playmaker and free-kick specialist **Christian Eriksen** is the latest in a proud tradition of creative young Danish soccer players, and another who has enjoyed a popular and successful association with Dutch giants Ajax Amsterdam. He followed the same career path as Danish stars, such as Soren Lerby and Frank Arnesen in the 1970s and 1980s, and the Laudrup brothers, Michael and Brian, in the late 1990s. Eriksen helped inspire the Amsterdam club to a hat-trick of title triumphs before crossing the North Sea to join Tottenham Hotspur in the summer of 2013. He ended his debut season being voted both player of the year and young player of the year by the London club's supporters. His Danish debut came in March 2010, having only turned 18 the previous month. It made him Denmark's fourth youngest debutant—and he was the youngest player at the 2010 FIFA World Cup. Eriksen's first international goal came in a win against Iceland in April 2011. One of Eriksen's biggest fans is Netherlands and Ajax legend Johan Cruyff, who said: "He's a player I really like with all my heart. You can compare him with Brian and Michael Laudrup."

TOP SCORERS

1	Poul Nielsen	52
=	Jon Dahl Tomasson	52
3	Pauli Jorgensen	44
4	Ole Madsen	42
5	Preben Elkjaer Larsen	38
6	Michael Laudrup	37
7	Henning Enoksen	29
8	Nicklas Bendtner	24
9	Michael Rohde	22
=	Ebbe Sand	22

QUICK DRAW

Ebbe Sand scored the fastest ever FIFA World Cup goal by a substitute. He netted a mere 16 seconds after coming onto the field in Denmark's 4-1 round-of-16 victory over Nigeria at the 1998 FIFA World Cup.

TAKING THE MICHAEL

One Danish player with unhappy memories of a spell with Ajax is Michael Krohn-Dehli, who made just four appearances for the Amsterdam club between 2006 and 2008. But if he felt any resentment for the Netherlands—or the injuries that hampered his progress there and also contributed to his omission from the 2010 FIFA World Cup—then the 2012 UEFA European Championship brought some solace. Krohn-Dehli scored the only goal in Denmark's surprise opening victory over the Netherlands. He said afterwards: "It's a little bit special for me as I played for eight years in Holland and I have a Dutch girlfriend, so I think the whole family was cheering in Holland." Manager Morten Olsen admitted afterwards that he should have taken Krohn-Dehli to the FIFA World Cup two years earlier. The only other Dane to score—and twice—at Euro 2012 was Nicklas Bendtner, though he was later fined $100,000 and banned for a game after celebrating his second by displaying underpants bearing the name of a betting firm.

THE UNEXPECTED IN 1992

Few Danish soccer fans will forget June 1992, the national team's finest hour, when it won the UEFA European Championship, despite not qualifying for the finals in Sweden. Ten days before the tournament opened, UEFA asked the Danes—runner-up behind to Yugoslavia in its qualifying group—to take Yugoslavia's place, following its exclusion in the wake of international sanctions over the Balkan War. Expectations were minimal, but then the inconceivable happened. Relying heavily on goalkeeper Peter Schmeichel, his defense, and the creative spark of Brian Laudrup, Denmark crafted one of the biggest shocks in modern soccer history by winning the tournament, culminating in a 2-0 victory over world champion Germany. This victory was all the more remarkable in that Brian's brother Michael, its best player, walked away during the qualifying competition, after falling out with coach **Richard Moller Nielsen**. Michael revived his international career in 1993, but Denmark failed to qualify for the 1994 FIFA World Cup. Among those paying their respects at Moller Nielsen's funeral after his death, aged 76, in February 2014, were Schmeichel, Brian Laudrup, and Euro 92 team-mates Preben Elkjaer Larsen and John Jensen.

BROTHERS IN ARMS

Brian (left) and Michael Laudrup are among the most successful soccer-playing brothers of modern times. As well as making a combined 186 international appearances, they played across Europe at club level. Michael (104 caps, 37 goals) played in Italy with Lazio and Juventus, and in Spain with Barcelona and Real Madrid. Brian (82 caps, 21 goals) starred in Germany with Bayer Uerdingen and Bayern Munich, Italy with Fiorentina and Milan, Scotland for Rangers, and England for Chelsea.

GREECE

There is no argument about Greece's proudest soccer moment: its shock triumph at the 2004 UEFA European Championship, one of the game's greatest international upsets. Guided by German coach Otto Rehhagel, it was only the Greeks' second appearance at a UEFA Euro finals. Greece also made the last eight at Euro 2012 in Poland and Ukraine. South Africa 2010 marked just its second qualification for the FIFA World Cup and Greece reached the knock-out stages for the first time in 2014.

TOP SCORERS

1	Nikos Anastopoulos	29
2	Angelos Charisteas	25
3	Theofanis Gekas	24
4	Dimitris Saravakos	22
5	Mimis Papaioannou	21
6	Nikos Machlas	18
7	Demis Nikolaidis	17
8	Panagiotis Tsalouchidis	16
9	Giorgos Sideris	14
10	Nikos Liberopoulos	13
=	Dimitris Salpingidis	13

SIMPLY THEO BEST

Theodoros "Theo" Zagorakis, born near Kavala on October 27, 1971, was captain of Greece when it won the UEFA European Championship in 2004 and the defensive midfielder also won the prize as the tournament's best player. He is the second most-capped Greek player of all time, with 120 caps. But it was not until his 101st international appearance—10 years and five months after his Greek debut—that he scored his first goal for his country, in a FIFA World Cup qualifier against Denmark in February 2005. He retired from international soccer after making a 15-minute cameo appearance against Spain in August 2007.

PARTY CRASHERS

Shock UEFA Euro 2004 winners Greece became the first team to beat both the holder and the host on its way to winning either a UEFA European Championship or FIFA World Cup. In fact, it beat host Portugal twice—in the opening game and the final. Greece beat defending champion France in the quarterfinal.

GORGEOUS GEORGE

Georgios Samaras won—and converted—the last-minute penalty that sent Greece into the knock-out stages of a FIFA World Cup for the first time, clinching a dramatic 2-1 victory over Group C opponent Ivory Coast at the 2014 tournament in Brazil. The goal, following a foul by Giovanni Sio, was the ninth for Samaras in internationals—his first had come on his debut against Belarus in February 2006. Samaras could actually have played international football for Australia, because his father, Ioannis, was born in Melbourne, and moved to Greece aged 13. Ioannis won 16 caps for Greece, between 1986 and 1990, but he is a long way behind his son, who has made 78 appearances.

ALL WHITE NOW

The triumph at UEFA Euro 2004 signaled a big change in Greek international soccer—it switched the first-choice team kit from blue to white. The former colors had been used since the Hellenic Football Federation was formed in 1926, but the success of Otto Rehhagel's men in its second kit prompted the permanent change of color. Blue is now the second kit.

TOP CAPS

1	Giorgos Karagounis	139
2	Theodoros Zagorakis	120
3	Kostas Katsouranis	114
4	Angelos Basinas	100
5	Stratos Apostolakis	96
6	Antonis Nikopolidis	90
7	Angelos Charisteas	88
8	Dimitris Salpingidis	80
9	Georgios Samaras	78
=	Dimitris Saravakos	78

HONESTY PAYS

Greece's 500th goal in international soccer was scored by Demis Nikolaidis at Old Trafford, Manchester, in October 2001, giving it an unexpected 2-1 lead away to England in its final 2002 FIFA World Cup qualifier—though David Beckham went on to tie the game with a famous last-minute free-kick. In March the following year, striker Nikolaidis was formally acclaimed by the FIFA International Committee for Fair Play for admitting to the referee that he handled the ball when scoring for AEK Athens in the final of the Greek Cup. His team still won the game, and the trophy.

DIMI MORE

Striker **Dimitrios Salpingidis** not only struck the only goal of Greece's 2010 FIFA World Cup qualifying play-off victory against Ukraine, sealing its place in South Africa, he later became the first Greek player ever to score at a FIFA World Cup, with a 44th-minute deflected strike in the 2-1 Group B triumph over Nigeria. Yet another notable achievement was added with his equalizer against Poland in the opening game of UEFA Euro 2012: this made him the first Greek ever to score at a FIFA World Cup and a UEFA European Championship.

GEKAS SETBACK

With only two goals, Greece was the lowest scoring team to reach the knockout stage at the 2014 FIFA World Cup. It faced its first tournament penalty shoot-out in the round-of-16, and lost to Costa Rica, 5-3 after a 1-1 tie. The only miss was by Theofanis Gekas, who at 34 years and 37 days, was the second-oldest man to miss in a FIFA World Cup shoot-out. Italy captain Franco Baresi was 33 days older when he missed in the 1994 FIFA World Cup final against Brazil.

TOP KAT

Greek football has enjoyed many Portuguese links. National coach Fernando Santos is Portuguese and took over in 2000 after being the Greek league's most successful manager in the 1990s. He was also boss of Portuguese giants Benfica, and their signings this century have included big Greek stars **Kostas Katsouranis** and Giorgios Karagounis. Both players were part of the Greek side that lifted the 2004 UEFA European Championship trophy at Benfica's Estadio da Luz in Lisbon. Katsouranis also played at UEFA Euro 2012, but squandered his best chance of a first goal in a finals tournament when he missed a penalty in the opening game against Poland.

GRIEF AND GLORY FOR GIORGOS

It was a bittersweet day for captain **Giorgos Karagounis** when he equaled the Greek record for international appearances, with his 120th cap against Russia in its final Group A game at the UEFA Euro 2012. The midfielder scored the only goal of the game, giving Greece a place in the quarterfinal at Russia's expense, but a second yellow card of the tournament ruled him out of the next game, which the Greeks lost to Germany. Karagounis was one of three survivors from Greece's Euro 2004 success, along with fellow midfielder Kostas Katsouranis and goalkeeper Kostas Chalkias—though it was only in Poland that Chalkias made his UEFA European Championship debut, having been an understudy in both 2004 and 2008. Manager Fernando Santos also surprised many by leaving the winning goalscoring hero of Euro 2004, Angelos Charisteas, out of the squad. Chalkias, at 38, Euro 2012's oldest player, announced his international retirement once the tournament ended.

KING OTTO

German coach Otto Rehhagel became the first foreigner to be voted "Greek of the Year" in 2004, after leading the country to glory at that year's UEFA European Championship. He was also offered honorary Greek citizenship. His nine years in charge, after being appointed in 2001, made him Greece's longest-serving international coach. The UEFA Euro 2004 triumph was the first time a country coached by a foreigner had triumphed at either the UEFA European Championship or FIFA World Cup. Rehhagel was aged 65 at UEFA Euro 2004, making him the oldest coach to win the UEFA European Championship, but that record was taken off him four years later, when 69-year-old Luis Aragones lifted the trophy with Spain.

HUNGARY

For a period in the early 1950s, Hungary possessed the most talented soccer team on the planet. It claimed the Olympic Games gold medal at Helsinki in 1952, and inflicted a crushing first-ever Wembley defeat on England the following year. It entered the 1954 FIFA World Cup, unbeaten in almost four years, and firm favorites to win the title. But, after losing to West Germany in the final. Hungary's world soccer fortunes have never been the same again.

TOP SCORERS

1	Ferenc Puskas	84
2	Sandor Kocsis	75
3	Imre Schlosser	59
4	Lajos Tichy	51
5	Gyorgy Sarosi	42
6	Nandor Hidegkuti	39
7	Ferenc Bene	36
8	Tibor Nyilasi	32
=	Gyula Zsengeller	32
10	Florian Albert	31

RETURN TO SANDOR

Sandor Egervari was assistant coach the last time Hungary played at a FIFA World Cup finals, in 1986, and was in charge for one of the success-starved country's most encouraging soccer moments in recent years: third place at the 2009 FIFA U-20 World Cup. Krisztian Nemeth scored the decisive spot-kick in a play-off defeat of Costa Rica, with only champion Ghana and runner-up Brazil performing better. His reward was promotion to manage the full national team in summer 2010, but he resigned following a national record 8-1 loss to the Netherlands in October 2013, and was succeeded by former international Attila Pinter. Hungary's only comparable defeats were 7-0 trouncings by England in 1908, England Amateurs in 1912 and Germany in 1941.

GERA'S SHARE OF THE SPOILS

While none could compare with Ferenc Puskas, the elegant left-footed playmaker **Zoltan Gera** has been one of Hungary's most noted players of recent decades— not only with his performances in the English Premier League (with Fulham and West Bromwich Albion), but also on the international stage. His tally of 76 caps could have been higher but for a brief international retirement in 2009 after a dispute with then-manager Erwin Koeman, after Gera had arrived late for a team meeting. He returned to the fold when Sandor Egervari took as coach in 2010, and was made captain. The first three of his 23 international goals all came in the same game, a 3-0 victory over San Marino in October 2002, eight months after his international debut.

GALLOPING MAJOR

Ferenc Puskas was one of the greatest players of all time, scoring a remarkable 84 goals in 85 international games for Hungary and 514 goals in 529 games in the Hungarian and Spanish leagues. Possessing arguable the most lethal left-foot shot in soccer history, he was nicknamed the "Galloping Major", as he played for the Hungarian army team, Honved, before joining Real Madrid. He also went on to play for Spain in internationals. During the 1950s Puskas was top scorer and captain of the legendary "Mighty Magyars" (the nickname given to the Hungarian national team), as well as Honved.

GOLDEN HEAD

Sandor Kocsis, top scorer in the 1954 FIFA World Cup finals with 11 goals, was so good in the air he was known as "The Man with the Golden Head." In 68 internationals he scored an incredible 75 goals, including a record seven hat-tricks. In the 1954 FIFA World Cup semifinal against Uruguay, Kocsis scored the two extra-time goals that gave Hungary a 4-2 win after the South Americans had forced an extra 30 minutes with two goals in the last quarter-hour of regulation time.

HUNGARY FOR IT

Hungary's 6-3 win over England at Wembley in 1953 remains one of the most significant international results of all time. Hungary became the first team from outside the British Isles to beat England at home, a record that had stood since 1901. The Hungarians had been undefeated for three years and had won the Olympic tournament the year before, while England were the so-called "inventors" of soccers. The British press dubbed it "The Match of the Century." In the event, the match revolutionized the game in England, Hungary's unequivocal victory exposing the naivete of English soccer tactics. England captain Billy Wright later summed up the humiliation by saying: "We completely underestimated the advances that Hungary had made, and not only tactically. When we walked out at Wembley ... I looked down and noticed that the Hungarians had on these strange, lightweight boots, cut away like slippers under the ankle bone. I turned to big Stan Mortensen and said: 'We should be all right here, Stan, they haven't got the proper kit.'"

EUROPEAN PIONEERS

While Argentina's game against Uruguay in July 1902 was the first international outside the British Isles, Hungary's 5-0 loss to Austria in Vienna three months later was the first in Europe between two non-UK sides. Ten of Hungary's first 16 internationals were against Austria, with the Hungarians winning four, tying one, and losing the other five. In total, Hungary has won 66, tied 30, and lost 40, against its Austrian neighbor.

GLORIOUS FAILURE

Hungary was a runaway favourite to win the 1954 FIFA World Cup in Switzerland. It arrived for the finals having been unbeaten for four years. In the first round it thrashed West Germany 8-3, despite finishing with ten men after skipper Ferenc Puskas injured an ankle.

GOODISON LESSON

In the 1966 FIFA World Cup, Hungary gave defending champion Brazil a soccer lesson at Goodison Park, running out 3-1 winners. Hungary's progress was halted by the Soviet Union in the quarterfinal. This was Brazil's first defeat in the FIFA World Cup since the 1954 quarterfinal, when it had lost 4-2 to ... Hungary.

YEARS OF PLENTY

Hungary's dazzling line-up of the early 1950s was known as the "*Aranycsapat*"— or "Golden Team". It set many records, including an unbeaten run of 31 consecutive international games between May 1950 and its July 1954 FIFA World Cup final loss to West Germany. A highlight of this run was winning the Olympic Games gold medal at Helsinki, Finland, in 1952. That record has since been overtaken, but only by Brazil and Spain. Another mark set by the Hungarians in the 1950s was for the most consecutive games scoring at least one goal—73. And Hungary's goals per game average of 5.4 at the 1954 FIFA World Cup remains the tournament's all-time best.

NERVES AND STEEL

Gabor Kiraly may now have won more caps, and earned more attention for his customary tracksuit bottoms—often compared to pajama trousers—but **Gyula Grosics** is still recognized as Hungary's greatest goalkeeper. Unusual for a goalkeeper of his era, he was comfortable with the ball at his feet, and was willing to rush out of his area. The on-field confidence was not always displayed off it, however, and he was thought to be a nervous character, a hypochondriac, and a loner. He allegedly asked to be substituted before the end at Wembley in 1953. He suffered after Hungary's surprise loss to West Germany in the 1954 FIFA World Cup final, being blamed for the equalizer.

TOP CAPS

1	Jozsef Bozsik	101
2	Laszlo Fazekas	92
3	Gabor Kiraly	90
4	Gyula Grosics	86
5	Ferenc Puskas	85
6	Imre Garaba	82
7	Sandor Matrai	81
8	Roland Juhasz	80
9	Vilmos Vanczak	78
10	Zoltan Gera	77
=	Ferenc Sipos	77

NORTHERN IRELAND

Northern Ireland has played as a separate country since 1921 (before that there had been an all-Ireland team). It has qualified for the FIFA World Cup finals on three occasions: in 1958 (when it became the smallest nation to reach the quarterfinal stage), 1982 (when it beat host nation Spain and reached the second round), and 1986.

GIANT JENNINGS

Pat Jennings's record of 119 appearances for Northern Ireland was also the most in international soccer for a while. The former Tottenham Hotspur and Arsenal goalkeeper made his international debut, aged just 18, against Wales on April 15, 1964, and played his final game in the 1986 FIFA World Cup, against Brazil, on his 41st birthday.

GEORGE BEST

One of the greatest players never to grace a FIFA World Cup, **George Best** (capped 37 times by Northern Ireland) nevertheless won domestic and European honors with Manchester United—including both a European Champions Cup medal and the European Footballer of the Year award in 1968. He also played in the United States, Hong Kong and Australia before he finally retired in 1984.

"PETER THE GREAT"

Former Manchester City and Derby County striker Peter Doherty, one of the most expensive players of his era, won the English league and FA Cup as a player, and earned 19 caps for Northern Ireland in a career interrupted by World War Two. His late goal to earn a 2-2 tie in 1947 ensured Northern Ireland avoided defeat against England for the first time. As coach, he led Northern Ireland to the quarterfinal of the 1958 FIFA World Cup—Northern Ireland remains the smallest nation ever to reach the last eight of the competition. It was defeated 4-0 by France, the eventual third-place finisher.

OH DANNY BOY

Northern Ireland's captain at the 1958 FIFA World Cup was Tottenham Hotspur's cerebral **Danny Blanchflower**—the first twentieth-century captain of an English club to win both the league and FA Cup in the same season, in 1960–61. When asked the secret of his national team's success in 1958, he offered the explanation: "Our tactic is to equalize before the others have scored." More famously, he offered the philosophy: "The great fallacy is that the game is first and foremost about winning. It's nothing of the kind. The game is about glory. It's about doing things in style, with a flourish, about going out and beating the other lot, not waiting for them to die of boredom."

TOP SCORERS

1	David Healy	36
2	Colin Clarke	13
=	Billy Gillespie	13
4	Gerry Armstrong	12
=	Joe Bambrick	12
=	Iain Dowie	12
=	Jimmy Quinn	12
8	Olphie Stanfield	11
9	Billy Bingham	10
=	Johnny Crossan	10
=	Jimmy McIlroy	10
=	Peter McParland	10

THE BOY DAVIS

Midfielder **Steven Davis** became Northern Ireland's youngest post-war captain when he led out the team against Uruguay in May 2006, aged just 21 years, five months and 20 days. He has remained captain under current coach Michael O'Neill, who replaced Nigel Worthington in 2012 to become Northern Ireland's first Catholic manager for half a century.

TOP CAPS

1	Pat Jennings	119
2	David Healy	95
3	Mal Donaghy	91
4	Aaron Hughes	90
5	Sammy McIlroy	88
=	Maik Taylor	88
7	Keith Gillespie	86
8	Jimmy Nicholl	73
9	Michael Hughes	71
10	Steven Davis	68

"PETER THE LATE"

Peter Watson is thought to have had the shortest Northern Ireland international career, spending two minutes on the field in a 5-0 UEFA European Championship qualifying win over Cyprus in April 1971. Born in Coventry, England, Watson was playing that season for Northern Irish club Distillery, in a team featuring law student and future international **Martin O'Neill**, who won 64 caps, and captained Northern Ireland at the 1982 FIFA World Cup.

HOSTILE HOSTS

Northern Ireland topped its first-round group at the 1982 FIFA World Cup, thanks to a 1-0 win over host Spain at a passionate Mestalla Stadium in Valencia. Watford striker Gerry Armstrong scored the goal and the Irish held on despite defender Mal Donaghy being sent off. A 4-1 second-round group loss to France denied Northern Ireland a semifinal place. Armstrong moved to Spain, joining Mallorca the following year and, predictably, was regularly booed by rival fans.

KEEPING CONNECTED

Maik Taylor is Northern Ireland's fourth most-capped player, though he has no family connection to the country. Born in Germany, to an English father and German mother, his British passport meant he could represent any of the Home Nations—and he chose Northern Ireland. The goalkeeper was skipper for his 88th and final appearance, against Italy, in October 2011.

YOUNG GUN

Norman Whiteside became the then-youngest player at a FIFA World Cup finals (beating Pele's record) when he represented Northern Ireland in Spain in 1982 aged 17 years and 41 days. He won 38 caps, scoring nine goals, before injury forced his retirement aged just 26.

STRIFE OF BRIAN

Brian McLean's Northern Ireland career began, and ended, with a second-half appearance against Estonia in March 2006. Born in Scotland, he had been thought eligible to play for Northern Ireland through family links, but he had played for Scotland Under-17s in a UEFA competition four years earlier and had not officially changed his allegiance until after the official deadline of his 21st birthday.

HERO HEALY

Northern Ireland's record scorer **David Healy** netted almost three times as many international goals as the next highest player on the list. He scored twice on his debut against Luxembourg on February 23, 2000, and all three when Northern Ireland shocked Spain 3-2 in a UEFA Euro 2008 qualifier on September 6, 2006.

He also got the winning goal against Sven-Goran Eriksson's England in September 2005, Northern Ireland's first victory over it since 1972. Healy endured a four-year, 24-game, scoring drought between October 2008 and November 2012. His final international goal came in a 2-1 home loss to Israel in March 2013. He retired from all football later that year, aged 34.

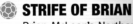

NORWAY

Although it played it first international, against Sweden, in 1908, and qualified for the 1938 FIFA World Cup, it would take a further 56 years, and the introduction of a direct brand of soccer, before Norway reappeared at a major international tournament. Success in such competitions has been rare, it has never progressed beyond the second round, but Norway retains the distinction of being the only nation in history never to have lost to Brazil.

JUVE DONE IT ALL

Jorgen Juve netted his national record 33 international goals in 45 appearances between 1928 and 1937. He did not score as Norway claimed a bronze medal at the Berlin 1936 Olympic Games, but was playing when Norway beat Germany 2-0 in the quarterfinal, prompting spectators Adolf Hitler and other Nazi leaders, to storm out in fury. After retiring in 1938, he worked as a legal scholar, sports journalist and author of books about the Olympics and soccer.

GOALS FOR EITHER IVERSEN

Steffen Iversen scored the only goal of Norway's only win at a UEFA European Championship—against Spain at the 2000 tournament. Iversen's father, Odd, had previously been one of the country's leading strikers, hitting memorable strikes in unexpected victories over Yugoslavia in a 1966 FIFA World Cup qualifier and away to France ahead of the 1970 tournament. Odd scored a total of 19 times in 45 games for Norway between 1967 and 1979. Steffen equaled his father's international scoring tally with a hat-trick against Malta in November 2007, and scored his next two goals against Iceland the following September. He ended his international career in 2011, aged 34, having won 79 caps and scored 21 goals.

TOP SCORERS

1	Jorgen Juve	33
2	Einar Gundersen	26
3	Harald Hennum	25
4	John Carew	24
5	Tore Andre Flo	23
=	Ole Gunnar Solskjaer	23
7	Gunnar Thoresen	22
8	Steffen Iversen	21
9	Jan Age Fjortoft	20
10	Odd Iversen	19
=	Oyvind Leonhardsen	19
=	Olav Nilsen	19

YOUR BOYS TOOK A HELL OF A BEATING

Bjorge Lillelien's famous commentary after Norway beat England 2-1 in a qualifier for the 1982 FIFA World Cup remains one of the iconic moments of European soccer. A commentator from 1957 until just before his death from cancer in 1987, he concentrated on winter sports and soccer. Roughly translated, it sounded as follows: "Lord Nelson, Lord Beaverbrook, Sir Winston Churchill, Sir Anthony Eden, Clement Attlee, Henry Cooper, Lady Diana, Maggie Thatcher, can you hear me? Your boys took a hell of a beating." Although the commentary was for Norwegian radio, it soon made its way to an English audience and has achieved cliché status. In 2002, Lillelien's words were designated the greatest piece of sports commentary ever by the *Observer* newspaper's sports supplement. Such is its place in British sporting culture, parodies of the commentary have been written to celebrate a vast array of domestic sporting victories.

LONG–DISTANCE RIISE

Fierce-shooting, ex-Liverpool, AS Monaco and AS Roma left-back Jon Arne Riise marked the game in which he matched Thorbjorn Svenssen's Norwegian appearances record, against Greece in August 2012, by getting onto the scoresheet, albeit in a 3-2 losing cause. He was also on the losing team when claiming the record for himself, a 2-0 loss in Iceland the following month, before scoring his 16th international goal in his 106th game, four days later, as Norway beat Slovenia 2-1. Midfielder Bjorn Helge Riise, Jon Arne's younger brother, was with him at English club Fulham, and has won more than 30 full international caps.

BOOT CAMPER

Egil Olsen, one of Europe's most eccentric coaches, was signed up for a surprise second spell as national manager when Norway put its faith in the direct-soccer specialist, trying to qualify for the 2010 FIFA World Cup. It was 15 years since he had led the unfancied Scandinavians to the 1994 finals—Norway's first appearance in the FIFA World Cup since 1938—and it went on to beat Brazil in the first round at France 98, making a hero out of the man in Wellington boots. He also guided Norway to No. 2 in the FIFA World rankings. Before answering his country's call for a second stint as manager, Olsen's previous job had been as coach of Iraq, but he left after only three months. Remarkably, in his first game back at the helm for Norway, he masterminded a 1-0 win away to Germany with his route-one tactics.

ERIK THE VIKING

Goalkeeper Erik Thorstvedt played at the Los Angeles 1984 Olympic Games, when Norway replaced the boycotting Poland and East Germany. He was also a key member of Norway's team that qualified for the 1994 FIFA World Cup in the US. Throrstvedt played a Norwegian goalkeeper-record of 97 internationals between 1982 and 1996.

GOAL HANGE

Norway's captain and fifth most-capped player, is commanding center-back **Brede Hangeland**. He was actually born 5,000 miles from Norway, in Houston, Texas, where his father worked for two years for an oil company, but spent most of his childhood in Stavanger, Norway, making his name with local team Viking, and then Danish club Copenhagen. His former Viking coach Roy Hodgson signed him in 2008 for English Premier League team Fulham, where Hangeland has become a fan favorite. He made his international debut in November 2002, but did not score his first goal until his 62nd appearance, against Iceland in September 2010. Another wait followed, before his second, third, and fourth came in quick succession between August and October 2012.

TOP CAPS

1	John Arne Riise	110
2	Thorbjorn Svenssen	104
3	Henning Berg	100
4	Erik Thorstvedt	97
5	John Carew	91
=	Brede Hangeland	91
7	Oyvind Leonhardsen	86
8	Kjetil Rekdal	83
9	Morten Gamst Pedersen	80
10	Steffen Iversen	79

LONG STAY TRAVELLERS

Norway's best finish at an international tournament was the bronze medal it won at the Berlin 1936 Summer Olympic Games. It lost to Italy in the semifinal, but beat Poland 3-2 in the bronze-medal game, thanks to an Arne Brustad hat-trick. That year's team has gone down in Norwegian soccer history as the "*Bronselaget*", or "Bronze Team." However, Norway had entered the tournament with low expectations, and was forced to alter their travel plans ahead of the semifinal against Italy on August 10, because Norwegian soccer authorities had originally booked its trip home for the previous day, not expecting the team to do so well. Italy beat Norway 2-1 in extra-time in that 1936 semifinal, and against in the first round of the 1938 FIFA World Cup. On both occasions Italy won the tournament.

GOLD TIMERS

Any Norway international who reaches 25 appearances for the country is traditionally awarded a gold watch by Norway's football association. This custom began with Gunnar Andersen after he reached his quarter-century on 29 June 1919. Andersen, Norway's football captain at the 1920 Summer Olympics in Antwerp, was also an accomplished ski-jumper.

THE WHOLE HOGMO

Per-Mathias Hogmo, appointed coach of Norway's men's national team in September 2013, also spent three years in charge of Norway's women's team. He coached the women's team from 1997 to 2000, taking it to a fourth-place finish at the 1999 FIFA Women's World Cup, and to gold medal glory at the 2000 Sydney Olympic Games. Hogmo then became coach of Norway's men's U-21 team, before returning to club soccer with Tromso, where the one-cap midfielder had ended his playing days in 1989. He succeeded Egil Olsen as Norway coach after the team failed to qualify for the 2014 FIFA World Cup. Hogmo, who combined coaching with doing a PhD in soccer at Tromso University, vowed: "I see myself as an innovator and will look to put my stamp on how Norway play."

POLAND

The history of Polish soccer is littered with tremendous highs and depressing lows. Olympic gold-medal success in 1972, and third-place finishes in the 1974 and 1982 FIFA World Cup, were followed by failure to qualify for any tournament until 1992. Poland qualified for the UEFA European Championship finals for the first time in 2008—and co-hosted the tournament with Ukraine in 2012—but went out in the first round both times.

STAYING ON LATER THAN LATO

Record-breaking Polish stalwart **Michal Zewlakow** bowed out of international soccer on familiar turf, even though his country was playing an away game. The versatile defender's 102nd and final appearance for his country was a scoreless exhibition tie in March 2011, in Greece, at the Karaiskakis stadium in Piraeus, where he used to play club soccer for Olympiacos. Zewlakow had overtaken Grzegorz Lato's appearances record for Poland in his previous game, an October 2010 exhibition against Ecuador. He had already helped make soccer history for his homeland when he and brother Marcin, a striker, became the first twins to line up together for Poland, against France in February 2000. Marcin would end his international career with 25 appearances and five goals.

TOP SCORERS

1	Wlodzimierz Lubanski	48
2	Grzegorz Lato	45
3	Kazimierz Deyna	41
4	Ernest Pol	39
5	Andrzej Szarmach	32
6	Gerard Cieslik	27
7	Zbigniew Boniek	24
8	Ernest Wilimowski	21
9	Dariusz Dziekanowski	20
=	Euzebiusz Smolarek	20

TYTON THE TITAN

Two straight 1-1 ties at the 2012 UEFA European Championship extended Poland's unbeaten run to eight games, and filled the tournament co-host with high hopes of reaching the knock-out stages for the first time, but a 1-0 defeat to the Czech Republic sealed its fate. But among the players to emerge from the tournament with credit was goalkeeper **Przemyslaw Tyton**. The stopper, with only five caps to his name, saved a penalty from Greece's Giorgos Karagounis just moments after coming on in the competition's opening match following a red card for first-choice goalkeeper Wojciech Szczesny, and kept his place in the team for the next two games. Szcesny had already conceded an equalizer to Greece's Dimitrios Salpingidis—ending a Polish record run of 512 minutes without allowing opponents to score, stretching back to a 2-1 victory over Hungary in November 2011.

LOVING LEWANDOWSKI

Star striker **Robert Lewandowski** is adept at proving people wrong. He was rejected by Legia Warsaw at the age of 16, and future Poland coach Franciszek Smuda saw nothing in him as a 20-year-old, chiding the man who had recommended him: "You owe me petrol money." Lewandowski's prolific form for Lech Poznan secured a big-money move to Germany's Borussia Dortmund in 2009. After struggling in his first Bundesliga season, he became one of Europe's top goalscorers, inspiring Dortmund to two Bundesliga titles and the 2013 UEFA Champions League final. Lewandowski was even warmly applauded by Dortmund's fans when he said goodbye in spring 2014, having agreed a move to Bayern Munich. He scored on his international debut, as a substitute against San Marino in September 2008, and also struck the opening goal of the 2012 UEFA European Championship. But his sporting exploits should not be a surprise: his father Krzysztof was a soccer player, and Polish judo champion; both his mother Iwona and his sister Milena have played high-level volleyball; and his partner Anna Stachurska is a karate champion.

TOP CAPS

1	Michael Zewlakow	102
2	Grzegorz Lato	100
3	Kazimierz Deyna	97
4	Jacek Bak	96
=	Jacek Krzynowek	96
6	Wladyslaw Zmuda	91
7	Antoni Szymanowski	82
8	Zbigniew Boniek	80
9	Wlodzimierz Lubanski	75
10	Tomasz Waldoch	74

LATO'S MISSION

Grzegorz Lato is not only second on the lists of both Poland's most-capped and top-scoring players, he is also the only Polish winner of the Golden Boot—with his seven goals at the 1974 FIFA World Cup—and a member of the gold medal-winning team at the Munich 1972 Olympic Games. He was also a leading figure in Poland's co-hosting, with Ukraine, of the 2012 UEFA European Championship, having become president of the country's soccer federation in 2008. He vowed: "I am determined to change the image of Polish soccer, to make it transparent and pure."

SUPER ERNEST

Ernest Wilimowski wrote his name into FIFA World Cup history in 1938, when he scored four goals, but still finished on the losing team. Poland went down 6-5 after extra-time to Brazil in a first-round tie in Strasbourg, France.

PUNCTUALITY PUNISHMENT

Kazimierz Gorski—capped once as a player— was the coach who led Poland to third place at the 1974 FIFA World Cup, having won gold at the Olympics in Munich, Germany, two years earlier. While winning a reputation for closeness with his players, Gorski could also be ruthless: key player Adam Musial was dropped from the team for a second-round game against Sweden at the 1974 tournament as punishment for turning up 20 minutes late to training. Poland still won the game, 1-0.

"LITTLE FIGO"

Jacub Blaszczykowski was one of the Polish players to come out of Euro 2012 with the most credit. He scored a spectacular equalizing goal against Russia, despite having gone into the tournament in testing circumstances. Before joining the rest of the squad at training camp, he had attended his father's funeral. His presence at this event was all the more noteworthy because, as a ten-year-old boy, Blaszyzkowski had witnessed his mother, Anna, being stabbed to death by his father, who served a 15-year prison sentence as a result. Polish great Zbigniew Boniek has dubbed Blaszczykowski "Little Figo," after the Portuguese winger Luis Figo, though he is more commonly known as "Kuba," the name he often wears on the back of his shirt. He had been encouraged to pursue soccer as a teenager by his uncle Jerzy Brzeczek, who also played for Dortmund and captained Poland, winning 42 caps between 1992 and 1999, and picking up an Olympic silver medal in 1992.

FIVE ASIDE

Poland had five different scorers when it beat Peru 5-1 at the 1982 FIFA World Cup: Wlodzimierz Smolarek, Grzegorz Lato, Zbigniew Boniek, Andrzej Buncol, and Wlodzimierz Ciolek. The feat was not repeated until Phillip Cocu, Marc Overmars, Dennis Bergkamp, Pierre van Hooijdonk, and Ronald de Boer gave the Netherlands a 5-0 win over South Korea at the 1998 FIFA World Cup.

COOL KEEPER

What is it with Polish goalkeepers? The country's outfield players may not always be household names worldwide, but Jerzy Dudek (Liverpool), Artur Boruc and Lukasz Zaluska (both Celtic), Lukasz Fabianski and Wojciech Szczesny (both Arsenal), and Tomasz Kuszczak (Manchester United) have all played roles at four of Britain's most successful clubs.

BONIEK

Zbigniew Boniek, arguably the best player Poland has ever produced, earned a place among soccer's legends for his role in the country's progress to third place at the 1982 FIFA World Cup. However, his absence from the tournament's semifinal will go down as one of the great "what ifs" of the competition. Robbed of its star forward through suspension, could Poland have upset both Italy and the odds and reached the final? Instead it lost the game 2-0.

PORTUGAL

Portugal's first experience of an international finals almost ended in triumph. Inspired by Eusebio, it marched through to the semifinal of the 1966 FIFA World Cup, only to lose to eventual champion England. A standout performance in the 1984 UEFA European Championship apart, more than 30 years would pass before Portugal enjoyed such giddy heights again. A "golden" generation of players arrived on the scene and since the turn of the century Portugal has become a consistent force on the world soccer stage.

TOP CAPS

1	Luis Figo	127
2	Cristiano Ronaldo	114
3	Fernando Couto	110
4	Rui Costa	94
5	Pauleta	88
6	Simao	85
7	Joao Pinto	81
8	Vitor Baia	80
9	Nuno Gomes	79
=	Ricardo	79

GOODISON GLORY

At the 1966 FIFA World Cup, Portugal beat North Korea 5-3 in an incredible quarterfinal at Everton's Goodison Park. The sensational Eusebio spurred an amazing comeback after the Koreans had gone 3-0 ahead in the first 25 minutes. He scored four goals to take Portugal to the semifinal in the nation's first-ever FIFA World Cup finals appearance. Despite the tears that flowed after a 2-1 loss to eventual winner England, Portugal rallied to claim third place with a **2-1 victory over the Soviet Union**.

HAPPY HUNDREDTH BIRTHDAY

Portugal celebrated its 100th birthday as a republic by beating recently crowned world champion Spain in a specially-arranged exhibiton in November 2010. The game not only marked this anniversary, but also celebrated the two countries' union in an ultimately unsuccessful bid to co-host the 2018 FIFA World Cup. Yet there was little equality on the field, as Portugal swept to a 4-0 win. It was tiny consolation for Portugal, which had lost to Spain in the FIFA World Cup round-of-16 five months earlier.

TOP SCORERS

1	Cristiano Ronaldo	50
2	Pauleta	47
3	Eusebio	41
4	Luis Figo	32
5	Nuno Gomes	29
6	Helder Postiga	27
7	Rui Costa	26
8	Joao Pinto	23
9	Nene	22
=	Simao	22

THE BLACK PANTHER

Born in Mozambique, **Eusebio** da Silva Ferreira was named Portugal's "Golden Player" to mark UEFA's 50th anniversary in 2004. Signed by Benfica in 1960 at the age of 18, he scored a hat-trick in his second game—against Santos in an exibition tournament in Paris—and outshone its young star, Pele. He helped Benfica to win a second European Cup in 1962, was named European Footballer of the Year in 1965, and helped Portugal to third place in the 1966 FIFA World Cup, finishing as top scorer with nine goals. A phenomenal striker, he scored 320 goals in 313 Portuguese league games, won the first European Golden Boot in 1968, and earned a second in 1973. The world of soccer united in paying tribute to Eusebio, after he died, aged 71, in January 2014. Portugal declared three days of mourning; his statue at Benfica's Estadio da Luz home was transformed into a shrine; his coffin was carried around the field; and Benfica's players wore his name on their backs during a 2-0 win over rival Porto.

PRESIDENTIAL POWER

Cristiano Ronaldo dos Santos Aveiro got his second name because his father was a great fan of US President Ronald Reagan. He grew up supporting Benfica, but began his career with arch-rival Sporting Clube before securing a move to Manchester United in 2003. His best season with United, in 2008, not only brought him the Golden Boot as well as Premier League and Champions League titles, but also helped him become only the second Portuguese player (after Luis Figo) to be named FIFA World Player of the Year (an award he scooped for a second time in 2013). Spanish giants Real Madrid paid €93.9 million to make him the most expensive player in history the following year. His club record 60 goals in 2011–12 steered Real to the La Liga title, before he scored three times for Portugal at the 2012 UEFA European Championship. Ronaldo ended the 2013–14 season with an extra-time goal as Madrid clinched the UEFA Champions League, in Lisbon. He then scored at his third FIFA World Cup—and sixth international tournament—with the winner against Ghana in Portugal's final group game. A few days earlier, against the United States, he had set up a last-gasp equalizer for Silvestre Varela: at 94 minutes and 33 seconds, the latest regulation-time goal in FIFA World Cup history, seven seconds later than Francesco Totti's penalty for Italy against Australia in the round-of-16 at the 2006 finals.

THE FAMOUS FIVE

Eusebio, Mario Coluna, Jose Augusto, Antonio Simoes, and Jose Torres, were the "Fabulous Five" in Benfica's 1960s Dream Team, which made up the spine of the Portuguese national team at the 1966 FIFA World Cup. Coluna, the "Sacred Monster," scored the vital third goal in the 1961 European Cup final and captained the national side in 1966. Jose Augusto scored two goals in the opening game against Hungary in 1966, and went on to manage both the men's and women's national teams. Antonio Simoes, the "Giant Gnome"—he was just 5ft 3in tall— made his debut for Portugal and Benfica in 1962, aged just 18. Jose Torres, the only one of the five not to win the European Cup—he played in the defeats in both 1963 and 1968—scored the winner against Russia in the 1966 third-place match, and went on to coach the national team in its next appearance at the FIFA World Cup finals in 1986.

THREE AND IN

After suffering a 4-0 trouncing against Germany in its opening game of the 2014 finals, its heaviest FIFA World Cup defeat, Portugal manager Paulo Bento replaced goalkeeper Rui Patricio with Beto for the next match, a 2-2 tie with the USA. Portugal ended its campaign by replacing the injured Beto with Eduardo for the final moments of a 2-1 victory over Ghana. It became only the fifth team to use all its goalkeepers in one FIFA World Cup finals—and the first since Greece had done so 20 years earlier—but the feat was matched by the Netherlands later in the tournament.

WAY TO GOMES

Portugal has provided three of the seven players to score at three different UEFA European Championships: Nuno Gomes (in 2000, 2004, and 2008) and Cristiano Ronaldo and **Helder Postiga** (both in 2004, 2008 and 2012). Gomes scored four at Euro 2000, the first of which—in a 3-2 victory over England—was actually the first of his 29 goals for Portugal, despite the fact he had made his international debut four years earlier. He was named in the official UEFA team of the tournament for the 2000 event, despite ending it in disgrace: he pushed referee Gunter Benko following Portugal's semifinal defeat to France and was handed a lengthy international ban.

REP. OF IRELAND

It took a combination of astute management and endless searching through ancestral records before the Republic of Ireland finally qualified for the finals of a major tournament, at the 20th time of asking. But ever since Jack Charlton took the team to UEFA Euro 88, Ireland has remained one of Europe's most dangerous opponents.

ROBBIE KEEN

The Republic of Ireland's all-time scoring record was taken by much-traveled striker **Robbie Keane** in October 2004 and he has been adding to it ever since, notably with last-minute equalizers against Germany and Spain at the 2006 FIFA World Cup. He marked the final game at the old Lansdowne Road with a hat-trick against San Marino in November 2006 and, four years later, marked the inaugural game at the revamped venue—now the Aviva Stadium—with his 100th cap against Argentina. Ireland's 2-1 win over Macedonia in March 2011 was Keane's 41st game as captain, equaling the record set by Andy Townsend. He followed this up with two more games as skipper, as Ireland beat Northern Ireland and Scotland in the British-based Carling Nations Cup. Keane also scored three goals in the two games, taking his overall tally to 49, before a double against Macedonia in June 2011 took him to 51. These made him the first player from the British Isles to score a half-century of international goals, and past England's 49-goal top scorer Bobby Charlton. Now with the Los Angeles Galaxy in the MLS, he still plays for Ireland, and has scored 62 times in 133 appearances.

KILBANE KEEPS ON AND ON

Only England's Billy Wright, with 70, played more consecutive internationals than **Kevin Kilbane**, whose 109th Republic of Ireland cap against Macedonia in March 2011 was also his 65th in a row, covering 11 years and five months. The run ended three days later, however, when the versatile left-sided player—nicknamed "Zinedine Kilbane" by fans—was given a rest for an exibition game against Uruguay.

KEANE CARRY—ON

Few star players have walked out on their country with quite the dramatic impact as Republic of Ireland captain **Roy Keane** in 2002 at its FIFA World Cup training camp in Saipan, Japan. The fiercely intense Manchester United skipper quit before a competitive ball had been kicked, complaining about a perceived lack of professionalism in the Irish preparations—and a loss of faith in manager Mick McCarthy. Ireland reached the round-of-16 without him, losing on penalties to Spain, but his behavior divided the nation. When McCarthy stepped down, Keane and the Irish football federation brokered a truce, and he returned to international duty in April 2004, under new boss Brian Kerr. Few expected his second comeback, however, when he was appointed assistant to new coach Martin O'Neill in November 2013. O'Neill, who played 64 times for Northern Ireland between 1971 and 1984, succeeded Italian veteran Giovanni Trapattoni, who resigned after failing to qualify for the 2014 FIFA World Cup finals.

CHAMPION CHARLTON

Jack Charlton became a hero after he took Ireland to their first major finals in 1988, defeating England 1-0 in their first game at the UEFA European Championship. Things got even better at their first FIFA World Cup finals two years later, where the unfancied Irish lost out only to hosts Italy in the quarter-finals.

IT'S A GIVEN

The Republic of Ireland's second-most-capped player, goalkeeper Shay Given, bowed out of international soccer at the 2012 UEFA European Championship finals, the first major tournament his country had reached since the 1994 FIFA World Cup—when Given also had been the first-choice in goal. Despite going into UEFA Euro 2012 on a 14-game unbeaten run, the Irish lost all three games, to Croatia, Spain, and Italy. The team's final game saw the captain's armband given to winger **Damien Duff**, as he became the fifth man to win a century of caps for Ireland. UEFA president Michel Platini praised the country's boisterous traveling fans, and promised them a special award for their enthusiasm. Given, who gave all his international match fees to charity, retired after recording 55 clean sheets in 125 appearances, though he did suggest, in January 2013, that he could be available for a comeback. One of Givens' rivals had been Millwall goalkeeper David Forde, who was 33 when he faced Sweden in a FIFA World Cup qualifier in March 2013, making him the oldest Ireland debutant in a competitive international.

MORE FOR MOORE

Paddy Moore was the first player ever to score four goals in a FIFA World Cup qualifier when Ireland came from behind to draw 4-4 with Belgium on February 25, 1934. Don Givens became the only Irishman to equal Moore's feat when he scored all four as Ireland beat Turkey 4-0 in October 1975.

CAPTAIN ALL-ROUND

Johnny Carey not only captained Matt Busby's Manchester United to the English league title in 1952, he also captained both Northern Ireland (nine caps) and later the Republic of Ireland (27 caps). He went on to coach the Republic of Ireland between 1955 and 1967.

HOORAY FOR RAY

Ray Houghton may have been born in Glasgow and spoke with a Scottish accent, but he scored two of Ireland's most famous goals. A header gave the Republic a shock 1-0 win over England at UEFA Euro 88 in West Germany and, six years later, his long-range strike was the only goal of the game against eventual finalist Italy, in the first round of the USA 1994 FIFA World Cup. It was exactly 18 years to the day from that 1994 shock that Ireland—now coached by Italian Giovanni Trapattoni—lost 2-0 to Italy in its third and final Group C game of the 2012 UEFA European Championship. Playing for Ireland that day was defender John O'Shea, who had previously been part of the Irish team which beat Italy 2-1 in the final of the 1998 UEFA European U-16s Championship final in Scotland. The Republic's only other continental title was the UEFA European U-19s Championship trophy it lifted by beating Germany, also in 1998.

TOP CAPS

1	Robbie Keane	133
2	Shay Given	125
3	Kevin Kilbane	110
4	Steve Staunton	102
5	Damien Duff	100
6	John O'Shea	96
7	Niall Quinn	92
8	Tony Cascarino	88
9	Paul McGrath	83
10	Richard Dunne	80
=	Packie Bonner	80

CROSSING THE CODES

Cornelius "Con" Martin played Irish Rules football, but his soccer exploits saw him expelled from the Gaelic Athletic Association—GAA players are strictly amateur and cannot be paid for playing any other football code. His versatility meant he was as good at center-half as he was in goal, both for his club, Aston Villa, and his country. In what was England's first home defeat to a non-British opponent, at Goodison Park in 1949, Martin played both in goal and in defense for the Republic of Ireland, scoring a penalty in that historic 2-0 victory.

TOP SCORERS

1	Robbie Keane	62
2	Niall Quinn	21
3	Frank Stapleton	20
4	John Aldridge	19
=	Tony Cascarino	19
=	Don Givens	19
7	Noel Cantwell	14
8	Gerry Daly	13
=	Kevin Doyle	13
=	Jimmy Dunne	13

ROMANIA

The history of Romanian soccer is littered with a series of bright moments, it was one of four countries (with Brazil, France, and Belgium) to appear in the first three editions of the FIFA World Cup, followed by significant spells in the doldrums. Since 1938, It has qualified for the FIFA World Cup finals only four times in 14 attempts. Romania's soccer highlight came in 1994 when, inspired by Gheorghe Hagi, it reached the quarterfinal of the FIFA World Cup.

TOP CAPS

1	Dorinel Munteanu	134
2	Gheorghe Hagi	125
3	Gheorghe Popescu	115
4	Ladislau Boloni	102
5	Razvan Rat	97
6	Dan Petrescu	95
7	Bogdan Stelea	91
8	Michael Klein	89
9	Bogdan Lobont	85
10	Marius Lacatus	83
=	Mircea Rednic	83

FAMOUS FOURSOME

Gheorghe Hagi, Florin Raducioiu, Ilie Dumitrescu, and **Gheorghe "Gica" Popescu** lit up the FIFA World Cup in the United States in 1994. Together they scored nine of Romania's ten goals—Raducioiu with four, Hagi three, and Dumitrescu two. All three successfully converted their penalties in the quarterfinal shoot-out against Sweden, but misses from Dan Petrescu and Miodrag Belodedici sent Romania crashing out. The trio made big-money moves for the following 1994–95 season: Hagi went from Brescia to Barcelona; Dumitrescu from Steaua Bucharest to Tottenham Hotspur; and Raducioiu went from warming the bench at Milan to the first team at Espanyol. Defender/midfielder Popescu followed Dumitrescu to Spurs, won the UEFA European Cup Winners' Cup with Barcelona, and was captain of Galatasaray when it became the first Turkish team to win a European trophy, the 2000 UEFA Cup. Popescu scored 16 goals in 115 appearances for Romania between 1998 and 2003, playing in the FIFA World Cups of 1990, 1994, and 1998, and the UEFA European Championships of 1996 and 2000. As well as being team-mates, Popescu and Hagi are also brothers-in-law: their wives, Luminita Popescu and Marlilena Hagi, are sisters.

BORDER CROSSING

Some 14 men played for both Romania, during the 1930s, and Hungary, during the 1940s, the most prolific being striker Iuliu Bodola. He scored 31 goals in 48 games for Romania, and played at the 1934 and 1938 FIFA World Cups. Bodola also four goals in 13 appearances for his adopted homeland Hungary.

YELLOW PERIL

Despite topping Group G, ahead of England, Colombia, and Tunisia, at the 1998 FIFA World Cup, Romania's players of that tournament might perhaps be best remembered for their collective decision to dye their hair blond ahead of the final group game. The **newly bleached Romanians** struggled to a 1-1 tie against Tunisia, before being knocked out by Croatia in the second round, 1-0.

TOP SCORERS

1	Gheorghe Hagi	35
=	Adrian Mutu	35
3	Iuliu Bodola	31
4	Viorel Moldovan	25
5	Ciprian Marica	24
6	Ladislau Boloni	23
7	Rodion Camataru	21
=	Dudu Georgescu	21
=	Anghel Iordanescu	21
=	Florin Raducioiu	21

CEMETERY SENTRY

It was second time luckier for former international striker Victor Piturca when he coached Romania at the 2008 UEFA European Championship in Austria and Switzerland, even though it was eliminated in the first round. He had previously been in charge when Romania qualified for the 2000 UEFA European Championship, but was forced out of the job before the tournament began, following disagreements with big-name players, such as Gheorghe Hagi. Piturca's cousin Florin Piturca was also a professional soccer player, but he died aged only 27 in 1978. Florin's father and Victor's uncle, Maximilian, a cobbler, not only built a mausoleum for Florin but also slept every night in the cemetery until his own death in 1994.

BROUGHT TO BUCHAREST

Romania's new national stadium in the capital Bucharest became the first in the country ever to stage a major European final, when it hosted the 2012 UEFA Europa League final, in which Atletico Madrid beat fellow Spanish club Athletic Bilbao. The 55,200-capacity Arena Nationala was opened in September 2011, when Romania tied 0-0 with France. It has also been used by Steaua Bucharest and Dinamo Bucharest for league games, Otelul Galati for UEFA Champions League games, and both Steaua and Rapid Bucharest for UEFA Europa League fixtures. The venue stands on the site of the old Stadionul National, built in 1953 and demolished 54 years later.

CENTURY MAN

Gheorghe Hagi, Romania's "Player of the [twentieth] Century," scored three goals and was named in the Team of the Tournament at the 1994 FIFA World Cup in the United States. Romania lost on penalties to Sweden after a 2-2 quarterfinal tie, its best post-war performance. Hagi made his international debut in 1983, aged just 18, scored his first goal aged 19 (in a 3-2 defeat to Northern Ireland) and remains Romania's joint-top scorer with 35 goals in 125 games. Despite retiring from international football after the 1998 FIFA World Cup, Hagi couldn't resist answering his country's call to play in UEFA Euro 2000. Sadly, two yellow cards in six minutes in the quarterfinal against Italy meant Hagi's final appearance for the national team ended with his premature dismissal. Farul Constanta, in Hagi's hometown, named its stadium after him in 2000, but fans stopped referring to it as such after he took the coach's job at fierce local rival Timisoara.

ENDURING DORINEL

Dorinel Munteanu has played for Romania more times than anyone else, although at one point his former team-mate Gheorghe Hagi's 125-cap record looked safe. Versatile defensive midfielder Munteanu was stuck on 119 caps throughout an 18-month absence from the international scene, before being surprisingly recalled—at the age of 37—by coach Victor Piturca in February 2005. He ended his international career two years later, having scored 16 times in 134 games. Yet many Romanians believe he was wrongly denied a goal when a shot against Bulgaria at the 1996 UEFA European Championship appeared to bounce over the goalline, but the goal was not given. The match ended 1-0 to Bulgaria, and Romania was eliminated in the first round with three defeats to its name.

ADRIAN'S AID

Romania has only lost once when **Adrian Mutu** has scored—a fact made all the better for it since, with 35 goals, he is (with Gheorghe Hagi) his country's all-time leading goalscorer. Mutu tied Hagi with a FIFA World Cup qualifying game equalizer against Hungary in March 2013, though this was his first international goal in 21 months. Unfortunately for Romania, controversy has followed its finest player of the 21st century: he has been banned twice for failed drugs tests. The first came after a test carried out by his club employer, Chelsea, in September 2004, showed traces of cocaine and brought about his dismissal. After a seven-month ban, he rehabilitated his career in Italy, first with Juventus, and then Fiorentina, before receiving a nine-month suspension, after he tested positive for a banned anti-obesity drug in January 2010. He did score against Italy at the 2008 UEFA European Championship, Romania's only goal at the last major tournament for which it qualified.

RUSSIA

Before the break-up of the Soviet Union (USSR) in 1992, the team was a world soccer powerhouse, winning the first UEFA European Championship in 1960, gold medals at the 1956 and 1988 Olympic Games, and qualifying for the FIFA World Cup on seven occasions. Playing as Russia since August 1992, the good times have eluded it, apart from being a UEFA Euro 2008 semifinalist. It did, however, reach the 2014 FIFA World Cup, under Italian coach Fabio Capello. But Russia will be hoping to do better than its first-round exit when it gets to host the tournament for the first time in 2018.

TOP SCORERS
(Russia only)

1	Vladimir Beschastnykh	26
=	Aleksandr Kerzhakov	26
3	Roman Pavlyuchenko	21
4	Andrei Arshavin	17
=	Valeri Karpin	17
6	Dmitri Sychev	15
7	Igor Kolyvanov	12
=	Roman Shorokov	12
9	Sergei Kiryakov	10
=	Aleksandr Mostovoi	10

KERZH LIFTS HIS CURSE

Only one man was in Russia's squads for the 2002 FIFA World Cup finals and the next time it qualified, in 2014: Aleksandr Kerzhakov. He was a teenager in 2002, having made his international debut three months earlier, and he played just eight minutes of the finals. Kerzhakov, still only 31 in Brazil, scored his 26th international goal to earn a 1-1 tie in Russia's opener against South Korea. He thus matched Russia's all-time scoring record set by 2002 team-mate Vladimir Beschastnykh. Kerzhakov, with five goals, was Russia's leading scorer in qualifying for the 2014 finals, but unlike in 2008, when he was five-goal top-scorer in UEFA European Championship qualifying, this time he was not omitted from the finals squad.

HOME RANGE

Russia was the only country at the 2014 FIFA World Cup to select its entire 23-man squad of men who played their club soccer domestically. Dynamo Moscow had six players, and CSKA Moscow five, including defender **Sergei Ignashevich** who reached a century of caps in the final Group H game against Algeria. Russia may also have had the highest-paid coach at the tournament, with Fabio Capello earning a reported $11 million per year. But for the second FIFA World Cup running Capello was undone by a goalkeeping error in the opening game: in 2010, he watched England's Rob Green fumble in a shot from the United States' Clint Dempsey; in Russia's 2014 opener, keeper Igor Akinfeev suffered similarly, with a long-range effort by South Korea's Lee Keun-Ho. And, by coincidence, both lapses were equalizers in 1-1 ties.

YOUNG PROMISE

Igor Akinfeev became post-Soviet Russia's youngest international soccer player when he made his debut in a friendly against Norway on April 28, 2004. The CSKA Moscow goalkeeper was just 18 years and 20 days old. The following season was perhaps just as memorable for him, clinching a domestic league and cup double with his club while also lifting the UEFA Cup as CSKA Moscow became post-Soviet Russia's first UEFA club trophy-winner. The youngest Soviet-era debutant was Eduard Streltsov, who hit a hat-trick on his debut against Sweden in June 1956, at the age of 17 years and 340 days, and then scored another treble in his second game, against India.

PUTTING ON THE STYLE

As a professional soccer player who has a diploma in fashion design, perhaps it is no surprise **Andrei Arshavin** could strut across the pitch with a certain flair as the most skillful of Russia's 21st-century players. Even after missing the first two games of the 2008 UEFA European Championship through suspension, Russia's captain dazzled with his performances in his team's next two games—especially a 3-1 quarterfinal triumph over the Netherlands. Just a month earlier, Arshavin had been central as Zenit St Petersburg won the UEFA Cup. A later spell with English club Arsenal proved patchier and he was released in summer 2013. Arshavin's image back home was tainted a little when he argued with fans after Russia's Euro 2012 first-round exit, and he then lost the captaincy under new coach Fabio Capello. Yet, on his day, this natty man with an eye for an outfit could prove a cut above the rest.

TOP CAPS

(Russia only)

1	Viktor Onopko	109
2	Sergei Ignashevich	100
3	Aleksandr Kerzhakov	84
4	Vasili Berezutskiy	81
5	Aleksandr Anyukov	77
8	Andrei Arshavin	75
7	Igor Akinfeev	72
=	Valeri Karpin	72
9	Vladimir Beschastnykh	71
10	Sergei Semak	65

PAV A GO HERO

Roman Pavlyuchenko's thumping strike as a substitute to wrap up a 4-1 victory over the Czech Republic in Russia's opening game of the 2012 UEFA European Championship took him to within five goals of Vladimir Beschastnykh's post-Soviet scoring record. Pavlyuchenko also scored Russia's first goal of Euro 2008, this time in a 4-1 defeat at the hands of eventual champion Spain. Despite the loss, Russia still managed to reach the semifinal that year; in 2012 it failed to make it beyond the group stage. Pavlyuchenko is Russia's top scorer in UEFA European Championships, with four overall, three in 2008 and one in 2012.

SUPER STOPPER

FIFA declared **Lev Yashin** to be the finest goalkeeper of the 20th century and, naturally, he made it into its Century XI team, too. In a career spanning 20 years, Yashin played 326 league games for Dynamo Moscow—the only club he ever played for—and won 78 caps for the Soviet Union, conceding an average of less than a goal a game (only 70 in total). With Dynamo, he won five Soviet championships and three Soviet cups, the last of which came in his final full season in 1970. He saved around 150 penalties in his long career, and kept four clean sheets in his 12 FIFA World Cup games. Such was Yashin's worldwide reputation, Chile's Eladio Rojas was so excited at scoring past the legendary Yashin in the 1962 FIFA World Cup that he gave the surprised keeper a big hug with the ball still sitting in the back of the net. Yashin was nicknamed the "Black Spider" for his distinctive black jersey and his uncanny ability to get a hand, arm, leg, or foot, in the way of shots and headers of all kinds. In 1963, Yashin became the first, and so far only, goalkeeper to be named European Footballer of the Year, the same year in which he won his fifth Soviet championship and starred for the Rest of the World XI in the English FA's centenary exhibition game at Wembley.

CAPPING IT ALL

Viktor Onopko, despite being born in the Ukraine, played all his career for the CIS and Russian national football teams. The first of Onopko's 113 international caps (four for the CIS, 109 for Russia) came in a 2-2 tie against England in Moscow on April 29, 1992. He played in the 1994 and 1998 FIFA World Cups, as well as the UEFA European Championship in 1996. He was due to join the squad for the UEFA European Championship in 2004 but missed out through injury. Onopko's club career spanned 19 years, and took him to Shakhtar Donetsk, Spartak Moscow, Real Oviedo, Rayo Vallecano, Alania Vladikavkaz, and FC Saturn. He was Russia's player of the year—in both both 1993 and 1994.

GOLDEN BOY

Igor Netto captained the Soviet Union to its greatest soccer successes: a gold medal at the Melbourne 1956 Olympic Games, and victory in the first-ever UEFA European Championship in France in 1960. Born in Moscow in 1930, Netto was awarded the Order of Lenin in 1957 and became a hockey coach after retiring from soccer.

SCOTLAND

A country with a vibrant domestic league and a rich soccer tradition—it played host to the first-ever international soccer game, against England, on November 30, 1872, Scotland has never put in the performances on the international stage to match its lofty ambitions. There have been moments of triumph, such as the unexpected 3-2 victory over the Netherlands at the 1978 FIFA World Cup, but far too many moments of despair. Scotland has not qualified for a major tournament finals since 1998.

TOP SCORERS

1	Kenny Dalglish	30
=	Denis Law	30
3	Hughie Gallacher	23
4	Lawrie Reilly	22
5	Ally McCoist	19
6	Kenny Miller	18
7	Robert Hamilton	15
=	James McFadden	15
9	Maurice Johnston	14
10	Bob McColl	13
=	Andrew Wilson	13

KING KENNY

Kenny Dalglish is Scotland's joint-top international goalscorer (with Denis Law) and remains the only player to have won more than a century of caps for the national team—102 in total, and 11 more than the next highest cap-winner, goalkeeper Jim Leighton. Despite growing up a Rangers fan (he was born in Glasgow on March 4, 1951), Dalglish made his name spear-heading Celtic's domestic dominance in the 1970s, winning four league titles, four Scottish Cups, and one League Cup. He then went on to become a legend at Liverpool, winning a hat-trick of European Cups (1978, 1981, and 1984), and leading the team as player-coach to its first-ever league and cup double in 1986. He later joined Herbert Chapman and Brian Clough as one of the few men to coach two different clubs to the league title—guiding Blackburn Rovers to the English Premier League in 1994–95. For Scotland, Dalglish scored at both the 1978 and 1982 FIFA World Cup finals, netting the first goal in the famous 3-2 victory over the eventual runner-up Netherlands in the 1978 group stage. He played his last international in 1986.

DON'T COME HOME TOO SOON

Scotland's 2-0 loss to Serbia in March 2013 gave it the unenviable record of being the first European nation to be eliminated from the 2014 FIFA World Cup. It denied Scotland the chance to go beyond the first round of a major finals for the first time. **Gordon Strachan**, who scored five goals in 50 games for Scotland in midfield between 1980 and 1992, had replaced the sacked Craig Levein in January 2013.

THE LAWMAN

Denis Law is joint top scorer for Scotland with Kenny Dalglish. He scored 30 goals in only 55 games, compared to the 102 it took Dalglish to do the same. Law twice scored four goals in a game for Scotland, first against Northern Ireland on November 7, 1962—helping to win the British Home Championship—and against Norway in an exhibition on November 7, 1963. Law clearly enjoyed playing against Norway, having grabbed a hat-trick in Bergen just five months earlier.

ROOM FOR ONE MORE?

Hampden Park, Scotland's national stadium, boasts the record for the highest-ever soccer attendance in Europe. The crowd was so large no one is sure how many squeezed in to watch Scotland play England in 1937, though the official figure is usually quoted as 149,415. Scotland won the British Home Championship game 3-1, but it ended runner-up behind Wales in the overall tournament. Since being redeveloped in 1999, Hampden Park has hosted almost all of Scotland's home internationals. The first to be played elsewhere was a 2008 UEFA European Championship qualifier against the Faroe Islands in September 2006, when Celtic Park, Glasgow, was used instead. Hampden had been pre-booked for a concert by pop star Robbie Williams.

DIVIDED LOYALTIES

Scottish-born winger Jim Brown played and scored for the US team which lost to Argentina in the first FIFA World Cup in 1930. He had moved to New Jersey three years earlier and qualified through his US citizen father. Two of his brothers also played professionally: younger brother John, a goalkeeper, was capped by Scotland, but Tom did not play at international level. Jim's son George appeared once for the US, in 1957, while two of John's sons, Peter and Gordon, both played rugby for Scotland. The first brothers to play for different countries were John and Archie Goodall, members of Preston North End's 1888–89 league and FA Cup double-winning squad, and although their parents were both Scottish, London-born John played for England and Belfast-born Archie represented Ireland. Another pair of brothers with Scottish parents were Joe and Jerry Baker, though Joe chose to play for England in the 1960s and Jerry appeared for Team USA.

TOP CAPS

1	Kenny Dalglish	102
2	Jim Leighton	91
3	Alex McLeish	77
4	Paul McStay	76
5	Tom Boyd	72
6	Kenny Miller	69
=	David Weir	69
8	Christian Dailly	67
9	Willie Miller	65
10	Darren Fletcher	62
=	Danny McGrain	62

I HAVEN'T FELT THIS GOOD SINCE ARCHIE GEMMILL SCORED AGAINST THE DUTCH

Archie Gemmill scored Scotland's greatest goal on the world stage in the surprise 3-2 victory over the Netherlands at the 1978 FIFA World Cup. He jinked past three defenders and chipped the ball neatly over Dutch goalkeeper Jan Jongbloed. Amazingly, in 2008, this magical moment was turned into a dance in the English National Ballet's "The Beautiful Game."

RECENT REMATCH

The world's oldest international fixture was staged for the first time in 14 years when England and Scotland met at Wembley in an August 2013 exhibition game. Gordon Strachan's Scotland twice came from behind, but lost 3-2 thanks to a late winner by England's debutant substitute Rickie Lambert. This was the first England–Scotland game in which both teams had scored at least twice since Scotland's famous 3-2 win in 1967.

WEIR ON THE BALL

Rugged Rangers center-back **David Weir** became Scotland's oldest international soccer player when he faced Lithuania in a 2012 UEFA European Championship qualifier on September 3, 2010. He was aged 40 years and 111 days, and it was his 66th appearance. He was still representing his country three caps and 39 days later, against reigning world and European champions Spain.

UNOFFICIAL WORLD CHAMPIONS

One of the victories most cherished by Scotland fans is the **3-2 triumph** over arch-rivals and reigning world champion England in April 1967 at Wembley—the first time Sir Alf Ramsey's team had lost since winning the 1966 FIFA World Cup. Scotland's man of the match that day was ball-juggling left-half/midfielder Jim Baxter, while it was also the first game in charge for Scotland's first full-time coach, Bobby Brown. Less fondly recalled is Scotland's 9-3 trouncing by the same opponents, at the same stadium in April 1961. It made unfortunate goalkeeper Frank Haffey the butt of a popular joke that did the rounds across the border in England: "What's the time? Nearly 10 past Haffey." The game was Haffey's second—and last—for Scotland.

SERBIA

The former Yugoslavia was one of the strongest soccer nations in eastern Europe. It reached the FIFA World Cup semifinal in 1930 and 1962, it was also runner-up in the UEFA European Championships of 1960 and 1968. In addition, Yugoslavia's leading club, Red Star Belgrade, was only the second team from eastern Europe (after Romania's Steaua Bucharest in 1986) to win the European Cup, when it beat Marseille on penalties in the 1991 final.

MAGIC DRAGAN

Yugoslavia's greatest player was Red Star left-winger **Dragan Dzajic**, who later went on to become the club's president. He made his international debut at 18, won a national record 85 caps and scored 23 goals. The most important was his last-minute winner against world champion England in the 1968 UEFA European Championship semifinal in Florence. It took Yugoslavia to the final against Italy. Pele said of Dzajic: "He's a real wizard. I'm sorry he's not Brazilian."

TOP CAPS

1	Dejan Stankovic	103
2	Savo Milosevic	102
3	Dragan Djazic	85
4	Dragan Stojkovic	84
5	Predrag Mijatovic	73
6	Branislav Ivanovic	71
7	Zlatko Vujovic	70
8	Branko Zebec	65
9	Slavisa Jokanovic	64
10	Stjepan Bobek	63
=	Sinisa Mihajlovic	63

SAVICEVIC STRIKES

Dejan Savicevic is Serbia's greatest player of the modern era. The attacking midfielder was a key member of Red Star Belgrade's 1991 European Cup-winning team. He also inspired it to three consecutive league championships. He moved on to AC Milan, and starred as his new club beat Barcelona 4-0 in the 1994 UEFA Champions League final. He created the opening goal, then crashed home a 35-yard volley. Savicevic later became a prominent supporter of the drive for Montenegrin independence from Serbia, and was credited with playing an influential role in the referendum vote on May 21, 2006 that led to the establishment of a separate Montenegrin state.

YUGOSLAVIA HIT BY BOYCOTT

The rivalry between Serbia and Croatia was apparent even in the early days of the old federation. Yugoslavia reached the semifinal of the inaugural FIFA World Cup in 1930, but it did so without any players from Croatia. They all boycotted the squad for the finals in protest at the new federal association headquarters being located in the Serbian capital, Belgrade.

TOP SCORERS

1	Stjepan Bobek	38
2	Mian Galic	37
=	Savo Milosevic	37
4	Blagoje Marjanovic	36
5	Rajko Mitic	32
6	Dusan Bajevic	29
7	Todor Veselinovic	28
8	Borivoje Kostic	26
=	Predrag Mijatovic	26
10	Zlatko Vujovic	25

STAN'S THE MAN

Midfielder **Dejan Stankovic** is the only man to have represented three different countries at separate FIFA World Cups. He played for Yugoslavia in 2002, Serbia and Montenegro in 2006, and Serbia in 2010. His pragmatic comment on his achievement was: "I'm happy with the record, but I'd rather win. It's OK to have been in three World Cups, but I would have liked to have better results." Stankovic scored twice on his international debut for Yugoslavia in 1998. In club soccer for Internazionale of Milan, he has twice scored memorable volleyed goals from close to the halfway line: first, against Genoa in 2009–10, a first-time shot from the Genoa goalkeeper's clearance; and, in the following season, against Germany's FC Schalke 04 in the UEFA Champions League. Stankovic equaled Savo Milosevic's Serbian appearances record with his final competitive international in October 2011, but went one better in October 2013, when playing the first ten minutes of a 2-0 exhibition defeat of Japan at Novi Sad.

SAV A GO HERO

Savo Milosevic was the first Serbian player to reach a century of international appearances. He has also played for his country in four different guises: he represented Yugoslavia before and after it broke up, Serbia and Montenegro, and finally Serbia alone. Milosevic's 100th international appearance was memorable for the wrong reasons, coming in a 6-0 defeat to Argentina at the 2006 FIFA World Cup. He returned to the fold for a final, farewell game, an exhibition against Bulgaria on November 19, 2008. Milosevic played only the first 34 minutes, but managed to score twice, and miss two penalties. He joked: "Maybe those 34 minutes sum up my career, in the best possible way, with good moments and bad times, when you are at the top and at the bottom. Believe me, I have never missed two penalties before—not even in training."

MILORAD'S MILESTONE

The first man to captain and then coach his country at the FIFA World Cup was Milorad Arsenijevic. He captained Yugoslavia to the semifinal at the inaugural tournament in Uruguay, in 1930, and then coached the Yugoslavia squad in Brazil 20 years later.

BRAN POWER

Versatile Chelsea defender and Serbia captain **Branislav Ivanovic** has enjoyed scoring significant late goals against Portuguese opposition. His first goal for his country was an 88th-minute equalizer in a UEFA European Championship qualifier away to Portugal in September 2007. His stoppage-time header gave Chelsea victory over Benfica in the final of the 2013 UEFA Europa League, a year after suspension ruled him out of the club's UEFA Champions League triumph over Bayern Munich.

GOING IT ALONE

After Serbia and Montenegro had competed at the 2006 FIFA World Cup, the 2010 tournament was the first featuring Serbia alone following Montenegro's independence. Topping its qualifying group ahead of France, Radomir Antic's Serbian team failed to make it through to the knockout stages in South Africa, despite a single-goal victory over Group D rival Germany. A Serbian working for an opposing team was partly to blame for its early exit: Milovan Rajevac was coach of the Ghana team which beat Serbia 1-0 in its opening first-round game. A mainstay in Serbia's defense was dominating center-back **Nemanja Vidic**, a 2008 UEFA Champions League-winner and hero at Manchester United. He announced his retirement from international soccer in October 2011.

SLOVAKIA

Slovakia has finally begun to claim bragging rights over its neighbor, the Czech Republic. A Slovak team did play games during the Second World War, but then had to wait until post-war Czechoslovakia split into Slovakia and the Czech Republic in 1993 before its next game. Slovakia returned to competitive action in qualifiers for the 1996 UEFA European Championship, finishing a promising third in its group. Continuing gradual progress culminated in qualification for its first FIFA World Cup final, in 2010. In South Africa, it upset defending champion Italy 3-2, and reached the round-of-16.

VLAD ALL OVER

Three relatives named Vladimir Weiss—different generations of the same family—have represented their country in international soccer, with two of them featuring at the 2010 FIFA World Cup. The first Vladimir won a soccer silver medal with Czechoslovakia at the 1964 Olympic Games, before his son Vladimir played for the same country at the 1990 FIFA World Cup. This second Vladimir then coached Slovakia at the 2010 FIFA World Cup, picking his Manchester City winger son—yet another Vladimir—for three of the team's four games. The first Vladimir won only three caps for Czechoslovakia, but it included the Tokyo 1964 Olympic Games final, and he had the misfortune to score an own goal as Hungary triumphed 2-1. The second Vladimir won 19 caps for Czechoslavakia and 12 for Slovakia. Aged 20 at the 2010 FIFA World Cup, the youngest Vladimir ended the summer of 2014 with 33 appearances. The coach at the 2010 FIFA World Cup described Slovakia's 3-2 victory over the defending champion Italy in South Africa as the second happiest day of his life—only beaten by the day his son was born. He stepped down as coach after failing to qualify for the 2012 UEFA European Championship.

HOMEMADE MARIAN

Marian Masny holds the international appearances record for Slovak-born players who represented the united Czechoslovakia, earning 75 caps between 1974 and 1982. Masny, from Rybany, was also the second-highest-scoring Slovak during the united Czechoslovakia era. His 18 goals were only bettered by the 22 in 36 games struck by Vrutky-born Adolf Scherer from 1958 to 1964. Scherer's tally included three at the 1962 FIFA World Cup, when Czechoslovakia finished runner-up. Scherer scored the winner against Hungary in the quarterfinal and Czechoslovakia's final goal in its 3-1 semifinal victory over Yugoslavia.

TOP SCORERS

1	Robert Vittek	23
2	Szilard Nemeth	22
3	Miroslav Karhan	14
=	Marek Mintal	14
5	Peter Dubovsky	12
=	Stanislav Sestak	12
7	Marek Hamsik	11
8	Martin Jakubko	9
=	Tibor Jancula	9
=	Lubomir Reiter	9

MAREK OFF THE MARK

Slovakia's biggest win is 7-0, a result it has achieved three times. Wing-back Marek Cech was the only man to play in all three games: against Liechtenstein in September 2004 and twice versus San Marino, in October 2007 and June 2009. He scored twice in last of these games and, in fact, four of his five international goals since his debut in 2004 came against San Marino—he also bagged a double in a 5-0 victory in November 2007.

CZECH EIGHT

Eight men from Slovakia played in Czechoslovakia's winning team in the 1976 UEFA European Championship final against West Germany. It included the captain Anton Ondrus and both its scorers in the 2-2 tie, Jan Svehlik and Karol Dobias. Three of the team's successful penalty-takers in the 5-3 shoot-out win were Slovak-born: Marian Masny, Ondrus, and substitute Ladislav Jurkemik. The other Slovaks to feature were Jan Pivarnik, Jozef Capkovic, and Jozef Moder. Defender Koloman Gogh was born in what is now the Czech Republic, but had Slovak family ties and played most of his club football for Slovan Bratislava in the Slovak capital.

TOP CAPS

1	Miroslav Karhan	108
2	Robert Vittek	80
3	Marek Hamsik	69
4	Martin Skrtel	66
5	Jan Durica	64
6	Filip Holosko	63
7	Szilard Nemeth	58
8	Radoslav Zabavnik	57
9	Stanislav Varga	54
10	Stanislav Sestak	53

SKRTEL'S A CERT

Slovakia captain and center-back **Martin Skrtel** has won his country's Footballer of the Year award more times than any other Slovak player, since it was introduced in 1993. He collected the prize in 2007, 2008, 2011, and 2012. National team-mate Marek Hamsik won it in 2009, 2010, and 2013. The only man to be named Slovak Footballer of the Year three years in a row was defender Dusan Tittel: in 1993, 1994, and 1995.

ROBERT THE HERO

Slovakia's **Robert Vittek** became only the fourth player from a country making its FIFA World Cup debut to score as many as four goals in one tournament, at the 2010 event in South Africa. He hit one against New Zealand, two against defending champion Italy, and a late penalty in a round-of-16 loss against the Netherlands. The previous three players to have done so were: Portugal's Eusebio in 1966, Denmark's Preben Elkjaer Larsen in 1986, and Croatia's Davor Suker in 1998. Vittek's last-minute penalty against the Netherlands made him Slovakia's all-time leading scorer with 23 goals, overtaking former Sparta Prague and Middlesbrough striker Szilard Nemeth. His 2010 FIFA World Cup form was all the more striking since he had failed to score at all in the qualifiers.

CUTTING EDGE HAMSIK

Playmaker Marek Hamsik was just 17 when he left Slovakia in 2004—after only six games for Slovan Bratislava—and moved to Italy, joining Brescia, then Napoli. After helping Napoli to win the 2012 Coppa Italia, he fulfilled a promise to shave off his Mohawk hairstyle. Hamsik captained Slovakia at the 2010 FIFA World Cup, where he helped to eliminate Italy in the opening round. It was a less happy story for Hamsik and Slovakia when it came to qualifying for the 2014 FIFA World Cup. Slovakia finished a disappointing third, behind Greece and group G winner Bosnia & Herzegovina. Hamsik scored twice in eight appearances, but was absent for the final two games.

BROKEN-DOWN KARHAN

Slovakia's defensive midfielder **Miroslav Karhan** helped his country qualify for the 2010 FIFA World Cup, taking his appearances tally to a national-record 95. But an Achilles tendon injury meant the team captain was ruled out of the tournament itself. After returning to action later in 2010, Karhan became the first Slovakia player to pass 100 caps.

SWEDEN

Eleven appearances at the FIFA World Cup finals (with a best result of runner-up, as tournament host, in 1958) and three Olympic medals (including gold at London in 1948), bear testament to Sweden's rich history on the world soccer stage. Recent success has been harder to find, however, with semifinal appearances at the 1992 UEFA European Championship (again as the host nation) and the 1994 FIFA World Cup the country's best performances in recent years.

GRE-NO-LI OLYMPIC AND ITALIAN GLORY

Having conquered the world by leading Sweden to gold in the 1948 Olympics in London, Gunnar Gren, Gunnar Nordahl, and **Nils Liedholm** were snapped up by AC Milan. Its three-pronged "Gre-No-Li" forward line led the Italian giants to its 1951 Scudetto win. Nordahl, who topped the Serie A scoring charts five times between 1950 and 1955, remains Milan's all-time top scorer with 221 goals in 268 games. Gren and Liedholm went on to appear for the Swedish national team at the 1958 FIFA World Cup. Sweden reached the final, but lost 5-2 to Brazil.

TOP CAPS

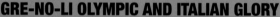

1	Anders Svensson	148
2	Thomas Ravelli	143
3	Olof Mellberg	117
4	Roland Nilsson	116
5	Bjorn Nordqvist	115
6	Andreas Isaksson	113
7	Kim Kallstrom	110
8	Niclas Alexandersson	109
9	Henrik Larsson	106
10	Zlatan Ibrahimovic	98

ONE MORE ENCORE, AGAIN!

One of the most famous and decorated Swedish players of modern times, **Henrik Larsson** (a star on the club scene with both Celtic and Barcelona) retired from international soccer after the 2002 FIFA World Cup ... and again after the 2006 FIFA World Cup in Germany. He then made a further comeback in the 2010 FIFA World Cup qualifiers. With 37 goals in his 106 appearances, including five in his three FIFA World Cups, fans and officials clamored for his return each time he tried to walk away. Sweden's failure to qualify for the tournament in 1998 meant a record-equaling 12 years elapsed between Larsson's first FIFA World Cup finals goal, against Bulgaria in 1994, and his last, a dramatic late equalizer in a 2-2 group-stage draw with England in 2006. After finally retiring for good in 2009, he became coach of Swedish second-tier club Landskrona BoIS.

TOP-STOPPER RAVELLI

Thomas Ravelli kept goal for Sweden a record 143 times—conceding 143 goals. He saved two penalties in a shoot-out against Romania in the 1994 FIFA World Cup quarterfinal to send Sweden into the last four, but it lost 1-0 to Brazil. Sweden went on to finish third, and was also the tournament's highest scorers with 15 goals in all, four more than eventual champion Brazil. Sweden's tally included five for Kennet Andersson, four for Martin Dahlin, and three for Tomas Brolin.

IBRA–CADABRA

Few players these days can claim such consistent success—or have as big an ego—as Swedish forward **Zlatan Ibrahimovic**. His proclamations have included: "There's only one Zlatan," "I am like Muhammad Ali," and, in response to criticism from Norway's John Carew, "What Carew does with a football, I can do with an orange." Yet his clubs, including Ajax in the Netherlands, Juventus, Internazionale, and AC Milan in Italy, Barcelona in Spain, and Paris Saint-Germain in France, have all benefited from his presence; he has won 11 league titles since 2002. He christened the newly built Friends Arena in Solna with all four goals as Sweden beat England 4-2 in a November 2012 exhibition—his final goal topping the lot, a 30-yard overhead kick that earned him the FIFA Ferenc Puskas goal of the year award. Ibrahimovic thus became the first player in 915 games to score four goals in one game against England. Other notable strikes include a back-heel volley against Italy at the 2004 UEFA European Championship and a long-range volley versus France at Euro 2012. Despite also qualifying for Bosnia and Croatia through his family, Malmo-born Ibrahimovic made his Sweden debut in January 2001 and has scored 48 goals in 98 appearances. His success in Paris since signing for €20million in 2012 prompted a local restaurateur to introduce a new €30 burger, "La Zlatan", comprising 17 oz of beef, three slices of cheese, and extravagant toppings of onions and ham.

ANDERS KEEPERS

Midfielder Anders Svensson celebrated equaling Thomas Ravelli's Sweden appearances record by scoring in both his 142nd and 143rd games for his country: a long-range strike as Norway were beaten 4-2 and then the winning goal against the Republic of Ireland in a qualifier for the 2014 FIFA World Cup. He then became his country's most-capped player in a 1-0 victory over Kazakhstan, but didn't score. Svensson retired from international soccer in 2013, aged 37, after Sweden lost to Portugal in the qualifying play-off. He made 148 appearances, and scored 21 goals.

MAGICAL MELL

Commanding center-back **Olof Mellberg** became one of only seven players to appear at four different UEFA European Championship finals when he took part at Euro 2012—and was the first Swede to achieve the feat. The 34-year-old also became Sweden's oldest UEFA European Championship goalscorer when he headed it into a 2-1 lead against England, ten minutes after his shot led to Glen Johnson scoring an own goal to draw the Swedes level. Unfortunately for Mellberg, and Sweden, however, England hit back to win 3-2. Mellberg's six previous goals for his country had all come in qualifying matches for either the UEFA European Championship or the FIFA World Cup.

TOP SCORERS

1	Sven Rydell	49
2	Zlatan Ibrahimovic	48
3	Gunnar Nordahl	43
4	Henrik Larsson	37
5	Gunnar Gren	32
6	Kennet Andersson	31
7	Marcus Allback	30
8	Martin Dahlin	29
9	Tomas Brolin	27
=	Agne Simonsson	27

FOUR SQUARE

In October 2012, Sweden became the first team to claw back a four-goal deficit against Germany, when it recovered from 4-0 down to finish 4-4 in a 2014 FIFA World Cup qualifier—thanks to second-half goals from Zlatan Ibrahimovic, Mikael Lustig, Johan Elmander, and Rasmus Elm.

MANAGER SWAP

The most successful coach Sweden has ever had was Englishman **George Raynor**. He led the team to the London 1948 Olympic Games gold medal and steered Sweden to third place in the 1950 FIFA World Cup, then the runner-up spot in the 1958 FIFA World Cup. Raynor got one over on the country of his birth when Sweden became only the second foreign team to win at Wembley, with a 3-2 victory over England in 1959. Working in the opposite direction, in 2001 Sven-Goran Eriksson left Serie A side Lazio to become England's first foreign coach. He took the team to three consecutive quarterfinals: in the FIFA World Cups of 2002 and 2006 and, in between, the 2004 UEFA European Championship. Eriksson, however, didnt achieve a win against his home country, recording three ties (1-1 in a 2001 exhibition; 1-1 in a 2002 FIFA World Cup group game; 2-2 in a 2006 FIFA World Cup group game) and a defeat (0-1 in a 2004 exhibition).

KLAS ACT

Midfielder Klas Ingesson helped Sweden finish third at the 1994 FIFA World Cup but after retiring in 2001, he opted for a very different career: working as a lumberjack on his farm and 815-hectare wood. Yet he was tempted back into soccer, in coaching, and pursued that path even after being diagnosed with an incurable form of cancer in 1999. He took joint charge of IF Elfsborg in September 2013, despite being told by doctors he would have to use a wheelchair.

SWITZERLAND

Switzerland set a record in 2006 when it became the first team in FIFA World Cup finals history to go out of the tournament without conceding a goal. It sums up the country's soccer history: despite three FIFA World Cup quarterfinal appearances (in 1934, 1938, and 1954, the last when it was tournament host) and the round-of-16 in 2006 and 2014, Switzerland has failed to establish itself on the international soccer stage. It co-hosted the 2008 UEFA European Championship, with Austria, and is better known as being the home of both FIFA and UEFA.

CLEAN SHEET WIPE-OUT

Switzerland made history in 2006 by becoming the first team to be eliminated from the FIFA World Cup without allowing a single goal. However, its round-of-16 game against Ukraine ended in a scoreless tie after 120 minutes and, in the shoot-out, Switzerland did not score a single penalty, and lost 3-0. Despite being beaten three times in the shoot-out, goalkeeper **Pascal Zuberbuhler**'s performances in Germany earned him a Swiss record for consecutive clean sheets at an international tournament.

DERDIYOK AT THE DOZEN

Nineteen-year-old striker **Eren Derdiyok** scored with his very first kick of the ball in international soccer after coming on as a substitute against England at Wembley in a February 2009 exhibition. But England won 2-1. He scored three of Switzerland's goals in a thrilling 5-3 exhibition victory over Germany in May 2012, making him the first player to score a hat-trick against the Germans since England's Michael Owen almost 11 years earlier. At the time, Derdiyok was playing his club soccer for German team Hoffenheim, and all three of his goals were set up by another Bundesliga-based player, Bayer Leverkusen's Tranquillo Barnetta.

TOP SCORERS

1	Alexander Frei	42
2	Max Abegglen	34
=	Kubilay Turkyilmaz	34
4	Andre Abegglen	29
=	Jacques Fatton	29
6	Adrian Knup	26
7	Josef Hugi	23
8	Charles Antenen	22
9	Lauro Amado	21
=	Stephane Chapuisat	21

LLAMA FARMER FREI-ING HIGH

After being compared to a llama by an angry Swiss sports press for spitting at Steven Gerrard at UEFA Euro 2004, **Alexander Frei**, Switzerland's all-time top scorer, adopted a llama at Basel zoo as part of his apology to the nation. Frei appeared to abandon all hope of adding to his record Swiss goal tally of 42 in 84 games when he announced his retirement from international soccer in April 2011, blaming abuse from his own fans during recent games. These included a scoreless tie against minnows Malta, when both Frei and team-mate Gokhan Inler missed penalties. Frei was joined in international retirement by strike partner Marco Streller, who had scored 12 goals in 37 games.

CHAMPION CHAPPI

Stephane "Chappi" Chapuisat, the third man to win 100 caps for Switzerland, was the first Swiss player to win a UEFA Champions League medal. The forward started the final for Borussia Dortmund in its 3-1 victory over Juventus in 1997, but maybe his most significant contribution in the game was to make way for Lars Ricken, whose goal with his first touch put the game beyond Juventus. Stephane's father, Pierre-Albert Chapuisat, was also a Swiss international, who earned 34 caps for the national team in the 1970s and 1980s. Pierre-Albert failed to reach the heights achieved by Stephane, who later added both the Club World Cup and the Swiss super league—the latter while playing for Grasshoppers—to his winners' medal collection.

YAK ATTACK

Brothers Murat and **Hakan Yakin** were both born in the Swiss city of Basel to Turkish parents and both opted to play for the country of their birth. Midfielder Murat, almost three years older than his brother, scored four goals and won 49 caps between 1994 and 2004, while Hakan, who played slightly further forward, made his international debut in 2000 and bowed out 11 years later. Hakan scored the opening goal of Switzerland's 2008 UEFA European Championship first-round 2-1 defeat to Turkey—in rain-soaked conditions and despite the ball sticking in the mud—but he declined to celebrate. Hakan ended his international career with 20 goals from 87 appearances.

SEF ESTEEM

Switzerland not only got its 2014 FIFA World Cup campaign off to a dramatic and victorious start, a 2-1 triumph over Ecuador in Brasilia, it did so thanks to a goal scored, three minutes into stoppage-time, by substitute striker Haris Seferovic. This new record for the latest winning goal recorded in the group stages of a FIFA World Cup lasted all of seven days: Portugal equalized in the fifth minute of added time against the United States.

SHAQIRI SHAQIRI

Twenty-two-year-old **Xerdan Shaqiri** scored the 50th hat-trick in FIFA World Cup finals history during Switzerland's 3-0 triumph over Honduras in Manaus, in the first round of the 2014 tournament. The Bayern Munich playmaker was the second Swiss player to register a FIFA World Cup treble, the previous one being Josef Hugi in its 7-5 defeat to Austria in the 1954 quarterfinal. Hugi remains the last Swiss goalscorer in the knock-out stages of a FIFA World Cup. Since 1954, it has lost 3-0 to Spain in 1994, on penalties following a round-of-16 scoreless tie with Ukraine in 2006, and 1-0 extra-time defeat against Argentina in 2014.

"MERCI KOBI"

Former Swiss international player and coach, **Jakob "Kobi" Kuhn**, was left close to tears as his players unfurled a "thank you" banner at the end of his final game in charge of the Swiss manager team—a 2-0 defeat of Portugal in its last group game at UEFA Euro 2008. How times had changed for Kuhn, the much-loved elder statesmen of the Swiss game. As a 22-year-old, he was sent home from the 1966 FIFA World Cup for missing a curfew. He was then banned from the national side for a year. The shoe had been on the other foot when Kuhn sent Alexander Frei home from UEFA Euro 2004 after the center-forward spat at England's Steven Gerrard. Kuhn spent most of his playing career, where he was described as playing "with honey in his boots," with FC Zurich, winning six league titles and five Swiss Cups. He played 63 times for the national team, scoring five goals. He then worked his way up through the coaching ranks of the Swiss national team, leading first the Under-18s, then the Under-21s and finally the senior national team. He retired, aged 64, with a record of 32 victories, 18 ties, and 23 defeats in 73 games as Swiss coach.

TOP CAPS

1	Heinz Hermann	117
2	Alain Geiger	112
3	Stephane Chapuisat	103
4	Johann Vogel	94
5	Hakan Yakin	87
6	Alexander Frei	84
7	Patrick Muller	81
8	Severino Minelli	80
9	Andy Egli	79
=	Ciriaco Sforza	79

THE ORIGINAL BOLT

Karl Rappan did so much for Swiss soccer, including founding its first national fan club, that it is often forgotten he was Austrian. After a moderately successful career as a player and coach in Austria, Rappan achieved lasting fame as an innovative coach in Switzerland, leading the national team in the 1938 and 1954 FIFA World Cups, as well as securing league titles and cups in charge of Grasshopper Club, FC Servette, and FC Zurich. He developed a flexible tactical system, one that allowed players to switch positions, depending on the situation, and putting greater pressure on their opponents. This revolutionary new idea became known as the "Swiss bolt" and helped the unfancied host defeat Italy on its way to the quarterfinal of the 1954 FIFA World Cup, before losing out to Rappan's home country, Austria. An early advocate of a European league, Rappan eventually settled for the simpler knockout tournament, the Intertoto Cup, which he helped devise and launch in 1961. Rappan was, until Kobi Kuhn, Switzerland's longest-serving and statistically most successful coach, with 29 wins in 77 games in charge.

TURKEY

Galatasaray's penalty shoot-out success over Arsenal in the 2000 UEFA Cup final signaled a change in fortune for Turkish soccer. Prior to that night in Copenhagen, Turkey had qualified for the FIFA World Cup only twice (in 1950, when it withdrew, and 1954), and had consistently underachieved on the world stage. Since 2000, however, Turkish fans have had plenty to cheer about, including a third-place finish at the 2002 FIFA World Cup in Japan and South Korea, and a semifinal appearance at the 2008 UEFA European Championship.

SPOREL SPORTS

Zeki Riza Sporel scored Turkey's first goal in international soccer, against Romania on October 26, 1923. He actually hit a double that day, in a 2-2 tie, the first of 16 games for Turkey in which he hit 15 goals. Turkey's captain for their first international was his older brother Hasan Kamil Sporel.

OLD GOLD

The last FIFA World Cup "golden goal" was scored by Turkey substitute **Ilhan Mansiz**, in the 94th minute of its 2002 quarterfinal against Senegal, giving his team a 1-0 win on its way to finishing third overall. The "golden goal" rule was abandoned ahead of the 2006 FIFA World Cup, which went back to two guaranteed 15-minute periods of extra-time if a knockout fixture ended level after 90 minutes.

QUICK OFF THE MARK

Hakan Sukur scored the fastest-ever FIFA World Cup finals goal, taking only 11 seconds to score Turkey's first goal in its third-place play-off game against South Korea at the 2002 FIFA World Cup. Turkey went on to win the game 3-2 to claim third place, its best-ever performance in the competition. Sukur's total of 51 goals, in 112 appearances, is more than double his nearest competitor in the national team ranking. His first goal came in only his second game, as Turkey beat Denmark 2-1 on April 8, 1992. He went on to score four goals in a game twice: a 6-4 defeat of Wales on August 20, 1997; and in a 5-0 crushing of Moldova on October 11, 2006.

GUESS WHO'S BACK?

Rustu Recber doesn't know the meaning of the word "quit." Less than a year after retiring from international soccer after UEFA Euro 2008, Turkey's most-capped player came out of retirement to join the national team once more in the qualifying campaign for the 2010 FIFA World Cup in South Africa. This was not his first international comeback: for UEFA Euro 2008, Rustu had been relegated to the bench, but played in the quarterfinal against Croatia after first-choice keeper Volkan Demirel was sent off in the final group game. Rustu was the hero of the penalty shoot-out, saving from Mladen Petric to send Turkey through to its first-ever UEFA European Championship semifinal, though it lost to Germany. Back in 1993, Rustu came back from an even more devastating set-back after he was seriously injured in a car crash that resulted in the death of a friend. The accident also scuppered a potential move to Besiktas, although he went on to star for Fenerbahce, winning five Turkish league titles in 12 years with it. With his distinctive pony-tail and charcoal-black war paint, Rustu has always stood out, but perhaps never more so than as a star performer in Turkey's third-place performance at the 2002 FIFA World Cup finals. He was elected into the Team of the Tournament and was named FIFA's Goalkeeper of the Year.

TWIN TURKS

Hamit Altintop (right) was born 10 minutes before identical twin brother **Halil** (left), and he has been just about leading the way throughout their parallel professional soccer careers since their birth in the city of Gelsenkirchen, Germany, on December 8, 1982. Both began playing for German amateur side Wattenscheid, before defender–midfielder Hamit signed for FC Schalke 04 in the summer of 2006 and striker Halil followed suit shortly afterward. Hamit would stay just one season at Schalke, though, before being bought by Bayern Munich. Thw twins helped Turkey reach the semifinal of the 2008 UEFA European Championship—losing to Germany—but only Hamit was voted among UEFA's 23 best players of the tournament.

TAKE FAT

Having coached Galatasaray to its UEFA Cup triumph in 2000, **Fatih Terim** led Turkey in its amazing run to the 2008 UEFA European Championship semifinal. Defeat to Portugal in the opening game left the Turks with an uphill task, but stunning consecutive comebacks, against Switzerland and the Czech Republic, took it into the quarterfinal. A 119th-minute goal seemed to have settled the quarterfinal in Croatia's favor, but, as its players celebrated, "Emperor" Fatih urged his players to get up, pick the ball out of the net and fight on to the very end. They did just that, and Semih Senturk's improbable equalizer took the game to a penalty shoot-out. The semifinal against Germany provided yet another rollercoaster ride, but this time there was no answer to the Germans' last-minute winner. When Fatih said "there is something special about this team," few could disagree. Terim followed this up with a third spell as Galatasaray coach, before returning to international duty in August 2013 for a third stint in charge of Turkey. He won eight games, and lost one, before stepping aside to become national team director. His record as Turkey coach showed 101 games, 51 wins, 26 ties, and 24 defeats.

TOP SCORERS

1	Hakan Sukur	51
2	Tuncay Sanli	22
3	Lefter Kucukandonyadis	21
4	Nihat Kahveci	19
=	Metin Oktay	19
=	Cemil Turan	19
7	Zeki Riza Sporel	15
8	Arda Turan	14
9	Burak Yilmaz	13
10	Arif Erdem	11
=	Ertugrul Saglam	11

TOP CAPS

1	Rustu Recber	120
2	Hakan Sukur	112
3	Bulent Korkmaz	102
4	Tugay Kerimoglu	94
5	Emre Belozoglu	91
6	Alpay Ozalan	90
7	Hamit Altintop	80
=	Tuncay Sanli	80
9	Ogun Temizkanoglu	76
10	Arda Turan	72

500 MILESTONE

Turkey played its 500th game in international soccer on November 14, 2012, an exhibition that ended in a 1-1 tie with Denmark. The game, played at Istanbul's Turk Telekom Arena, was preceded by pop star Hadise's performance, and appearances by Turkish soccer legends. Turkey's first international game was also a tie in Istanbul: 2-2 with Romania on October 26, 1923.

WORK HARD, PLAY ARDA

Wing wizard **Arda Turan** has survived cardiac arrhythmia, swine flu, and a car crash to emerge as one of Turkish soccer's leading lights. His international achievements include key goals at the 2008 UEFA European Championship, the first a stoppage-time winner against Switzerland, then Turkey's late opener when overturning a two-goal deficit against the Czech Republic in a first-round qualification decider. After leaving boyhood club Galatasaray for Spain's Atletico Madrid in 2011, he has helped the club to glory in the UEFA Europa League and UEFA Super Cup in 2013, and La Liga in 2014, as well as the 2013–14 UEFA Champions League final, though he missed that game through injury. He mixes in prestigious circles—guests at his June 2013 wedding to TV presenter Sinem Kobal included the Turkish prime minister, Recep Tayyip Erdogan.

UKRAINE

Ukraine has been a stronghold of soccer in eastern Europe for many years. A steady flow of talent from Ukraine clubs with a rich European pedigree, such as Dynamo Kiev, provided the Soviet Union team with many standout players before independence. Since separating from the Soviet Union in 1991, Ukraine has become a soccer force in its own right. It qualified for the FIFA World Cup for the first time in 2006, and reached the quarterfinal in Germany.

DEVASTATING DEVIC

Ukraine enjoyed its biggest win on September 6, 2013 thrashing San Marino 9-0 in a FIFA World Cup qualifier, and rubbed salt into the wounds by winning 8-0 away to the same team the following month, on October 25, 2013. There were eight different scorers in the first game, with the opening goal coming from striker Marko Devic, who then went on to register a hat-trick in San Marino. Devic was actually born in Belgrade, and was brought up in Serbia, but joining Ukrainian club Volyn Lutsk in 2005, and switching nationalities three years later.

ROCKET MAN

Andriy Shevchenko beat team-mate **Anatoliy Tymoshchuk** to become the first Ukrainian player to reach a century of international appearances, but the defensive midfielder later overtook the striker to become the country's most-capped player with 132 caps. He also enjoyed the rare honor of seeing his name in space, when Ukrainian cosmonaut Yuri Malenchenko launched into orbit wearing a Zenit St Petersburg shirt with "Tymoshchuk" on the back in 2007. After leaving Zenit in 2009 for Bayern Munich, he won the 2013 UEFA Champions League with the German club before deciding to return to his former St Petersburg club.

YURI-KA MOMENT

Denys Harmash and Dmytro Korkishko scored the goals against England that gave Ukraine its first major international soccer title, in the final of the 2009 UEFA Under-19 European Championship. The coach was Yuri Kalitvintsev, later assistant to Oleg Blokhin with the senior international team.

HARD START

With the newly independent Ukraine unable to register with FIFA in time for the qualifying rounds for the 1994 FIFA World Cup, many of its stars opted to play for Russia, and went to the finals in the United States representing that country. Andrei Kanchelskis, Viktor Onopko, Sergei Yuran, and Oleg Salenko could all have played for the new Ukraine side, but decided not to. Ukraine then failed to qualify for an international tournament until the **2006 FIFA World Cup** in Germany, where it lost 3-0 in the quarterfinal to eventual winner Italy.

SUPER SHEVA

In 2004, **Andriy Shevchenko** became the third Ukrainian to win the Ballon D'Or. The first to do so, in 1975, was his 2006 FIFA World Cup coach Oleg Blokhin (second was Igor Belanov in 1986), but he was the first to win the award since Ukraine's independence from the Soviet Union. Born on September 29, 1976, Shevchenko was a promising boxer as a youngster, before deciding to focus on soccer full-time. He has won trophies at every club he's played for, including five titles in a row with Dynamo Kiev, the Serie A and the Champions League with AC Milan, and even two cups in his "disappointing" time at Chelsea. Shevchenko is Ukraine's second most-capped player and leading goalscorer, with 48 goals in 111 games. This includes two at the 2006 FIFA World Cup, where he captained his country in its first-ever major finals appearance, and a double to secure a 2-1 comeback win over Sweden in Ukraine's first game as co-host of the 2012 UEFA European Championship.

LEADING FROM THE FRONT

Oleg Blokhin, Ukraine's coach on its first appearance at a major tournament finals, made his name as a star striker with his hometown club Dynamo Kiev. Born on November 5, 1952, when Ukraine was part of the Soviet Union, Blokhin scored a record 211 goals in another record 432 appearances in the USSR national league. He also holds the goals and caps records for the USSR, with 42 in 112 games. He led Kiev to two victory in the European Cup-Winners' Cup in 1975 and 1986, scoring in both finals, and was named the 1975 European Footballer of the Year. Always an over-achiever, Blokhin coached Ukraine to the finals of the 2006 FIFA World Cup in Germany, where it lost out to eventual winner Italy 3-0 in the quarterfinal, after winning a penalty shoot-out against Switzerland in the round-of-16. Blokhin was renowned for his speed: when Olympic gold medalist Valeriy Borzov trained the Kiev squad in the 1970s, Blokhin recorded a 100 meters time of 11 seconds, just 0.46 seconds slower than Borzov's own 1972 medal-winning run. Blokhin resigned as Ukraine coach in December 2007, but returned to the job in April 2011. Ukraine's coach, since December 2012, has been former USSR international defender Mykhaylo Fomenko, whose 24 caps for the Soviet Union included reaching the final of the 1972 UEFA European Championship and winning a bronze medal at the Montreal 1976 Olympic Games.

REBROV REBORN

Serhiy Rebrov, who retired in 2009, was Andriy Shevchenko's dynamic strike partner for both club and country. The forward pair starred for Dynamo Kiev in the late 1990s before making big-money moves across Europe. Like Shevchenko at Chelsea, Rebrov struggled in London, first at Tottenham Hotspur, and then West Ham United. But after returning to Ukraine in 2005, he earned a recall to the national team—scoring with a memorable long-range strike against Saudi Arabia at the 2006 FIFA World Cup. He then crossed the border and—now playing in midfield—helped outsiders Rubin Kazan win its first Russian league title in 2008. But Rebrov, a keen amateur radio "ham", remains the Ukrainian Premier League's all-time leading scorer, with 125 goals in 268 games.

TOP SCORERS

1	Andriy Shevchenko	48
2	Serhiy Rebrov	15
=	Andriy Yarmolenko	15
4	Oleh Husyev	13
5	Serhiy Nazarenko	12
6	Andriy Husin	9
=	Yevhen Seleznyov	9
=	Andriy Vorobey	9
9	Tymerlan Huseynov	8
=	Yevhen Konoplyanka	8
=	Artem Milevskiy	8
=	Andriy Voronin	8

PY IN THE SKY

Goalkeeper **Andriy Pyatov** set a national record by going 752 minutes without conceding a goal for his country, between March 2013 and November 2013. The previous best had been Oleksandr Shovkovskiy's 728 minutes. Pyatov's resistance was finally ended by Mamadou Sakho's opener in a 3-0 play-off defeat that took France instead of Ukraine to the 2014 FIFA World Cup.

TOP CAPS

1	Anatoliy Tymoshchuk	132
2	Andriy Shevchenko	111
3	Oleksandr Shovkovskiy	92
4	Oleh Husyev	91
5	Serhiy Rebrov	75
6	Ruslan Rotan	74
=	Andriy Voronin	74
7	Andriy Husin	71
=	Andriy Vorobey	68
10	Andriy Nesmachniy	67

WALES

In a land where rugby union remains the national obsession, Wales has struggled to impose itself on the world of international soccer. Despite having produced a number of hugely talented players, Wales has only ever qualified for the finals of one major tournament: the 1958 FIFA World Cup finals in Sweden. It went on to reach the quarterfinal, only to lose to eventual winner Brazil.

GOOD ON RAMSEY

Arsenal midfielder **Aaron Ramsey** became Wales's youngest captain when appointed to the role in March 2011 by new manager Gary Speed. Ramsey was 20 years and 90 days old when he led the side out for the first time at Cardiff's Millennium Stadium in a 2012 UEFA European Championship qualifier that ended in a 2-0 win for England. The record had previously been held by center-back Mike England, who was 22 years and 135 days old when skipper against Northern Ireland in April 1964. Ramsey had not long returned to full fitness after a potentially career-threatening broken leg suffered while playing for Arsenal against Stoke City in February 2010.

WHERE'S OUR GOLDEN BOY?

One of the most skillful and successful players never to appear at the FIFA World Cup, **Ryan Giggs** somehow missed 18 consecutive exhibition games for Wales. He made his Manchester United debut in 1990, and appeared in his 1,000th competitive game in a 2-1 UEFA Champions League defeat to Real Madrid. His tally by then included 932 club games, 64 for Wales and four for Great Britain at the London 2012 Olympic Games. Giggs finally retired, aged 40 at the end of the 2013–14 season, the last four games of which he had spent as Manchester United's caretaker-boss following the dismissal of David Moyes. He made the announcement as the club revealed he would now be assistant to new coach Louis Van Gaal.

BRICKS TO BRILLIANCE

Goalkeeper **Neville Southall** made the first of his record 92 appearances for Wales in a 3-2 win over Northern Ireland on May 27, 1982. The former hod-carrier and bin man kept 34 clean sheets in 15 years playing for Wales and won the English Football Writers' Player of the Year in 1985 thanks to his performances alongside Welsh captain Kevin Ratcliffe at Everton. In his final match for Wales, on August 20, 1997, he was substituted halfway through a 6-4 defeat against Turkey in Istanbul.

RUSH FOR GOAL

Ian Rush is Wales's leading goalscorer, with 28 goals in 73 games. His first came in a 3-0 win over Northern Ireland on May 27, 1982; he scored the 28th and final goal in a 2-1 win over Estonia in Tallinn in 1994.

CAUGHT ON CAMERA

Pioneer movie-makers Sagar Mitchell and James Kenyon captured Wales v Ireland in March 1906, making it the first filmed international soccer game.

TOP CAPS

1	Neville Southall	92
2	Gary Speed	85
3	Craig Bellamy	78
4	Dean Saunders	75
5	Peter Nicholas	73
=	Ian Rush	73
7	Mark Hughes	72
=	Joey Jones	72
9	Ivor Allchurch	68
10	Brian Flynn	66

TOP SCORERS

1	Ian Rush	28
2	Ivor Allchurch	23
=	Trevor Ford	23
4	Dean Saunders	22
5	Craig Bellamy	19
6	Robert Earnshaw	16
=	Mark Hughes	16
=	Cliff Jones	16
9	John Charles	15
10	John Hartson	14

KEEPING UP WITH THE JONESES

Cliff Jones, left-winger for Wales at the 1958 FIFA World Cup and for Tottenham Hotspur's league and cup "Double" winners in 1961, was part of a Welsh soccer dynasty. His father Ivor Jones had previously played for Wales, as did Ivor's brother Bryn. Cliff's cousin Ken, a goalkeeper, was another member of the 1958 FIFA World Cup squad, but never actually played for his country.

ALL HAIL BALE

Wales' long wait to return to a major international tournament continues, but it can now boast one of the world's authentic soccer superstars, and the most expensive player of all-time. Blessed with dramatic bursts of acceleration and piledriving long-range shooting, wing wizard **Gareth Bale** cost Real Madrid $140 million to buy from England's Tottenham Hotspur in August 2013. Yet even that extravagant sum looked like money well-spent when he scored the crucial extra-time goal that put Real Madrid ahead in the 2014 UEFA Champions League final against rivals Atletico Madrid. Real went on to win the game in Lisbon 4-1. Bale had previously scored a stunning solo winner in that season's Spanish Cup final against Barcelona. He began his career at Southampton as a left-back, then blossomed as a dynamic left-winger at Spurs before flourishing as an all-round forward. He was named English football's player of the year in 2011 and 2013, chosen by both the Premier League's players and the nation's soccer writers, thanks to dazzling performances and goals for both Spurs and Wales. Despite being eligible to play for England through one grandmother, the Cardiff-born patriot became Wales' youngest international when making his debut against Trinidad and Tobago in May 2006, aged 16 years and 315 days.

HAT-TRICK HERO

Welsh striker Robert Earnshaw holds the remarkable record of having scored hat-tricks in all four divisions of English soccer, the FA Cup, the League Cup, as well as scoring three for the national team against Scotland on February 18, 2004.

SHOCK LOSS OF A MODEL PROFESSIONAL

Welsh and world soccer were united in shock and grief at the sudden death of Wales manager **Gary Speed** in November 2011. Former Leeds United, Everton, Newcastle United, and Bolton Wanderers midfielder Speed, the country's most-capped outfield player, was found at his home in Cheshire, England. The 42-year-old had been manager for 11 months, overseeing a series of encouraging performances that saw a rise in the world rankings from 116th to 48th and a prize for FIFA's "Best Movers" of 2011. An official memorial game was played in Cardiff in February 2012 between Wales and Costa Rica, the country against which he had made his international debut in May 1990. Among the tributes paid to Speed was one from FIFA president Sepp Blatter, who called him "a model professional and a fantastic ambassador for the game." Former Wales center-back Chris Coleman was appointed as Speed's successor.

OTHER TEAMS EUROPE

For the major European soccer powers, a qualifying campaign for one of the sport's major international tournaments would not be the same without an awkward trip to one of the former Eastern Bloc countries or the chance of a goal-fest against the likes of San Marino or Luxembourg. For these countries' players, the thrill of representing their nation is more important than harboring dreams of world domination.

SELVA SERVICE

San Marino, with a population of fewer than 30,000, is the smallest country to be a member of UEFA. Striker **Andy Selva** is San Marino's top scorer with eight goals and, for a long time, he was the country's only player to score twice. That was until midfielder Manuel Marani followed up his February 2007 goal against the Republic of Ireland with another, against Malta, in August 2012.

MOSQUITO STINGS

Malta ended a 20-year wait for an away win in a competitive international when it shocked Armenia 1-0 in a 2014 FIFA World Cup qualifier in June 2013. Appropriately enough, the decisive strike came from veteran forward **Michael Mifsud**—his country's captain and all-time leading scorer, who made his international debut in February 2000 and made his name in Germany with Kaiserslautern, and in England with Coventry City. Nicknamed "Mosquito," the 5ft 5in-tall player's international exploits include five goals in a 7-1 trouncing of Liechtenstein in March 2008, including a hat-trick within the first 21 minutes. Before Armenia, the last time Malta won a FIFA World Cup or UEFA European Championship away qualifier had been a 1-0 success in Estonia in May 1993.

UNDERDOGS HAVE THEIR DAY

Slovenia was the only unseeded team to win a UEFA qualifying play-off for the 2010 FIFA World Cup, beating Russia. It lost 2-1 in Moscow, but Nejc Pecnik did tally late in the first leg. Thus, when Ztlatko Dedic scored the only goal in Maribor, it gave Slovenia victory on away goals, the aggregate score being 2-2. With a population of two million and 429 registered professional players, Slovenia was the smallest nation in the finals.

LIT'S A KNOCK-OUT

Perhaps it's not be too surprising that **Jari Litmanen** should have become a soccer star. Both his parents played for the Lahti-based club Reipas, while Litmanen's father, Olavi, also won five caps for the national team. But Jari's skills and achievements far outstripped them both—and, arguably, any other player in Finnish history. It was fitting that Litmanen became the first Finnish player to get his hands on the UEFA European Cup—or Champions League trophy—when his Ajax Amsterdam side beat AC Milan in 1995. Litmanen had left Finland at the age of 21 to make his name and did so at the legendary Dutch club Ajax. He inherited the great Dennis Bergkamp's support-striker role—and his number 10 shirt. Litmanen scored in the 1996 UEFA Champions League final, though Ajax lost on penalties to Juventus. He remains the Dutch club's record scorer in European competition, with 24 goals in 44 games. Litmanen joined Barcelona in 1999, and then Liverpool, two years later, though his time in England was hampered by a wrist injury suffered on international duty, and he returned to Ajax in 2002. Despite a series of injuries, he remained dedicated to his country, captaining the team between 1996 and 2008, and was still playing and scoring for Finland in 2010 at the age of 39. In all, Litmanen notched up more international goals and games than any other Finn, scoring 32 times in 137 appearances.

GIVING IT UP

Lithuania and Estonia did not bother playing their final group game against each other in the 1934 FIFA World Cup qualifying competition. Sweden had already guaranteed itself top spot, and the sole finals place available, by beating Lithuania 2-0 and Estonia 6-2.

BEYOND THE IRON CURTAIN

The break-up of the Soviet Union in 1990 led to 15 new soccer nations, though initially Russia played on at the 1992 UEFA European Championship as CIS, or the Commonwealth of Independent States—but without players from Estonia, Latvia, or Lithuania. Over the next few years, UEFA and FIFA approved the creation of separate teams for Russia, Armenia, Azerbaijan, Belarus, Estonia, Georgia, Kazakhstan, Kyrgyzstan, Latvia, Lithuania, Moldova, Tajikstan, Turkmenistan, Ukraine, and Uzbekistan. Upheavals in the early 1990s also fragmented the former Yugoslavia into Croatia, Serbia, Bosnia-Herzegovina, Macedonia, Slovenia, and Montenegro, while Czechoslovakia split into Slovakia and the Czech Republic.

YEAR AFFILIATED TO FIFA

Albania	1932
Andorra	1996
Austria	1905
Belarus	1992
Bosnia-Herzegovina	1996
Cyprus	1948
Estonia	1923
Faroe Islands	1988
Finland	1908
Georgia	1992
Greece	1927
Iceland	1947
Israel	1929
Kazakhstan	1994
Latvia	1922
Liechtenstein	1974
Luxembourg	1910
Macedonia	1994
Malta	1959
Moldova	1994
Montenegro	2007
San Marino	1988
Slovenia	1992

REBORN BOURG

A long and painful wait finally ended for traditional whipping-boys Luxembourg when it beat Northern Ireland 3-2 in September 2013. It was the "Red Lions'" first home win in a FIFA World Cup qualifier for 41 years, since overcoming Turkey 2-0 in October 1972. It was also five years to the day since its last FIFA World Cup qualifying victory, a 2-1 win in Switzerland in 2008. Luxembourg's goals came from Aurelien Joachim, Stefano Bensi, and **Mathias Janisch**. The winning goal, with three minutes remaining, was the first of Janisch's international career.

THE FULL MONTY AND THE FULL MONTY

Estonia may have lost its June 2012 exhibition against France 4-0, despite the presence of all-time top scorer **Andres Oper**, but it did make history that night, becoming the first country to play all 52 fellow UEFA nations. The 52nd addition to the UEFA family was Montenegro, which became a FIFA member in 2007, a year after competing as part of Serbia and Montenegro in the 2006 FIFA World Cup. Both Estonia and Montenegro came close to a major tournament in their own rights by reaching the play-offs for the 2012 UEFA European Championship, but lost over two legs to the Republic of Ireland and the Czech Republic, respectively. In 2013 Gibraltar became UEFA's 54th member.

TRAVELLING MEN

Israel looked like qualifying for the 1958 FIFA World Cup without kicking a ball, because scheduled opponents Turkey, Indonesia, and Sudan, all refused to play it. But FIFA ordered it into a two-legged play-off against a European side, which Israel lost 4-0 on aggregate to Wales. Israel was unfortunate, again, in the 2006 FIFA World Cup qualifiers. It completed its qualifying group unbeaten—but failed even to make the play-offs, as it finishing third in its group behind France and Switzerland. Coach Avram Grant later went on to be in charge at Chelsea, where he lost the 2008 UEFA Champions League final on penalties to Manchester United. Israel hosted, and won, the 1964 Asian Nations Cup, and qualified for the 1970 FIFA World Cup through a combined Asia/Oceania qualifying competition, but is now a member of the European confederation.

HIT AND SWISS

When defender Elsad Zverotic made his 44th appearance, he passed Simon Vukcevic to become Montenegro's most-capped international. He was born in Behane, in what is now Serbia, but played for Switzerland U-18s, where he had also played his club soccer from 2004. Zverotic moved to English Premier League Fulham in 2013.

AD ENOUGH

Temuri Ketsbaia scored 16 times for Georgia, more than anyone, other than 26-goal Shota Arveladze, and was also the first coach to lead a Cypriot side—Anorthosis Famagusta—into the UEFA Champions League, before taking over as Georgia's national coach in 2009. Yet to many fans, those in England especially, he might be best remembered for his bizarre celebration after scoring a last-minute winner for Newcastle United against Bolton Wanderers in January 1998. Instead of looking pleased, he flung off his shirt, and furiously kicked out at pitchside advertizing boards. After receiving the ball when the game kicked off again, he instantly booted it high into the crowd.

MORE SIND AGAINST

Austria's star player **Matthias Sindelar** refused to play for a new, merged national team when Germany annexed Austria in 1938. Sindelar, born in modern-day Czech Republic in February 1903, was the inspirational leader of Austria's so-called Wunderteam of the 1930s. He scored 27 goals in 43 games for Austria, which went 14 internationals unbeaten between April 1931 and December 1932, won the 1932 Central European International Cup, and the silver medal at the 1936 Olympic Games. During a special reunification match between the Austrian and German teams in Vienna in April 1938, Sindelar disobeyed orders and scored a spectacular solo goal. Austria went on to win 2-0 in a game which might have been expected to end in a diplomatic tie. Sindelar was mysteriously found dead from carbon monoxide poisoning in his Vienna apartment in January 1939.

YURA STAR

Armenia equaled its biggest ever win with a 4-0 triumph away to Denmark in FIFA World Cup qualifying in June 2013. **Yura Movsisyan** opened the scoring after only 24 seconds, later added another goal, and was applauded off even by the home fans when substituted with seven minutes remaining. The Spartak Moscow forward used to play club soccer in Denmark, for Randers. He began his career in the United States, having moved there as a child with his Armenian family after being born in the capital of Azerbaijan, Baku. Armenia's unexpected and emphatic victory over the Danes came just four days after an embarrassing 1-0 defeat to Malta, only its opponents' fifth ever victory in competitive games.

THE GUD SON

Iceland striker **Eidur Gudjohnsen** made history on his international debut, away to Estonia in April 1996, by coming on as a substitute for his own father, Arnor Gudjohnsen. Eidur was 17 at the time, his father 34—though both were disappointed they did not get to be on the field at the same time. The Icelandic Football Association thought they would get a chance to do so in Iceland's next home game, but Eidur was ruled out by an ankle injury and the opportunity never arose again.

REIM AND REASONING

Before being overtaken by Latvia's Vitalijs Astafjevs, the European record for most international appearances was held by another Baltic veteran: Estonian holding midfielder Martin Reim scored 14 goals in 157 games for his country between June 1992 and June 2009. Yet he could even have closed in on an unprecedented double-century of international appearances, had he not missed 40 games following a dispute with Latvia's Dutch coach Jelle Goes between 2004 and 2007. He retired from international soccer after matching the 150-cap record of Germany's Lothar Matthaus in February 2007, but was persuaded to return by new national boss Viggo Jensen. His 157th and final game, a testimonial played in his honor, came against Equatorial Guinea on June 6, 2009, a day that was also said to mark the centenary of soccer in Estonia.

VITAL VITALIJS

Midfielder Vitalijs Astafjevs put Latvia on the map when he became the most-capped European soccer player of all time, with 167 appearances for his country—including three at the 2004 UEFA European Championship. He also scored 16 goals for Latvia. Astafjevs made his international debut in 1992, the year the Latvian soccer team was revived after independence following the break-up of the Soviet Union. He was still playing for his country at the age of 38 in November 2009, when his appearance in an exhibition game against Honduras saw him to overtake Estonian Martin Reim's record for most European caps.

MOST INTERNATIONAL APPEARANCES

Albania	Altin Lala	79
Andorra	Oscar Sonejee	97
Austria	Andreas Herzog	103
Belarus	Alyaksandr Kulchy	102
Bosnia-Herz.	Zvejzdan Misimovic	83
Cyprus	Ioannis Okkas	106
Estonia	Martin Reim	157
Faroe Islands	Oli Johannesen	83
Finland	Jari Litmanen	137
Georgia	Levan Kobiashvili	100
Iceland	Runar Kristinsson	104
Israel	Yossi Benayoun	96
Kazakhstan	Ruslan Baltiev	73
Latvia	Vitalijs Astafjevs	167
Liechtenstein	Mario Frick	113
	Martin Stocklasa	113
Lithuania	Andrius Skerla	84
Luxembourg	Jeff Strasser	98
Macedonia	Goce Sedloski	100
Malta	David Carabott	121
Moldova	Radu Rabeja	74
Montenegro	Elsad Zverotic	47
San Marino	Damiano Vannucci	68
Slovenia	Zlatko Zahovic	80

ED BOY

Edin Dzeko became Bosnia-Herzegovina's all-time leading scorer with a second-half hat-trick in an 8-1 2014 FIFA World Cup qualifier victory over Liechtenstein in September 2012. The goals not only took him past previous record-holder Elvir Bolic, but also ahead of team-mate Zvejdan Misimovic, whose double, earlier in the game, had briefly put him in the lead. Midfielder Misimovic drew level with Dzeko again in the following game, scoring twice in a 4-1 win, before Dzeko's last-minute strike restored his advantage. Dzeko's feat is not bad for a forward sold by Bosnian club Zeljeznicar to the Czech Republic's FK Teplice for a cut-price $35,000 in 2005—and six years before English club Manchester City handed over $40 million to sign him from Germany's VfL Wolfsburg. Dzeko's off-field activities include a role as a UNICEF ambassador, and he donated almost $35,000 in 2012 towards the care of a 17-year-old Bosnian boy fighting bone marrow disease.

SUPER PAN

Macedonia celebrated 100 years of soccer in the country with an exhibition game against world champion Spain in August 2009. Star striker **Goran Pandev** marked the occasion by becoming his country's all-time leading scorer. His first-half double gave the hosts a 2-0 lead and although Spain came back to win 3-2, he replaced 16-goal Gorgi Hristov at the top of Macedonia's scoring charts. Pandev has played the majority of his club career in Italy, after signing for Internazionale from local team FK Belasica as an 18-year-old in 2001. Pandev helped Inter win a treble of the UEFA Champions League, Serie A, and the Coppa Italia in 2009–10, before scoring in its 2010 FIFA Club World Cup victory. Now with Napoli, he also played for Ancona and Lazio.

LAT'S ENTERTAINMENT

The 1938 FIFA World Cup went ahead with 15 instead of 16 teams after qualifier Austria found itself annexed by Germany. It was a big frustration for Latvia, which had finished as runner-up in the Austrians' qualification group. Latvia was subsumed by the Soviet Union between 1940 and 1991, but qualified for its first major finals by beating Turkey in a play-off to reach the 2004 UEFA European Championship. Its squad at the finals featured all-time leading scorer Maris Verpakovskis—still playing for Latvia in 2013—and its most-capped player Vitalijs Astafjevs.

BASKET CASE

Captain **Rashad Sadygov** not only secured Azerbaijan's most notable win in its history when he scored the only goal against Turkey in a UEFA Euro 2012 qualifier in October 2010. He also delivered a blow against the country in which he was making his living. Having previously played for Turkish top-flight side Kayserispor, he had since moved on to rivals Eskisehirspor. Not every transfer has worked out well for Sadygov: he missed the transfer deadline when signing for Azeri side PFC Neftchi in 2006, so he decided to play basketball for a season to keep himself fit until allowed to resume soccer.

MOST INTERNATIONAL GOALS

Albania	Erjon Bogdani	18
Andorra	Ildefons Lima	7
Austria	Toni Polster	44
Belarus	Maksim Romashenko	20
Bosnia-Herz.	Edin Dzeko	36
Cyprus	Michalis Konstantinou	32
Estonia	Andres Oper	38
Faroe Islands	Rogvi Jacobsen	10
Finland	Jari Litmanen	32
Georgia	Shota Arveladze	26
Iceland	Eidur Gudjohnsen	24
Israel	Mordechai Spiegler	33
Kazakhstan	Ruslan Baltiev	13
Latvia	Maris Verpakovskis	29
Liechtenstein	Mario Frick	16
Lithuania	Tomas Danilevicius	19
Luxembourg	Leon Mart	16
Macedonia	Goran Pandev	26
Malta	Michael Mifsud	39
Moldova	Serghei Clescenco	11
Montenegro	Mirko Vucinic	15
San Marino	Andy Selva	8
Slovenia	Zlatko Zahovic	35

TU-WHIT TWO-NIL

Finland's adopted lucky mascot is an eagle owl called "Bubi." He occasionally swoops down on the Helsinki Olympic Stadium during international games, having made his "debut" during a 2-0 UEFA European Championship qualifying group win over Belgium in June 2007. Bubi held up the game for several minutes as he flew about the over and perched on goalposts. The eagle owl was later voted the Finnish capital's "Resident of the Year."

HIGH LIFE

At 64°09'N, Reykjavik, in Iceland, is the northernmost city to host a FIFA World Cup match—though so far only in qualifiers. The northernmost FIFA World Cup finals venue is Sandviken in Sweden, at 60°37'N. Christchurch in New Zealand (43°32'S) holds the record for southernmost FIFA World Cup venue, with the finals record held by Mar del Plata in Argentina (38°01'S). Iceland's 9,800-seater national stadium, the Laugardalsvollur, was opened in 1958 and then renovated 39 years later.

BOHEMIAN RHAPSODY

Striker **Josef "Pepi" Bican** is, for many Austrian fans, the most prolific goalscorer of all time. Some authorities put his total tally in officially recognized games at 805 goals, higher in the rankings than Romario, Pele and Gerd Muller. Bican played for Austrian clubs Rapid Vienna and Admira in the 1930s, but the bulk of his goals came for Czech-based Slavia Prague between 1937 and 1948. He also scored 19 goals in 19 games for Austria from 1933 to 1936, before switching citizenship and netting 21 in 14 matches for Czechoslovakia between 1938 and 1949. Although he reached the semifinal of the 1934 FIFA World Cup with Austria, an administrative error meant he was not registered with his new country in time for the 1938 tournament. He also played one international game for a representative Bohemia and Moravia side in 1939, scoring a hat-trick.

LIVING HAND TO FOOT

The part-time international soccer players of the Faroe Islands have a motley collection of day jobs, and other sporting achievements. Bobble hat-wearing goalkeeper **Jens Martin Knudsen,** man of the match in its shock 1-0 win over Austria in 1989, made his living as a forklift truck driver—while also winning a national gymnastics title and playing handball. Team-mates who have also played both soccer and handball include journalist/musician Uni Arge, the Faroes' fourth-top-scorer, and third-placed John Petersen.

POWER GAME

Albert Gudmundsson was Iceland's first professional soccer player. He enjoyed a distinguished career in the 1940s and 1950s, including spells with Rangers in Scotland, Arsenal in England, and AC Milan in Italy. After retiring from soccer, he entered politics and ran, unsuccessfully, for president in 1980 before being appointed minister for finance in 1983, and minister for industry two years later. His son Ingi Bjorn Albertsson played as a striker for Iceland in the 1970s then joined his father as a member of parliament in 1987.

A SEQUEL TO HAMLET

Striker Hamlet Mkhitaryan played twice for post-Soviet state Armenia in 1994, though he died two years later from a brain tumour at the age of just 33. His son Henrikh, aged seven when his father died, has gone on to become the country's all-time leading scorer, and he who often dedicates his achievements to his late parent. The younger Mkhitaryan became Armenia's joint top scorer, alongside Artur Petrosyan, with a goal against Denmark in June 2013. While Petrosyan's goals came in 69 games, Mkhitaryan's 11 were scored in 39. He pulled away on his own, with a 12th international strike, in a 2-2 tie with Italy in October 2012. **Henrikh Mkhitaryan** made his Armenia debut in 2007, and his international career overlapped with an unrelated player also named Hamlet Mkhitaryan—a midfielder who won 56 caps between 1994 and 2008.

RECORD WINS

Albania	5-0	v Vietnam (A, December 2003);
	6-1	v Cyprus (H, August 2009)
Andorra	2-0	v Belarus (H, April 2000);
	2-0	v Albania (H, April 2002)
Austria	9-0	v Malta (H, April 1977)
Belarus	5-0	v Lithuania (H, June 1998)
Bosnia-Herzegovina	7-0	v Estonia (H, September 2008)
Cyprus	5-0	v Andorra (H, November 2000)
Estonia	6-0	v Lithuana (H, July 1928)
Faroe Islands	3-0	v San Marino (H, May 1995)
	4-1	v Gibraltar (A, March 2014)
Finland	10-2	v Estonia (H, August 1922)
Georgia	7-0	v Armenia (H, March 1997)
Iceland	9-0	v Faroe Islands (H, July 1985)
Israel	9-0	v Chinese Taipei (A, March 1988)
Kazakhstan	7-0	v Pakistan (H, June 1997)
Latvia	8-1	v Estonia (A, August 1942)
Liechtenstein	4-0	v Luxembourg (A, October 2004)
Luxembourg	6-0	v Afghanistan (A, July 1948)
Macedonia	11-1	v Liechtenstein (A, November 1996)
Malta	7-1	v Liechtenstein (H, March 2008)
Moldova	5-0	v Pakistan (A, August 1992)
Montenegro	6-0	v San Marino (A, September 2012)
San Marino	1-0	v Liechtenstein (H, April 2004)
Slovenia	7-0	v Oman (A, February 1999)

RECORD DEFEATS

Albania	0-12	v Hungary (A, September 1950)
Andorra	1-8	v Czech Republic (A, June 2005);
	0-7	v Croatia (A, October 2006)
Austria	1-11	v England (H, June 1908)
Belarus	0-5	v Austria (A, June 2003)
Bosnia-Herzegovina	0-5	v Argentina (A, May 1998)
Cyprus	0-12	v West Germany (A, May 1969)
Estonia	2-10	v Finland (A, August 1922)
Faroe Islands	0-7	v Yugoslavia (A, May 1991);
	0-7	v Romania (A, May 1992);
	0-7	v Norway (H, August 1993);
	1-8	v Yugoslavia (H, October 1996)
Finland	0-13	v Germany (A, September 1940)
Georgia	0-5	v Romania (A, April 1996);
	1-6	v Denmark (A, September 2005)
Iceland	2-14	v Denmark (A, August 1967)
Israel*	1-7	v Egypt (A, March 1934)
Kazakhstan	0-6	v Turkey (H, June 2006);
	0-6	v Russia (A, May 2008)
Latvia	0-12	v Sweden (A, May 1927)
Liechtenstein	1-11	v Macedonia (H, November 1996)
Luxembourg	0-9	v England (H, October 1960);
	0-9	v England (A, December 1982)
Macedonia	0-5	v Belgium (H, June 1995)
Malta	1-12	v Spain (A, December 1983)
Moldova	0-6	v Sweden (A, June 2001)
Montenegro	0-4	v Romania (A, May 2008)
	0-4	v Ukraine (H, June 2013)
San Marino	0-13	v Germany (H, September 2006)
Slovenia	0-5	v France (A, October 2002)

* Played under the British Mandate of Palestine.

KULCHY COUP

Midfielder **Alyaksandr Kulchy** became the first player to win 100 caps for Belarus, skippering the team against Lithuania in a June 2012 exhibition. He also ended ex-Arsenal and Barcelona playmaker Alexander Hleb's run of four successive Belarus player of the year awards by claiming the prize in 2009. Hleb, whose younger brother Vyacheslav has also played for Belarus, had previously won the accolade in both 2002 and 2003. The all-time leading goalscorer for Belarus, Maksim Romashenko, won it in 2004.

NO-SCORE ANDORRA

Since playing its first international on New Year's Day 1996, a 6-1 home defeat against Estonia, Andorra has won only three games, two of them exhibitions. Its only competitive triumph was a 1-0 success over Macedonia in an October 2004 FIFA World Cup qualifying game, when left-back Marc Bernaus struck the only goal. Perhaps its lack of strength should come as no surprise, because the principality is the sixth-smallest country in Europe, with a population of only 71,822. It has played its most high-profile games, against England, across the Spanish border in Barcelona.

CAUGHT SHORT

If Montenegro are scoring, then fans can "put their shirt" on captain and all-time leading scorer **Mirko Vucinic** being among the goals. He celebrated scoring the winner against Switzerland in a UEFA Euro 2012 qualifier by removing not his top, but his shorts—and wearing them on his head, antics that earned him a yellow card. Vucinic had previously celebrated a goal for his Italian club side by taking off both his shorts and his shirt, revealing another AS Roma shirt underneath.

MASSIMO BETTER BLUES

Massimo Bonini was unable to inspire a win or even a tie as San Marino coach between 1996 and 1998. But his own playing career was far more effective, including seven years, 192 games and three Serie A league titles at Italian giants Juventus during the 1980s. Bonini played all 90 minutes of Juventus's 1-0 victory over Liverpool in the 1985 UEFA European Cup final, making him the only San Marino player to lift the trophy, or even feature at such a high-blown soccer occasion.

SARG'S 20-YEAR SERVICE

Armenia's first international was a scoreless tie at home to Moldova on October 14, 1992. In its starting line-up that day was center-back Sargis Hovsepyan, who went on to win a record 132 caps for the country before his international retirement in November 2012. He was then appointed the Armenian national team's soccer director.

SOUTH AMERICA

Brazil hosted a spectacularly vivid and exciting FIFA World Cup in 2014, returning there for the first time since 1950. Appropriately one of the continent's giants reached the final, albeit arch-enemy and neighbor Argentina. Brazil has won the trophy five times and Argentina twice, as has Uruguay, the inaugural FIFA World Cup host and winner. Argentina and Uruguay may bid to co-host the centenary tournament in 2030. A special centenary Copa America is due in 2016, with central and north American teams joining in, and the US will host it.

Brazil's high hopes for a sixth FIFA World Cup were not fulfilled in 2014 but it was not for any lack of passion, fervor, and support from its home fans.

ARGENTINA

Copa America champions on 14 occasions, FIFA Confederations Cup winners in 1992, Olympic gold medallists in 2004 and 2008 and, most treasured of all, FIFA World Cup winners in 1978 and 1986: few countries have won as many international titles as Argentina. The country has a long and rich soccer history (the first Argentine league was contested in 1891) and it has produced some of the greatest ever to have played the game.

LONGEST–SERVING MANAGERS

Guillermo Stabile	1939–60
Cesar Luis Menotti	1974–83
Carlos Bilardo	1983–90
Alfio Basile	1990–94
	2006–08
Marcelo Bielsa	1998–2004
Jose Maria Minella	1964–68
Daniel Passarella	1994–98
Manuel Seoane	1934–37
Juan Jose Pizzuti	1969–72
Alejandro Sabella	2011–14

HAPPY AND SAB

Argentina's 2014 FIFA World Cup squad received a rapturous welcome home from thousands of fans and national president Cristina Fernandez de Kirchner after its final loss to Germany. There had already been mass celebrations and relief across Argentina at qualifying for its first FIFA World Cup final since 1990. The 2014 coach was **Alejandro "Alex" Sabella**, who succeeded Sergio Batista in 2011. Sabella, who stepped down after the tournament, led the first Argentina side to win all of its first five games at a FIFA World Cup, before relying on the penalty saves of goalkeeper Sergio Romero in the semifinal. Sabella's two predecessors, Batista and Diego Maradona, were both FIFA World Cup winners as Argentina players in 1986—two years after midfielder Sabella won the last of his eight caps.

FRINGE PLAYERS

Daniel Passarella was a demanding captain when he led his country to glory at the 1978 FIFA World Cup. He was the same as coach. After taking over the national side in 1994, he refused to pick anyone unless they had their hair cut short—and ordered striker Claudio Caniggia to get rid of his "girl's hair."

GONZALO'S HIGHS AND LOWS

Striker Gonzalo Higuain ended the longest scoring drought of his international career—528 minutes and six games—when he netted the only goal with an opportunist's strike against Belgium in the 2014 FIFA World Cup quarterfinal. Higuain was born in Brest, France, where his ex-soccer player father Jorge Higuain was playing, but left the country aged ten months. Higuain holds dual French-Argentina nationality, but took up Argentine citizenship in 2007. His goal against Belgium was his only one of the 2014 FIFA World Cup but he thought he had given Argentina the lead in the final against Germany, only for it to be ruled out for offside.

WORTH WAITING FOR

Argentina's national stadium, "El Monumental" in Buenos Aires, hosted its first game in 1938. But the original design was not completed until 20 years later—largely thanks to the £97,000 River Plate received for a transfer fee from Juventus for **Omar Sivori**. The stadium is a must-see stop on the itinerary of many global soccer tourists for the "Superclasico" derby between hosts River Plate and cross-city rivals Boca Juniors.

NUMBERS GAME

Argentina's FIFA World Cup squads of 1978 and 1982 were given numbers based on alphabetical order rather than positions, which meant the No. 1 shirt was worn by midfielders Norberto Alonso in 1978 and Osvaldo Ardiles in 1982. The only member of the 1982 squad whose shirt number broke the alphabetical order was No. 10, Diego Maradona.

DO YOU COME HERE OFTEN?

Argentina and Uruguay have played each other more often than any other two nations, beginning with Argentina's 3-2 victory in Uruguay's capital Montevideo in 1901, the first international staged outside the United Kingdom. The two teams have clashed another 179 times in official international games since then, with Argentina winning 82 times in all, Uruguay 54, and 44 ending as ties.

A ROUND DOZEN

Argentina were responsible for the biggest win in Copa America history, when five goals by Jose Manuel Moreno helped it thrash Ecuador 12-0 in 1942. The much-traveled Moreno won domestic league titles in Argentina, Mexico, Chile and Colombia.

CHINA IN YOUR HAND

In an unusual move, the two 2008 Olympics soccer finalists Argentina and Nigeria were allowed to take two drinks breaks during the gam, which was watched by 89,102 spectators. The game was played in stifling heat in Chinese host city Beijing. Angel Di Maria scored the only goal for Argentina, allowing it to retain the title it won in Athens—for the first time—four years earlier.

THE KIDS ARE ALL RIGHT

Sergio Aguero struck in the final, and ended the tournament as six-goal top scorer, when Argentina won the FIFA World U-20 Championship for a record sixth time in 2007, in Canada, beating the Czech Republic 2-1. Two years later, Aguero married Giannina Maradona, the youngest daughter of Argentina legend Diego, and in February 2009 she gave birth to Diego's first grandchild, Benjamin. Sergio Aguero is widely known by his nickname of "Kun," after a cartoon character he was said to resemble as a child.

BEGINNER'S LUCK

Aged just 27 years and 267 days old, Juan Jose Tramutola became the FIFA World Cup's youngest-ever coach when Argentina opened its 1930 campaign by beating France 1-0. Argentina went on to reach the final, only to lose 4-2 to Uruguay. Top-scorer at the 1930 FIFA World Cup was Argentina's Guillermo Stabile, with eight goals in four games, the only internationals he played. He later won six Copa America titles as his country's longest-serving coach between 1939 and 1960.

TARNISHED GOLD

Despite winning Olympics soccer gold in 2004 and 2008—with **Javier Mascherano** becoming the first male soccer player since 1928 to collect two Olympic golds—Argentina surprisingly failed to qualify for the 2012 tournament in London. South America's two places went instead to Brazil and Uruguay, based on performances at the 2011 South American Youth Championship staged in Peru. Argentina had finished third in the final group of six.

MAJOR TOURNAMENTS

FIFA WORLD CUP Winners (2)	16 appearances – 1978, 1986
COPA AMERICA Winners (14)	39 appearances – 1921, 1925, 1927, 1929, 1937, 1941, 1945, 1946, 1947, 1955, 1957, 1959, 1991, 1993
CONFEDERATIONS CUP Winners (1)	Three appearances – 1992
FIRST INTERNATIONAL	Uruguay 2 Argentina 3 (Montevideo, Uruguay, May 16, 1901)
BIGGEST WIN	Argentina 12 Ecuador 0 (Montevideo, Uruguay, January 22, 1942)
BIGGEST DEFEATS	Czechoslovakia 6 Argentina 1 (Helsingborg, Sweden, June 15, 1958); Argentina 0, Colombia 5 (Buenos Aires, September 5, 1993) Bolivia 6 Argentina 1 (La Paz, Bolivia, April 1, 2009)

YELLOW GOODBYE

Some 20 years before France were forced to wear local Argentine club Atletico Kimberly's kit at the 1978 FIFA World Cup, Argentina itself faced similar embarrassment for its first-round game against West Germany. The Argentines had neglected to bring along a second kit and a color-clash with its opponent meant borrowing the yellow shirts of Swedish side IFK Malmo. Despite taking a third-minute lead, Argentina lost 3-1 and went out of the tournament, at the bottom of Group A.

PEOPLE'S FAVORITE

Lionel Messi may be acclaimed as the finest soccer player in the world, and one of the best of all-time, yet back home in Argentina the real hero for many fans is three-time South American Footballer of the Year **Carlos Tevez**. When Argentina staged the 2011 Copa America, team line-up announcements in stadia described Messi as "the best in the world" but Tevez as "the player of the people." Tevez grew up in poverty in Buenos Aires' tough "Fuerte Apache" neighborhood and still bears scars on his neck from when boiling water was spilled on him as a child. Yet he ended the 2011 Copa America as a villain—his missed penalty gave Uruguay shoot-out victory in the quarterfinal. Tevez failed even to make Argentina's squad for the 2014 FIFA World Cup, despite having scored 21 club goals the preceding season and been named Juventus's player of the year as it won its third consecutive Italian league title.

SPOT-KICK FLOP

If at first you don't succeed, try and try again. Unfortunately Martin Palermo missed all three penalties he took during Argentina's 1999 Copa America clash with Colombia. The first hit the crossbar, the second flew over the bar and the third was saved. Colombia won the gam 3-0.

WINNING TOUCH

Midfielder Marcelo Trobbiani played just two minutes of FIFA World Cup soccer, the last two minutes of the 1986 final, after replacing winning goalscorer Jorge Burruchaga. Trobbiani touched the ball once, a backheel. The former Boca star ended his international career with 15 caps and one goal to his name.

TOP SCORERS

1	Gabriel Batistuta	56
2	Lionel Messi	42
3	Hernan Crespo	35
4	Diego Maradona	34
5	Luis Artime	24
6	Gonzalo Higuain	22
=	Leopoldo Luque	22
=	Daniel Passarella	22
9	Sergio Aguero	21
=	Herminio Masantonio	21
=	Jose Sanfilippo	21

SECOND TIME LUCKY

Luisito Monti is the only man to play in the the FIFA World Cup final for two different countries. The center-half, born in Buenos Aires on May 15, 1901, but with Italian family origins, was highly influential in Argentina's run to the 1930 final. It lost the game 4-2 to Uruguay—after Monti allegedly received mysterious pre-game death threats. Following a transfer to Juventus the following year, he was allowed to play for Italy and was on the winning side when the *Azzurri* beat Czechoslovakia in the 1934 final. Another member of the 1934 team was Raimundo Orsi, who had also played for Argentina before switching countries in 1929.

DIVINE DIEGO

To many people **Diego Armando Maradona** is the greatest soccer player the world has ever seen, better even than Pele. The Argentine legend, born in Lanus on October 30, 1960, first became famous as a ball-juggling child during half-time intervals at Argentinos Juniors games. He was distraught to be left out of Argentina's 1978 FIFA World Cup squad and was then sent off for retaliation at the 1982 tournament. Maradona, as triumphant Argentina captain in Mexico in 1986, scored the notorious "Hand of God" goal and then a spectacular individual strike within five minutes of each other in a quarterfinal win over England. He again captained Argentina to the final in 1990, in Italy, the country where he inspired Napoli to Serie A and UEFA Cup success. He was thrown out of the 1994 FIFA World Cup finals in disgrace after failing a drugs test. Maradona captained Argentina 16 times in FIFA World Cup games, a record, and was surprisingly appointed national coach in 2008, despite scant previous experience in that role

FITTER, JAVIER

Javier Zanetti is Argentina's most-capped player, with 145 international appearances, despite being surprisingly left out of squads for both the 2006 and 2010 FIFA World Cups. Zanetti, who can play at full-back or in midfield, has also played more Serie A games than any other non-Italian, and all for Internazionale of Milan, where he won the treble of Italian league, Italian Cup and UEFA Champions League in 2009–10. Despite those achievements, he and Inter team-mate Esteban Cambiasso failed to make Diego Maradona's squad for the 2010 FIFA World Cup. However, Zanetti returned to the fold under Maradona's successor, Sergio Batista, and captained Argentina at the 2011 Copa America. Zanetti made his 600th appearance in Italy's Serie A in March 2013.

THE ANGEL GABRIEL

Gabriel Batistuta, nicknamed "Batigol," and Argentina's all-time leading scorer, is the only man to have scored hat-tricks in two separate FIFA World Cups. He scored the first against Greece in 1994 and the second against Jamaica four years later. Hungary's Sandor Kocsis, France's Just Fontaine and Germany's Gerd Muller all scored two hat-tricks in the same FIFA World Cup finals. Batistuta, born in Reconquista on February 1, 1969, also set an Italian league record during his time with Fiorentina, by scoring in 11 consecutive Serie A games at the start of the 1994–95 season.

SUPER MARIO

Mario Kempes, who scored twice in the 1978 FIFA World Cup final and won the Golden Boot, was the only member of Cesar Menotti's squad who played for a non-Argentine club. Playing for Valencia, he had been the Spanish league's top scorer for the previous two seasons.

LEO BRAVO

Lionel Messi passed the international appearances total of Diego Maradona during the 2014 FIFA World Cup, having edged ahead of him in goalscoring a year earlier. But his wait to lift the FIFA World Cup, as his predecessor did, goes on, after Argentina lost the final in Rio de Janeiro 1-0 to Germany. The FIFA World Cup remains a rare accolade to have escaped Messi's grasp and he left the Maracana with the Golden Ball prize after being named tournament's best player. As coach, Maradona made Messi Argentina's youngest-ever captain, giving him the armband, two days before his 23rd birthday, during the 2010 FIFA World Cup. He was captain under both of Maradona's successors, Sergio Batista and Alejandro Sabella, as he continued to be a world superstar. He scored four times at the 2014 FIFA World Cup, including a last-minute winner in the first-round against Iran. His four Man Of The Match awards were the most in finals. But the four-time FIFA Ballon d'Or winner may have just one more shot to win the FIFA World Cup, in Russia in 2018 when he will be 31.

TOP CAPS

1	Javier Zanetti	145
2	Roberto Ayala	115
3	Diego Simeone	106
4	Javier Mascherano	105
5	Oscar Ruggeri	97
6	Lionel Messi	93
7	Diego Maradona	91
8	Ariel Ortega	87
9	Gabriel Batistuta	78
10	Juan Pablo Sorin	76

SAINTED PALERMO

Veteran striker Martin Palermo waited 10 years between international appearances before being called up again by his former Boca Juniors team-mate Diego Maradona in 2009. He justified the surprise recall with a stoppage-time winner in the penultimate FIFA World Cup qualifier against Peru, prompting Maradona to take a celebratory dive in rain-sodden mud on the touchline and then hail it as "the miracle of St Palermo." Palermo also became his country's oldest-ever FIFA World Cup scorer, at the 2010 finals in South Africa. He was 36 years and 227 days old when he came on as a substitute in the first round against Greece and completed the scoring in a 2-0 victory—a year and 358 days older than Maradona had been when scoring against the same country 16 years earlier.

BRAZIL

No country has captured the soul of the game to the same extent as Brazil. The country's distinctive yellow-shirted players have thrilled generations of soccer fans and produced some of the game's greatest moments. No FIFA World Cup tournament would be the same without Brazil, the nation that gave birth to Pele, Garrincha, Zico, Ronaldo and Kaka. The only nation to appear in every FIFA World Cup finals and competition winners a record five times, Brazil's widely-admired hosting of the 2014 tournament did not end with the sixth triumph it craved.

FIERCEST RIVALS

Brazil's oldest club classic is Fluminense versus Botafogo in Rio de Janeiro. The clubs faced each other for the first time on October 22, 1905, when Fluminense won 6-0. One particular game stirred a controversy that lasted 89 years. The two teams disagreed on the result of the 1907 championship, whose title was disputed up to 1996 ... when they finally decided to share it.

CLOSE ENCOUNTERS

Brazil has been involved in many memorable games. Its 3-2 defeat to Italy in 1982 is regarded as one of the classic games in FIFA World Cup finals history. Paolo Rossi scored all three of Italy's goals with Brazil coach Tele Santana much criticized for going all out in attack when only a 2-2 draw was needed. Brazil's 1982 squad, with players such as **Socrates**, Zico and **Falcao**, is considered one of the greatest teams never to win the tournament. In 1994, a 3-2 win over the Netherlands in the quarterfinal—its first competitive meeting in 20 years—was just as thrilling, with all the goals coming in the second half. Socrates, a qualified medical doctor, as well as elder brother to 1994 FIFA World Cup-winner Rai, was mourned across the globe when he died at the age of 57 in December 2011.

TAKING AIM WITH NEYMAR

Brazil's triumph in the 2013 FIFA Confederations Cup, a record third in a row, was consolation for its failure in 2012 to break its Olympic hoodoo when Mexico beat it in the London Games final. This remains the only FIFA-approved prize to elude Brazil but it will be the hosts at Rio de Janeiro in 2016. **Neymar** was nine-goal top scorer at London 2012, voted South American Footballer of the Year for the second successive year and then, in 2013, was named player of the FIFA Confederations Cup. Those were his last games as a Santos player before he joined Spanish giants Barcelona. He was Brazil's undoubted star man at the 2014 FIFA World Cup, with four goals in four games before suffering a tournament-ending broken bone in his back during the quarterfinal win against Colombia.

BRAZIL'S RECORD

FIFA WORLD CUP	20 appearances (every finals)
Games (104)	W70, D17, L17, GF221, GA102
Winners (5)	1958, 1962, 1970, 1994, 2002
Runners-up (2)	1950, 1998
Third place (2)	1938, 1978
Fourth place (1)	1974, 2014
COPA AMERICA	33 appearances
Winners (8)	1919, 1922, 1949, 1989,
	1997, 1999, 2004, 2007
CONFEDERATIONS CUP	Seven appearances
Winners (4)	1997, 2005, 2009, 2013
FIRST INTERNATIONAL	Argentina 3 Brazil 0
	(Buenos Aires, September 20, 1914)
BIGGEST WIN	Brazil 10 Bolivia 1 (Sao Paulo,
	April 10, 1949)
HEAVIEST DEFEAT	Uruguay 6 Brazil 0 (Vina del
	Mar Chile, September 18, 1920)
	Brazil 1, Germany 7
	(Belo Horizonte, July 8, 2014)

LAND OF SOCCER

No country is more deeply identified with soccer success than Brazil, which has won the FIFA World Cup a record five times: in 1958, 1962, 1970, 1994, and 2002. It is also the only team never to have missed a FIFA World Cup finals and is a favorite virtually every time the competition is staged. After winning the trophy for a third time in Mexico in 1970, Brazil kept the **Jules Rimet Trophy** permanently. Sadly, it was stolen from the federation's headquarters in 1983, and was never recovered. Brazilians often refer to its country as "o país do futebol" ("the country of soccer"). It is the favorite pastime of youngsters, while general elections are often held in the same year as the FIFA World Cup, with critics arguing that political parties try to take advantage of the nationalistic surge created by soccer and bring it into politics. Charles Miller, the son of a Scottish engineer, is credited with bringing soccer to Brazil in 1894. Yet the sport would only truly become Brazilian when blacks were able to play at the top level in 1933. At first, because of the game's European origin, it was the sport of Brazil's urban white elite. However, it quickly spread among the urban poor as Brazilians realized the only thing it needed to play was a ball, which could be substituted inexpensively with a bundle of socks, an orange, or even a cloth filled with paper.

CAPTAIN TO COACH

Brazil's 1994 FIFA World Cup-winning captain **Dunga** was appointed national coach in 2006 despite having no previous management experience. He led the team to 2007 Copa America and 2009 FIFA Confederations Cup success. But he lost his job after Brazil were knocked out of the 2010 FIFA World Cup in a 2-1 quarterfinal defeat to the Netherlands. Dunga, real name Carlos Caetano Bledorn Verri, but widely known by the Portuguese for "Dopey," had already faced criticism back home for his team's defensive style and decisions not to take Ronaldinho, Adriano or Alexandre Pato to South Africa.

TOP OF THE FLOPS

Brazil's dreams of winning a sixth FIFA World Cup, but first on home soil, became a nightmare in 2014, 64 years on from the trauma caused by Uruguay's surprise triumph at Rio de Janeiro's Maracana stadium. Luiz Felipe Scolari's 2014 vintage set a series of unenviable records as it crashed out, 7-1 to Germany, in the semifinal in Belo Horizonte. This was not only Brazil's heaviest FIFA World Cup defeat, but also the biggest any semifinalist had ever suffered. It equaled the 6-0 trouncing by Uruguay at the 1920 Copa America as Brazil's worst defeat of all-time. Finally, it was Brazil's first home loss in a competitive international since Peru beat it 3-1—also in Belo Horizonte—in a 1975 Copa America semifinal. A 3-0 setback against the Netherlands in the third-place play-off meant Brazil lost consecutive internationals at home for the first time since 1940, when Argentina, 3-0, and Uruguay 4-3, were victorious. The 14 goals Brazil conceded was its worst ever in a FIFA World Cup, three worse than in 1938, and it became the first FIFA World Cup hosts to concede the most goals in a tournament.

EYE FOR GOAL

Center-forward **Tostao**, full name Eduardo Goncalves de Andrade, was one of the stars of Brazil's legendary 1970 FIFA World Cup-winning team but almost did not make the tournament. He had suffered a detached retina when hit in the face by a soccer ball the previous year, prompting some doctors' warnings that he should be left out. Tostao eventually retired at the age of 26 in 1973, after another eye injury, and went to work as a doctor instead. His 1970 team-mate Pele also experienced failing eyesight.

JOY OF THE PEOPLE

Garrincha, one of Brazil's greatest legends, was really Manuel Francisco dos Santos at birth but his nickname meant "Little Bird," inspired by his slender, bent legs. Despite the legacy of childhood illness, he was a star right-winger at Botafogo from 1953 to 1965. He and Pele were explosively decisive newcomers for Brazil at the 1958 FIFA World Cup finals. In 1962 Garrincha was voted player of the tournament four years later. He died in January 1983 at just 49. His epitaph was the title often bestowed on him in life: "The Joy of the People."

TOP CAPS

1	Cafu	142
2	Roberto Carlos	125
3	Lucio	105
4	Claudio Taffarel	101
5	Djalma Santos	98
=	Ronaldo	98
=	Ronaldinho	98
7	Gilmar	94
9	Gilberto Silva	93
10	Pele	92
=	Rivelino	92

TOP SCORERS

1	Pele	77
2	Ronaldo	62
3	Romario	55
4	Zico	48
5	Bebeto	39
6	Neymar	35
7	Rivaldo	34
8	Jairzinho	33
=	Ronaldinho	33
10	Ademir	32
=	Tostao	32

THE KING

Pele is considered by many as the greatest player of all time, a sporting icon *par excellence* and not only for his exploits on the pitch. When, for instance, he scored his 1,000th goal, Pele dedicated it to the poor children of Brazil. He began playing for Santos at the age of 15 and won his first FIFA World Cup two years later, scoring twice in the final. Despite numerous offers from European clubs, the economic conditions and Brazilian soccer regulations at the time allowed Santos to keep hold of its prized asset for almost two decades, until 1974. All-time leading scorer of the Brazilian national team, he is the only player to be a member of three FIFA World Cup-winning teams. Despite being in the Brazilian squad at the start of the 1962 tournament, an injury suffered in the second game meant he was not able to play on and, initially, he missed out on a winner's medal. However, FIFA announced in November 2007 that he would be awarded a medal retrospectively. After the disastrous 1966 tournament, when Brazil fell in the first round, Pele said he did not wish to play in the FIFA World Cup again. He was finally talked round and ended up, in 1970, playing a key role in what is widely considered as one of the greatest sides ever. Since his retirement in 1977, Pele has been a worldwide ambassador for soccer, as well as undertaking various acting roles and commercial ventures.

PARTY ANIMAL

Brazil's captain when it played Argentina (twice), Costa Rica and Mexico in autumn 2011 was a man many had not even expected to be in the international team again: former two-time FIFA World Footballer of the Year, Ronaldinho. Having amazed the world with his fancy footwork and prolific goalscoring for Paris Saint-Germain in France, Barcelona in Spain and AC Milan in Italy, he returned to his homeland with Flamengo in 2011, but was widely accused of being more interested in partying than playing. But a return to form won him a recall under Mano Menezes. Ronaldinho's goal against Mexico took him to 33, level with 1970 FIFA World Cup winner Jairzinho. When he played in his next game—his 94th for Brazil—he equaled the caps tally of 1958 and 1962 FIFA World Cup champion goalkeeper Gilmar. Ronaldinho himself was a FIFA World Cup winner in 2002, aged 22. In the quarterfinal, his long-range goal against England gave Brazil victory. However, he was sent off a few minutes later, so was suspended for the semifinal, but was able to return for the final.

WHITHER RONALDO?

Only one person knows exactly what happened to **Ronaldo** in the hours before the 1998 FIFA World Cup final: the man himself. He sparked one of the biggest mysteries in FIFA World Cup history when his name was left off the teamsheet before the game, only for it to reappear just in time for kick-off. It was initially reported that Ronaldo had an ankle injury, and then a upset stomach. Finally team doctor Lidio Toledo revealed the striker had been rushed to hospital after suffering a convulsion in his sleep, but that he had been cleared to play after neurological and cardiac tests. The most dramatic account came from Ronaldo's roommate Roberto Carlos. "Ronaldo was scared about what lay ahead. The pressure had got to him and he couldn't stop crying," said the legendary full-back. "At about four o'clock, he became ill. That's when I called the team doctor and told him to get over to our room as fast as he could."

HOME COMFORTS

The host of the FIFA World Cup has never lost its first game of that tournament, and Brazil continued that run by beating Croatia 3-1 in what was also the opening game of the 2014 FIFA World Cup. It was Brazil's ninth consecutive victory in its finals opener. Neymar scored twice against Croatia, making him the first Brazil player to grab a double in his FIFA World Cup debut.

THAT'S MY BOY

When Bebeto scored for Brazil against the Netherlands in its 1994 FIFA World Cup quarterfinal, he and strike partner Romario celebrated with a "cradling the baby" dance that would be much-imitated for years to come. Bebeto's wife had just given birth to its son Matheus, who would grow up to become a soccer player himself, joining Flamengo's youth set-up in 2011. By this time, both **Bebeto** (middle) and **Romario** (right, Mazinho is left) were in tandem again—as elected politicians in Brazil.

INAUSPICIOUS START

Left-back/left-winger **Marcelo** achieved the dubious "honour" of being the first player to score the opening goal of a FIFA World Cup finals in his own net. He inadvertently gave Croatia the lead in the 2014 tournament's curtain-raiser in Sao Paulo, but Brazil did come back to win 3-1, thanks to a pair of goals from Neymar and one from Oscar. Marcelo, who a couple of weeks earlier had scored for his club, Real Madrid, as it won the UEFA Champions League final, also became the first Brazil player ever to score an own goal in the FIFA World Cup finals.

BRAZIL'S YOUNGEST PLAYERS

1 Pele, 16 years and 257 days
   (v Argentina, July 7, 1958)
2 Ronaldo, 17 years and 182 days
   (v Argentina, March 24, 1994)
3 Adriano, 17 years and 272 days
   (v Australia, November 17, 1999)
4 Toninho, 17 years and 343 days
   (v Uruguay, April 28, 1976)
5 Carvalho Leite, 18 years and 26 days
   (v Bolivia, July 22, 1930)
6 Diego, 18 years and 60 days
   (v Mexico, April 30, 2003)
7 Marcelo, 18 years and 115 days
   (v Wales, September 5, 2006)
8 Philippe Coutinho, 18 years and 116 days
   (v Iran, October 7, 2010)
9 Doria, 18 years and 149 days
   (v Bolivia, April 6, 2013)
10 Neymar, 18 years and 186 days
   (v USA, August 10, 2010)

ROLLING RIVA

Brazilian legend **Rivaldo** was still playing in his fifth decade, ten years after the highlight of his career, helping Brazil to win the 2002 FIFA World Cup. He scored 34 goals in 74 games for his country between 1993 and 2003, including three goals at the 1998 FIFA World Cup and five more in Japan and South Korea four years later. His 2002 FIFA World Cup was marred only by blatant play–acting that helped get Turkey's Hakan Unsal sent off and earned Rivaldo a fine. Rivaldo, full name Rivaldo Vitor Borba Ferreira, became one of the world's finest soccer players despite suffering malnourishment in a poverty-stricken childhood. His individual achievements including FIFA World Footballer of the Year and European Footballer of the Year prizes in 1999 while playing for Spanish giants Barcelona. His later clubs included AC Milan in Italy, Olympiacos and AEK Athens in Greece, Bunyodkor in Uzbekistan, Kabuscorp in Angola and, in 2013, at the age of 40, Brazilian second division side Sao Caetano.

WORLD–BEATING SAINTS

Right-back **Djalma Santos** is one of only two players to be voted into the official all-star team of a FIFA World Cup on three different occasions. He was honoured for his performances at the 1954, 1958 and 1958 finals, even though his only appearance in 1958 was in the final. West Germany's Franz Beckenbauer was the other, chosen in 1966, 1970 and 1974. On the opposite flank to Djalma Santos was the left-back Nilton Santos—no relation— who also played in 1954, 1958 and 1962 and had also been a member of Brazil's runners-up squad on home turf in 1950.

ON THE SLIDE?

As 2014 FIFA World Cup hosts, Brazil qualified automatically and so saw little competitive action after the 2012 Copa America. This explained its plunge out of the FIFA World Rankings top ten, to 11th, in July 2012. Brazil reached an all-time low of 22nd in June 2013, but went into the 2014 FIFA World Cup third behind Spain and Germany. It fell to seventh in the first post-tournament update.

YELLOW FEVER

The world-renowned yellow and blue kit now worn by Brazil was not adopted until 1954, as a replacement for its former all-white strip. The *Correio da Manha* newspaper organized a design competition which was won by 19-year-old Aldyr Garcia Schlee and the new colors were worn for the first time in March 1954 against Chile. Schlee was from Pelotas, close to Brazil's border with Uruguay and actually supported Uruguayan sides against Brazil.

THE OLD RIVALS: BRAZIL V ARGENTINA

Games played: 95
Brazil wins: 35
Argentina wins: 36
Draws: 24
Brazil goals: 145
Argentina goals: 151
First game: Argentina 3 Brazil 0 (September 20, 1914)
Latest game: Argentina 2 Brazil 1 (November 21, 2012)
Biggest Brazil win: Brazil 6 Argentina 2 (December 20, 1945)
Biggest Argentina win: Argentina 6 Brazil 1 (March 5, 1940)

GRAND ACHIEVEMENT

Brazil played its 1,000th game on November 14, 2012, with Neymar's second-half equalizer securing a 1-1 tie against Colombia in New Jersey, United States. Brazil's first game is considered generally to have been a 2-0 victory over visiting English club Exeter City on July 21, 1914, at the Estadio das Laranjeiras in Rio de Janeiro—a venue still used by Fluminense. Brazil won that day despite star striker **Arthur Friedenreich** losing two teeth in a collision. Brazil's first international against another country was a 3-0 defeat to Argentina on September 20, 1914.

LUIZ STREAK

Crazy-haired Brazil center-back **David Luiz** went 39 international appearances without a goal. His first goal came against Chile in the 2014 FIFA World Cup second-round, and his second came in the next game, a long-range free-kick, in the quarterfinal win over Colombia. Just before the tournament began he had left English club Chelsea for France's Paris Saint-Germain, where he would play next to his regular Brazil central defensive partner Thiago Silva. Luiz stood in as captain for the suspended Silva in the 7-1 semifinal defeat to Germany.

BRAZIL'S 2014 WORLD CUP STADIA

1 Maracana, Rio de Janeiro (76,804)
2 Brasilia, Estadio Nacional Mane Garrincha (70,064)
3 Mineirao, Belo Horizonte (62,547, Atletico Mineiro and Cruzeiro)
4 Arena Corinthians, Sao Paulo (65,807)
5 Estadio Castelao, Fortaleza (64,846)
6 Estadio Beira-Rio, Porto Alegre (48,849)
7 Arena Fonte Neva, Salvador (48,747)
8 Arena Pernambuco, Recife (46,000)
9 Arena Pantanal, Cuiaba (42,968)
10 Arena da Amazonia, Manaus (42,374)
11 Arena das Dunas, Natal (42,086)
12 Arena da Baixaba, Curitiba (41,456)

BRAZIL HAS HAD ITS PHIL

The return of "Big Phil" **Luiz Felipe Scolari** as Brazil coach in November 2012 was meant to culminate, in 2014, with a repeat of his success spearheading the country to triumph at the 2002 FIFA World Cup. Yet although his second reign did bring glory at the 2013 FIFA Confederations Cup, the following year's FIFA World Cup on home turf will be remembered for the many unwanted records his team set, and the embarrassing way its tournament ended, most notably, the 7-1 defeat by Germany in its Belo Horizonte semifinal. Scolari was relieved of his role just days after a 3-0 defeat to the Netherlands in the third-place play-off. However, the tournament gave him a second fourth-place finish, matching achievement when he was coach of Portugal in 2006, and he became the first coach to be in charge of a team in three FIFA World Cup semifinals.

LETTING LUCIO

Elegant center-back **Lucio** set a FIFA World Cup record during the 2006 tournament by playing for 386 minutes without conceding a foul, only ending in Brazil's 1-0 quarterfinal defeat to France. While mostly noted for leadership and control at the back. Lucio also had an eye for goa. He headed the late winner that gave Brazil a 3-2 triumph over the United States in the 2009 FIFA Confederations Cup final. The following year he was part of Italian club Internazionale's treble success, clinching the Italian league and cup as well as the UEFA Champions League.

SUPER-POWERS' POWER CUT

There was a new addition to the annual international calendar in 2011: the Superclasico de los Americas, a two-legged event between Brazil and Argentina. Brazil were the first winners, thanks to a goalless draw followed by a 2-0 win. It dramatically retained the crown in 2012. Brazil won the first leg at home, 2-1, but the return game in Chaco was postponed after a power cut, possibly because Brazil's team bus hit an electricity trailer. The rearranged game ended 2-1 to Argentina, but Brazil won 4-3 on penalties, its goal being scored by Fred, while strike partner Neymar netted the winning spot-kick. For Brazil's coach Mano Menezes, however, his "reward" was the sack. There was no Superclasico in 2013 and the next edition was due to be a one-off game, in the Chinese capital Beijing in October 2014.

CHILE

Chile were one of four founding members of CONMEBOL, South America's soccer confederation, in 1916. It played in the first game at a South American soccer championship, losing the opener of the unofficial 1910 tournament 3-0 to Uruguay—and it played in the first official Copa America, in 1916. Never a winner, Chile has been a runner-up on four occasions: in 1955, 1956, 1979, and 1987. Its greatest glory was hosting, and taking third place at, the 1962 FIFA World Cup.

TOP SCORERS

1	Marcelo Salas	37
2	Ivan Zamorano	34
3	Carlos Caszely	29
4	Alexis Sanchez	24
5	Leonel Sanchez	23
6	Jorge Aravena	22
7	Humberto Suazo	21
8	Juan Carlos Letelier	18
9	Enrique Hormazabal	17
10	Matias Fernandez	14

BRAVO, BEAUSEJOUR

Chile went precisely 48 years between victories at a FIFA World Cup, from a 1-0 third-place play-off success against Yugoslavia on June 16, 1962, to a first-round victory by the same scoreline over Honduras on June 16, 2010. That long-awaited winner in South Africa came from **Jean Beausejour**, who then scored Chile's third goal in its opening-game 3-1 win over Australia in Brazil four years later. It meant he became the first Chilean player ever to score at more than one FIFA World Cup. Goalkeeper and captain at both tournaments was Claudio Bravo, Chile's second-most-capped player.

CENTER-BACK'S HAT-TRICK

The first player to be named South American Footballer of the Year three times was not Pele, Garrincha or Diego Maradona but Chilean center-back **Elias Figueroa**, who took the prize in three consecutive years from 1974 to 1976 while playing for Brazilian club Internacional. The only players to emulate such a hat-trick were Brazil's Zico, in 1977, 1981 and 1982, and Argentina forward Carlos Tevez, in 2003, 2004 and 2005. Two more Chileans have won the award: Marcelo Salas in 1997 and Matias Fernandez in 2006. Outside of Brazil and Argentina, the most winners of the prize have come from Chile and Paraguay, with five apiece. Although Figueroa started and ended his playing career in Chile, he also played for clubs in Brazil, Uruguay and the US, while also representing his country for 16 years from 1966 to 1982, including FIFA World Cup appearances in 1966, 1974 and 1982.

ALEXIS IS YOUNGEST

Chile's youngest-ever international is now its most exciting star, Arsenal winger **Alexis Sanchez**. He was 17 years and four months old when he made his debut against New Zealand in April 2006, a month before he left South America to sign for Italy's Udinese. He spent loan spells back in Chile and Argentina before making his breakthrough in Serie A with eye-catching displays that earned a move to Barcelona in 2011. Sanchez is now fourth on Chile's leading goalscorers list, with 24, his tally including three in qualifying for the 2010 FIFA World Cup and two in the finals four years later, when it again reached the round-of-16. Chile won many admirers with its attacking style of play, though its tougher edge could be found in the nicknames of other stars, such as Gary "The Pitbull" Medel and Arturo "The Warrior" Vidal. Sanchez showed more tender emotions after scoring Chile's final goal, in a 4-0 exhibition victory over Estonia in June 2011. He revealed a T-shirt bearing a photo of his adoptive father Jose Delaigue, who had died days earlier.

TOP CAPS

1	Leonel Sanchez	84
3	Claudio Bravo	83
2	Nelson Tapia	73
4	Alexis Sanchez	71
5	Alberto Fouilloux	70
=	Marcelo Salas	70
7	Fabian Estay	69
=	Gonzalo Jara	69
=	Ivan Zamorano	69
10	Pablo Contreras	67

SALAS DAYS

Chile's all-time leading scorer **Marcelo Salas** formed a much-feared striking partnership with Ivan Zamorano during the late 1990s and early 21st century. Salas scored four goals as Chile reached the second round of the 1998 FIFA World Cup in France despite not winning a game. The striker spent two years in international retirement, from 2005 to 2007, but returned for the first four games of qualification for the 2010 FIFA World Cup. His scored twice in Chile's 2-2 draw with Uruguay on November 18, 2007, but his international career ended for good three days later, following a 3-0 defeat to Paraguay.

HAPPY SAMP

Chile had never reached the knock-out stages of consecutive FIFA World Cups until its 2014 vintage in Brazil gamed the 2010 squad's achievement. And both times it had coaches from Argentina: Marcelo Bielsa was in charge in 2010 and Jorge Sampaoli four years later, and another compatriot, Claudio Borghi, served a spell in between. Sampaoli retired from playing aged 19, because of tibia and fibula injuries, and devoted himself to a coaching career that took in Peru and Ecuador before he took the Chilean hotseat in 2012.

SURFACE APPEAL

Soccer helped keep up the spirits of 33 Chilean miners trapped underground for 69 days after an explosion at a mine in the Atacama desert on August 5, 2010. The men were initially given up for dead, but after news of their survival emerged, supplies sent underground included footage of Chile's 2-1 defeat to Ukraine in an exhibition on September 7. Some of the rescued miners played "keepy-uppies" with soccer balls on finally emerging into daylight at the surface and, two weeks later, played an exhibition game against their rescuers.

LUCKY LEO

Leonel Sanchez holds the Chilean record for international appearances, scoring 23 goals in 84 games. But he was lucky to remain on the pitch for one of it. Sanchez escaped an early bath despite punching Italy's Humberto Maschio in the face during its so-called "Battle of Santiago" clash at the 1962 FIFA World Cup, when English referee Ken Aston could have sent off more than just the two players he did dismiss. Sanchez, a left-winger born in Santiago on April 25, 1936, finished the tournament as one of its six four-goal leading scorers, along with Brazilians Garrincha and Vava, Russian Valentin Ivanov, Yugoslav Drazan Jerkovic and Hungarian Florian Albert.

URUGUAY

Uruguay was the first country to win a FIFA World Cup, in 1930, and with a population of under four million, it remains the smallest to do so. It claimed the game's greatest prize for a second time in 1950, having already won Olympic gold in 1924 and 1928. Recent years were less productive, until a fourth-place finish at the 2010 FIFA World Cup and a record-breaking 15th Copa America triumph the following year.

TOP SCORERS

#	Player	Goals
1	Luis Suarez	40
2	Diego Forlan	36
3	Hector Scarone	31
4	Angel Romano	28
5	Oscar Miguez	27
6	Sebastian Abreu	26
7	Pedro Petrone	24
8	Carlos Aguilera	22
=	Edinson Cavani	22
=	Fernando Morena	22

FORLAN HERO

Diego Forlan was Uruguay's star man at the 2010 FIFA World Cup, scoring five goals, including three from outside the penalty area, the first player to achieve that feat at a FIFA World Cup since Germany's Lothar Matthaus in 1990. He also hit the crossbar with a free-kick, the final touch of his country's 3-2 defeat to Germany in the 2010 third-place play-off. Uruguay's fourth-place finish in South Africa meant Diego fared better than his father Pablo, who had played in the Uruguay team that was knocked out in the first round of the 1974 FIFA World Cup.

GET IN, GODIN

Center-back **Diego Godin's** crucial late headed goal gave Uruguay a 1-0 Group D win over Italy at the 2014 FIFA World Cup and a place in the second round at Italy's expense. Godin developed an knack for crucial strikes in 2014: his goal secured a first Spanish league title in 18 years for Atletico Madrid in May 2014 and he gave it the lead in the UEFA Champions League final, only to lose ultimately 4-1 to Real Madrid.

DIFFERENT BALL GAME

Uruguay was the inaugural host, and first winner, of the FIFA World Cup in 1930, having won soccer gold medals at the Paris 1924 and Amsterdam 1928 Olympic Games. Among the players who won all three of those titles was forward Hector Scarone, who remains Uruguay's second-highest scorer with 31 goals in 52 internationals. Uruguay beat arch-rivals Argentina 4-2 in the 1930 final, in a game which used two different soccer balls: Argentina's choice in the first half, after which it led 2-1, before Uruguay's choice was used for its second-half comeback.

HAPPY ANNIVERSARY

A so-called "Mundialito," or "Little World Cup," was staged in December 1980 and January 1981 to mark the 50th anniversary of the FIFA World Cup—and, as in 1930, Uruguay emerged triumphant. The tournament was meant to involve all six countries who had previously won the tournament, though 1966 champions England turned down the invitation and was replaced by the 1978 runner-up Netherlands. Uruguay beat Brazil 2-1 in the final, a repeat of the scoreline from the two teams' final game of the 1950 FIFA World Cup. The Mundialito-winning Uruguay side was captained by goalkeeper Rodolfo Rodriguez and coached by Roque Maspoli, who had played in goal in that 1950 final.

TOP CAPS

1. Diego Forlan   112
2. Diego Lugano   95
3. Maxi Pereira   93
4. Diego Perez   89
5. Diego Godin   81
6. Luis Suarez   79
7. Rodolfo Rodriguez   78
8. Cristian Rodriguez   77
9. Fabian Carini   74
10. Enzo Francescoli   73

CAV FAITH

It took just three minutes for **Edinson Cavani** to score his first international goal, after coming on as a substitute for his Uruguay debut against Colombia in February 2008. He not only helped Uruguay finish fourth at the 2010 FIFA World Cup and win a record 15th Copa America in 2011, but his scoring exploits in club soccer for Italy's Napoli and Paris Saint-Germain in France have established him as one of the world's finest modern strikers. Cavani, a devout Christian, received high praise from the Archbishop of Naples, Crescenzio Sepe, who said: "God serves himself by having Cavani score goals." The forward was given his Uruguay debut by Oscar Tabarez, a former schoolteacher known as "The Maestro," whose second spell as international boss began in 2006. Cavani was aged just three when Tabarez led Uruguay at its most recent FIFA World Cup before 2010, reaching the second round in 1990.

BITE RETURN

Notoriety has cast many shadows over the career of **Luis Suarez** and the controversy he caused at the 2010 FIFA World Cup was mild compared to what followed in Brazil four years later. Uruguay's all-time leading scorer is one of the world's most talented strikers but is also a danger not only to others but to himself and team-mates. He earned infamy with a deliberate goal-line handball to concede a penalty when Uruguay and Ghana were level in its 2010 FIFA World Cup quarterfinal—then celebrated wildly when Asamoah Gyan missed—and Uruguay won the resulting shoot-out. Worse followed, however, at the 2014 FIFA World Cup, when he bit into the shoulder of Italian defender Giorgio Chiellini, earning himself a nine-game international ban and a four-month suspension from all soccer. Astonishingly, this was the third time Suarez had bitten someone on the soccer field—having previously done so while playing for both Ajax Amsterdam and Liverpool. His scoring instincts, are much more admirable: his 40 international goals include four during Uruguay's triumphant 2011 Copa America campaign. Suarez does inspire loyalty among supporters and team-mates, who even pegged his shirt up in the dressing-room before their 2014 second-round clash with Colombia, despite his enforced departure from Brazil the previous day.

BOYS IN BLUE

Uruguay's 3-2 home loss to Argentina, in Montevideo on May 16, 1901, was the first international game staged outside the UK. The second, on July 20, 1902, ended 6-0 to Argentina—still the *Celeste*'s heaviest loss. They have played each other another 178 times in official internationals, a world record, with Uruguay winning 53, Argentina 81, and 44 ties. Before an agreed kit-swap in 1910, Uruguay often wore vertical light-blue and white stripes and arch-rivals Argentina would don pale-blue shirts.

OLE, FRANCESCOLI

Until Diego Forlan passed him in 2011, no outfield player had represented Uruguay more often than **Enzo Francescoli** (73 caps), and few can have taken the field quite so gracefully as the playmaker whose club career included stints with River Plate in Argentina, Racing and Marseille in France and Cagliari and Torino in Italy. His international swansong for Uruguay brought Copa America glory in 1995, when he starred as both midfielder and emergency striker and also scored one of Uruguay's spot-kicks in its penalty shoot-out final victory over Brazil. Among Francescoli's high-profile fans was Zinedine Zidane, who later named his first-born son Enzo, in honour of the Uruguayan maestro.

TRAVEL SICKNESS

Despite winning the 1930 FIFA World Cup, Uruguay turned down the chance to defend its crown four years later, when the tournament was held in Italy. Uruguayan soccer authorities were unhappy that only four European countries had made the effort to travel to Uruguay and take part in 1930.

OTHER TEAMS SOUTH AMERICA

GOING CARACAS FOR SOCCER

Baseball and boxing may have held more sway with Venezuelans in recent decades but soccer fever has been on the rise in the twenty-first century, given a big boost by the country staging its first Copa America in 2007. This not only saw extravagant investment in new stadia but also Venezuela's first Copa America victory since 1967, and unprecedented progress into the knock-out stages. **Juan Arango,** a popular success in Spain with La Liga club RCD Mallorca, scored Venezuela's goal in a 4-1 quarterfinal loss to Uruguay. It followed this relative breakthrough by finishing eighth out of 10 in South America's qualification campaign for the 2010 FIFA World Cup, then sixth of nine for 2014, above Peru, Bolivia and Paraguay.

NATIONAL STADIUMS

Bolivia:
Estadio Hernando Siles,
La Paz (45,000 capacity)

Chile:
Estadio Nacional,
Santiago (63,379)

Colombia:
Estadio El Campin,
Bogota (48,600)

Ecuador:
Estadio Olimpico Atahualpa,
Quito (40,948)

Paraguay:
Estadio Defensores del Chaco,
Asuncion (36,000)

Peru:
Estadio Nacional,
Lima (45,574)

Venezuela:
Estadio Polideportivo
de Pueblo Nuevo,
San Cristobal (38,755)

BOLIVIA LEAVE IT LATE

Bolivia has only ever won the Copa America once, but did so in dramatic and memorable style when playing host in 1963. It was the only team to finish the competition unbeaten in all six games, topping the league table. But it almost threw away glory on the competition's final day, twice squandering two-goal leads against Brazil. Bolivia led 2-0 before being pegged back to 2-2, then saw a 4-2 advantage turn to 4-4, before Maximo Alcocer scored what proved to be Bolivia's winning goal with four minutes remaining.

ENNER THE OTHER VALENCIA

Ecuador striker **Enner Valencia**'s hot scoring streak in 2014 saw him find the net six times across five consecutive games, including three strikes at that summer's FIFA World Cup. His brace in the 2-1 Group E win over Honduras made him the first Ecuadorian to score more than once in a FIFA World Cup game. His fortunes were in stark contrast to those of his namesake, Ecuador captain Antonia Valencia. The Manchester United winger was sent off in its final first-round game against France, and it was his second red card in four internationals, having been dismissed in a pre-tournament exhibition against England.

YEP MAN

Two of Colombia's most-capped players are **Carlos Valderrama** (first, with 111 appearances) and Leonel Alvarez (third, with 101). Valderrama led the criticism when Alvarez was fired after just three games as national coach in 2011. But his successor, ex-Argentina boss Jose Pekerman, led Colombia to the 2014 FIFA World Cup quarterfinal, its best ever performance. Colombia defender Mario Yepes, at 38 one of the finals' oldest players, won four more caps to take him to 102. He had been worried about playing on, but right-back Camilo Zuniga said: "You have to be there— we'll do the running for you."

RE-ENTER THE MONDRAGON

Colombia goalkeeper **Faryd Mondragon** set a number of records at the 2014 FIFA World Cup. He became the oldest player to appear in the finals when he came on as a substitute with five minutes remaining of its first-round game against Japan, on June 24, aged 43 years and three days, breaking the record formerly held by Cameroon's 42-year-old Roger Milla in 1994. Mondragon also set a new mark for the longest gap between FIFA World Cup appearances, two days short of 16 years. His last game had been in Colombia's final game at the 1998 tournament, a 2-0 defeat to England. This was actually Mondragon's third FIFA World Cup finals, spanning a record 20 years, but he did not appear in the 1994 tournament.

BIGGEST WINS

Bolivia 7 Venezuela 0
(August 22, 1993)

Argentina 0 Colombia 5
(September 5, 1993)

Colombia 5 Uruguay 0
(June 6, 2004)

Colombia 5 Peru 0
(June 4, 2006)

Ecuador 6 Peru 0
(June 22, 1975)

Paraguay 7 Bolivia 0
(April 30, 1949)

Hong Kong 0 Paraguay 7
(November 17, 2010)

Peru 9 Ecuador 1
(August 11, 1938)

Venezuela 6 Puerto Rico 0
(December 26, 1946)

ABOVE-PAR PARAGUAY

In its eighth appearance at a FIFA World Cup, Paraguay topped its first-round group for the first time in 2010. Not only that, it went on to reach a later stage of the tournament than ever before, the quarterfinal, before narrowly losing 1-0 to Spain. Its penalty shoot-out victory over Japan in the second round (Oscar Cardozo converting the decisive kick) meant four South American countries made the quarterfinal, outnumbering the three European nations, for the first time. That said, there were no quarterfinals in 1930, 1950, 1974, 1978 or 1982. Paraguay followed up its impressive FIFA World Cup display by reaching the final of the following year's Copa America, only losing in the end to Uruguay (3-0).

TIM'S TIME

Peru was coached at the 1982 FIFA World Cup by Tim, who had been waiting an unprecedented 44 years to return to the FIFA World Cup finals. He played once, as a striker, for his native Brazil in the 1938 tournament.

HIGH LIFE

Bolivia and Ecuador play its home internationals at higher altitudes than any other teams on earth. Bolivia's showpiece Estadio Hernando Siles stadium, in the capital La Paz, is 3,637 metres (11,932ft) above sea level, while Ecuador's main Estadio Olimpico Atahualpa, in Quito, sits 2,800 metres (9,185ft) above sea level. Opposing teams have complained that the rarefied nature of the air makes it difficult to breathe, let alone play, but a FIFA ban on playing competitive internationals at least 2,500 metres (8,200ft) above sea level, first introduced in May 2007, was amended a month later, adjusting the limit to 3,000 metres (9,840ft) and allowing Estadio Hernando Siles to be used as a special case. The altitude ban was suspended entirely in May 2008. FIFA had changed its mind after protests by Bolivia, Ecuador and other affected nations Colombia and Peru. Other campaigners to overturn the law included Argentina legend Diego Maradona. He may have regretted his decision. In March 2009 Bolivia scored a 6-1 home win against Argentina in a FIFA World Cup qualifier. The Argentina coach was ... Maradona.

STUDYING THE FORM

Peru captain **Claudio Pizarro** is the highest-scoring foreign-born player in Germany's Bundesliga, his successful spells, two apiece, with Werder Bremen and Bayern Munich bringing him 176 goals in 370 league games, as well as a 2012–13 UEFA Champions League winners' medal with Bayern. His international career has been patchier, hampered by a fractured skull suffered against Venezuela at the 2004 Copa America and a three-month ban for joining a hotel party while on international duty in 2007. But he did score Peru's fastest international goal, after 18 seconds of its 3-1 exhibition victory over Mexico in August 2003. He has also enjoyed success off the soccer field and on the racing track, as co-owner, with English soccer player Joey Barton, of a racehorse named Crying Lightning, after a song by the rock band the Arctic Monkeys.

BIGGEST DEFEATS

Brazil 10 Bolivia 1
(April 10, 1949)

Brazil 9 Colombia 0
(March 24, 1997)

Argentina 12 Ecuador 0
(January 22, 1942)

Argentina 8 Paraguay 0
(October 20, 1926)

Brazil 7 Peru 0
(June 26, 1997)

Argentina 11 Venezuela 0
(August 10, 1975)

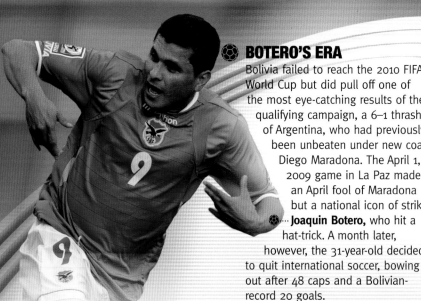

BOTERO'S ERA

Bolivia failed to reach the 2010 FIFA World Cup but did pull off one of the most eye-catching results of the qualifying campaign, a 6–1 thrashing of Argentina, who had previously been unbeaten under new coach Diego Maradona. The April 1, 2009 game in La Paz made an April fool of Maradona but a national icon of striker **Joaquin Botero,** who hit a hat-trick. A month later, however, the 31-year-old decided to quit international soccer, bowing out after 48 caps and a Bolivian-record 20 goals.

ELITE CUB

Peru forward Teofilo Cubillas became the first player to twice end a FIFA World Cup finals with at least five goals—he scored five apiece in 1970 and 1978, but did not win the Golden Boot on either occasion. Germany's Miroslav Klose emulated the achievement, scoring five times in both 2002 and 2006, as did compatriot, Thomas Muller, who scored five in 2010 and 2014. Klose and Muller, however, did win the Golden Boot, Klose in 2006 and Muller four years later.

COOL DUDAMEL

Venezuela suffered some bad defeats when missing out on the 1998 FIFA World Cup. It ended with no wins and 13 defeats in 16 games, scoring 13 and conceding 41 goals. The losses included 4–1 to Peru, 6–1 to Bolivia and 6–0 to Chile, for whom Ivan Zamorano scored five. But its goalkeeper Rafael Dudamel had a moment to savor against Argentina in October 1996, when he scored with a direct free-kick late in the game. Venezuela still lost 5–2.

HOT ROD

Colombia's second-most expensive ever player was cruelly denied a role at the 2014 FIFA World Cup. Star striker Radamel Falcao failed to recover in time from a knee injury suffered at the start of that year. This gave the chance for his AS Monaco team-mate **James Rodriguez** to emerge not only as Colombia's main man, but also one of the most dazzling players at the whole tournament. The 22-year-old playmaker scored in all five of Colombia's games, six goals in all. It included a long-range volley against Uruguay, which opposing manager Oscar Tabarez described as one of the finest the FIFA World Cup had ever seen. Rodriguez joined Monaco for €45 million from FC Porto in May 2013. There he was joined, a few weeks later, by compatriot Falcao, who cost Monaco €60 million when it signed him from Atletico Madrid. The striker—named after the 1980s Brazil midfielder Falcao—has scored 20 goals in 57 games for Colombia, behind only Arnoldo Iguaran who managed 25 in 68.

CHRISTIAN TRIBUTE

Ecuador's players dedicated its 2014 FIFA World Cup campaign to former team-mate Christian "Chucho" Benitez, who died suddenly from a cardiac arrest in July 2013 at the age of only 27. Team-mate, and Ecuador's captain at the 2014 FIFA World Cup finals, Antonio Valencia had Benitez's number 11 tattooed on his arm in tribute and the number was officially "retired" by the Ecuador FA. FIFA World Cup rules, however, meant the number had to be worn, and it was given to striker Felipe Caicedo at the 2014 finals.

MOST INTERNATIONAL CAPS

Bolivia	Luis Cristaldo	93
	Marco Sandy	93
Colombia	Carlos Valderrama	111
Ecuador	Ivan Hurtado	167
Paraguay	Paulo Da Silva	112
Peru	Roberto Palacios	128
Venezuela	Juan Arango	120

FIVE–STAR PARAGUAY

The South American Footballer of the Year award dates back to 1971 and has been dominated by players from Brazil and Argentina. However, five Paraguayan players have won the award, all since 1985, and the honors have come roughly every five years. The first was attacking midfielder Romerito (Julio Cesar Romero), the only Paraguayan named in Pele's top 125 living players in 2004, who claimed the prize in 1985. Five years later, it went to Raul Vicente Amarilla who, although Paraguayan, did not win a cap for his country (he had won two Spanish Under-21 caps when playing club soccer over there). Prolific goalscoring goalkeeper Jose Luis Chilavert won the award in 1996 and he was followed by two strikers, Jose Cardozo, in 2002, and Salvador Cabanas, in 2007.

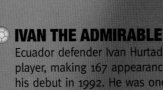

IVAN THE ADMIRABLE

Ecuador defender Ivan Hurtado is South America's most-capped player, making 167 appearances—scoring five goals—since his debut in 1992. He was one of Ecuador's most influential players at its first FIFA World Cup finals, in 2002, and was captain when it advanced to the round-of-16 four years later.

MEDELLIN MURDER

Tragic Colombian defender Andres Escobar, 27, was shot dead outside a Medellin bar ten days after scoring an own goal in a 1994 FIFA World Cup first-round game against the United States. Colombia lost the game 2-1 and were eliminated from a tournament some observers—including Pele—had tipped it to win.

MARKSMAN SPENCER

Ecuador's greatest player of all time is arguably prolific striker **Alberto Spencer,** even though he played much of his club soccer in Uruguay. Spencer holds the record for most goals in South America's Copa Libertadores club championship, scoring 54 times between 1960 and 1972 and lifting the trophy three times with Uruguay's Penarol. He also scored four goals in 11 games for Ecuador and once in four appearances for Uruguay. Spencer was nicknamed "Magic Head" and was even praised as a better header of the ball than Pele—the tribute coming from Pele himself.

MOST INTERNATIONAL GOALS

Bolivia	Joaquin Botero	20
Colombia	Arnoldo Iguaran	25
Ecuador	Agustin Delgado	31
Paraguay	Roque Santa Cruz	29
Peru	Teofilo Cubillas	26
Venezuela	Juan Arango	22
	Giancarlo Maldonado	22

SAFE HANDS OSCAR

Keeping clean sheets for Colombia all the way through the 2001 Copa America was **Oscar Cordoba**, who went on to become his country's most-capped goalkeeper, with 73 appearances between 1993 and 2006.

HIGHS AND LOWS FOR LOLO

Teodoro "Lolo" Fernandez scored six goals in two games for Peru at the 1936 Summer Olympics, including five in a 7–3 defeat of Finland and another in a 4–2 victory over Austria. But Peru were outraged when the Austrians claimed that fans had been invading the pitch and were even more upset when officials ordered the game to be replayed. Peru withdrew from the tournament in protest, while Austria went on to claim silver. But Fernandez and his team-mates had a happier ending at the Copa America three years later, with Peru crowned champions and Fernandez finishing as top scorer with seven goals. Only Teofilo Cubillas, with 26 goals in 81 games, has scored more for Peru than Fernandez's 24 from 32 appearances.

CANIZA CAN DO

Center-back and captain Denis Caniza, 36, became the first Paraguayan to play at four different FIFA World Cups, with his one appearance against New Zealand during the 2010 tournament. The same event brought a milestone for team-mate Roque Santa Cruz, his goal in the first-round game against Brazil equaled Jose Saturnino Cardozo's all-time Paraguayan scoring record of 25. Fellow striker Salvador Cabanas missed out on the tournament after being shot in the head with a gun in a nightclub five months earlier. Thankfully, he recovered well enough to return to professional soccer in 2012.

AFRICA

The African confederation organized its inaugural Cup of Nations in 1957, only a year after it was founded. Egypt, with a record seven victories, was the first winner while more recent ones include first-timers Zambia then Nigeria in 2013. In the FIFA World Cup, South Africa, in 2010, was Africa's first finals host, but it is still waiting for a semifinalist—Cameroon, Senegal, and Ghana have all lost in the quarterfinal. And, in 2014, only two teams made it to the round-of-16, and, unfortunately, both Algeria and Nigeria were beaten at that stage.

Ghana reached the quarterfinal of the FIFA World Cup in 2010 but, despite colourful vocal support, the Black Stars failed narrowly to progress beyond the group stage at Brazil 2014.

NORTH AFRICA FIFA WORLD CUP RECORDS

FAWZI'S FIRST

Abdelrahman Fawzi became the first African footballer to score at a FIFA World Cup, when he pulled a goal back for Egypt against Hungary in the first round of the 1934 tournament. He scored an equalizer eight minutes later, to make it 2-2 at half-time. Egypt went on to lose the game 4-2, and would not return to the finals for another 56 years.

PLAY-OFF PIQUE

Morocco's qualification for the 1970 FIFA World Cup ended a 36-year African exile from the finals. No African country even played in the 1966 FIFA World Cup qualifying competetion—the 16 possible countries all boycotted the event because FIFA wanted the top African team to face a team from Asia or Oceania in a qualification play-off.

HAIL HALLICHE

Algeria became the first African nation to score four goals in one game at a FIFA World Cup finals when it defeated South Korea 4-2 at Porto Alegre in a Group H contest in the Brazil 2014 tournament. The Algerians went on to finish second in the group, behind winners Belgium, and thus qualified for the knock-out stages for the first time. In the round-of-16, it faced one of the tournament favorites, Germany, and Algeria only departed after losing a thrilling game 2-1 after extra time. One of Algeria's scorers in the victory over South Korea on June 22—it had raced into a 3-0 half-time lead—was center-back **Rafik Halliche** (he headed the second goal). By the end of the 2014 tournament, Halliche had made eight FIFA World Cup appearances—a new Algerian record.

AGELESS ALI

Tunisian goalkeeper **Ali Boumnijel** played in all three of his country's games at the 2006 FIFA World Cup, making him not only the oldest player to feature in Germany, but also only the fifth man over the age of 40 to appear in a FIFA World Cup finals. Boumnijel conceded six goals in those three games, against Saudi Arabia (two, in a 2-2 tie), Spain (three, in a 3-1 defeat), and Ukraine (one, in a 1-0 loss).

REDS IN A ROW

When Antar Yahia was sent off for a second bookable offence, three minutes into stoppage-time of Algeria's 1-0 loss to the United States at the 2010 FIFA World Cup, it was the latest red card shown in any World Cup game, not featuring extra-time. It meant also that at least one player had been sent off on eight consecutive days of the 2010 tournament—a record run for any FIFA World Cup.

DJAB FAB

Barring penalty shoot-outs, no African has scored a later FIFA World Cup goal than Algerian midfielder **Abdelmoumene Djabou**. His consolation strike in the 2-1 round-of-16 loss to Germany on June 30, 2014, was timed at 120 minutes and 50 seconds. It was the third meeting between the two teams. Algeria had followed a 2-0 exhibition win, in 1964, with a shock 2-1 success at the 1982 FIFA World Cup.

MOROCCAN ROLL

Morocco was the first North African country to reach the second round of a FIFA World Cup, though it was knocked out, 1-0, by eventual finalist West Germany. It was in Mexico in 1986 that Morocco became the first African team to top a FIFA World Cup group, finishing above England, Poland, and Portugal. Crucial was its 3-1 victory over Portugal in the final group game, following scoreless ties against the other two teams, including the England team that lost its captain Bryan Robson, to a dislocated shoulder, and vice-captain Ray Wilkins, to a red card. **Abderrazak Khairi** scored two of the goals against Portugal, while Lothar Matthaus's winning strike for Germany came with just three minutes remaining.

NORTH AFRICAN COUNTRIES' BEST FIFA WORLD CUP PERFORMANCES

ALGERIA:	Second round 2014
EGYPT:	First round 1934, 1990
MOROCCO:	Second round 2006
TUNISIA:	First round 1978, 1998, 2002, 2006

NORTH AFRICAN COUNTRIES' FIFA WORLD CUP QUALIFICATIONS

ALGERIA:	4 (1982, 1986, 2010, 2014)
MOROCCO:	4 (1970, 1986, 1994, 1998)
TUNISIA:	4 (1978, 1998, 2002, 2006)
EGYPT:	2 (1934, 1990)

NORTH AFRICA: TOP FIFA WORLD CUP GOALSCORERS

Salah Assad	(Algeria)	2
Salaheddine Bassir	(Morocco)	2
Abdelmoumene Djabou	(Algeria)	2
Abdelrahman Fawzi	(Egypt)	2
Abdeljalil Hadda	(Morocco)	2
Abderrazak Khairi	(Morocco)	2
Islam Slimani	(Algeria)	2

NO WAITING GAME

Morocco's 2-1 defeat to Saudi Arabia in 1994 was one of the last two games to be played simultaneously at a FIFA World Cup, without falling on a final match-day of a group. Belgium was defeating the Netherlands 1-0 at the same time, with every team in Group F having still one game to play. At later tournaments, every match has been played separately until the climactic two fixtures of any group.

HOMEGROWN HERO

Of the six African countries at the 2010 FIFA World Cup, Algeria's was the only squad with an African coach: **Rabah Saadane**, in his fifth separate stint in charge since 1981. He previously led his country to the 1986 FIFA World Cup in Mexico, where it was also eliminated in the first round. Algeria, along with Honduras, were the only two countries which failing to score a single goal in the finals. However, Algeria conceded only two goals in its three games: 1-0 defeats to Slovakia and the United States, and a surprise scoreless tie with England, Algeria's first-ever FIFA World Cup clean sheet.

MOKHTAR RUNS AMOK

Egypt had to play only two games to qualify for the 1934 FIFA World Cup, becoming the first African representatives at the tournament. Both games were against a Palestine side under the British mandate. The Egyptians won both games easily: 7-1 in Cairo, and 4-1 in Palestine. Captain and striker Mahmoud Mokhtar scored a hat-trick in the first leg, and two in the return game. Turkey was also meant to contest qualifiers against the two teams, but it withdrew, leaving the path to the finals free for Egypt.

TUNISIA IN TUNE

Tunisia became the first African team to win a game in the FIFA World Cup finals, when it beat Mexico 3-1 in Rosario, Argentina, in 1978, thanks to goals from Ali Kaabi, Nejib Ghommidh and Mokhtar Dhouib. While it shares with Morocco and Algeria the North African record of reaching four different FIFA World Cups, it is the only only one of them to have qualified for three consecutive finals: in 1998, 2002, and 2006. Among the players to feature in all three tournaments were 2006 captain Riadh Bouazizi, Hatem Trabelsi and **Radhi Jaidi**.

FRENCH CONNECTIONS

Algeria was the only North African country to qualify for the 2014 FIFA World Cup, as Ethiopia, Egypt, and Tunisia, all fell short in the final play-offs. The Algerians' victory over Burkina Faso gave its Bosnian coach Vahid Halilhodzic the chance to finally manage at a finals, having led the Ivory Coast through qualifying four years earlier, only to be fired before the finals. All three Algeria goalscorers against Burkina Faso were born in France, but with family connections to Algeria: Sofiane Feghouli, former France U21s captain Carl Medjani, and skipper **Madjid Bougherra**.

ABOUD AWAKENING

After the political upheaval in Libya in 2011, little was expected of the country's players at the 2012 Africa Cup of Nations. Yet it brought some joy to its supporters with a surprise 2-1 win against Senegal in its final first-round game, the first time Libya had ever won an Africa Cup of Nations game outside of its own country. The Algerian kit bore the new flag of the country's National Transitional Council. Among the star performers were Ihaab al Boussefi, scorer of both goals against Senegal, and goalkeeper and captain **Samir Aboud**—at 39 the oldest player at the tournament. Libya played its first competitive home game in the capital Tripoli since 2010, when it hosted the Democratic Republic of Congo in a 2014 FIFA World Cup qualifier in June 2013, the game ending in a 0-0 tie.

OFFICIAL INFLUENCE

The first African to referee a FIFA World Cup final was Morocco's **Said Belqola**, who controlled the 1998 climax in which hosts France beat Brazil 3-0. Perhaps his most notable moment was sending off France's **Marcel Desailly** in the 68th minute, brandishing only the third red card to be shown in a FIFA World Cup final. Belqola was 41 at the time. Sadly, Belqola died from cancer just under four years later.

FOUNDING FATHERS

The Confederation of African Football was officially established at a meeting in the Sudanese capital Khartoum, in the city's Grand Hotel on February 7, 1957, three days before the first Africa Cup of Nations kicked off in the same city. Representatives of Sudan, South Africa, Ethiopia, and Egypt were present at the first assembly, and Egypt's Abdel Aziz Salem became CAF's first president.

SUDAN IMPACT

After two second-place and one third-place finishes, Sudan became the third and last of the Africa Cup of Nations founders to lift the trophy, when it beat Ghana in the 1970 final. Hosts Sudan left it late to reach the final, with two goals from El-Issed, the second 12 minutes into extra-time, seeing off Egypt. The same player scored the only goal of the final, after 12 minutes.

NORTH AFRICA: SELECTED TOP GOALSCORERS

ALGERIA: Abdelhafid Tasfaout		35
EGYPT: Hossam Hassan		68
LIBYA: Tarik El Taib		23
MOROCCO: Ahmed Faras		42
SUDAN: Haytham Tambal		26
TUNISIA: Issam Jemaa		36

THE BLACK EAGLES HAVE LANDED

The Confederation of African Football welcomed a new and 54th member state on February 10, 2012, when the newly-independent nation of South Sudan created a new team and soccer association. The "Black Eagles" were not admitted in time to take part in qualifiers for the 2013 Africa Cup of Nations but hope to take part in future events, and gain FIFA membership as well. Soccer association president Oliver Benjamin said: "We are a country that has just come out of war. We lack even the balls and the T-shirts—we don't have these in our country. Some of our players use their socks, put clothes in them, wrap them up and play with them. That is our love of soccer."

HURRAH FOR SALAH

Egypt has a rising star in **Mohamed Salah**. His performances at the London Olympic Games helped him to win the African Football Confederation's 2012 Most Promising Talent award. A week before his 21st birthday, in June 2013, he scored a hat-trick against Zimbabwe in a 4-2 FIFA World Cup qualifier win and ended the campaign with six goals – only equaled by compatriot Mohamed Aboutrika and Ghana's Asamoah Gyan in Africa's 2014 qualifying rounds. His performances for both country and Swiss club Basel earned him a $17.5 million move to English Premier League giants Chelsea in January 2014.

HEAD–TO–HEAD

The international career of Algeria's leading scorer **Abdelhafid Tasfaout** came to an end at the 2002 Africa Cup of Nations, though it could have been a lot worse. Tasfaout was knocked out in a collision with Mali defender Boubacar Diarra. It caused him to swallow his tongue and prompted fears that he might not even survive. Thankfully, he has recovered. Tasfaout, who played French league soccer for six years, scored 34 goals in 62 games for Algeria between 1990 and 2002.

SORE LOSERS

Libya could claim the record for highest-scoring victory by an African team, having racked up a 21-0 lead over Oman during the Arab Nations Cup in April 1966. But the Oman players walked off with 10 minutes remaining, in protest at Libya being awarded a penalty, and played no further part in the competition.

NORTH AFRICA: SELECTED TOP APPEARANCES

ALGERIA: Lakhdar Belloumi	101
EGYPT: Ahmed Hassan	184
LIBYA: Tarik El Taib	77
MOROCCO: Abdelmajid Dolmy	140
SUDAN: Haitham Mustafa	103
TUNISIA: Radhi Jaidi	105

STRIKING RIVALS

A homegrown hero is back at the top of Tunisia's scoring ranks after Gabes-born **Issam Jemaa** overtook Francileudo Santos, and now has 34 goals from 73 appearances since his debut in 2005. Jemaa began his career with Esperance, but since 2005 has played his club soccer in France, for Lens and Auxerre. Brazil-born Santos, by contrast, did not visit Tunisia until his late teens and only accepted citizenship at the age of 24 in 2004. Within weeks he was helping his new nation not only to host, but win, the 2004 Africa Cup of Nations, scoring four goals including the opener in the final against Morocco. Both Jemaa and Santos were hampered by injury ahead of the 2006 FIFA World Cup: Santos played only 11 minutes at the tournament, while Jemaa missed out all together. He has recovered to continue scoring ever since, including the winner against Niger at the 2012 Africa Cup of Nations.

MAD FOR "MADIBA"

Apart from the Dutch and Spanish teams competing in the 2010 FIFA World Cup final, one of the star attractions in Johannesburg's Soccer City stadium on July 11, 2010, was South Africa's legendary former president **Nelson Mandela**. The frail 91-year-old, known affectionately by his tribal name of "Madiba," was driven on to the field before the game in a golf cart and given a rapturous reception by the crowd. It marked his one and only public appearance at the tournament. Mandela had hoped to attend the opening ceremony and game on June 11, but was mourning the death of his 13-year-old great-granddaughter in a car crash the previous evening. He had been a high-profile presence at the FIFA vote in 2004 which awarded South Africa hosting rights for 2010.

GOING FOR A SONG

Two players have been sent off at two separate FIFA World Cups: Cameroon's Rigobert Song, against Brazil in 1994 and Chile four years later, and France's Zinedine Zidane, red-carded against Saudi Arabia in 1998 and against Italy in the 2006 final. Song's red card against Brazil made him the youngest player to be dismissed at a FIFA World Cup, aged just 17 years and 358 days. Born in Nkanglikock on July 1, 1976, Song is Cameroon's most-capped player, with 137 appearances, including winning displays in the 2000 and 2002 finals of the Africa Cup of Nations. He has been joined in the national team by his nephew, Alexandre Song Billong of Barcelona.

MORE FOR ASAMOAH

Ghana's Asamoah Gyan has scored more FIFA World Cup goals than any other player representing an African nation. He took his overall tally to six— one ahead of Cameroon's Roger Milla—with two strikes at the Brazil 2014 FIFA World Cup. He also became the first African to score at three separate FIFA World Cups, and his 11 appearances took him level with Cameroon's Francois Omam-Biyik for the most games.

JOLLY ROGER

Cameroon striker **Roger Milla**, famous for dancing around corner flags after each goal, became the FIFA World Cup's oldest scorer against Russia in 1994, aged 42 years and 39 days. He came on as substitute during that tournament with his surname handwritten, rather than printed, on the back of his shirt. Milla, born in Yaounde on May 20, 1952, had retired from professional soccer for a year before Cameroon's president, Paul Biya, persuaded him to join the 1990 FIFA World Cup squad. His goals in that tournament helped him win the African Footballer of the Year award for an unprecedented second time, 14 years after he had first received the trophy. He finally ended his international career after the 1994 FIFA World Cup in the United States, finishing with 102 caps and 28 goals to his name.

SUB–SAHARAN AFRICAN COUNTRIES' BEST FIFA WORLD CUP PERFORMANCES

ANGOLA:	First round 2006
CAMEROON:	Quarter-finals 1990
GHANA:	Quarter-finals 2010
IVORY COAST:	First round 2006, 2010, 2014
NIGERIA:	Second round 1994, 1998, 2014
SENEGAL:	Quarter-finals 2002
SOUTH AFRICA:	First round 1998, 2002, 2010
TOGO:	First round 2006
ZAIRE/CONGO DR:	First round 1974

SUB–SAHARAN AFRICAN COUNTRIES' FIFA WORLD CUP QUALIFICATIONS

CAMEROON:	7	(1982, 1990, 1994, 1998, 2002, 2010, 2014)
NIGERIA:	5	(1994, 1998, 2002, 2010, 2014)
SOUTH AFRICA:	3	(1998, 2002, 2010)
GHANA:	3	(2006, 2010, 2014)
IVORY COAST:	3	(2006, 2010, 2014)
ANGOLA:	1	(2006)
SENEGAL:	1	(2002)
TOGO:	1	(2006)
ZAIRE/CONGO DR:	1	(1974)

OH NO, YOBO

Nigeria captain Joseph Yobo set two national records when he played in the round-of-16 game against France at the 2014 FIFA World Cup. However, his late own goal in a 2-0 defeat may make it a game he would rather forget. His appearance that day not only made him the first Nigerian international to reach a century of caps, but also meant he had played 10 FIFA World Cup games, one more than previous national record-holder Jay-Jay Okocha.

RATOMIR GETS IT RIGHT

Ghana went through four different coaches during qualifiers for the 2006 FIFA World Cup, with Serbian coach Ratomir Dujkovic finally clinching the country a place at the finals for the first time. He led it through the whole of 2005 unbeaten, winning a FIFA prize for being the most-improved team of the year. Ghana was the only African country to make it through the first round of both the 2006 and 2010 FIFA World Cups, despite having the youngest average age of any squad each time. It was again coached by a Serb in 2010, this time Milovan Rajevac.

BROTHERS AT ARMS

The Boateng brothers made FIFA World Cup history in playing against each other at the 2010 finals in South Africa. Both were also selected for the "replay" in 2014. In 2010 Jerome played left-back for Germany while elder half-brother **Kevin-Prince**, who had switched nationalities a month earlier, was in the Ghana midfield. In the group match in 2010, Jerome Boateng switched to right-back. Germany won 1-0 in South Africa, while the return in Brazil ended in a 2-2 tie. Kevin-Prince was the only brother to play the full 90 minutes in South Africa. He was substituted during the game in Brazil, but Jerome was replaced during both games. In the two games they were on field together for 117 of the 180 minutes.

SUB–SAHARAN AFRICAN COUNTRIES: TOP FIFA WORLD CUP GOALSCORERS

Asamoah Gyan (Ghana) 6
Roger Milla (Cameroon) 5
Papa Bouba Diop (Senegal) 3
Samuel Eto'o (Cameroon) 3
Daniel Amokachi (Nigeria) 2
Emmanuel Amunike (Nigeria) 2
Andre Ayew (Ghana) 2
Shaun Bartlett (South Africa) 2
Wilfried Bony (Ivory Coast) 2
Henri Camara (Senegal) 2
Aruna Dindane (Ivory Coast) 2
Didier Drogba (Ivory Coast) 2
Gervinho (Ivory Coast) 2
Patrick Mboma (Cameroon) 2
Benni McCarthy (South Africa) 2
Sulley Muntari (Ghana) 2
Ahmed Musa (Nigeria) 2
Francois Omam-Biyik (Cameroon) 2

KESHI JOB

Nigeria's Stephen Keshi became the first African manager to reach the knock-out stages of a FIFA World Cup when he steered his country through Group F at the 2014 tournament in Brazil. The feat also meant Nigeria was the first African country to reach the round-of-16 at three FIFA World Cups, having previously done so in 1994—when Keshi was in the team—and 1998. He announced his resignation after its 2-0 round-of-16 loss to France, which came despite one of several brave displays by goalkeeper **Vincent Enyeama**.

THE FOURMOST

The only two African soccer players to appear at four FIFA World Cups—and the only three to be named in the squads for four—are all from Cameroon. Striker Samuel Eto'o became the latest in 2014, after playing in 1998, 2002, and 2010. He emulated defender Rigobert Song, who was in the Cameroon team in 1994, 1998, 2002, and 2010. Goalkeeper Jacques Songo'o was named in the country's squads for the four FIFA World Cups between 1990 and 2002, but he only actually played in the 1994 and 1998 versions.

SUB-SAHARAN AFRICA NATIONAL RECORDS

HOT DROG

Didier Drogba may have been raised in France, but he was born in Ivory Coast and remains one of the African country's favorite sons for his actions both on and off the field. The Ivory Coast captain has a record 65 goals in 104 appearances for the Elephants. He has been credited with influence off the field, too, when he called for a ceasefire in the civil war-torn nation. He also pushed for an Africa Cup of Nations qualifier against Madagascar in June 2007 to be moved from the capital Abidjan to rebel army stronghold Bouake, in an effort to encourage reconciliation. Drogba, a two-time CAF African Footballer of the Year, captained the Ivory Coast team at the three FIFA World Cups it has reached, in 2006, 2010, and 2014, but he started only in the third game in 2014.

SUB—SAHARAN AFRICA: SELECTED TOP GOALSCORERS

ANGOLA: Akwa	36
BOTSWANA: Jerome Ramatlhakwane	19
CAMEROON: Samuel Eto'o	56
GHANA: Asamoah Gyan	42
IVORY COAST: Didier Drogba	65
NIGERIA: Rashidi Yekini	37
SENEGAL: Henri Camara	29
SOUTH AFRICA: Benni McCarthy	32
TOGO: Emmanuel Adabayor	27
ZAMBIA: Godfrey Chitalu	79
ZIMBABWE: Peter Ndlovu	38

KNOCKED OUT ON PENALTIES

Botswana goalkeeper and captain Modiri Marumo was sent off in the middle of a penalty shoot-out against Malawi in May 2003, after punching the opposing goalkeeper Philip Nyasulu in the face. Botswana defender Michael Mogaladi had to go in goal for the rest of the shoot-out, which Malawi won 4-1.

FIFTEEN LOVE

Samuel Kuffour became the youngest man to win an Olympic Game soccer medal when Ghana took bronze at the 1992 Olympics in Barcelona. It was 27 days before his 16th birthday.

EAGLETS SOAR

The first African country to win an official FIFA tournament was Nigeria, when its "Golden Eaglets" beat West Germany 2-0 in the final of the 1985 World Under-17 Championships.

SO LONG, PITSO

South Africa went through four different foreign coaches—in five separate spells—between 2004 and 2010, before the top job went to South African Pitso Mosimane. He had previously won four caps as a player, then assisted Brazilian Carlos Alberto Parreira at the 2010 FIFA World Cup. Mosimane's first nine games in charge brought six wins, two ties and just one defeat, but he lost the post in 2012 after a nine-game winless streak cost South Africa any chance of competing at the 2014 FIFA World Cuo. He was replaced by Gordon Igesund.

GENEROUS GEORGE

In 1995 Liberia's George Weah became the first African to be named FIFA World Player of the Year, an award that recognized his prolific goalscoring exploits for Paris Saint-Germain and AC Milan. That same year, he added the European Footballer of the Year and African Footballer of the Year prizes to his collection. Weah not only captained his country, but often funded the team's travels—though he remains the only FIFA World Player of the Year whose country has never qualified for a FIFA World Cup. After retiring in 2003 after 60 caps and 22 international goals, he moved into politics and ran unsuccessfully for the Liberian presidency in 2005.

SUPER FRED

In 2007, **Frederic Kanoute** became the first non-African-born player to be named African Footballer of the Year. The striker was born in Lyon, France, and played for France U-21s. But the son of a French mother and Malian father opted to play for Mali in 2004, scoring 23 goals in 37 appearances, before retiring from international soccer after the 2010 Africa Cup of Nations. As well as going down in history as one of Mali's greatest-ever players, he is also a hero to fans of Spanish club Sevilla, with which he scored 143 goals, and won two UEFA Cups along the way. Only three men have scored more goals for the club.

SUB–SAHARAN AFRICA: SELECTED TOP APPEARANCES

Country	Player	Appearances
ANGOLA:	Akwa	80
BOTSWANA:	Mompati Thuma	66
CAMEROON:	Rigobert Song	137
GHANA:	Richard Kingson	90
IVORY COAST:	Didier Zokora	121
NIGERIA:	Joseph Yobo	100
SENEGAL:	Henri Camara	99
SOUTH AFRICA:	Aaron Mokoena	107
TOGO:	Dare Nibombe	71
ZAMBIA:	David Chabala	108
ZIMBABWE:	Peter Ndlovu	100

DRAMATIC TURNAROUNDS

Ghana managed to concede three goals in one minute to world champions Germany in an April 1993 exhibition. Ghana had been leading 1-0 with 20 minutes left, but lost the game 6-1. In the 1989 FIFA World Youth Championships, Nigeria was 4-0 down with 25 minutes remaining in its quarterfinal against the Soviet Union, but hit back to tie 4-4 before winning 5-3 on penalties.

MAESTRO'S MEMORIALS

Didier Zokora, the Ivory Coast's most-capped player, bears several tattoos cherishing members of his family—chiefly his tragic younger brother Armand, whose name is inked on Didier's right forearm. The duo had both just signed professional contracts with local club ASEC Mimosas when Armand, aged just 14, drowned off a beach in 1997. On his left forearm, Zokora—himself nicknamed "Maestro"—has the names of his children, Sarah and Nadya, while a tattoo of his wife Mariam is just above his heart. Zokora has scored just once in 121 international appearances, in a 4-0 FIFA World Cup qualifier victory over Botswana in June 2008.

MAD FOR "MADIBA"

The world of soccer united in paying tribute to one of the sport's greatest fans, when former South African president and anti-apartheid leader Nelson Mandela died aged 94 on December 5, 2013. His final public appearance had been at the 2010 FIFA World Cup final, when he and wife Graca Machel were driven around the field and given a rapturous reception by the crowd. Mandela, known affectionately by his tribal name of "Madiba," had played a crucial role in convincing FIFA to award the 2010 hosting rights to South Africa. He had often spoken of how, when imprisoned on Robben Island, he and fellow inmates kept their spirits up by playing soccer. He recalled: "The only access to the World Cup was on radio. Soccer was the only joy to prisoners." Former South Africa captain Lucas Radebe described Mandela as "my hero," David Beckham said meeting him was "the highlight of my career," and Pele called him "one of the most influential people in my life." The week of Mandela's death, every UEFA Champions League game began with the unfurling of giant banners proclaiming: "Madiba, the world will never forget you."

ASIA & OCEANIA

Asia wrote a major chapter in soccer history in 2002 when Japan and South Korea became the FIFA World Cup's first co-hosts, and the Koreans produced Asia's best-ever finish, fourth. Asia's World Cup strength improved when Australia moved from Oceania in 2006. However, the 2014 FIFA World Cup was depressing for the Asian region as all four nations went out at the group stage, and Oceania was not even represented. Asia's two most populous nations, China and India, have yet to catch up with their neighbours in football terms.

Korea's dynamic fans proved as much of a sensation as their team did co-hosting the 2002 FIFA World Cup with Japan, but there was no such luck at Brazil 2014, as Korea went home after the group stage.

AUSTRALIA

Victims, perhaps, of an overcomplicated qualifying system that once limited the country's FIFA World Cup finals appearances, and hampered by its geographical isolation that, in the early years, saw other sports prosper in the country at soccer's expense, it has taken many years for Australia to establish itself on the world soccer map. However, driven by a new generation of players, many based with top European clubs, the Socceroos delivered for the first time at the 2006 FIFA World Cup and briefly was the No. 1 ranked team in Asia.

AUSTRALIA RECORDS

Honours: Oceania champions 1980, 1996, 2000, 2004
First international: v New Zealand (lost 3-1), Auckland, June 17, 1922
Biggest win: 31-0 v American Samoa, Coffs Harbour, April 11, 2001
Biggest defeat: 7-0 v Croatia, Zagreb, June 6, 1998

NATIVE HERO

Harry Williams holds a proud place in Australian soccer history as the first Aboriginal player to represent the country in internationals. He made his debut in 1970, and was part of the first Australian squad to compete at a FIFA World Cup finals, in West Germany in 1974.

MOMENTOUS MORI

Damian Mori's then-Australian record total of 29 goals, in just 45 internationals, included no fewer than five hat-tricks: three against Fiji and Tahiti, four against the Cook Islands and Tonga, and five in Australia's 13-0 trouncing of the Solomon Islands in a 1998 FIFA World Cup qualifier. His international career spanned from 1992 to 2002, but he never played in a FIFA World Cup finals as Australia didn't qualify. He did, though, claim a world record for scoring the fastest goal—after just 3.69 seconds—for his club, Adelaide City, against Sydney United in 1996.

NEILL APPEAL

Tough-tackling Australia veteran **Lucas Neill** had to wait until his 91st international appearance before scoring his first goal for his country: the final strike in a 4-0 victory over Jordan in June 2013 to boost the Socceroos' chances of reaching the 2014 FIFA World Cup. Qualification was clinched in the next game, thanks to a lone goal by Josh Kennedy to defeat Iraq. It made Australia the third team, after host Brazil and Japan, to secure a place at the finals. Former Blackburn Rovers, West Ham United, and Galatasary defender Neill made his Australia debut in October 1996, becoming the country's third-youngest international. His scoring record, though, pales alongside that of fellow center-back Robbie Cornthwaite, his goal against Romania in February 2013 was his third in his first six games for Australia.

TOP CAPS

1	Mark Schwarzer	109
2	Lucas Neill	96
3	Brett Emerton	95
4	Alex Tobin	87
5	Paul Wade	84
6	Luke Wilkshire	80
7	Mark Bresciano	76
=	Tony Vidmar	76
9	Tim Cahill	71
10	Scott Chipperfield	68

CAHILL MAKES HISTORY

Tim Cahill's FIFA World Cup goals total is only one fewer than all other Australians combined. He scored the Socceroos' first ever finals goals, netting in the 84th (and 89th) minutes of a comeback 3-1 win over Japan in 2006. His most spectacular goal was his last, a first-time volley in a 3-2 defeat to the Netherlands at Porto Alegre in 2014. Sadly for Cahill he later received his second yellow card of the finals and so missed Australia's final game. He scored twice in 2006, once in 2010, and twice in 2014. Australia's other FIFA World Cup finals scorers are: Brett Holman (two), John Aloisi, Craig Moore, Harry Kewell, and Mile Jedinak (all one).

AUSTRALIA'S SHOOT-OUT RECORD

Australia is the only team to reach the FIFA World Cup finals via a penalty shoot-out – in the final qualifying play-off in November 2005. It had lost the first leg 1-0 to Uruguay in Montevideo. Mark Bresciano's goal leveled the aggregate score, which remained 1-1 after extra-time. Goalkeeper **Mark Schwarzer** made two crucial saves as Australia won the shoot-out, 4-2, with John Aloisi scoring the winning spot-kick. Schwarzer passed Alex Tobin to become Australia's most-capped player with his 88th appearance, in January 2011, in the AFC Asian Cup final defeat to Japan. Tobin had been in defense when Schwarzer made his Australia debut against Canada in 1993.

COME TO A LAND DOWN UNDER

After reaching the quarterfinal of its first AFC Asian Cup in 2007, and finishing runner-up to Japan four years later, Australia will want to make it third time lucky at the 2015 tournament—especially as this time the country will be playing host. Australia was the only country to bid for staging rights.

THREE-CARD TRICK

Graham Poll, in 2006, was not the first referee at a FIFA World Cup to show the same player three yellow cards. It happened in another game involving Australia, when its English-born midfielder Ray Richards was belatedly sent off against Chile at the 1974 FIFA World Cup. Reserve official Clive Thomas, from Wales, informed Iranian referee Jafar Namdar he had booked Richards three times without dismissing him. Richards played four unwarranted minutes before eventually receiving his marching orders.

PRECEDENT KENNEDY

Australian newspapers acclaimed a player nicknamed "Jesus" as the country's "savior" when Josh Kennedy's 83rd-minute goal against Iraq in June 2013 clinched Australia's place at the 2014 FIFA World Cup—ensuring a third consecutive finals appearance. Lofty striker Kennedy, given the nickname for his former styling of long hair and a beard, had entered the field just six minutes earlier, as a replacement for Tim Cahill. It was his 16th, and most important, goal in 30 appearances for Australia.

BET ON BRETT

Brett Holman's goal against Ghana, in a 1-1 tie at the 2010 tournament, made him Australia's youngest marksman at a FIFA World Cup. He was 26 years and 84 days old at the time, 105 days younger than Tim Cahill had been when he scored against Japan in 2006. Holman added to his tally five days later, when Australia beat Serbia 2-1. Cahill himself was also on the scoresheet, though goal difference meant Australia failed to reach the round-of-16.

TOP SCORERS

1	Tim Cahill	34
2	Damian Mori	29
3	Archie Thompson	28
4	John Aloisi	27
5	Attila Abonyi	25
=	John Kosima	25
7	Brett Emerton	20
=	David Zdrilic	20
9	Graham Arnold	19
10	Ray Baartz	18

KEWELL THE TOPS

Harry Kewell (born on September 22, 1978) is widely regarded as Australia's best-ever player. The left winger scored 13 goals in 39 international appearances, including the equalizer against Croatia that took Australia into the round-of-16 at the 2006 FIFA World Cup. Kewell enjoyed a successful European club career, with Leeds United, Liverpool, and Galatasaray. He is also the only Australian-born player to gain a Champions League winner's medal, with Liverpool in 2005. He endured an unhappier time at the 2010 FIFA World Cup, when he lasted just 22 minutes before being sent off for handball against Ghana. It was the finals' 150th red card.

JAPAN

The past two decades have seen great breakthroughs for Japanese soccer. Until the first professional league was introduced in 1993, clubs had been amateur, and it was overshadowed in Japan's affections by other sports such as baseball, martial arts, table tennis, and golf. Even more significantly, Japan co-hosted the 2002 FIFA World Cup, and the team reached the round-of-16 for the first time. Japan's four AFC Asian Cup wins, in 1992, 2000, 2004, and 2011 were celebrated keenly as proof of surging standards.

TOP SCORERS

1	Kunishige Kamamoto	80
2	Kazuyoshi Miura	55
3	Shinji Okazaki	39
4	Hiromi Hara	37
5	Takuya Takagi	27
6	Kazushi Kimura	26
7	Shunsuke Nakamura	24
8	Keisuke Honda	23
=	Naohiro Takahara	23
10	Masashi Nakayama	21

NAKATA BLAZES THE TRAIL

Hidetoshi Nakata ranks among Japan's best-ever players. The midfielder set up all three goals in a 3-2 FIFA World Cup qualifying play-off win over Iran in November 1997. Nakata moved to Perugia in Italy after the 1998 finals, becoming the first Japanese player to star in Europe, and won a Serie A championship medal with Roma in 2001. He was followed abroad by international team-mates, such as Shinji Ono, who joined Feyenoord in the Netherlands, and midfielder Shunsuke Nakamura, whose European employers included Reggina in Italy, Celtic in Scotland, and Espanyol in Spain. Nakata played in three FIFA World Cup finals, making ten appearances and scoring one goal—the second in a 2-0 win over Tunisia that took Japan into the round-of-16 in 2002. Nakata won 77 caps and scored 11 goals, before surprisingly retiring from all forms of soccer after the 2006 FIFA World Cup, aged just 29.

PLAYING POLITICS

Japan was a surprise bronze medalist at the 1968 Olympic Games soccer tournament in Mexico City, and star striker **Kunishige Kamamoto** finished top scorer overall with seven goals. He remains Japan's all-time leading scorer, with 76 goals in 75 games. Since retirement, he has combined coaching with being elected to Japan's parliament and serving as vice-president of the country's soccer association.

HONDA INSPIRES

Japan was the first country—after host Brazil—to qualify for the 2014 FIFA World Cup. Keisuke Honda's late penalty secured the required point from a 1-1 tie with Australia in June 2013. Honda won two man-of-the-match awards at the 2010 FIFA World Cup, and was named player of the tournament when Japan, under Italian-born coach Alberto Zaccheroni, won the 2011 AFC Asian Cup. He scored Japan's first goal at the 2014 finals, against Ivory Coast, but it lost 2-1 and was eliminated after two defeats and a tie, leading to Zaccheroni's resignation. Honda was the first Japanese player to score at two FIFA World Cups and the first to reach three goals.

TOP CAPS

1	Yasuhito Endo	146
2	Masami Ihara	122
3	Yoshikatsu Kawaguchi	116
4	Yuji Nakazawa	110
5	Shunsuke Nakamura	98
6	Kazuyoshi Miura	89
7	Kunishige Kamamoto	84
8	Yasuyuki Konno	83
9	Junichi Inamoto	82
=	Alessandro Santos	82

CLEAN SWEEP

Japan's players may not have made much of an impact on the field at the 2014 FIFA World Cup—all four Asian teams went out in the first round, the first time this had happened since FIFA expanded the World Cup allocation to four. But its supporters certainly made a good impression in the stands. Fans were widely acclaimed for staying after each of its three group games to tidy the stands around them. One "Blue Samurai" supporter, Kei Kawai, said: "We try to do a little bit of clean-up to show respect to the host country and just, you know, show off how clean things are in Japan. And we like to make it so here, too."

THREE AND IN

Japan's 3-1 Group E win over Denmark in Bloemfontein at the 2010 FIFA World Cup made it the first Asian team to score three times in one FIFA World Cup game, since North Korea's 5-3 defeat to Portugal in its 1966 quarterfinal. Japan's goals came from Keisuke Honda, Yasuhito Endo, and Shinji Okazaki. Honda and Endo both scored directly from free-kicks, the first time a team has managed such a feat in a FIFA World Cup game since Yugoslavia scored with three free-kicks in the 9-0 rout of Zaire. Endo became Japan's most-capped player, passing Masami Ihara, when playing in an October 2012 exhibition against Brazil.

SHINJI BENEFITS

Playmaker **Shinji Kagawa** became the first Japanese player to be part of an English league championship-winning side, when securing the Premier League title with Manchester United in 2012–13, 12 months after helping his former club Borussia Dortmund to win Germany's Bundesliga. Kagawa was named 2012 AFC International Player of the Year. But he suffered for his art during Japan's triumphant 2011 AFC Asian Cup campaign. He scored twice in a quarterfinal victory, only to break his foot in the semi-final, and miss the final win against Saudi Arabia.

TA–DA, TADANARI

The goalscoring hero whose extra-time strike clinched a record fourth AFC Asian Cup for Japan in 2011 was a man who had not even played for his country before the tournament began. Striker Tadanari Lee made his international debut in the first-round match against Jordan, and conjured perfect timing for his first Japan goal, with 11 minutes of extra-time remained in the final against Australia. His midfield team-mate **Kaisuke Honda** took the prize for the event's most valuable player, while forward Shinji Okazaki's first-round hat-trick against Saudi Arabia helped earn him a place in the team of the tournament.

JAPANESE GOAL GLUT

No team has scored more goals in one AFC Asian Cup finals than Japan's 21 in six games on its way to winning the title for the second time, in Lebanon in 2000. The final, against Saudi Arabia, however, was settled with just a single goal, from Shigeyoshi Mochizuki. Nine different Japanese players scored during the tournament, including Akinori Nishizawa and Naohiro Takahara, both netting five. Their team-mate Ryuzo Morioka scored once, but in his own goal. Japan's most emphatic victory of the tournament came in the first round, 8-1 against Uzbekistan, with both Nishizawa and Takahara hitting hat-tricks.

SOUTH KOREA

"Be the Reds!" was the rallying cry of South Korea's fervent fans as the nation co-hosted the 2002 FIFA World Cup—and they saw their energetic team become the first Asian team to reach the semifinal, ultimately finishing fourth. South Korea also won the AFC Asian Cup the first two times it was staged (in 1956 and 1960). It could well claim to be the continent's leading soccer team, even if AFC Asian Cup triumphs have been thin on the ground since then. The country's professional K-League is making progress and South Korean teams have won the Asian club championship 10 times.

HWANG'S THE MAN

A rare veteran among South Korea's young guns at the 2002 FIFA World Cup was 33-year-old **Hwang Sun-Hong**, after Cha Bum-Kun the only other player to score a half-century of goals for the country. His 50th goal came in the 2-0 win over Poland that clinched South Korea's place in the second round. Hwang had also played in the 1990 and 1994 FIFA World Cups, but missed the 1998 event through injury. Eight of Hwang's goals came in one game, an 11-0 crushing of Nepal in October 1994. South Korea's record win was also against poor Nepal, in September 2003—this time ending 16-0, with five for Park Jin-Sub and three each for Woo Sung-Yong and Kim Do-Hoon.

HERE COMES THE SON

South Korea has played more FIFA World Cup finals games than any other Asian team, taking its total to 31 with three in 2014, although it finished bottom of Group H. Only twice has South Korea made it past the first round and its overall record is five wins, nine ties and 17 losses. Its 30th game, which fell on June 22, 2014, a 4-2 loss to Algeria, was an unhappier outcome than their two previous games on the same date: a penalty shoot-out victory over Spain in a 2002 quarterfinal, and a 2-2 group-stage tie with Nigeria eight years later. South Korea's second goal against Algeria was scored by Bayer Leverkusen striker **Son Heung-Min**. His father, Son Woong-Chun, himself a former international soccer player, had unsuccessfully urged coaches during qualifying to leave his son out of the team and allow him more time to develop as a player.

SPIDER CATCHER

Goalkeeper **Lee Woon-Jae**—nicknamed "Spider Hands"—made himself a national hero by making the crucial penalty save that took co-host South Korea into the semifinal of the 2002 FIFA World Cup. He blocked Spain's fourth spot-kick, taken by winger Joaquin, in a quarterfinal shoot-out. Lee, who also played in the 1994, 2006, and 2010 FIFA World Cups, provided more penalty saves at the 2007 AFC Asian Cup, stopping three spot-kicks in shoot-outs on South Korea's way to third place. Lee's form restricted his frequent back-up, Kim Byung-Ji, to just 62 international appearances. But Kim did at least set a new South Korean top-flight landmark of 200 clean sheets in June 2012, at the age of 42.

PARK LIFE

The tirelessly-energetic midfielder **Park Ji-Sung** can claim to be the most successful Asian
soccer player of all time. He became the first Asian player to be part of UEFA Champions
League winning team, when his club, Manchester United, beat Chelsea in 2008—although
Park missed the final. He also became the first Asian player to score at three successive
FIFA World Cups, beginning on home turf in 2002, when his goal broke the deadlock in a
first-round game against Portugal. It helped to put South Korea through to the knock-
out stages for the first time ever. At the time, team-mate Ahn Jung-Hwan and Saudi
Arabia's Sami Al-Jaber were the only other other Asian players to have scored three FIFA
World Cup finals goals. Park became the eighth South Korean to reach a century of caps
when he captained the team in its 2011 AFC Asian Cup semifinal defeat to Japan, before
announcing his international retirement to allow a younger generation to emerge.

TOP CAPS

1	Hong Myung-Bo	136
2	Lee Woon-Jae	132
3	Lee Young-Pyo	127
4	Yoo Sang-Chul	122
5	Cha Bum-Kun	121
6	Kim Tae-Young	106
7	Hwang Sun-Hong	103
8	Park Ji-Sung	100
9	Lee Dong-Gook	99
10	Kim Nam-Il	98

TOP SCORERS

1	Cha Bum-Kun	55
2	Hwang Sun-Hong	50
3	Park Lee-Chun	36
4	Kim Jae-Han	33
5	Kim Do-Hoon	30
=	Lee Dong-Gook	30
=	Choi Soon-Ho	30
8	Huh Jung-Moo	29
9	Choi Yong-Soo	27
10	Park Chu-Young	24

HONG SETS FIFA WORLD CUP RECORD

South Korea defender **Hong Myung-Bo** was the first
Asian player to appear in four consecutive FIFA World
Cup finals tournaments. He played all three games
as South Korea lost to Belgium, Spain, and Uruguay
in 1990. He scored twice in three appearances in
1994, when his goal against Spain sparked a Korean
fightback from 2-0 down to tie 2-2. In 1998 he started
all three group games as South Korea was eliminated
at the group stage. Four years later, on home soil,
he captained South Korea to fourth place, and was
voted third-best player of the tournament. Hong
coached South Korea's U-23 side to Olympic bronze
at the 2012 Summer Games – beating Japan 2-0 in
the medal play-off. Those goals were scored by Park
Chu-Young and Koo Ja-Cheol. Hong became South
Korea coach in June 2013, and was in charge of the
team at the 2014 FIFA World Cup. One of the Koreans'
group games was against Belgium, a repeat of a 1998
FIFA World Cup meeting, when Hong and his Belgian
counterpart, Marc Wilmots, played against each other.

CHA BOOM AND BUST

Even before South Korea made its FIFA World Cup
breakthrough under Guus Hiddink, the country had a
homegrown hero of world renown: thunderous striker
Cha Bum-Kun, known for his fierce shots and
suitable nickname "Cha Boom." He helped to pave
the way for more Asian players to make their name
in Europe by signing for German club Eintracht
Frankfurt in 1979, and later playing for Bundesliga
rivals Bayer Leverkusen. His achievements in
Germany included two UEFA Cup triumphs,
with Frankfurt in 1980 and with Leverkusen
eight years later, while his performances
helped make him a childhood idol for
future German internationals, such as
Jurgen Klinsmann and Michael Ballack.
His record 55 goals for the national team, in 121
appearances, included a seven-minute hat-trick
against Malaysia in the 1977 Park's Cup tournament—
leveling the score after South Korea had been trailing
4-1. "Cha Boom" later served as national coach,
winning 22, losing 11 and tying eight, between January
1997 and June 1998. There was an unhappy end for Cha,
as he was fired two games into the 1998 FIFA World Cup,
after a 5-0 loss to the Netherlands.

OTHER ASIAN COUNTRIES

The lesser-known Asian nations represent the true backwaters of world soccer. These may well be the countries in which true soccer obsession has yet to take hold, but competition between, and achievements by, these teams are no less vibrant. The regions are the home to many of the game's record-breakers—from the most goals in a single game to the most career appearances—and some of these records may never be broken.

SAUDIS MAKE FLYING START

Saudi Arabia reached the last 16 in its first FIFA World Cup finals appearance in 1994. **Saeed Owairan**'s winner against Belgium enabled it to finish level on points with the Netherlands in Group F. After the Saudis lost its opening game 2-1 to the Dutch, Sami Al-Jaber and Fuad Amin then scored in a 2-1 win over Morocco before it lost 3-1 to Sweden in the round-of-16. Substitute Fahad Al-Ghesheyan scored in the 85th minute after the Swedes led 2-0. Kennet Andersson then grabbed Sweden's decisive third goal three minutes later. Saudi Arabia has failed to advance beyond the group stages in its three subsequent appearances.

IRAN TOP SCORERS

1	Ali Daei	109
2	Karim Bagheri	50
3	Ali Karimi	38
4	Javad Nekounam	37
5	Gholam Hossein Mazloomi	19
=	Farshad Pious	19
7	Nasser Mohammadkhani	18
=	Ali Asghar Modir Roosta	18
9	Vahid Hashemian	15
10	Hamid Alidoosti	14

NEK'S THE NEXT IN LINE

Iran midfielder Javad Nekounam is second behind striker Ali Daei not only in caps won, but also in matches as captain. He led Iran 49 times in 143 games, compared to 149-cap Daei's 80 as skipper. Only Ali Parvin, in 1978, can match Nekounam for the most FIFA World Cup games as Iran captain, three. But only two Iran players have appeared in six FIFA World Cup games: Mehdi Mahdavikia (in 1998 and 2006) and Andranik Teymourian (in 2006 and 2014).

IRAN'S WINNING RUN

Iran won all 13 matches across its hat-trick of AFC Asian Cup triumphs, in 1968, 1972, and 1976, and its 8-0 crushing of South Yemen in 1976 remains a tournament record. Among the players who enjoyed repeat success was Homayoun Behzadi, who scored in all four games in 1968 and was again on the winning team four years later. Iran's coach in 1976 was Heshmat Mohajerani, who also led the team to the quarterfinal of that year's Olympic Games in Montreal, before steering Iran to its first-ever FIFA World Cup appearance in 1978. Iran's captain at the FIFA World Cup in Argentina was midfielder Ali Parvin, scorer the only goal of the 1976 AFC Asian Cup final against Kuwait.

RANK OUTSIDERS

North Korea only narrowly lost its first game of the 2010 FIFA World Cup, 2-1 to Brazil. **Ji Yun-Nam** scored a late consolation for the Koreans. The game matched the tournament's highest- and lowest-ranked qualifying teams. Brazil was in first place in the FIFA rankings, while North Korea was in 105th.

IRAN TOP CAPS

1	Ali Daei	149
2	Javad Nekounam	143
3	Ali Karimi	127
4	Mehdi Mahdavikia	111
5	Hossein Kaebi	89
6	Jalal Hosseini	88
7	Karim Bagheri	87
8	Mohammad Nosrati	83
9	Hamid Reza Estili	82
=	Andranik Taymourian	82

APPEARANCES IN THE FIFA WORLD CUP FINALS

Saudi Arabia	4	(1994, 1998, 2002, 2006)
New Zealand	2	(1982*, 2010*)
North Korea	2	(1966, 2010)
China	1	(2002)
Indonesia**	1	(1938)
Iraq	1	(1986)
Israel	1	(1970)
Kuwait	1	(1982)
United Arab Emirates	1	(1990)

* Qualified for FIFA World Cup as Oceania Confederation member
** Played in the 1938 FIFA World Cup as Dutch East Indies

SHAKEN SHEIKH

Kuwait has qualified for the FIFA World Cup just once, in 1982, but it was certainly memorable. The team almost walked off the field during a first-round group game against France in protest at a decision. Kuwait's chief Olympic official, Sheikh Fahad Al-Ahmed, even stormed on to the field in Valladolid, Spain, when France's Alain Giresse scored a goal that would have given *Les Bleus* a 4-1 lead. The Kuwaitis claimed they had heard a whistle, and stopped playing, They ultimately convinced referee Myroslav Stupar to disallow the strike. The game still finished 4-1 to France, and Kuwait was eliminated in the first round.

CHINA YET TO REALIzE POTENTIAL

China, the world's most populous nation, has qualified just once for the FIFA World Cup finals, in 2002. It topped its final qualifying group by eight points from the United Arab Emirates, but coach Bora Milutinovic's team slumped in the finals, failing to score in defeats by Costa Rica (2-0), Brazil (4-0), and Turkey (3-0). Leading appearance-maker, **Li Weifeng**—with 112,—and top-scorer Hao Haidong (37 goals) were both in China's 2012 squad.

IRAN STOP AT 19

Iran holds the record for the highest score in an Asian zone FIFA World Cup qualifier. It thrashed Guam 19-0 in Tabriz on November 24, 2000. Karim Bagheri scored six goals and Ali Karimi four. Future national coach Ali Daei and Farhad Majidi both netted three. This was two goals better than Iran's previous highest qualifying win, 17-0 against the Maldives on June 2, 1997, during which Bagheri scored seven times. Two days after its 19-goal thrashing, Guam crashed 16-0 to Tajikistan.

PALESTINE THE PIONEERS

Palestine, then under British rule, was the first Asian team to enter the FIFA World Cup qualifiers. It lost 7-1 away to Egypt on March 16, 1934, and lost the return leg, at home, on April, 6, 4-1. Four years later, its was eliminated by Greece, after losing 3-1 in Tel Aviv and 1-0 in Greece.

WORLD'S WORST

On the same day that Brazil and Germany contested the FIFA World Cup final on 30 June 2002, the two lowest-ranked FIFA countries were also taking each other on. Asian side Bhutan ran out 4-0 winners over CONCACAF's Montserrat, in a match staged in the Bhutan capital Thimphu. The winning side's captain, striker Wangay Dorji, scored a hat-trick.

IRAQ AND ROLL

One of the greatest—and most heart-warming—surprises of recent international soccer was Iraq's unexpected triumph at the 2007 AFC Asian Cup, barely a year after the end of the war that had ravaged the country and forced it to play "home" games elsewhere. Despite disrupted preparations, Iraq eliminated Vietnam and South Korea on the way to the 2007 final, in which captain **Younis Mahmoud**'s goal proved decisive against Saudi Arabia. It failed to retain irs title four years later, losing to Australia in the quarterfinal. Mahmoud retired from international soccer in March 2014, ending his Iraq career with 50 goals in 124 matches, second in both categories, behind only Hussein Saeed, who scored 61 goals in 126 appearances between 1977 and 1990.

AI–DEAYEA CAPS THEM ALL

Saudi goalkeeper Mohamed Al-Deayea had to choose between soccer and handball as a youngster. He was persuaded by his elder brother Abdullah to pick soccer and he went on to make 181 appearances for his country: the first coming against Bangladesh in 1990, and the last against Belgium in May 2006. He also appeared in the FIFA World Cup finals tournaments of 1994, 1998, and 2002. He played his last finals game in a 3-0 defeat by the Republic of Ireland on June 11, 2002, and although Al-Deayea was recalled to the squad for the 2006 finals, he did not play.

HAPPY DAEI

Iran striker **Ali Daei** became the first player to score a century of international goals, when his four in a 7-0 defeat of Laos on November 17, 2004 took him to 102. He ended his career having scored 109 times for Iran in 149 internationals between 1993 and 2006, though none came during his two FIFA World Cup finals—in 1998, and 2006. He is also the all-time leading scorer in the AFC Asian Cup, with 14 goals, despite failing ever to win the tournament. His time as national coach was less auspicious: he lasted only a year from March 2008 to March 2009 before being fired, as Iran struggled in vain to qualify for the 2010 FIFA World Cup.

ONE OF BARCA'S BEST

The first Asian soccer player ever to appear for a European club was also, for almost a century, Spanish giants Barcelona's all-time leading scorer. Paulino Alcantara, from the Philippines, scored 369 goals in 357 matches for the Catalan club between 1912 and 1927, a record finally overtaken by Lionel Messi in March 2014. He made his debut aged just 15, and remains Barcelona's youngest-ever first-team player. Alcantara was born in the Philippines, but had a Spanish father, and appeared in internationals for Catalonia, Spain, and the Philippines—featuring in the Philippines' record 15-2 victory over Japan in 1917. Alcantara became a doctor after retiring from soccer at the age of 31, though he did briefly coach Spain in 1951.

SURPRISE SEVEN

The top scorer in the Asian qualification campaign for the 2014 FIFA World Cup was Japan's eight-goal Shinji Okazaki, but he was followed by players from outside the Asian Confederation's traditional superpowers. Tied on seven goals apiece were Iraq's Younis Mahmoud, Jordan's Ahmad Hayel, and Hassan Abdel-Fattah, and Vietnam's **Le Cong Vinh**, whose strikes helped him to an all-time national record of 31. Jordan, in the fourth and final round of AFC qualifiers for the first time, was coached by Adnan Hamad, who had previously served five different stints as coach of his native Iraq.

KUWAIT IN GOLD

Kuwait's one and only AFC Asian Cup triumph came in 1980, when it also hosted the tournament. It beat South Korea 3-0 in the final, having lost by the same scoreline, to the same opponent, in a first-round group game. Faisal Al-Dakhil was Kuwait's hero in the final, scoring two of the goals, his fourth and fifth of the tournament. He had also struck what proved to be the winner in a 2-1 sem-final victory over Iran.

THE JONG TURNING

North Korea's star striker at the 2010 FIFA World Cup, Jong Tae-Se, sobbed when its anthem was played before the first game against Brazil, but he had never actually visited the country he was playing for. Jong was born in Japan, where he continues to play his club soccer for Kawasaki Frontale, and has parents who are South Korean citizens. But he chose to pursue his family right to a North Korean passport.

AFC ASIAN CUP ALL-TIME TOP SCORERS

1	**Ali Daei** (Iran)	14
2	**Lee Dong-Gook** (South Korea)	10
3	**Naohiro Takahara** (Japan)	9
4	**Jassem Al-Houwaidi** (Kuwait)	8
5	**Behtash Fariba** (Iran)	7
=	**Hossein Kalani** (Iran)	7
=	**Choi Soon-Ho** (South Korea)	7
=	**Faisal Al-Dakhil** (Kuwait)	7
9	**Yasser Al-Qahtani** (Saudi Arabia)	6
=	**Alexander Geynrikh** (Uzbekistan)	6

PAK STRIKE MAKES HISTORY

North Korea's **Pak Doo Ik** earned legendary status by scoring the goal that eliminated Italy from the 1966 FIFA World Cup finals. The shockwaves caused by the victory were comparable to those when the United States defeated England 1-0 in Belo Horizonte, Brazil, in 1950. Pak scored the only goal of the game in the 42nd minute at Middlesbrough on July 19. North Korea became the first Asian team to reach the quarterfinal. Pak, an army corporal, was promoted to sergeant after the victory and later became a gymnastics coach.

ASIAN FOOTBALLER OF THE YEAR

Year	Player	Country
1988	Ahmed Radhi	Iraq
1989	Kim Joo-Sung	South Korea
1990	Kim Joo-Sung	South Korea
1991	Kim Joo-Sung	South Korea
1992	not awarded	
1993	Kazuyoshi Miura	Japan
1994	Saeed Owarain	Saudi Arabia
1995	Masami Ihara	Japan
1996	Khodadad Azizi	Iran
1997	Hidetoshi Nakata	Japan
1998	Hidetoshi Nakata	Japan
1999	Ali Daei	Iran
2000	Nawaf Al Temyat	Saudi Arabia
2001	Fan Zhiyi	China
2002	Shinji Ono	Japan
2003	Mehdi Mahdavikia	Iran
2004	Ali Karimi	Iran
2005	Hamad Al-Montashari	Saudi Arabia
2006	Khalfan Ibrahim	Qatar
2007	Yasser Al-Qahtani	Saudi Arabia
2008	Server Djeparov	Uzbekistan
2009	Yasuhito Endo	Japan
2010	Sasa Ognenovski	Australia
2011	Server Djeparov	Uzbekistan
2012	Lee Keun-Ho	South Korea
2013	Zheng Zhi	China

SO NEAR AND SO FAR

The Asian Confederation's two third-placed teams in the final qualifying group for the 2014 FIFA World Cup, Uzbekistan and Jordan, had to meet for the right to play in the inter-continental playoff. The Uzbeks finished behind group runner-up South Korea with an inferior goal difference of on,e despite a 5-1 win over Qatar, when substitute Basodir Nasimov equalized just 18 seconds after coming on. Jordan, with **Amer Shafi** heroic in goal, won 9-8 on penalties, after two 1-1 ties, but lost to Uruguay 5-0 on aggregate and missed out on the finals.

AFC ASIAN CUP–WINNING COACHES

1956	**Lee Yoo-Hyung** (South Korea)	
1960	**Wi Hye-Deok** (South Korea)	
1964	**Gyula Mandl** (Israel)	
1968	**Mahmoud Bayati** (Iran)	
1972	**Mohammad Ranjbar** (Iran)	
1976	**Heshmat Mohajerani** (Iran)	
1980	**Carlos Alberto Parreira** (Kuwait)	
1984	**Khalil Al-Zayani** (Saudi Arabia)	
1988	**Carlos Alberto Parreira** (Saudi Arabia)	
1992	**Hans Ooft** (Japan)	
1996	**Nelo Vingada** (Saudi Arabia)	
2000	**Philippe Troussier** (Japan)	
2004	**Zico** (Japan)	
2007	**Jorvan Vieira** (Iraq)	
2011	**Alberto Zaccheroni** (Japan)	

AL-JABER TO THE FORE

Sami Al-Jaber (born on December 11, 1972, in Riyadh) became only the second Asian player to appear in four FIFA World Cup finals tournaments, when he started against Tunisia in Munich on June 14, 2006. He scored in a 2-2 tie, his third goal in nine appearances at the finals. Al-Jaber played only one game in 1998, before he was rushed to hospital with a burst appendix, which ruled him out of the competition. He became Saudi Arabia's record scorer, with 44 goals in 163 matches.

A LONG JOURNEY FOR A BEATING

The first Asian country to play in a FIFA World Cup finals was Indonesia, who played in France in 1938 as the Dutch East Indies. The tournament was a straight knockout and, on 5 June in Reims, Hungary beat it 6-0, with goals from Gyorgy Sarosi, Gyula Zsengeller (two each), Vilmos Kohut and Geza Toldi.

A RESULT FOR REZA

No AFC nation reached the 2014 FIFA World Cup knock-out stages for the first time since 1998. Japan, South Korea, Australia, and Iran all went out in the first-round, but Iran forward **Reza Ghoochannejhad**'s consolation goal in its final game, a 3-1 loss to Bosnia-Herzegovina, meant that all the finalists had scored. This had not happened at a FIFA World Cup since 1998, when the tournament first expanded to 32 teams. Ghoochannejhad also scored Iran's goal in the 1-0 win against South Korea in June 2013 that ensured it finished at the top of its final Asian qualification group.

FOREIGN DOUBLE AGENT

Brazilian Carlos Alberto Parreira is the only coach to win the AFC Asian Cup twice, and he did so with two different countries. His Kuwait team won in 1980, and he got his hands on the trophy again, eight years later, this time in charge of Saudi Arabia.

LOCAL COACHES MAKE THEIR MARK

No one has won the AFC Coach of the Year award more than once since it was introduced in 1994, though Asians have claimed the prize every year except when it went to Japan's French boss Philipppe Troussier in 2000, and South Korea's Dutch coach Guus Hiddink two years later. Women's soccer was recognized, with triumphs for China coach Ma Yuanan in 1996, North Korea's U-20 manager Choe Kwang-Sok ten years later, and Japan's FIFA Women's World Cup-winning coach Norio Sasaki in 2011. The award 12 months later went to Kim Ho-Gon, coach of South Korean club Ulsan Hyundai.

HIGHEST ... AND LOWEST

The highest attendance for an Asian country in a home FIFA World Cup qualifying game was the 130,000 who watched Iran tie 1-1 with Australia in the Azadi Stadium, Tehran, on November 22, 1997. The game was the first leg of a final playoff for the last place at the 1998 finals. Iran advanced on away goals after tying the second leg 2-2 in Melbourne. The lowest attendance was the "crowd" of 20 that turned out for Turkmenistan's 1-0 win over Taiwan, played in Amman, Jordan, on May 7, 2001.

HUGE FOLLOWING FOR SOCCER IN CHINA

China's national team boasts a massive fan base, as was demonstrated when it reached the FIFA World Cup finals for the only time in 2002. Between its qualification on October 19, 2001, and its opening game of the finals against Costa Rica on June 4, 2002, an estimated 170 million new television sets were sold throughout China. TV audiences for the team's three gamees regularly topped 300 million, even though China lost all three games and failed to score a goal.

CHINA'S 4X4

Four teams carry the name of China. The China national team receives the most attention, but Hong Kong (a former British colony) and Macau (a former Portuguese colony) both retain their autonomous status for socer, as Hong Kong China and Macau China, respectively. Meanwhile, the independent island state of Taiwan competes in the FIFA World Cup and other competitions as Chinese Taipei.

ABOUT UZ

Uzbekistan's four most-capped internationals are still active: midfielders Timur Kapadze (109 appearances) and two-time Asian Footballer of the Year Server Djeparov (100), striker Alexander Geynrikh (84), and goalkeeper Ignatiy Nesterov (83). Striker **Maksim Shatskikh** leads the nation's scoring list, with 34 goals in 61 games. He has also enjoyed success in Ukraine with several teams, including Dynamo Kiev, where he became the second Uzbek, after Mirjalol Qosimov, to score in UEFA club competitions. Qosimov, who scored 31 goals for Uzbekistan, is now the national team coach.

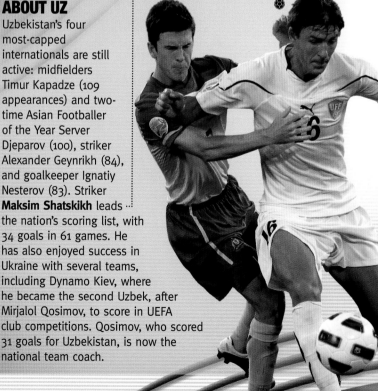

UAE KO ZAGALLO

Brazilian great Mario Zagallo, who won the FIFA World Cup as both player and manager, coached the United Arab Emirates when it qualified for its one and only FIFA World Cup finals in 1990. But despite his success in the Asian qualifiers, he was sacked on the eve of the FIFA World Cup itself. Zagallo was replaced by Polish coach Bernard Blaut, and the UAE team lost all three games at Italia 90. Other big names to have managed the UAE over the years include Brazil's Carlos Alberto Parreira (another FIFA World Cup winner with Brazil), England's Don Revie and Roy Hodgson, Ukraine's Valery Lobanovsky, and Portugal's Carlos Queiroz.

SOVIET REPUBLICS FIND NEW HOME

The break-up of the former Soviet Union swelled the ranks of the Asian Football Confederation in the early 1990s. Former Soviet republics Kazakhstan, Kyrgyzstan, Tajikistan, Turkmenistan, and Uzbekistan, all joined in 1994, though Kazakhstan joined UEFA in 2002. **Uzbekistan** has been the most successful in the Asian Cup, reaching the quarterfinal in 2004 and 2007, and finishing fourth in 2011. Australia was the AFC's 46th, and newest, member, switching from Oceania, on January 1, 2006, a few months after East Timor had become the 45th.

DOUBLE AGENT

Although North Korea's Kim Myong-Won usually plays as a striker, he was named as one of three goalkeepers in the country's 23-man squad for the 2010 FIFA World Cup. FIFA told North Korea he would only be able to play in goal, rather than outfield, though he failed to make it on to the pitch in any form during his country's three Group G matches.

THE ISRAEL ISSUE

Israel is, geographically, an Asian nation. It hosted, and won, the Asian Cup in 1964. But, over the years, many Asian confederation countries have refused to play Israel, citing political and/or safety reasons. When Israel reached the 1970 FIFA World Cup finals, it came through a qualifying tournament involving two Asian nations, Japan and South Korea, and two from Oceania, Australia and New Zealand. In 1989, Israel topped the Oceania group, but lost a final play-off to Colombia for a place in the 1990 finals. It switched to the European zone qualifiers in 1992 and has been a full member of the European confederation, UEFA, since 1994.

ASIAN CUP WINNERS

The Asian Cup is Asia's continental championship

Year	Winners
1956	South Korea
1960	South Korea
1964	Israel
1968	Iran
1972	Iran
1976	Iran
1980	Kuwait
1984	Saudi Arabia
1988	Saudi Arabia
1992	Japan
1996	Saudi Arabia
2000	Japan
2004	Japan
2007	Iraq
2011	Japan

FROZEN OUT

Mongolia went 38 years without playing a single international—between 1960 and 1998—and the country still barely stages any action, international or domestic, due to below-freezing conditions between October and June.

OCEANIA

Soccer in Oceania can claim some of the most eye-catching statistics—though not necessarily in a way many there would welcome, especially the long-suffering goalkeepers from minnow islands on the end of cricket-style scorelines. The departure to the Asian Football Confederation of Australia, seeking more testing competition, was a morale blow—but benefited New Zealand out on the field. The finals tournament of the 2010 FIFA World Cup was the first to feature both Australia and New Zealand.

KAREMBEU THE FIFA WORLD CUP WINNER

Christian Karembeu, born in New Caledonia, is the only FIFA World Cup winner to come from the Oceania region. He started for France in its 3-0 final victory over Brazil on July 12, 1998. The defensive midfielder had earlier played against Denmark (group), Italy (quarterfinal), and Croatia (semifinal). He played 53 times for France, scoring one goal, and was also a double UEFA Champions League winner with Real Madrid, in 1998 in 2000.

RYAN'S SISTER

New Zealand's captain **Ryan Nelsen** flew back from Blackburn in England to his native city of Christchurch in March 2011 after the city was devastated by an earthquake. Nelsen was worried for the safety of his family, especially his pregnant sister Stephanie Martin— but after being "knocked down" by the 6.3-magnitude quake, she safely gave birth to a healthy baby boy.

PAIA FIRE IN VAIN

No team from Oceania, other than Australia or New Zealand, has ever qualified for the men's soccer tournament at the Olympic Games, but Fiji came close to reaching the 2012 event, only losing 1-0 to New Zealand in the qualifying competition final. The top scorers were the Solomon Islands, but it didn't make it out of its opening group. It recorded a best first-round goal difference of +12, thanks to a 16-1 destruction of American Samoa, which included seven goals from Ian Paia. However, losses to Fiji and Vanuatu left it third in the four-team section.

TOP CAPS: NEW ZEALAND

1	Ivan Vicelich	88
2	Simon Elliott	69
3	Vaughan Coveney	64
4	Ricki Herbert	61
5	Chris Jackson	60
6	Brian Turner	59
7	Duncan Cole	58
=	Steve Sumner	58
9	Chris Zoricich	57
10	Leo Bertos	56
=	Ceri Evans	56

TOP SCORERS: NEW ZEALAND

1	Vaughan Coveney	28
2	Shane Smeltz	23
3	Steve Sumner	22
4	Brian Turner	21
5	Jock Newall	17
6	Chris Killen	16
=	Keith Nelson	16
8	Grant Turner	15
9	Darren McClennan	12
=	Michael McGarry	12
=	Wynton Rufer	12
=	Chris Wood	12

RETURNING RICKI

Ricki Herbert is the only soccer playerer from New Zealand to reach a FIFA World Cup twice. He played at left-back in the 1982 tournament in Spain, then coached the country to its second World Cup appearance, in 2010. Qualification, second time around, came courtesy of a play-off win over Asian Football Confederation representatives Bahrain. Herbert, born in Auckland in 1961, combined qualifying for the 2010 FIFA World Cup with coaching New Zealand-based club Wellington Phoenix, which plays in Australia's A-League. The New Zealand soccer authorities recently have been pondering whether to follow Australia in defecting from Oceania and joining the AFC.

TEHAU ABOUT THAT?

The Pacific Island underdogs of Tahiti finally broke the stranglehold Australia and New Zealand had on the OFC Nations Cup by winning the tournament when it was held for the ninth time in 2012, following four previous triumphs for Australia and four for New Zealand. Tahiti scored 20 goals in its five games at the event in the Solomon Islands, 15 of which came from the Tehau family: brothers Lorenzo (five), Alvin and **Jonathan Tehau** (four each), and their cousin Teaonui (two). Steevy Chong Hue scored the only goal of the final, against New Caledonia, to give the team caoched by Eddy Etaeta not only the trophy but a place at the 2013 FIFA Confederations Cup in Brazil.

PIERRE'S PERFECT START

The very first goal of the 2010 FIFA World Cup was scored, in qualifying, by New Caledonia's Pierre Wajoka – the only strike of an August 2007 game against Tahiti, the country of his birth.

BAD LUCK OF THE DRAW

Despite featuring at only its second-ever FIFA World Cup, and their first since 1982, New Zealand did not lose a game in South Africa in 2010. It tied all three first-round games, against Slovakia, Italy, and Paraguay. The three points were not enough to secure a top-two finish in Group F, but third-placed New Zealand did finish above defending world champion Italy. The only other three teams to be eliminated despite going unbeaten in three first-round group games were: Scotland (in 1974), Cameroon (in 1982), and Belgium (in 1998).

LAUGHING ALL THE WAY TO THE BANK

New Zealand went to the 2010 FIFA World Cup with four amateur players in its 23-man squad. Midfielder **Andy Barron**, who worked as an investment adviser at a bank in Wellington, even made it on to the pitch as a stoppage-time substitute against reigning world champion Italy.

"WORLD'S WORST TEAM" TO SILVER SCREEN

Nicky Salapu was in goal when American Samoa set an unwanted international record, losing 31-0 to Australia in April 2001, two days after Australia had crushed Tonga 22-0. Passport problems had denied American Samoa some of its best players for the Australia game and it had to field three 15-year-olds in a team with an average age of 18. Salapu was also playing when American Samoa finally won its first competitive international, 2-1 against Tonga in November 2011, thanks to goals by Ramin Ott and Shamin Luani. This was followed by a 1-1 tie with the Cook Islands, during a 2014 FIFA World Cup qualification campaign during which American Samoa was coached by a Dutchman, Thomas Rongen, and followed by film crews making a documentary movie, *Next Goal Wins*. It was released in 2014 to widespread critical acclaim—including for Jaiyah Saelua, the world's first transgender international soccer player. He was born biologically male, but is from the Fa'afafine people, a traditional American Samoan group with both masculine and feminine traits, and often described as "third-gender".

THE WHITE STUFF

New Zealand's national soccer team is known as the "All-Whites". This is not just a recognition of its kit colors, but also a counterpoint to the "All-Blacks" nickname of the country's more famous and successful rugby union side.

CONCACAF

The power and passion of soccer in the Caribbean, central and North America was illustrated dramatically at the 2014 FIFA World Cup finals. Costa Rica, Mexico, and the United States, all progressed beyond the group stage in Brazil, with the popular adventurers of Costa Rica going the furthest. "Los Ticos" reached the quarterfinal for the first time, and only lost to 2010 finalist, the Netherlands, on the lottery of a penalty shoot-out. Keeping CONCACAF squarely in focus, Canada will be the host of the FIFA Women's World Cup in 2015.

Record television ratings back home followed the United States' run to the round-of-16 at the 2014 FIFA World Cup in Brazil, where US fans also topped the foreign tickets "ranking."

MEXICO

Mexico may well be the powerhouse of the CONCACAF region, and it is a regular qualifier for the FIFA World Cup—it has not played in the finals on just four occasions (1934, 1974, 1982, and 1990). But Mexico has always struggled to impose itself on the international stage. Two FIFA World Cup quarterfinal appearances (both times when it was the tournament host, in 1970 and 1986) represent its best performances to date. This soccer-mad nation expects more.

TOP SCORERS

1	Jared Borghetti	46
2	Cuauhtemoc Blanco	39
3	Javier Hernandez	35
=	Carlos Hermosillo	35
=	Luis Hernandez	35
6	Enrique Borja	31
7	Luis Roberto Alves	30
8	Luis Flores	29
=	Benjamin Galindo	29
=	Luis Garcia	29
=	Hugo Sanchez	29

VICTOR HUGO

Jared Borgetti may hold the record as Mexico's all-time leading scorer, but perhaps the country's most inspirational striker remains **Hugo Sanchez,** famed for his acrobatic bicycle-kick finishes and somersault celebrations. Sanchez played for Mexico at the 1978, 1986, and 1994 FIFA World Cups and would surely have done so had it qualified in 1982 and 1990. During spells in Spain, with Atletico Madrid and Real Madrid, between 1985 and 1990, he finished as La Liga's top scorer five years out of six. He was less successful as Mexico coach from 2006 to 2008, the best result being third in the 2007 Copa America.

MAKING HIS MARQUEZ

Commanding center-back **Rafael Marquez** made history in 2014 as the first player to captain his country at four consecutive FIFA World Cups. His four games in 2014 took him to 16 FIFA World Cup appearances, beyond Antonio Carbajal, whose 11 were spread across five not four tournaments. Marquez scored against Cameroon in 2014, having also registered in 2006 and 2010, making him the second Mexican to score at three different FIFA World Cups, after Cuauhtemoc Blanco.

PRECOCIOUS PEREZ

Mexico's youngest international remains midfielder **Luis Ernesto Perez,** who won the first of his 69 caps at the age of 17 years and 308 days, against El Salvador on November 17, 1998. Less impressive was his red card in Mexico's third first-round game against Portugal at the 2006 FIFA World Cup. Hugo Sanchez was the nation's oldest player, 39 years and 251 days old for his final international, against Paraguay on March 19, 1998, though this was a farewell game for Sanchez, four years after his previous Mexico appearance, and he was replaced in the first minute by Luis Garcia.

TOP CAPS

1	Claudio Suarez	178
2	Pavel Pardo	148
3	Gerardo Torrado	146
4	Jorge Campos	130
5	Rafael Marquez	124
=	Carlos Salcido	124
7	Ramon Ramirez	121
8	Cuauhtemoc Blanco	120
9	Alberto Garcia-Aspe	109
10	Andres Guardado	108

LITTLE PEA FROM A POD

When Javier Hernandez appeared for Mexico against South Africa on June 11, 2010, he became the third generation of his family to play at a FIFA World Cup. Hernandez, nicknamed "Chicharito," or "Little Pea," is the son of Javier Hernandez, who reached the quarterfinal with Mexico in 1986, and the grandson of Tomas Balcazar, a member of the country's 1954 squad. Another Mexican pair were the first grandfather-grandson pairing to each play at the finals. Luis Perez represented Mexico in 1930 in Uruguay. His grandson Mario Perez played for Mexico, on home soil, 40 years later. Hernandez scored all three of Mexico's goals at the 2013 FIFA Confederations Cup, in a 2-1 loss to Italy and a 2-1 win over Japan, taking him to joint-third in his country's scoring ranks, alongside Carlos Hermosillo and Luis Hernandez. Chicharito reached the tally in 53 games, compared to Hermosillo's 90 and Luis Hernandez's 85.

FAMILY SPLIT

Winger **Giovani dos Santos** was distraught when Mexico's 30-man preliminary squad was reduced to 23 for the 2010 FIFA World Cup, but not for the obvious reason. He actually made the cut, and played in all four of Mexico's games, but his brother, Jonathan dos Santos, was left out by coach Javier Aguirre. Gio was again the only brother to make the cut in 2014, when he was among Mexico's most impressive performers and looked like putting it through to the quarterfinal with a stunning volley against the Netherlands. But Mexico conceded two goals in the last minutes and was eliminated.

MEXICO BEATS EARTHQUAKE

Mexico stepped in to host the 1986 FIFA World Cup finals after the original choice, Colombia, pulled out in November 1982. FIFA chose Mexico as the replacement venue because of its stadiums and infrastructure, still in place from the 1970 finals. The governing body turned down rival bids from Canada and the United States. Mexico had to work overtime to be ready for the finals, after the earthquake of September 19, 1985, which killed an estimated 10,000 people in central Mexico and destroyed many buildings in Mexico City.

SUAREZ IS NUMBER TWO ALL-TIME

Only Egyptian midfielder Ahmed Hassan played more internationals than Mexico defender **Claudio Suarez**, who made 178 appearances. Suarez—nicknamed "The Emperor"—played in all of Mexico's four games at the 1994 and the 1998 FIFA World Cups, but had to miss the 2002 finals after suffering a broken leg. He was a member of the squad for the 2006 tournament in Germany, but did not play.

ROSAS NETS HISTORIC PENALTY

Mexico's Manuel Rosas scored the first penalty ever awarded in the FIFA World Cup finals when he converted a 42nd-minute spot-kick in his country's match against Argentina in 1930. Rosas scored again in the 65th minute, but it was too little and too late for the Mexicans: it crashed to a 6-3 defeat.

SO NEAR, SO FAR

Mexico has become expert at getting out of the first round at the FIFA World Cup but, in recent years it has been a matter of thus far, and no further. It has now gone out at the round-of-16 stage six tournaments in a row, the latest being its last-gasp 2-1 defeat to the Netherlands in Fortaleza in 2014. The coach in 2014 was the excitable **Miguel Herrera**, whose extravagant touchline antics caught the eye almost as compellingly as the on-pitch action. Herrera, who played 14 times for Mexico in 1993 and 1994, took charge in October 2013—the country's fourth different coach within the space of a month, at a time when qualification for Brazil 2014 had seemed unlikely. But he guided the team into the finals, after beating New Zealand 9-3 in a playoff.

UNITED STATES

Some of soccer's biggest names, from Pele to David Beckham, have graced the United States' domestic leagues over the years, and the country is one of only 15 countries to have had the honor of hosting a FIFA World Cup. Although soccer is still considered a minority sport in the world's most powerful nation, following impressive performances on the world stage, especially at the Brazil 2014 World Cup, and a huge upsurge in support, this situation may well change in the very near future.

TOP CAPS

1	Cobi Jones	164
2	Landon Donovan	156
3	Jeff Agoos	134
4	Marcelo Balboa	128
5	DaMarcus Beasley	120
6	Claudio Reyna	112
7	Carlos Bocanegra	110
=	Paul Caligiuri	110
9	Clint Dempsey	109
10	Eric Wynalda	106

ALTIDORE OPENS THE FLOODGATES

Jozy Altidore became the United States' youngest scorer of an international hat-trick in a 3-0 victory over Trinidad and Tobago on April 1, 2009, aged 19 years and 146 days. But after a 15-month barren spell between November 2011 and June 2013, he scored the opener in a 4-3 defeat of Germany in a Washington DC exhibition game. He then scored against Jamaica, Panama, and Honduras to equal a national record of scoring four games in a row, joining William Lubb, Eric Wynalda, Eddie Johnson, **Brian McBride**, and Landon Donovan. Altidore's scoring spree came in a 2012–13 season in which he also set a US record for goals in a European club league, with 31 for Dutch club AZ Alkmaar. Sadly his 2014 FIFA World Cup was ended by a hamstring injury 23 minutes into the opening game against Ghana.

CALIGIURI'S SHOT MAKES HISTORY

The US's FIFA World Cup qualifying win in Trinidad, on November 19, 1989, is regarded as a turning point in the country's soccer history. The team included just one full-time professional, Paul Caligiuri, of West German second division club Meppen. He scored the only goal of the game with a looping shot after 31 minutes to take the United States to its first finals for 40 years. Trinidad's goalkeeper, Michael Maurice, claimed to have been blinded by the sun, but the win raised the profile of the US team hugely, despite a first-round elimination in the 1990 FIFA World Cup.

LANDON HOPE AND GLORY

The US's all-time leading scorer **Landon Donovan** was the undoubted star of their 2010 FIFA World Cup campaign. He scored three goals in four games, including a stoppage-time winner against Algeria that a result that saw the team finish top of Group C. His four displays at the tournament meant he had featured in 13 FIFA World Cup games for the USA, two ahead of compatriots Earnie Stewart and Cobi Jones. His successful penalty in a second-round defeat to Ghana also made him the United States' leading scorer in the competition, with five goals, one more than 1930 hat-trick hero Bert Patenaude. Donovan was the first player to score more than one hat-trick for the US, having hit four goals against Cuba in July 2003, then trebles versus Ecuador in March 2007 and Scotland in May 2012—at which time only nine other players had registered even one hat-trick.

HIGH-POWERED BACKING

US president Barack Obama was among the millions of Americans who enthused over the 2014 FIFA World Cup like never before. Many millions tuned in to watch the games in their homes, it was estimated 25 million for the team's 2-2 tie with Portugal in the group stage, and millions more watched in bars and clubs. Team USA also faced Joachim Low's Germany in the first-round, pitting US coach Jurgen Klinsmann against his native land, the country he had led at the 2006 FIFA World Cup, with Low as his assistant. Low's men won 1-0 to top Group G, with Team US second. Then some 28,000 fans crowded into Chicago's Soldier Field for big-screen coverage of the US's round-of-16 game against Belgium. It lost, bravely, 2-1 after extra-time, despite goalkeeper Tim Howard making a FIFA World Cup record 16 saves.

PAYING HIS DEUCE

Clint Dempsey got Team USA's 2014 FIFA World Cup off to the ideal start by scoring against Ghana after just 30 seconds. This was not only the fifth fastest goal in the tournament's history but also made him the first man to score for the US at three different FIFA World Cups. The striker, nicknamed "Deuce," is second only to Landon Donovan in the nation's international scoring records. Donovan, having played at the 2002, 2006, and 2010 finals, was contentiously left out of the 2014 squad by coach Jurgen Klinsmann, meaning that DaMarcus Beasley became the first USA player to appear in four FIFA World Cup finals.

ENGLAND STUNNED BY GAETJENS

The United States' 1-0 defeat of England on June 29, 1950, ranks among the biggest surprises in FIFA World Cup history. England, along with hosts Brazil, were joint favorites to win the trophy. The US had lost their last seven matches, scoring just two goals. Joe Gaetjens scored the only goal, in the 37th minute, diving to head Walter Bahr's cross past goalkeeper Bert Williams. England dominated the game, but US keeper Frank Borghi made save after save. Defeats by Chile and Spain eliminated the US at the group stage, but its victory over England remains the best result in the country's soccer history.

MILITARY SUB

Berlin-born defender **John Brooks**, who represented both the USA and Germany at U20s level, opted to play full international soccer for the American homeland of his armed forces-serving parents. His first goal for his country proved decisive in its first 2014 FIFA World Cup game against Ghana, securing a 2-1 victory in the 86th minute at Natal's Estadio das Dunas. Brooks also became the first USA substitute to score in the FIFA World Cup, after replacing Matt Besler for the second half.

TOP SCORERS

1	Landon Donovan	57
2	Clint Dempsey	39
3	Eric Wynalda	34
4	Brian McBride	30
5	Joe-Max Moore	24
6	Jozy Altidore	23
7	Bruce Murray	21
8	Eddie Johnson	19
9	DaMarcus Beasley	17
=	Earnie Stewart	17

"OLD MAN" HAHNEMANN

Goalkeeper Marcus Hahnemann became the United States' oldest international when he faced Paraguay on March 29, 2011, at the age of 38 years and 286 days. That was the last of his nine caps, testament to the US's strength in depth when it comes to goalkeepers in recent years – Kasey Keller (101 caps), Tim Howard (103), and Brad Friedel (82) were among the competition. Hahnemann's debut was in 1994, followed by two more appearances that year, but he then had to wait until 2004 for his next international action.

KEEPING UP WITH JONES

His dreadlocked hair helped catch the attention, but **Cobi Jones**'s raiding runs down the wing also made him one of the host country's most high-profile performers at the 1994 FIFA World Cup. Jones went on to become the US's most-capped player, with 164 international appearances between 1992 and 2004. When he finally retired from all forms of the game in 2007, his number 13 shirt was officially "retired" by the Los Angeles Galaxy, the first time a Major League Soccer club had honored a player in such a way. Jones had been with the Galaxy since the MLS was launched in 1996 and later served the club as assistant coach and caretaker manager.

CONCACAF OTHER TEAMS

Mexico and the United States (with 25 FIFA World Cup finals appearances between them) are clearly the powerhouses of the CONCACAF region, which takes in North and Central America, and the Caribbean. But Mexico only reached the 2014 finals via a play-off, after finishing behind automatic qualifiers USA, Honduras, and Costa Rica. The surprising Costa Ricans were one of the standout performers in the finals, outdoing their Confederation rivals by reaching the quarterfinal.

KEYLOR IS KEY

Costa Rica made its FIFA World Cup finals debut in 1990 and goalkeeper Luis Gabelo Conejo shared the best goalkeeper award with Argentina's Sergio Goycochea as his displays helped his team reach the knock-out stages. "Los Ticos" did even better in 2014, and while goalscorers **Joel Campbell** and Bryan Ruiz impressed, again a goalkeeper was crucial: **Keylor Navas** was named man of the match four times in five games. Costa Rica went to the quarterfinal, but lost to Netherlands, only after a penalty shoot-out. Costa Rica had topped the so-called "Group Of Death" by beating two former FIFA World Cup winners, Uruguay and Italy, and tying with another, England. Navas conceded only two goals at the finals and his penalty shoot-out save from Theofanis Gekas helped his team to overcome Greece in the round-of-16. Costa Rica became only the second CONCACAF team, after Mexico in 1986, to be eliminated without losing a game in regulation-time.

PAVON ... AND ON ... AND ON

Striker **Carlos Pavon**, with 101, is one of four Honduras players to win 100 caps. The others are defender Maynor Figueroa (108), goalkeeper Noel Valladares (125), and midfielder Amado Guevara (138). Guevara, in 2010, and Valladares, in 2014, also captained Honduras in the FIFA World Cup finals. Pavon scored seven goals in the 2010 qualifying tournament, as Honduras reached its first FIFA World Cup finals since 1982. But then aged 36, he played just 60 minutes in the finals. Nicknamed "The Shadow," Pavon played club soccer in seven countries before he retired in 2013: Honduras, Mexico, Spain, Italy, Colombia, Guatemala, and the US, where he was an LA Galaxy team-mate of David Beckham.

WAITING GAMES

Patience is the watchword for many of Central America's smaller nations when it comes to soccer achievement—or even participation. International games are rare in Montserrat due to the risk of volcanic activity on the 5,000-population Caribbean island. The team has played just 15 international matches in the 21st century, none between November 2004 and March 2008. More positively, Puerto Rico finally ended a 14-year wait for a win when it beat Bermuda 2-0 in January 2008, before reaching the second round of CONCACAF's qualifiers for the 2010 FIFA World Cup. The British Virgin Islands was eliminated from those qualifiers despite not losing a game, as its two-legged first-round tie against the Bahamas ended 5-5 on aggregate, but the British Virgin Islands was knocked out on away goals.

COSTA RICA WIN WITHOUT A CROWD

The lowest-ever attendance for a CONCACAF FIFA World Cup qualifier was for the Costa Rica–Panama game on March 26, 2005. FIFA ordered the game, staged at the Saprissa Stadium, San Jose, to be played behind closed doors after missiles were thrown at visiting players and the match officials when Mexico won there 2-1 on February 9. The game was known as "the ghost match." Costa Rica beat Panama 2-1, thanks to a **Roy Myrie** goal in the first minute of stoppage time.

CONCACAF TEAMS IN THE FIFA WORLD CUP FINALS

Appearances made by teams from the CONCACAF region at the FIFA World Cup finals

1	Mexico	15
2	US	10
3	Costa Rica	4
4	Honduras	3
5	El Salvador	2
6	Canada	1
=	Cuba	1
=	Haiti	1
=	Jamaica	1
=	Trinidad & Tobago	1

CELSO LIKE HIS FATHER

Costa Rica playmaker Celso Borges was delighted, in 2014, to emulate his father by reaching the knock-out stages of the FIFA World Cup. He actually went one better as he scored the first penalty of "Los Ticos'" 5-3 shoot-out win against Greece in the round-of-16. His Brazilian-born father, Alexandre Borges Guimares, played at the 1990 FIFA World Cup. He set up the late winner scored by Hernan Medford against Sweden to take the FIFA World Cup finals debutants beyond the first round. The man affectionately known as "Guima" was Costa Rica's coach at both the 2002 and 2006 FIFA World Cup finals, but it failed to go beyond the group stage on either occasion.

REGGAE BOYZ STEP UP

In 1998, Jamaica became the first team from the English-speaking Caribbean to reach the FIFA World Cup finals. The "Reggae Boyz," as Jamaica was nicknamed, included several players based in England. It was eliminated at the group stage, despite beating Japan 2-1 in its final game thanks to two goals by **Theodore Whitmore**. Jamaica had earlier lost 3-1 to Croatia and 5-0 against Argentina.

BROTHERS IN ARMS

Honduras became the first team to field not one, not two, but three siblings at a FIFA World Cup, when it selected defender Johnny, midfielder Wilson, and striker Jerry Palacios in its 2010 squad. There was an older brother, too, Milton Palacios, who played 14 times as a defender for Honduras between 2003 and 2006. Stoke City defensive midfielder Wilson was perhaps the most famous and acclaimed player in the first Honduras team to reach a FIFA World Cup in 28 years. However, just like the 1982 side, Reinaldo Rueda's men did not win a game. Both Jerry and Wilson made it into the 2014 FIFA World Cup squad, but it was not a happy time, especially for Wilson, who was sent off in the opening game against France. Honduras lost all three games, but did at least score in the defeat against Ecuador.

CUBA SHOW THE WAY

In 1938, Cuba became the first island state of the CONCACAF region to reach the FIFA World Cup quarterfinal. It tied 3-3 with Romania after extra-time in the first round, and won the replay 2-1, with goals by Hector Socorro and Carlos Oliveira, after trailing at half-time. Cuba was routed 8-0 by Sweden in the last eight. Haiti was the next Caribbean island to play in the finals, in 1974. It lost all three group games, 3-1 to Italy, 7-0 against Poland, and 4-1 to Argentina.

RUIZ ON TARGETS

Guatemala's all-time leading scorer **Carlos Ruiz** had double cause for celebration when scoring in a 3-3 tie with Paraguay in August 2012: he completed a century of international games, and a half-century of goals in the game. Nicknamed "Pescado," or "Fish," he announced his international retirement two months later, finishing with a record of 104 appearances and 55 goals.

STERN OPPOSITION

Only eight internationals have claimed more goals than the 70 in 114 games scored by Trinidad and Tobago's **Stern John** between his debut in 1995 and his final appearance for his country in 2011. The former Columbus Crew, Nottingham Forest, and Sunderland striker was Trinidad and Tobago's top scorer and second-highest appearance-maker, behind midfielder Angus Eve. John was part of the country's squad for the 2006 FIFA World Cup, though Eve missed out, prompting him to retire from international soccer after 117 appearances.

TRINIDAD'S FIRST TIME

Trinidad & Tobago reached the FIFA World Cup finals for the first time in 2006 after a marathon qualifying competition that ended with their 1-0 play-off victory in Bahrain. The team, nicknamed the "Socca Warriors", held Sweden 0-0 in their opening game, but lost 2-0 to England and 2-0 to Paraguay.

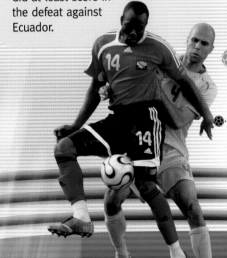

PART 3: UEFA EUROPEAN CHAMPIONSHIP

THE UEFA European Championship finals have gone from being a four-team curiosity, snubbed by major nations, to perhaps the third-biggest sports event on earth, behind only the FIFA World Cup and the Summer Olympic Games. UEFA, the European soccer confederation, was founded during the 1954 FIFA World Cup in Switzerland and initially set itself the task of creating a championship for national teams. Many major European nations—such as Italy, West Germany and England—refused to take part in the initial competition, launched in 1958, because their national associations feared fixture congestion. So the first finals, featuring four nations, were staged in France, and saw the Soviet Union end up as first winners, after defeating Yugoslavia in the final in Paris's original Parc des Princes.

Now the map of Europe has changed so remarkably that, while UEFA's membership has more than doubled, the Soviet Union and Yugoslavia no longer exist. The Soviets also reached the second finals in 1964 but lost their crown in the final against their Spanish hosts in the Estadio Bernabeu in Madrid. Spain's playmaker Luis Suarez, from Italy's Internazionale, thus became the first player to win the European Championship and the European Cup in the same season.

In the tournament's early years, qualifying was based on a simple two-legged knockout system, but this was amended to a group-based format and then, in 1980, the finals were expanded to eight nations. That year saw West Germany win for a second time, having previously triumphed in 1972. The next expansion, to 16 teams in England in 1996, saw unified Germany win its record third title, defeating the Czech Republic (once half of Czechoslovakia) with an extra-time golden goal.

Belgium and the Netherlands organized the first co-hosted finals in 2000. Eight years later Austria and Switzerland were co-hosts, and Spain then became the first team to retain the trophy when it triumphed again at Euro 2012, a tournament co-hosted behind the old Iron Curtain in Poland and Ukraine. France is due to stage the 2016 event with, for the first time, 24 teams.

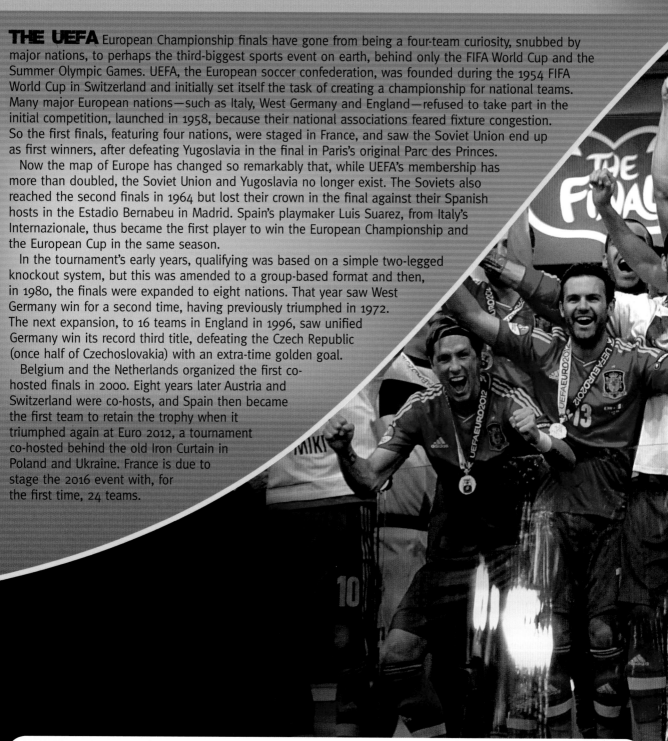

Goals from David Silva, Jordi Alba, Fernando Torres, and Juan Mata meant Spain's goalkeeper-captain Iker Casillas lifted the Henri Delaunay Trophy, his third international cup in a row, at the climax of Euro 2012.

UEFA EUROPEAN CHAMPIONSHIP TEAM RECORDS

FANCY SEEING YOU AGAIN

When Spain and Italy met in the 2012 final it was the fourth time UEFA European Championship opponents had faced each other twice in the same tournament. Each time, it followed a first-round encounter. The Netherlands lost to the Soviet Union, then beat it in the final in 1988; Germany beat the Czech Republic twice at Euro 96, including the final; and Greece did the same to Portugal in 2004. Spain and Italy drew in Euro 2012's Group C, with Cesc Fabregas replying to Antonio Di Natale's opener for Italy. Their second showdown was rather less even.

THREE OFF AS CZECHS ADVANCE

Czechoslovakia's 3-1 semifinal win over the Netherlands in Zagreb, on June 16, 1976, featured a record three red cards. The Czechs' Jaroslav Pollak was dismissed for a second yellow card—for a foul on Johan Neeskens—after an hour. Neeskens followed him off in the 76th minute—for kicking Zdenek Nehoda. Wim van Hanegem became the second Dutchman dismissed, for dissent, after Nehoda had scored the Czechs' second goal with six minutes remaining in extra-time.

DENMARK'S UNEXPECTED TRIUMPH

Denmark was the unlikely winner of UEFA Euro 1992. It had not even expected to take part after finishing behind Yugoslavia in its qualifying group, but it was invited to complete the final eight when Yugoslavia was barred because of security fears following the country's collapse. Goalkeeper **Peter Schmeichel** was the Danes' hero—in the semifinal shoot-out win over the Netherlands and again in the final against Germany, when goals by John Jensen and Kim Vilfort earned Denmark a 2-0 win.

GERMANS DOMINATE AS COMPETITION TAKES OFF

In 52 years, the UEFA European Championship has grown to become the most important international soccer tournament after the FIFA World Cup. Only 17 teams entered the first tournament, won by the Soviet Union in 1960, yet 51 took part in qualifying for the right to join co-hosts Poland and Ukraine at Euro 2012. Germany (formerly West Germany) and Spain have each won the competition three times, though the Germans have played and won more matches (43 and 23, respectively), as well as scoring and conceding more goals (63 and 45) than any other country. Defender Berti Vogts is the only man to win the tournament as a player (1972) and coach (1996), both with the Germans, the latter after unification. Some of Europe's most famous nations have under-achieved: Italy only claimed the title on home soil in 1968, and England has never reached the final, finishing third in 1968 and reaching the semifinals in 1996.

DOMENGHINI RESCUES ITALY

The most controversial goal in the history of the final came on June 8, 1968. Host Italy was trailing 1-0 to Yugoslavia with ten minutes left. The Yugoslavs seemed still to be organizing their defensive wall when Angelo Domenghini curled a free-kick past goalkeeper Ilja Pantelic for the equalizer. Yugoslavia protested, but the goal was allowed to stand. Italy won the only replay in finals history 2-0, two days later, with goals from Gigi Riva and Pietro Anastasi.

FRANCE BOAST PERFECT RECORD

France, on home soil in 1984, is the only team to win all its matches since the finals expanded beyond four teams. It won them without any shoot-outs, too, beating Denmark 1-0, Belgium 5-0 and Yugoslavia 3-2 in its group, Portugal 3-2 after extra-time in the semifinal and Spain 2-0 in the final.

CZECHS WIN LONGEST SHOOT-OUT

The longest penalty shoot-out in finals history came in the 1980 third-place play-off between host Italy and Czechoslovakia, in Naples on June 21. The Czechs won 9-8, following a 1-1 draw. After eight successful spot-kicks each, Czech goalkeeper **Jaroslav Netolicka** saved Fulvio Collovati's kick.

FRANCE STRIKE, WITHOUT STRIKERS

France still hold the record for the most goals scored by one team in a finals tournament, 14 in 1984. Yet only one of those goals was netted by a recognized striker—Bruno Bellone, who hit the second in its 2-0 final win over Spain. France's inspirational captain, Michel Platini, supplied most of the French firepower, scoring an incredible nine goals in five appearances. He hit hat-tricks against Belgium and Denmark and a last-gasp winner in the semi-final against Portugal. Midfielders Alain Giresse and Luis Fernandez chipped in with goals in the 5-0 win over Belgium. Defender Jean-Francois Domergue gave France the lead against Portugal in the semi-finals, and added another in extra-time after Jordao had put Portugal 2-1 ahead.

SAME OLD SPAIN

Spain not only cruised its way to the largest winning margin of any UEFA European Championship final by trouncing Italy 4-0 in the climax to 2012—it also became the first country to successfully defend its title. David Silva, **Jordi Alba**—with his first international goal—and two substitutes, Fernando Torres and Juan Mata, got the goals in Kiev's Olympic Stadium on July 1. Spain thus landed its third major trophy in a row, having won Euro 2008 and the 2010 FIFA World Cup.

TOP TEAM SCORERS IN THE FINALS

1960	Yugoslavia	6
1964	Spain, Soviet Union, Hungary	4
1968	Italy	4
1972	West Germany	5
1976	West Germany	6
1980	West Germany	6
1984	France	14
1988	Netherlands	8
1992	Germany	7
1996	Germany	10
2000	France, Netherlands	13
2004	Czech Republic	9
2008	Spain	12
2012	Spain	12

BIGGEST WINS IN THE FINALS

Netherlands 6, Yugoslavia 1, 2000
France 5, Belgium 0, 1984
Denmark 5, Yugoslavia 0, 1984
Sweden 5, Bulgaria 0, 2004

SPAIN REFUSE TO MEET SOVIETS

Political rivalries wrecked the planned clash between Spain and the Soviet Union in the 1960 quarter-finals. The fascist Spanish leader, General Francisco Franco, refused to allow Spain to go to the communist Soviet Union—and banned the Soviets from entering Spain. The Soviet Union was handed a walkover on the grounds that Spain had refused to play. Franco relented four years later, allowing the Soviets to come to Spain for the finals. He was spared the embarrassment of having to present the trophy to the Soviet Union, however, as Spain beat it 2-1 in the final.

UEFA EUROPEAN CHAMPIONSHIP WINNERS

3 West Germany/Germany
(1972, 1980, 1996)
Spain
(1964, 2008, 2012)
2 France (1984, 2000)
1 Soviet Union (1960)
Czechoslovakia (1976)
Italy (1968)
Netherlands (1998)
Denmark (1992)
Greece (2004)

DELLAS TIMES IT RIGHT FOR GREECE

Greece scored the only "silver goal" victory in the history of the competition in the UEFA Euro 2004 semifinals. The silver goal rule meant that a team leading after the first period of extra-time won the game. Traianos Dellas headed Greece's winner, seconds before the end of the first period of extra-time against the Czech Republic in Porto on July 1. Both golden goals and silver goals were abandoned for UEFA Euro 2008, and drawn knockout matches reverted to being decided over the full 30 minutes of extra-time, and penalties if necessary.

TOSS FAVORS HOSTS ITALY

Italy reached the 1968 final on home soil thanks to the toss of a coin. It was the only game in finals history to be decided in this fashion. Italy drew 0-0 against the Soviet Union after extra-time in Naples on June 5, 1968. The Soviet captain, Albert Shesternev, made the wrong call at the toss—so Italy reached the final where it beat Yugoslavia.

PLAYER RECORDS

SHEARER TALLY BOOSTS ENGLAND

Alan Shearer is the only Englishman to top the finals scoring chart. Shearer led the scorers with five goals as England went out on penalties to Germany in the Euro 96 semifinal at Wembley. He netted against Switzerland, Scotland, and the Netherlands (2) in the group, and gave England a third-minute lead against the Germans. Shearer added two more goals at Euro 2000, to stand second behind Michel Platini in the all-time scorers' list.

ILYIN GOAL MAKES HISTORY

Anatoly Ilyin of the Soviet Union scored the first goal in UEFA European Championship history when he netted after four minutes against Hungary on September 29, 1958. A crowd of 100,572 watched the Soviets win 3-1 in the Lenin Stadium, Moscow. The Soviet Union went on to win the first final, in 1960.

GOLDEN ONE–TOUCH

Spain striker **Fernando Torres** claimed the UEFA Euro 2012 Golden Boot, despite scoring the same number of goals—three—as Italy's Mario Balotelli, Russia's Alan Dzagoev, Germany's Mario Gomez, Croatia's Mario Mandzukic, and Portugal's Cristiano Ronaldo. The decision came down to the number of assists—with Torres and Gomez level on one apiece—then the amount of time played. The 92 minutes spent on the field by Torres, compared to Gomez, meant his contributions were deemed better value for the prize.

VONLANTHEN BEATS ROONEY RECORD

The youngest scorer in finals history was Switzerland midfielder **Johan Vonlanthen**. He was 18 years 141 days when he netted in a 3-1 defeat by France on June 21, 2004. He beat the record set by England forward Wayne Rooney four days earlier. Rooney was 18 years 229 days when he scored the first goal in England's 3-0 win over the Swiss. Vonlanthen retired from soccer at the age of 26 in May 2012 due to a knee injury.

GROOM FOR SUCCESS

Spanish playmaker Andres Iniesta, scorer of the winner in the 2010 FIFA World Cup, followed that tournament in style by being named the best player of Euro 2012—despite not appearing on the scoresheet in any of his team's six matches. Six days after the final against Italy, Iniesta had more cause for celebration. This time the occasion was back home in Spain, where he got married in a ceremony attended by international teammates Cesc Fabregas and Sergio Busquets.

KIRICHENKO NETS QUICKEST GOAL

The fastest goal in the history of the finals was scored by Russia forward Dmitri Kirichenko. He netted after just 67 seconds to give his side the lead against Greece on June 20, 2004. Russia won 2-1, but Greece still qualified for the quarterfinals—and went on to become shock winners. The fastest goal in the final was Spain midfielder Jesus Pereda's sixth-minute strike in 1964, when Spain beat the Soviet Union 2-1.

TOP SCORERS IN FINALS HISTORY

1	Michel Platini (France)	9
2	Alan Shearer (England)	7
3	Nuno Gomes (Portugal)	6
=	Thierry Henry (France)	
=	Patrick Kluivert (Netherlands)	
=	Zlatan Ibrahimovic (Sweden)	
=	Cristiano Ronaldo (Portugal)	
=	Ruud van Nistelrooy (Netherlands)	
9	Milan Baros (Czech Republic)	5
=	Jurgen Klinsmann (W Germany/Germany)	
=	Savo Milosevic (Yugoslavia)	
=	Wayne Rooney (England)	
=	Fernando Torres (Spain)	
=	Marco van Basten (Netherlands)	
=	Zinedine Zidane (France)	

BIERHOFF NETS FIRST "GOLDEN GOAL"

Germany's **Oliver Bierhoff** scored the first golden goal in the history of the tournament when he hit the winner against the Czech Republic in the Euro 96 final at Wembley on June 30. The golden goal rule—like sudden death—meant the first goal in extra-time won the game. Bierhoff netted in the fifth minute of extra-time. His shot from 20 yards deflected off defender Michal Hornak and slipped through goalkeeper Petr Kouba's fingers.

PONEDELNIK'S MONDAY MORNING FEELING

Striker Viktor Ponedelnik headed the Soviet Union's extra-time winner to beat Yugoslavia 2-1 in the first final on July 10, 1960—and sparked some famous headlines in the Soviet media. The game in Paris kicked off at 10pm, Moscow time, on Sunday, and it was running into Monday morning in Moscow when Ponedelnik—whose name means "Monday" in Russian—scored. He said: "When I scored, all the journalists wrote the headline 'Ponedelnik zabivayet v Ponedelnik' ('Monday scores on Monday')."

MARCHING ORDERS

Only one man has ever been sent off in a UEFA European Championship final: France defender Yvon Le Roux, who received a second yellow card with five minutes remaining of his team's 2-0 triumph over Spain in 1984. The most red cards were shown at Euro 2000, when the ten dismissals included Romania's Gheorghe Hagi, Portugal's **Nuno Gomes**, Italy's Gianluca Zambrotta, and the Czech Republic's Radoslav Latal—an unprecedented second sending-off for Latal, who was also given his marching orders at Euro 96.

VASTIC THE OLDEST

The oldest scorer in finals history is Austria's Ivica Vastic. He was 38 years and 257 days old when he equalized in the 1-1 draw with Poland at UEFA Euro 2008.

TOP SCORERS IN THE FINALS

1960	Francois Heutte (France)	2
	Milan Galic (Yugoslavia)	
	Valentin Ivanov (Soviet Union)	
	Drazan Jerkovic (Yugoslavia)	
	Slava Metreveli (Soviet Union)	
	Viktor Ponedelnik (Soviet Union)	
1964	Ferenc Bene (Hungary)	2
	Dezso Novak (Hungary)	
	Jesus Pereda (Spain)	
1968	Dragan Dzajic (Yugoslavia)	2
1972	Gerd Muller (West Germany)	4
1976	Dieter Muller (West Germany)	4
1980	Klaus Allofs (West Germany)	3
1984	Michel Platini (France)	9
1988	Marco van Basten (Netherlands)	5
1992	Dennis Bergkamp (Netherlands)	3
	Tomas Brolin (Sweden)	
	Henrik Larsen (Denmark)	
	Karlheinz Riedle (Germany)	
1996	Alan Shearer (England)	5
2000	Patrick Kluivert (Netherlands)	5
	Savo Milosevic (Yugoslavia)	
2004	Milan Baros (Czech Republic)	5
2008	David Villa (Spain)	4
2012	Mario Balotelli (Italy)	3
	Alan Dzagoev (Russia)	
	Mario Gomez (Germany)	
	Mario Mandzukic (Croatia)	
	Cristiano Ronaldo (Portugal)	
	Fernando Torres (Spain)	

MATTHAUS MIRRORS TOURNAMENT GROWTH

The career of Lothar Matthaus straddles the growth of the European Championship. He appeared in four tournaments between 1980 and 2000. He missed Euro 92 because of injury and stayed at home for Euro 96 after falling out with coach Berti Vogts and skipper Jurgen Klinsmann. He had made his entry as a 19-year-old substitute for Bernd Dietz in West Germany's 3-2 group win over the Netherlands in Naples on June 14, 1980. That was the first tournament which involved eight teams and two groups rather than the previous four semifinalists. He ended his association with the Championship at the age of 39, playing for the reunified Germany, as it was eliminated 3-0 by Portugal at Euro 2000. By now the tournament had expanded to include 16 teams in four groups. Despite featuring in four tournaments, Matthaus made only 11 appearances in total. He did, however, enter the tournament when it was taking its first steps to expansion and left it when the European Championship had become second only to the FIFA World Cup as soccer's most important international competition.

BROTHERS IN ARMS

Four pairs of brothers went to Euro 2000: Gary and Phil Neville (England), Frank and Ronald de Boer (Netherlands), Daniel and Patrik Andersson (Sweden), and Belgium's Emile and Mbo Mpenza.

BECKENBAUER'S 100th ENDS IN DEFEAT

West Germany legend Franz Beckenbauer won his 100th cap in the 1976 final against Czechoslovakia. After his side's shoot-out defeat, he played only three more games for his country before retiring from international soccer.

PORTUGAL TRIO BANNED FOR THE LONGEST

The longest suspensions in the history of the finals were handed out to three Portugal players after its Euro 2000 semifinal defeat by France. Zinedine Zidane's "Golden Goal" penalty infuriated the Portuguese, who surrounded referee Gunter Benko and assistant Igor Sramka. The three Portuguese players— **Abel Xavier**, Nuno Gomes and Paulo Bento—were banned for "physically and verbally intimidating" the officials. Xavier was suspended from European soccer for nine months. Gomes, who was also sent off, was banned for eight months. Bento received a six-month suspension.

CLEAN SHEETS FOR CASILLAS

Spain saw out the 2012 tournament conceding just one goal, emulating the achievement of Italy in 1980 and Norway in 2000—neither of whom achieved what Spain did and lifted the trophy. That successful 2012 campaign took Spanish captain and goalkeeper Iker Casillas to nine clean sheets in UEFA European Championships, from 14 games—equaling the record held by the Netherlands' Edwin van der Sar, with his nine clean sheets from 16 matches.

MOST FINALS TOURNAMENTS PLAYED

Eight players have appeared in four finals tournaments:

Lothar Matthaus	(West Germany/Germany)	1980, 1984, 1988, 2000
Peter Schmeichel	(Denmark)	1988, 1992, 1996, 2000
Aron Winter	(Netherlands)	1988, 1992, 1996, 2000
Alessandro del Piero	(Italy)	1996, 2000, 2004, 2008
Edwin van der Sar	(Netherlands)	1996, 2000, 2004, 2008
Lilian Thuram	(France)	1996, 2000, 2004, 2008
Olof Mellberg	(Sweden)	2000, 2004, 2008, 2012
Iker Casillas	(Spain)	2000, 2004, 2008, 2012

MULLERY THE FIRST TO GO

Wing-half Alan Mullery became the first England player ever to be sent off when he was dismissed in the 89th minute of its 1-0 semifinal defeat by Yugoslavia in Florence on June 5, 1968. Mullery was sent off for a foul on Dobrivoje Trivic, three minutes after Dragan Dzajic had scored Yugoslavia's winner. His dismissal came in England's 424th official international match.

HAGI'S JOURNEY ENDS IN RED

Romania's greatest player, Gheorghe Hagi, won the last of his 125 caps in a 2-0 UEFA Euro 2000 quarterfinal defeat by Italy on June 24. However, his international career would end in sad circumstances: he was sent off in the 59th minute for two yellow-card offences. Hagi had previously been booked against Germany and Portugal—and had missed Romania's 3-2 group win over England through suspension.

MOST MATCHES PLAYED IN THE FINALS

16	Edwin van der Sar (Netherlands)
	Lilian Thuram (France)
14	Iker Casillas (Spain)
	Luis Figo (Portugal)
	Nuno Gomes (Portugal)
	Philipp Lahm (Germany)
	Karel Poborsky (Czech Republic)
	Cristiano Ronaldo (Portugal)
	Zinedine Zidane (France)

BACK OF THE WRONG NET

Glen Johnson became only the fifth man to score an own goal at a UEFA European Championship, when the England right-back put through his own net against Sweden in a Euro 2012 first-round clash. The earlier unfortunates were Czechoslovakia's Anton Ondrus in 1976, Bulgaria's Dimitar Penev in 1996, Yugoslavia's Dejan Govedarica in 2000 and Portugal's Jorge Andrade in 2004.

ARAGONES THE VETERAN COACH

Luis Aragones, Spain's coach in 2008, is the oldest coach of a European champion team. Aragones (born in Madrid on July 28, 1938, and who died in 2014) was 29 days short of his 70th birthday when Spain beat Germany 1-0 in the final on June 29. That was his last match in charge. He had taken over the national team after Euro 2004.

KADLEC FATHER AND SON

Czech defenders Miroslav and Michal Kadlec are the only father and son to have played in the finals. Miroslav (born on June 22, 1964, in Uherske Hradiste) captained the Czech Republic team that finished as runners-up to Germany at Euro 96. He also scored the winning penalty in the semifinal shoot-out against France. Michal (born on December 13, 1984, in Vyskov) made his first appearance as an 80th-minute substitute for Jaroslav Plasil in the Group A game against Turkey in Geneva on June 15, 2008.

SUAREZ GAINS FIRST DOUBLE

The first man to earn winners' medals in the European Championship and the European Cup in the same season was Spain's **Luis Suarez**. He helped Spain beat the Soviet Union 2-1 in the final on June 21, 1964. A few weeks earlier, Suarez had been in the Internazionale team which beat Real Madrid 3-1 in the European Cup final. Four players were in both PSV Eindhoven's 1988 European Cup final victory over Benfica and the Netherlands' UEFA Euro 88 final defeat of Russia. Nicolas Anelka won the Champions League with Real Madrid in 2000 and was in the France squad that won Euro 2000, but he did not appear in the final.

KARAGOUNIS A GONER

The yellow card shown to Greece's Giorgos Karagounis in its final first-round match of Euro 2012, against Russia, achieved even more than ruling him out of the quarterfinal against Germany. It was also his eighth in UEFA European Championship history, a competition record. He had previously been able to play in the final of Euro 2004 after collecting two bookings beforehand.

MATTHAUS THE OLDEST

The oldest player to appear in a game at the UEFA European Championship finals was Germany's Lothar Matthaus. He was 39 years 91 days when he played in a 3-0 defeat by Portugal on June 20, 2000.

LOW CONQUERS ALMOST ALL

Germany coach Joachim Low claimed the record for most UEFA European Championship victories in charge, when his team beat Greece 4-2 in a Euro 2012 quarterfinal. It took him to eight wins from ten games, across Euro 2008 and Euro 2012. The semifinal defeat against Italy also equaled Berti Vogts's record of 11 UEFA European Championship games as a manager.

NAMES ON THEIR SHIRTS

Players wore their names as well as their numbers on the back of their shirts for the first time at Euro 92. They had previously been identified only by numbers.

REPEAT PROENCA

Portuguese official Pedro Proenca achieved the double feat of refereeing the 2012 UEFA Champions League final between Chelsea and Bayern Munich and the 2012 UEFA European Championship final between Spain and Italy. He also became the third man to referee four matches in one UEFA European Championship, after Sweden's Anders Frisk (2004) and Italy's Roberto Rosetti (2008). Frisk's eight matches overall is a UEFA European Championship record.

GREEKS HAND ALBANIA WALKOVER

When Greece were drawn against Albania in the first round of the 1964 tournament, the Greeks immediately withdrew, handing Albania a 3-0 walkover win. The countries had technically been at war since 1940. The Greek government did not formally lift the state of war until 1987, although diplomatic relations were re-established in 1971.

RECORD EURO GOAL DROUGHT

Between **Xabi Alonso**'s added-time penalty in Spain's 2-0 quarterfinal defeat of France and Mario Balotelli's 20th-minute semifinal strike for Italy in its 2-1 victory against Germany, Euro 2012's goalless spell lasted 260 minutes—a UEFA European Championship record.

ITALY HOSTS TWICE

Italy was the first country to host the finals twice—in 1968 and 1980. It was awarded the finals in 1968 in recognition of the 60th anniversary of the Italian soccer federation. Belgium has also hosted the finals twice: first, alone, in 1972, and then in partnership with the Netherlands for Euro 2000.

ELLIS BLOWS THE WHISTLE

English referee **Arthur Ellis** took charge of the first UEFA European Championship final between the Soviet Union and Yugoslavia in 1960. Ellis had also refereed the first-ever European Cup final, between Real Madrid and Reims, four years earlier. After he retired from soccer officiating, he became the "referee" on the British version of the Europe-wide TV game show *It's a Knock-out*.

FINALS HOSTS

1960	France
1964	Spain
1968	Italy
1972	Belgium
1976	Yugoslavia
1980	Italy
1984	France
1988	West Germany
1992	Sweden
1996	England
2000	Netherlands and Belgium
2004	Portugal
2008	Austria and Switzerland
2012	Poland and Ukraine

HOSTS WITH (ALMOST) THE MOST

In 2000, Belgium and the Netherlands began the trend for dual hosting the UEFA European Championship finals—it was the first time the tournament was staged in more than one country. The opening game was Belgium's 2-1 win over Sweden in Brussels on June 10, with the final in Rotterdam. Austria and Switzerland co-hosted Euro 2008, starting in Basel and climaxing in Vienna, before Poland and Ukraine teamed up in 2012. Warsaw staged the opening game and ceremony and Kiev was the host city for the final.

SINGING IN UKRAINE

The eight venues—four apiece—in Poland and Ukraine matched the number used when Belgium and the Netherlands shared hosting rights at Euro 2000, and when Austria and Switzerland did likewise eight years later. Only Euro 2004, in Portugal, had more venues (10). Poland's 56,070-capacity National Stadium in Warsaw staged the opening game between Poland and Greece, while Kiev's 64,640-seater Olympic Stadium was the setting for the final. France will stage Euro 2016, while the final tournament in 2020 will be played—for the first time—in as many as 13 different cities across 13 different countries.

WELL DONE, WELBECK

Perhaps surprisingly, the biggest official attendance at UEFA Euro 2012 was not for the final, but for a first-round Group D game, when 64,640 saw England beat Sweden 3-2, thanks to a late back-heeled winner by **Danny Welbeck**.

UEFA EUROPEAN CHAMPIONSHIP FINAL REFEREES

1960   Arthur Ellis (England)
1964   Arthur Holland (England)
1968   Gottfried Dienst (Switzerland)
          Replay: Jose Maria Ortiz de Mendibil (Spain)
1972   Ferdinand Marschall (Austria)
1976   Sergio Gonella (Italy)
1980   Nicolae Rainea (Romania)
1984   Vojtech Christov (Czechoslovakia)
1988   Michel Vautrot (France)
1992   Bruno Galler (Switzerland)
1996   Pierluigi Pairetto (Italy)
2000   Anders Frisk (Sweden)
2004   Markus Merk (Germany)
2008   Roberto Rosetti (Italy)
2012   Pedro Proenca (Portugal)

THE "ITALIAN JOB"

The 1968 finals in Italy were used as the backdrop to a famous English-language film—*The Italian Job*—starring Michael Caine, about a British gang who use the cover of the finals to stage a daring gold robbery in Turin. The film's English release was on June 2, 1969.

GOALS AREN'T EVERYTHING

Despite being widely praised for the quality of attacking soccer on display, Euro 2012 actually had the lowest average of goals per game for any UEFA European Championship since Euro 96 in England, when the tournament expanded to 16 teams. The 76 goals across 31 games in Poland and Ukraine was one fewer than was scored at each of the 2004 and 2008 tournaments, and meant an average of 2.45 goals per game. It was not until the fourth of the four quarterfinals that Euro 2012 witnessed its first goalless draw, between England and Italy, but it was followed by another stalemate in the next game, three days later, between Spain and Portugal in the first semifinal.

KEEPING IT CLEAN

Only three red cards were shown during Euro 2012: Greece's Sokratis Papastathopoulos and Poland's **Wojciech Szczesny** saw red in the opening game, as did Keith Andrews for the Republic of Ireland against Italy. This equaled the sendings-off total in the 2008 UEFA European Championship but was half of the tally at Euro 2004.

PART 4: COPA AMERICA

THE WORLD'S OLDEST surviving international championship finds its rich history repeating itself even in a modern world much-transformed since the inaugural Copa America—with both the 1916 and 2011 tournaments being won by Uruguay. Its 15th Copa America triumph in 2011 made Uruguay the competition's most successful country—flying high on the soccer field once more.

When Uruguay first lifted the trophy, there was no such thing as long-distance air travel, and it was one of the factors that made a continental championship such a worthwhile idea for its South American founders. Before jet travel became commonplace in the last half-century, major soccer events were difficult to organize. This played an influence in FIFA's founding membership, in 1904 being entirely European. Although South American nations such as Brazil, Argentina and Uruguay were not slow in signing up, the opportunities available to them to play against their European cousins were scarce, and open only to those willing to endure laborious journeys by sea.

The South Americans thus decided to organize their own international competitions, which led to the creation, in 1916, of the South American Championship, now known as the Copa America. Of course, communications were not what they are today, and tournament organization was far from simple, so some of the early championships are now considered unofficial. Further problems arose over scheduling, which meant that countries could not secure the release of their best players who were under contract to European clubs. Argentina was the champion in 1957 and considered a favorite for the following year's FIFA World Cup. But it lost all of its inspirational forward trio—Humberto Maschio, Antonio Valentin Angelillo and Enrique Omar Sivori—to Italian clubs.

Now, however, the club-versus-country issue has been largely resolved by FIFA's enforcement of a unified international calendar, recognizing the priority status of the Copa America.

Uruguay might have been South America's most successful nation at the 2010 FIFA World Cup, but its 2011 Copa America triumph, in Argentina, was still considered a big surprise.

COPA AMERICA TEAM RECORDS

LITTLE NAPOLEON

In 1942, Ecuador, and its goalkeeper Napoleon Medina, conceded more goals in one tournament than any other team, when they allowed 31 goals across six games—and all six ended in defeat. Three years later, Medina and his team-mates finally managed to keep a clean sheet, in a scoreless draw against Bolivia, but still managed to concede 27 goals in its five other games.

LUCK OF THE DRAW

Paraguay reached the 2011 final despite not winning a single game in normal play. It drew all three matches in the first-round group stage, then needed penalties to win its quarterfinal against Brazil and semifinal versus Venezuela, after both games had ended scoreless. It was hardly a surprise that Paraguay's captain **Justo Villar** was voted the tournament's best goalkeeper.

HOSTING RIGHTS BY COUNTRY

Argentina	9	(1916, 1921, 1925, 1929, 1937, 1946, 1959, 1987, 2011)
Uruguay	7	(1917, 1923, 1924, 1942, 1956, 1967, 1995)
Chile	6	(1920, 1926, 1941, 1945, 1955, 1991)
Peru	6	(1927, 1935, 1939, 1953, 1957, 2004)
Brazil	4	(1919, 1922, 1949, 1989)
Ecuador	3	(1947, 1959, 1993)
Bolivia	2	(1963, 1997)
Paraguay	1	(1999)
Colombia	1	(2001)
Venezuela	1	(2007)

EXTRA TIME

The longest match in the history of the Copa America was the 1919 final between Brazil and Uruguay. It lasted 150 minutes, 90 minutes of regular time plus two extra-time periods of 30 minutes each.

COPA AMERICA WINNERS

1916	Uruguay (league format)
1917	Uruguay (league format)
1919	Brazil 1 Uruguay 0
1920	Uruguay (league format)
1921	Argentina (league format)
1922	Brazil 3 Paraguay 1
1923	Uruguay (league format)
1924	Uruguay (league format)
1925	Argentina (league format)
1926	Uruguay (league format)
1927	Argentina (league format)
1929	Argentina (league format)
1935	Uruguay (league format)
1937	Argentina 2 Brazil 0
1939	Peru (league format)
1941	Argentina (league format)
1942	Uruguay (league format)
1945	Argentina (league format)
1946	Argentina (league format)
1947	Argentina (league format)
1949	Brazil 7 Paraguay 0
1953	Paraguay 3 Brazil 2
1955	Argentina (league format)
1956	Uruguay (league format)
1957	Argentina (league format)
1959	Argentina (league format)
1959	Uruguay (league format)
1963	Bolivia (league format)
1967	Uruguay (league format)
1975	Peru 4 Colombia 1 (on aggregate, after three games)
1979	Paraguay 3 Chile 1 (on aggregate, after three games)
1983	Uruguay 3 Brazil 1 (on aggregate, after two games)
1987	Uruguay 1 Chile 0
1989	Brazil (league format)
1991	Argentina (league format)
1993	Argentina 2 Mexico 1
1995	Uruguay 1 Brazil 1 (Uruguay won 5-3 on penalties)
1997	Brazil 3 Bolivia 1
1999	Brazil 3 Uruguay 0
2001	Colombia 1 Mexico 0
2004	Brazil 2 Argentina 2 (Brazil won 4-2 on penalties)
2007	Brazil 3 Argentina 0
2011	Uruguay 3 Paraguay 0

HOW IT STARTED

The first South American "Championship of Nations", as it was then known, was held in Argentina from July 2–17, 1916, during the country's independence centenary celebrations. Uruguay was the first winner, tying Argentina in the last match of the tournament. It was an inauspicious beginning, as the July 16 encounter had to be abandoned at 0-0 when fans invaded the pitch and set the wooden stands on fire. The match was continued at a different stadium the following day and still ended goalless ... but Uruguay ended up topping the mini-league table and was hailed the first champions. Isabelino Gradin was the inaugural tournament's top scorer. The South American confederation, CONMEBOL, was also founded during this competition, at a meeting on July 9. From that point on the tournament was held every two years, though some tournaments are now considered to have been unofficial. There was a three-year gap between the 2001, 2004 and 2007 tournaments, and it was next staged in 2011. Chile will be Copa America host in 2015, while, in 2016, a special cententary tournament, will be played outside the CONMEBOL confederation, in the United States.

SUB–STANDARD

During the 1953 Copa America, Peru was awarded a walkover win when Paraguay tried to make one more substitution than it was allowed. Would-be substitute Milner Ayala was so incensed, he kicked English referee Richard Maddison and was banned from soccer for three years. Yet Paraguay remained in the tournament and went on to beat Brazil in the final—minus, of course, the disgraced Ayala.

ROTATING RIGHTS

The Campeonato Sudamericano de Selecciones was rebaptized the Copa America from 1975. Between then and 1983 there was no host nation. CONMEBOL then adopted a policy of rotating the right to host the Copa America among the ten member federations. The first rotation was complete after Venezuela hosted the 2007 edition. Argentina played host for the ninth time in 2011, but Chile have swapped with Brazil to be host in 2015.

HISTORY MEN

The Copa America, the world's oldest surviving international soccer tournament, launched in 1916 with four participating nations: Argentina, Brazil, Chile, and Uruguay. Since then, Bolivia, Colombia, Ecuador, Paraguay, Peru, and Venezuela have become tournament regulars. In 1910, an unofficial South American championship was won by Argentina, beating Uruguay 4-1 in the decider, though the final game was delayed a day after rioting fans burned down a stand at Buenos Aires' Gimnasia stadium.

FALLEN ANGELS

Argentina's 1957 Copa America-winning forward trio of Humberto Maschio, Omar Sivori and Antonio Valentin Angelillo became known by the nickname, "the angels with dirty faces." At least one of them scored in each of the team's six games, Maschio finished with nine, Angelillo eight and Sivori three. Argentina's most convincing performance was an opening 8-2 win over Colombia, in which Argentina scored four goals and missed a penalty within the first 25 minutes. The dazzling displays made Argentina, not eventual winners Brazil, favorites for the following year's FIFA World Cup. However, Maschio, Sivori and Angelillo were all lured away to Europe by Italian clubs and the Argentine federation subsequently refused to pick any of them for the trip to Sweden for the FIFA World Cup. Sivori and Maschio ultimately made it to the FIFA World Cup, in 1962. However, to fury back home, they did so wearing not the light blue-and-white stripes of Argentina, but the Azzurri blue of their newly adopted Italy.

CONSISTENT COLOMBIANS

In 2001, Colombia, which went on to win the trophy for the first and only time in its history, became the only country to go through an entire Copa America campaign without conceding a single goal. Colombia scored 11 goals itself, more than half of them from six-goal tournament top scorer **Victor Aristazabal**. Keeping the clean sheets was goalkeeper Oscar Cordoba, who had previously spent much of his international career as back-up to the eccentric Rene Higuita. Just a month earlier, Cordoba had won the South American club championship, the Copa Libertadores, with Argentine team Boca Juniors.

TRIUMPHS BY COUNTRY

Uruguay 15 (1916, 1917, 1920, 1923, 1924, 1926, 1935, 1942, 1956, 1959, 1967, 1983, 1987, 1995, 2011)
Argentina 14 (1921, 1925, 1927, 1929, 1937, 1941, 1945, 1946, 1947, 1955, 1957, 1959, 1991, 1993)
Brazil 8 (1919, 1922, 1949, 1989, 1997, 1999, 2004, 2007)
Peru 2 (1939, 1975)
Paraguay 2 (1953, 1979)
Bolivia 1 (1963)
Colombia 1 (2001)

MORE FROM MORENO

Argentina was not only responsible for the Copa America's biggest win, but also the tournament's highest-scoring game, when it put 12 past Ecuador in 1942, without reply. Jose Manuel Moreno's five strikes in that game included the 500th goal in the competition's history. Moreno, born in Buenos Aires on August 3, 1916, ended that tournament as joint-top goalscorer with team-mate Herminio Masantonio—with seven apiece. Both men ended their international careers with 19 goals for Argentina, though Moreno did so in 34 appearances—compared to Masantonio's 21. Masantonio scored four in the Ecuador thrashing.

URUGUAY AGAIN

Uruguay, the first ever winners of the Copa America, once more became the competition's most successful side by claiming its 15th triumph in 2011—pulling one clear of neighbor and rival Argentina. What might have made the glory even sweeter was that it came on Argentine turf and included a quarterfinal victory, on penalties, over Argentina. Brazil and Argentina had gone into the event as favorites, with many expecting them to contest the final for the third consecutive tournament. Instead, both were knocked out in the quarterfinals, producing an unlikely last four of Uruguay, Paraguay, Venezuela, and Peru.

FROG PRINCE

Chilean goalkeeper Sergio Livingstone holds the record for most Copa America appearances, with 34, across the 1941, 1942, 1945, 1947, 1949, and 1953 tournaments. Livingstone, nicknamed "The Frog," was voted player of the tournament in 1941—becoming the first goalkeeper to win the award—and might have played even more Copa America games had he not missed out on the 1946 edition. Livingstone, born in Santiago on March 26, 1920, spent almost his entire career in his home country, except for one season, 1943–44, with Argentina's Racing Club. Overall, he played 52 times for Chile between 1941 and 1954, before retiring and becoming a popular TV journalist and commentator.

CHILE'S ILL FORTUNE

The first Copa America own goal was scored by Chile's Luis Garcia, giving Argentina a 1-0 win in 1917, in the second edition of the tournament. Even more unfortunately for Chile, Garcia's error was the only goal scored by one of its players throughout the tournament, making Chile the first team to fail to score a single goal in a Copa America competition.

MOST GAMES PLAYED

1	Sergio Livingstone (Chile)	34
2	Zizinho (Brazil)	33
3	Leonel Alvarez (Colombia)	27
4	Carlos Valderrama (Colombia)	27
5	Alex Aguinaga (Ecuador)	25
6	Claudio Taffarel (Brazil)	25
7	Teodoro Fernandez (Peru)	24
8	Angel Romano (Uruguay)	23
9	Djalma Santos (Brazil)	22
10	Claudio Suarez (Mexico)	22

OVERALL TOP SCORERS

1	Norberto Mendez (Argentina)	17
=	Zizinho (Brazil)	17
3	Teodoro Fernandez (Peru)	15
=	Severino Varela (Uruguay)	15
5	Ademir (Brazil)	13
=	Jair da Rosa Pinto (Brazil)	13
=	Gabriel Batistuta (Argentina)	13
=	Jose Manuel Moreno (Argentina)	13
=	Hector Scarone (Uruguay)	13

REPEATING THE FEAT

Uruguay's Pedro Petrone (in 1923 and 1924) and **Gabriel Batistuta** of Argentina (in 1991 and 1995) are the only players to finish as top scorers in the Copa America on two occasions. Batistuta made his Argentina debut just a few days before the 1991 Copa America, in which his starring performances—including the second goal in the 2-1 final defeat of Colombia—helped to earn him a transfer from Boca Juniors to Italy's Fiorentina.

LIKE GRANDFATHER, LIKE FATHER, LIKE SON

Diego Forlan's two goals in the 2011 Copa America final helped Uruguay to a 3-0 victory over Paraguay and its record 15th South American championship. The goals also ensured he followed in family footsteps in lifting the trophy—his father **Pablo** was part of the Uruguay team which won in 1967, when his grandfather Juan Carlos Corazzo was the triumphant coach. Corazzo had previously coached Uruguay's winning team in 1959. The brace against Paraguay put the youngest Forlan level with Hector Scarone as Uruguay's all-time leading scorer, with 31 goals. Yet it was Forlan's strike partner Luis Suarez, scorer of the final's opening goal, who was voted best player of the 2011 tournament.

MAGIC ALEX

When Alex Aguinaga lined up for Ecuador against Uruguay in his country's opening game at the 2004 event, he became only the second man to take part in eight different Copa Americas, joining legendary Uruguayan goalscorer Angel Romano. Aguinaga, a midfielder born in Ibarra on July 9, 1969, played a total of 109 times for Ecuador—25 in the Copa America, a competition that yielded four of his 23 international goals. His Copa America career certainly began well: Ecuador was unbeaten in his first four appearances, at the 1987 and 1989 events, but his luck had ran out by the time his career was coming to an end: he and Ecuador lost all of his final seven Copa America matches.

START TO FINISH

Playmaker Carlos Valderrama and defensive midfielder **Leonel Alvarez** played in all 27 of Colombia's Copa America games between 1987 and 1995, winning ten, drawing ten and losing seven. They also enjoyed third-place finishes in 1987, 1993, and 1995. Valderrama's only two Copa America goals came in his first and last appearances in the competition: a 2-0 win over Bolivia in 1987; and a 4-1 thrashing of the United States eight years later.

GUERRERO'S RARE ACHIEVEMENT

Peru endured a disastrous qualification campaign for the 2010 FIFA World Cup, finishing bottom of the South American table—which made its third-place finish at the 2011 Copa America all the more remarkable. There was even more joy for striker **Paolo Guerrero,** whose five goals made him only the third Peruvian ever to finish top scorer at a Copa America, following Teodoro Fernandez in 1939 and Eduardo Malasquez in 1983. Guerrero's haul included a hat-trick in a 4-1 defeat of Venezuela in the third-place play-off.

FANTASTIC FIVES

Four players have scored five goals in one Copa America game: Hector Scarone in Uruguay's 6-0 win over Bolivia in 1926; Juan Marvezzi in Argentina's 6-1 win over Ecuador in 1941; Jose Manuel Moreno in Argentina's 12-0 win over Ecuador in 1942; and Evaristo de Macedo in Brazil's 9-0 win over Colombia in 1957.

LOW-KEY JOSE

The first-ever Copa America goal, in 1916, was scored by Jose Piendibene. It set Uruguay on its way to a 4-0 triumph over Chile. But he is not thought to have marked the moment with any great extravagance. Piendibene, renowned for his sense of fair play, made a point of not celebrating goals, to avoid offending his opponents.

PELE'S INSPIRATION

Brazilian forward **Zizinho** jointly holds the all-time goalscoring record for the Copa America, along with Argentina's Norberto Mendez. Both men struck 17 goals, Zizinho across six tournaments and Mendez three, including the 1945 and 1946 tournaments, which featured both men. Mendez was top scorer once and runner-up twice, but he won championship-winners' medals on all three occasions, 1945, 1946, and 1947. Zizinho's goals helped Brazil take the title only once, in 1949. Pele's soccer idol, Zizinho emerged from the 1950 FIFA World Cup as Brazil's top scorer and was also voted the tournament's best player, but he was forever traumatized by the hosts' surprise defeat to Uruguay in the decisive Final Group game that cost Brazil the title.

SUCCESSFUL INVADERS

Only two foreign coaches have led a country to Copa America glory: Brazilian Danilo Alvim, whose Bolivia team won in 1963; and Englishman Jack Greenwell, coach of Peru in 1939. Alvim, who won the Copa America as a player—he was a center-half—with Brazil in 1949, not only coached Bolivia to its one and only Copa America triumph, he did it by beating his native land 5-4 in the final match.

HOME COMFORTS

Uruguay has a unique record in remaining unbeaten in all its 38 Copa America games played on home turf—and all in the country's capital Montevideo—comprising 31 wins, seven draws. The last tournament game it hosted—the 1995 final—was both a draw and a win, but it was 1-1 tie with Brazil in 1995. Uruguay emerged as champions, 5-3 on penalties, when Fernando Alvez saved Tulio's penalty.

INVITED GUESTS

1993	Mexico (runners-up), United States
1995	Mexico, United States (fourth)
1997	Costa Rica, Mexico (third)
1999	Japan, Mexico (third)
2001	Costa Rica, Honduras (third), Mexico (runners-up)
2004	Costa Rica, Mexico
2007	Mexico (third), United States
2011	Costa Rica, Mexico

WRONG JUAN

It took 21 years, but Uruguay's Juan Emilio Piriz became the first Copa America player sent off, against Chile in 1937—the first of 191 dismissals to date. Some 148 of those disgraced players have had a red card flourished in their face, since FIFA introduced the card system for referees in 1970.

MULTI–TASKING

Argentina's **Guillermo Stabile** not only holds the record for most Copa America triumphs as coach, he trounces all opposition. He led his country to the title on no fewer than six occasions: in 1941, 1945, 1946, 1947, 1955, and 1957. No other coach has lifted the trophy more than twice. Stabile coached Argentina from 1939 to 1960, having been appointed at the age of just 34. He was in charge for 123 games, winning 83 of them. However, he also managed to coach three clubs on the side at different times throughout his reign. He remained as Red Star Paris manager during his first year in the Argentina role, led Argentine club Huracan for the next nine years, and then led domestic rivals Racing Club from 1949 to 1960. Stabile's Argentina may have, unusually, missed out on Copa America success in 1949, but that year brought the first of three consecutive Argentina league championships for Stabile's Racing Club.

CAPTAIN CONSISTENT

Uruguay's 1930 FIFA World Cup-winning captain **Jose Nasazzi** is the only man to be voted player of the tournament at two different Copa Americas. Even more impressively, he achieved the feat 12 years apart, first taking the prize in 1923, then again in 1935. He played on four Cup-winning teams, in 1923, 1924, 1926, and 1935. Nasazzi also captained Uruguay to victory in the 1924 and 1928 Olympic Games and in the 1930 FIFA World Cup.

TROPHY—WINNING COACHES

6 Guillermo Stabile (Argentina 1941, 1945, 1946, 1947, 1955, 1957)
2 Alfio Basile (Argentina 1991, 1993)
Juan Carlos Corazzo (Uruguay 1959, 1967)
Ernesto Figoli (Uruguay 1920, 1926)
1 Jorge Pacheco and Alfredo Foglino (Uruguay 1916)
Ramon Platero (Uruguay 1917)
Pedro Calomino (Argentina 1921)
Lais (Brazil 1922)
Leonardo De Lucca (Uruguay 1923)
Ernesto Meliante (Uruguay 1924)
Americo Tesoriere (Argentina 1925)
Jose Lago Millon (Argentina 1927)
Francisco Olazar (Argentina 1929)
Raul V Blanco (Uruguay 1935)
Manuel Seoane (Argentina 1937)
Jack Greenwell (Peru 1939)
Pedro Cea (Uruguay 1942)
Flavio Costa (Brazil 1949)
Manuel Fleitas Solich (Paraguay 1953)
Hugo Bagnulo (Uruguay 1956)
Victorio Spinetto (Argentina 1959)
Danilo Alvim (Bolivia 1963)
Marcos Calderon (Peru 1975)
Ranulfo Miranda (Paraguay 1979)
Omar Borras (Uruguay 1983)
Roberto Fleitas (Uruguay 1987)
Sebastiao Lazaroni (Brazil 1989)
Hector Nunez (Uruguay 1995)
Mario Zagallo (Brazil 1997)
Wanderlei Luxemburgo (Brazil 1999)
Francisco Maturana (Colombia 2001)
Carlos Alberto Parreira (Brazil 2004)
Dunga (Brazil 2007)
Oscar Washington Tabarez (Uruguay 2011)

EXTENDED INVITE

Japan—albeit in one appearance as a guest team—has appeared in the fewest games in the Copa America, playing three times in 1999. It was invited to take part in the 2011 tournament, but was forced to withdraw following the devastating 9.0 magnitude earthquake and tsunami that struck the country four months earlier. Costa Rica replaced Japan and its up-and-coming stars included striker **Joel Campbell,** who signed for English giants Arsenal just after the tournament.

GOALS AT A PREMIUM

In terms of goals per game, the 2011 Copa America was the second tightest of all time—with only 54 strikes hitting the back of the net in 26 matches, an average of 2.08 per game. Only the 1922 tournament, in Brazil, saw fewer, with 22 goals in 11 games, an average of two. Both competitions were a far cry from the most—on average—prolific 1927 event in Peru, where 37 goals across six games averaged out at 6.17.

SEEING RED

Brazil has the worst disciplinary record in the FIFA World Cup, but neighboring Uruguay assumes that unenviable position in the Copa America. Uruguayan players have been dismissed 31 times, followed by Peru on 24 dismissals, Argentina (23), Brazil and Venezuela (20) apiece, Chile (17), Bolivia and Paraguay (13 each), Colombia, Ecuador, and Mexico (nine each), and Costa Rica, Honduras, and Japan (one apiece). Only the United States has, so far, made its way through all three of its Copa America participations with 11 men on the field throughout. Despite its overall record, however, Uruguay won the Fair Play Award for the 2011 tournament. Venezuela's Tomas Rincon, by contrast, suffered double disgrace: he received not one but two straight red cards in matches that tournament.

MARKARIAN MAKES HIS MARK

The 2011 Copa America was not only a Uruguayan success story for the eventual champion, but also for third-placed Peru, which was coached by a Uruguayan, **Sergio Markarian.** Uruguay's winning coach. Oscar Washington Tabarez, had Markarian as his club coach at Bella Vista in the 1970s. Markarian could also claim some credit for Paraguay's runners-up finish, having been a successful and influential coach in that country during the 1980s, 1990s and early 21st century.

PART 5:
AFRICA CUP OF NATIONS

THE AFRICAN governing socer confederation—Confederation Africaine de Football (or CAF)—is three years younger than UEFA, yet its cross-continental tournament, the Africa Cup of Nations, kicked off before the first European Championship. Formed on February 8, 1957, the CAF announced the first championship just three days later.

Egypt's ultimate triumph in that inaugural tournament set an appropriate pattern, as the "Pharaohs" have won a record number of championships overall (seven), but the competition has changed, and progressed, plenty since then.

Only three teams entered in 1957, but 47 nations vied for 15 qualification spots at the last event, in 2013, alongside already-qualified hosts South Africa, which was replacing the original choice, Libya. The global prominence of the Africa Cup of Nations has also grown, especially as the spotlight falls on major African stars taking time off from European club duties every other January. There have been mounting calls for the competition to be moved to the middle of the year, to avoid disrupting European league seasons, but these have been rejected for climatic and seasonal reasons.

Whatever the place in the calendar, the trophy—now in its third physical incarnation—will always be contested with vivacious skills and fierce local pride. More different countries have won the ACN than any other continental championship, with glory being shared among 14 separate nations, including Africa's three largest countries—Sudan, Algeria, and Congo DR—as well as mid-sized entrants such as Cameroon, Morocco, Ivory Coast, and early standard-setters Ghana, plus surprise 2012 champions Zambia.

And extra significance was achieved when the preliminary rounds for the 2010 event were integrated into Africa's FIFA World Cup 2010 qualification competition.

Nigeria's long and painful 19-year wait for a third Africa Cup of Nations triumph came to a happy end when it was crowned champions in 2013, reawakening the optimism of its glory days.

TEST OF ENDURANCE

The Ivory Coast has won the two highest-scoring penalty shoot-outs in full international history. It beat Ghana 11-10 over 24 penalties in the 1992 Africa Cup of Nations final, and Cameroon 12-11, over the same number of kicks, in the quarterfinals of the 2006 Africa Cup of Nations.

GHANA AGAIN

Ghana's "Black Stars" became the first country to reach the final of four consecutive Africa Cup of Nations, lifting the trophy in 1963 and 1965, and finishing runners-up in 1968 and 1970. It has now reached eight finals in all, a tally matched only by Egypt. The two countries have also staged the tournament four times apiece.

FROM TRAGEDY TO TRIUMPH

Zambia's unexpected glory at the 2012 Africa Cup of Nations was both fitting and poignant as the setting for its glory was just a few hundred yards from the scene of earlier calamity. The 2012 players spent the day before the final against **Ivory Coast** laying flowers in the sea in tribute to the 30 people killed when a plane crashed off the coast of Gabonese city Libreville on April 27, 1993. Victims that day included 18 Zambian internationals flying to Senegal for a FIFA World Cup qualifier. French coach Herve Renard dedicated the 2012 victory to the dead, after watching his team beat Ivory Coast 8-7 on penalties following a goalless tie after extra-time. Center-back Stoppila Sunzu struck the decisive spot-kick, after Ivory Coast's Kolo Toure had his penalty saved by Kennedy Mweene and Gervinho blazed his over the bar. Both teams were competing in their third Africa Cup of Nations final, Ivory Coast having won in 1992 and lost in 2006, while Zambia had finished runners-up in 1974 and 1994. Zambia's success was the climactic surprise of a tournament that produced shocks when traditional powerhouses Egypt, Cameroon, Nigeria, and South Africa all failed to even make the finals, then Senegal, Angola and Morocco were knocked out in the first round.

REIGNING PHARAOHS

Egypt dominate the major Africa Cup of Nations team records. It won the first tournament, in 1957, having been helped by a bye to the final, when semifinal opponent South Africa was disqualified, and has emerged as champions another six times since, three more than any other country. Its victories 2006, 2008, and 2010 make it the only country to lift the trophy three times in a row. Egypt has also qualified for a record 22 tournaments and played 84 games—10 more than the nearest challenger, Nigeria. It has also won more matches, 51 in all, followed by Ghana and Nigeria on 46 apiece, Cameroon on 37, and Ivory Coast on 36.

BAFANA BAFANA

The Africa Cup of Nations has been won by the host country on 11 separate occasions—including three times by Egypt and twice by Ghana. But perhaps the most surprising host-country triumph was South Africa's in 1996. The country had returned to international soccer only four years earlier, post-apartheid, when an 82nd-minute penalty by Theophilus "Doctor" Khumalo gave it a win over Cameroon on July 7, 1992. In February 1996, substitute Mark Williams scored both goals against Tunisia as South Africa won the Africa Cup of Nations trophy—lifted by white captain **Neil Tovey**, and handed over by the country's president Nelson Mandela—in Johannesburg's Soccer City stadium. South Africa was not even meant to be the host, but stepped in for original choice Kenya which was stripped of staging rights after falling behind on new stadium-building.

GIMME GUINEA GIMME

Guinea equaled the record for biggest ever win in the Africa Cup of Nations finals when it beat Botswana 6-1 in a first-round match in 2012—though both teams failed to make it out of Group D. Guinea was also only the third team to score six times in one match at a finals, following Egypt's 6-3 win over Nigeria in 1963, and Ivory Coast's 6-1 defeat of Ethiopia seven years later. The only other game to match the record winning margin saw Guinea not as the victors but the victims, going down 5-0 to Ivory Coast in 2008.

EQUATORIAL DEBUTANTS

Equatorial Guinea took part in an Africa Cup of Nations finals for the first time in 2012, thanks to co-hosting the tournament with Gabon. Equatorial Guinea had never managed to qualify before, while Gabon had reached the finals only four times previously. Botswana and Niger were the 2012 competition's other first-timers. The opening game of the 2012 competition was staged in Equatorial Guinea, in Bata, while the final was played in Gabonese city Libreville. The 2012 event was only the second to be shared between two host nations, after Ghana and Nigeria shared duties in 2000. Libya was awarded the right to host the Africa Cup of Nations, for a second time, in 2013, but turmoil in the country meant it was switched to South Africa, despite Nigeria initially being nominated as first reserve. Morocco has been selected to host its second ACN in 2015, and Libya is penciled in for 2017.

TOURNAMENT TRIUMPHS

7 Egypt (1957, 1959, 1986, 1998, 2006, 2008, 2010)
4 Ghana (1963, 1965, 1978, 1982)
  Cameroon (1984, 1988, 2000, 2002)
3 Nigeria (1980, 1994, 2013)
2 Zaire/Congo DR (1968, 1974)
1 Algeria (1990)
  Congo (1972)
  Ethiopia (1962)
  Ivory Coast (1992)
  Morocco (1976)
  South Africa (1996)
  Sudan (1970)
  Tunisia (2004)
  Zambia (2012)

TOURNAMENT APPEARANCES

22 Egypt
20 Ivory Coast
19 Ghana
17 Nigeria
16 Cameroon, Zaire/Congo DR, Tunisia, Zambia
15 Algeria, Morocco
12 Senegal
10 Ethiopia, Guinea
9 Burkina Faso
8 Mali, South Africa, Sudan
7 Angola, Togo
6 Congo
5 Gabon, Kenya, Uganda
4 Mozambique
3 Benin, Libya
2 Liberia, Malawi, Namibia, Niger, Sierra Leone, Zimbabwe
1 Botswana, Equatorial Guinea, Mauritius, Rwanda, Tanzania

FOUR SHAME

Host nation **Angola** was responsible for perhaps the most dramatic collapse in Africa Cup of Nations history, when it threw away a four-goal lead in the opening game of the 2010 tournament. Even more embarrassingly, it was leading 4-0 against Mali with just 11 minutes left, in the capital Luanda's Estadio 11 de Novembro. Mali's final two goals, by Barcelona's Seydou Keita and Boulogne's Mustapha Yatabare, were scored deep into stoppage-time. Mali failed to make it through the first round, while Angola went out in the quarterfinals.

MAGIC CAPE

The only country making its finals debut in the 2003 Africa Cup of Nations tournament was Cape Verde. Few expected the newcomers to go beyond the first round, yet Cape Verde qualified for the quarterfinals, where it lost 2-0 to competition veterans Ghana. The first Cape Verde goal at the finals was struck by **Luis Carlos Almada Soares** **(right)** in its opening 1-1 tie with Morocco—though the player who grew up in the French capital Paris is more popularly known by his nickname, after the France soccer legend: "Platini".

YO, YOBO

Nigeria's legendary **Joseph Yobo**—whose club career has encompassed spells in Belgium, France, Spain, England, and Turkey—was brought on to acclaim for the final few minutes over its final victory against Burkina Faso, while taking part in his sixth Africa Cup of Nations. He then had the honor of hoisting the trophy above his head as skipper. The record for most Africa Cup of Nations tournaments remains, however, with Cameroon's Rigobert Song. He appeared in the 1996, 1998, 2000, 2002, 2004, 2006, 2008, and 2010 tournaments, and also played in an unprecedented 35 ACN games in a row. Ivory Coast goalkeeper Alain Gouamene played at seven tournaments from 1988 to 2000.

REVOLUTION #9

No player has scored more goals in one Africa Cup of Nations than Zaire's Ndaye Mulamba's nine during the 1974 tournament. Three months later he was sent off at the FIFA World Cup in West Germany, as his team crashed to a 9-0 defeat against Yugoslavia.

STAR STRUCK

Gabon's Chiva Star Nzigou became the Africa Cup of Nations' youngest-ever player when he took the field against South Africa in January 2000, aged 16 years and 91 days. Gabon lost the game 3-1 and finished bottom of Group B without a win from three games.

PROLIFIC POKOU

Ivory Coast striker Laurent Pokou scored a record five goals in one Africa Cup of Nations match, as his team trounced Ethiopia 6-1 in the first round of the 1968 tournament. He finished top scorer at that tournament, and the following one, but ended both without a winners' medal. Only modern-day Cameroon star Samuel Eto'o has overtaken Pokou's overall Africa Cup of Nations tally of 14 goals.

OPENING GOAL

The first Africa Cup of Nations goal was a penalty scored by Egypt's Raafat Ateya in the 21st minute of its 2-1 semi-final win over Sudan in 1957. But his team-mate Mohamed Diab El-Attar would soon take over, as he not only added Egypt's second goal that day, but scored all four goals in the final against Ethiopia.

TOURNAMENT TOP SCORERS

Year	Player	Goals
1957	Mohamed Diab El-Attar (Egypt)	5
1959	Mahmoud Al-Gohari (Egypt)	3
1962	Abdelfatah Badawi (Egypt) Mengistu Worku (Ethiopia)	3
1963	Hassan El-Shazly (Egypt)	6
1965	Ben Acheampong (Ghana) Kofi Osei (Ghana) Eustache Mangle (Ivory Coast)	3
1968	Laurent Pokou (Ivory Coast)	6
1970	Laurent Pokou (Ivory Coast)	8
1972	Salif Keita (Mali)	5
1974	Ndaye Mulamba (Zaire)	9
1976	Keita Aliou Mamadou 'N'Jo Lea' (Guinea)	4
1978	Opoku Afriyie (Ghana) Segun Odegbami (Nigeria) Philip Omondi (Uganda)	3
1980	Khaled Al Abyad Labied (Morocco) Segun Odegbami (Nigeria)	3
1982	George Alhassan (Ghana)	4
1984	Taher Abouzaid (Egypt)	4
1986	Roger Milla (Cameroon)	4
1988	Gamal Abdelhamid (Egypt) Lakhdar Belloumi (Algeria) Roger Milla (Cameroon) Abdoulaye Traore (Ivory Coast)	2
1990	Djamel Menad (Algeria)	4
1992	Rashidi Yekini (Nigeria)	4
1994	Rashidi Yekini (Nigeria)	5
1996	Kalusha Bwalya (Zambia)	5
1998	Hossam Hassan (Egypt) Benni McCarthy (South Africa)	7
2000	Shaun Bartlett (South Africa)	5
2002	Julius Aghahowa (Nigeria) Patrick Mboma (Cameroon) Rene Salomon Olembe (Cameroon)	5
2004	Francileudo Santos (Tunisia) Frederic Kanoute (Mali) Patrick Mboma (Cameroon) Youssef Mokhtari (Morocco) Jay-Jay Okocha (Nigeria)	4
2006	Samuel Eto'o (Cameroon)	5
2008	Samuel Eto'o (Cameroon)	5
2010	Mohamed Nagy 'Gedo' (Egypt)	5
2012	Pierre-Emerick Aubameyang (Gabon), Cheick Diabate (Mali), Didier Drogba (Ivory Coast), Christopher Katongo (Zambia), Houssine Kharja (Morocco), Manucho (Tunisia), Emmanuel Mayuka (Zambia)	3
2013	Emmanuel Emenike (Nigeria), Mubarak Wakaso (Ghana)	4

TOP KATONGO

Zambia captain **Christopher Katongo** not only lifted the 2012 Africa Cup of Nations trophy, but also took home with him the prize for best player of the tournament. Katongo, who played his club soccer in China for Henan Construction, had got the final penalty shoot-out off to the perfect start for his team by successfully converting his spot-kick. His younger brother Felix Katongo also scored in the shoot-out, having come on as a 74th-minute substitute. Midfielder Felix had been playing earlier in the year for Libyan club Al-Ittihad, but Zambian authorities arranged for a plane to fly him out of the country as civil war raged. Another Zambian forward was awarded the Golden Boot for top scorer, though Emmanuel Mayuka was level on three goals with six other players: strike partner Christopher Katongo, as well as Pierre-Emerick Aubameyang (Gabon), Cheick Diabate (Mali), Didier Drogba (Ivory Coast), Houssine Kharja (Morocco), and Manucho (Angola).

PITROPIA REPRIEVE

Flying winger **Jonathan Pitroipa** was voted best player of the 2013 Africa Cup of Nations, despite finishing on the losing side when Burkina Faso fell short against Nigeria in the final. He took part in that showpiece game only after a reprieve following a red card in the semifinal victory over Ghana. His second yellow card—for simulation in the 117th minute—was judged harsh by officials at an appeal hearing. Pitroipa, who plays his club soccer for Stade Rennais in France, struck Burkina Faso's extra-time winner against Togo in the quarterfinals.

SAM THE MAN

Cameroon's Samuel Eto'o, who made his full international debut—at Costa Rica on March 9, 1997—one day short of his 16th birthday, is the Africa Cup of Nations' all-time leading goalscorer. He was part of Cameroon's victorious teams in 2000 and 2002, but had to wait until 2008 to pass Laurent Pokou's 14-goal Africa Cup of Nations record. That year's competition took his overall tally to 16 goals, only for the former Real Madrid, Barcelona, Internazionale, Anzi Makhachkala, and Chelsea striker to add another two in 2010. In 2005, Eto'o became the first player to be named African Footballer of the Year three years running. He also won an Olympic Games gold medal with Cameroon in 2000 and the UEFA Champions League three times: with Barcelona in 2006 and 2009—scoring in both finals—and with Inter, in 2010.

AFRICA CUP OF NATIONS ALL−TIME TOP SCORERS

1	Samuel Eto'o (Cameroon)	18
2	Laurent Pokou (Ivory Coast)	14
3	Rashidi Yekini (Nigeria)	13
4	Hassan El-Shazly (Egypt)	12
5	Didier Drogba (Ivory Coast)	11
=	Hossam Hassan (Egypt)	11
=	Patrick Mboma (Cameroon)	11
8	Kalusha Bwalya (Zambia)	10
=	Ndaye Mulamba (Zaire)	10
=	Francileudo Santos (Tunisia)	10
=	Joel Tiehi (Ivory Coast)	10
=	Mengistu Worku (Ethiopia)	10

NO HASSLE FOR HASSAN

Egypt's **Ahmed Hassan** not only became the first man to play in the final of four different Africa Cup of Nations in 2010, he also became the first to collect his fourth winners' medal. Earlier in the same tournament, his appearance in the quarterfinal against Cameroon gave him his 170th cap—a new Egyptian record. Hassan marked the game with three goals, one in his own net and two past Cameroon goalkeeper Carlos Kameni, although one of the two at the correct end appeared not to cross the line.

AFRICA CUP OF NATIONS OTHER RECORDS

AFRICA CUP OF NATIONS: FINALS

1957	(Host country: Sudan) Egypt 4 Ethiopia 0
1959	(Egypt) Egypt 2 Sudan 1
1962	(Ethiopia) Ethiopia 4 Egypt 2 (aet)
1963	(Ghana) Ghana 3 Sudan 0
1965	(Tunisia) Ghana 3 Tunisia 2 (aet)
1968	(Ethiopia) Zaire/Congo DR 1 Ghana 0
1970	(Sudan) Sudan 1 Ghana 0
1972	(Cameroon) Congo 3 Mali 2
1974	(Egypt) Zaire/Congo DR 2 Zambia 2
	Replay: Zaire/Congo DR 2 Zambia 0
1976	(Ethiopia) Morocco 1 Guinea 1 (Morocco win mini-league system)
1978	(Ghana) Ghana 2 Uganda 0
1980	(Nigeria) Nigeria 3 Algeria 0
1982	(Libya) Ghana 1 Libya 1 (aet; Ghana win 7-6 on penalties)
1984	(Ivory Coast) Cameroon 3 Nigeria 1
1986	(Egypt) Egypt 0 Cameroon 0 (aet; Egypt win 5-4 on penalties)
1988	(Morocco) Cameroon 1 Nigeria 0
1990	(Algeria) Algeria 1 Nigeria 0
1992	(Senegal) Ivory Coast 0 Ghana 0 (aet; Ivory Coast win 11-10 on penalties)
1994	(Tunisia) Nigeria 2 Zambia 1
1996	(South Africa) South Africa 2 Tunisia 0
1998	(Burkina Faso) Egypt 2 South Africa 0
2000	(Ghana & Nigeria) Cameroon 2 Nigeria 2 (aet; Cameroon win 4-3 on penalties)
2002	(Mali) Cameroon 0 Senegal 0 (aet; Cameroon win 3-2 on penalties)
2004	(Tunisia) Tunisia 2 Morocco 1
2006	(Egypt) Egypt 0 Ivory Coast 0 (aet; Egypt win 4-2 on penalties)
2008	(Ghana) Egypt 1 Cameroon 0
2010	(Angola) Egypt 1 Ghana 0
2012	(Gabon & Equatrorial Guinea) Zambia 0 Ivory Coast 0 (aet; Zambia 8-7 on pens)
2013	(South Africa) Nigeria 1 Burkina Faso 0

GEDO BLASTER

Egypt's hero in 2010 was Mohamed Nagy, better known by his nickname "Gedo"—Egyptian Arabic for "Grandpa." He scored the only goal of the final, against Ghana, his fifth of the tournament, giving him the Golden Boot. Yet he did all this without starting a single game. He had to settle for coming on as a substitute in all six of Egypt's matches, playing a total of 135 minutes in all. Gedo, born in Damanhur on October 3, 1984, made his international debut only two months earlier, and had played just two friendlies for Egypt before the tournament proper.

TOGO'S TRAGIC FATE

Togo were the victims of tragedy shortly before the opening of 2010 Africa Cup of Nations—followed by expulsion from the event. The team's bus was fired on by Angolan militants three days before its first scheduled match, killing three people: the team's assistant coach, press officer and bus driver. The team returned home to Togo for three days of national mourning, and was then thrown out of the competition by the CAF as punishment for missing its opening game against Ghana. Togo was later expelled from the next two competitions, but this sanction was overturned on appeal in May 2010.

RENARD REDEEMED

Herve Renard, the coach of 2012 champions Zambia, was in his second spell in charge, having previously led them between 2008 and 2010. His decision to resign after a run to the quarter-finals of the 2010 Africa Cup of Nations (to become Angola's coach) meant his return to Zambia in October 2011 wasn't uniformly welcomed. But all was forgiven when Zambia won its first title. Renard's celebrations included carrying injured defender Joseph Musonda on to the pitch—he had limped off after only ten minutes—and handing his winner's medal to Kalusha Bwalya, probably Zambia's greatest ever player. Bwalya had missed the doomed 1993 flight because he was playing club soccer for PSV Eindhoven in the Netherlands. He later coached Zambia but, by the time of the 2012 triumph, Bwalya was president of his country's soccer association.

UNFINISHED BUSINESS

Beware, if you go to see Nigeria play Tunisia, you may not get to see the full 90 minutes played. Nigeria was awarded third place at the 1978 Africa Cup of Nations after the Tunisian team walked off after 42 minutes of the third-place play-off, with the score at 1-1. Tunisia was protesting about refereeing decisions, but its action gave Nigeria a 2-0 victory by default. Oddly enough, it was Nigeria which walked off when the two teams met in the second leg of a qualifier for the 1962 tournament. Its action came when Tunisia equalized after 65 minutes. The punishment was a 2-0 win in Tunisia's favor—giving it a 3-2 victory on aggregate.

INTERNATIONAL EXILE

South Africa was disqualified from the four-team Africa Cup of Nations in 1957 after refusing to pick a multi-racial squad.

MEET THE NEW (BIG) BOSS, SAME AS THE OLD (BIG) BOSS

Stephen Keshi—known to admiring fans as "Big Boss"—became only the second man to win the Africa Cup of Nations as both player and manager, when leading Nigeria to the title in 2013. He previously lifted the trophy as captain in 1994. The Nigerian soccer association, for so long mired in corruption and mismanagement claims, had its grudging faith in Keshi vindicated in summer 2013, though he was its 19th manager in 19 years. Before Keshi, the only man to win the tournament both as a player and manager was Egypt's Mahmoud Al-Gohary, who was top scorer in 1959 and in charge 39 years later. Hassan Shehata, striker when Egypt finished third in 1970, then won a record-breaking three times as his country's coach.

TUNED IN TO SUDAN

The 1970 Africa Cup of Nations in Sudan marked the first time the tournament was televised. Ghana reached the final for what was then an unprecedented fourth consecutive time, but it was beaten 1-0 by the host nation.

RECENT AFRICA CUP OF NATIONS—WINNING COACHES

1988	Claude Le Roy (Cameroon)
1990	Abdelhamid Kermali (Algeria)
1992	Yeo Martial (Ivory Coast)
1994	Clemens Westerhof (Nigeria)
1996	Clive Barker (South Africa)
1998	Mahmoud El-Gohary (Egypt)
2000	Pierre Lechantre (Cameroon)
2002	Winfried Schafer (Cameroon)
2004	Roger Lemerre (Tunisia)
2006	Hassan Shehata (Egypt)
2008	Hassan Shehata (Egypt)
2010	Hassan Shehata (Egypt)
2012	Herve Renard (Zambia)
2013	Stephen Keshi (Nigeria)

LOCK DEFENCE

Liberia's military leader Samuel Doe threatened to jail the national team if it lost at an Africa Cup of Nations qualifier to Gambia in December 1980, a game that also doubled as a FIFA World Cup qualifier. The players escaped punishment by achieving a 0-0 draw, though neither side went on to reach either the Africa Cup of Nations or the 1982 FIFA World Cup.

MISSING THE POINT

The absences of Cameroon, Nigeria, and reigning champions Egypt from the 2012 African Cup of Nations were surprising—though all could at least comfort themselves on not missing out in quite such embarrassing circumstances as **South Africa.** It appeared happy to play out a goalless tie with Sierra Leone in its final qualifier, believing that would be enough to go through, and greeted the final whistle with celebrations on the pitch. But South Africa was mistaken in thinking goal difference would be used to separate teams level on points in its group, because Niger qualified instead, thanks to a better head-to-head record. South Africa's distraught coach Pitso Mosimane admitted misinterpreting the rules and deliberately targeting his team's tactics towards a tie. The South African soccer association initially appealed against elimination, claiming goal difference should be the decider, but ultimately decided not to pursue the matter.

DOUBLE FAULTED

Stephen Keshi was not the only coach going into the 2013 Africa Cup of Nations hoping to become only the second to triumph both as player and manager. James Kwesi Appiah, in charge of his native Ghana, was on the winning side in 1982, the last time his nation was the continental champion. This time, however, his luck was out as Burkina Faso prevailed in a semi-final penalty shoot-out.

PART 6:
OTHER FIFA TOURNAMENTS

AROUND three billion people are involved in soccer in one way or another. The passion and ambition explains just why the international game's competitive structure has expanded to meet demand. The value of all the other FIFA championships is that the competitive structure is devolved down to a regional level—whether in Africa or Europe or Oceania.

That brings world competition down to a local level, and increasingly imaginative concepts for tournament hosting means that more and more nations enjoy the opportunity to welcome the world. An obvious example was the FIFA Under-17 Women's World Cup staged in Azerbaijan—a relatively new member of the world soccer family—in autumn 2012. Such events encourage and acknowledge the work of enthusiasts at grassroots levels across the world. Regional confederations organize international championships for players in a wide range of age groups.

In 1977, FIFA extended its worldwide development programme with the launch of the FIFA World Youth Cup. The Soviet Union beat Mexico in the first final, in Tunisia. Eight years later came the FIFA Under-17 World Cup. Simultaneously, the Olympic Games men's soccer tournament became an Under-23 event with an exception for teams in the finals to field up to three over-age players. In 2000, FIFA stepped into the senior club sphere with the launch of FIFA Club World Cup. The establishment of such events at the top of world soccer encouraged regional confederations to create their own matching tournaments, so their teams could take to the world stage and face elite opponents.

Bayern Munich's captain Philipp Lahm leads the FIFA Club World Cup celebration in Marrakech, Morocco, after the German and European champions had defeated the host nation's Raja Casablanca, 2-0, in the 2013 final.

FIFA U-20 WORLD CUP

First staged in 1977 in Tunisia and known as the FIFA Youth World Championship until 2005, the FIFA U-20 World Cup is the world championship for players under the age of 20. It has featured some of the game's most notable names. Staged in alternate years, the tournament's most successful team has been Argentina, which has lifted the trophy on six occasions.

FULL HOUSES

The 2011 tournament saw record crowds, with 1,309,929 fans attending the 52 games at eight venues across eight Colombian cities, meaning the average attendance was 25,191 per match. The overall tally exceeded the 1,295,299 going to games at the finals in Egypt two years earlier, though the average crowd of 36,099 for the 32 games in Mexico in 1983 remains a record too. That 2009 tournament did feature a record 167 goals, two more than in Malaysia 12 years earlier. The 3.21 goals per game in Egypt was marginally higher than the Malaysian edition's 3.17. Poor Tahiti helped keep the goal rate high, conceding 21 goals in three group games in Egypt without managing to score for itself.

DOMINANT DOMINIC

Ghana became the first African country to lift the trophy when it upset Brazil in the 2009 final, despite playing 83 of the 120 minutes with just 10 men, following Daniel Addo's red card. The final finished goalless, one of only two games in which **Dominic Adiyiah** failed to score. He ended the tournament as top scorer with eight goals and also won the Golden Ball prize for best player. Immediately afterward, a further reward came with a transfer from Norway's Fredrikstad to Italy's AC Milan. The Silver Ball went to Brazil's Alex Teixeira, even though it was his missed penalty, when the final shoot-out went to sudden death, which handed Ghana victory.

SUPER SUB

The Soviet Union became the first winners of the FIFA Under-20 World Cup when it beat hosts Mexico 9-8 on penalties after a 2-2 tie in the 1977 final. Its shoot-out hero was substitute goalkeeper Yuri Sivuha, who had replaced Aleksandre Novikov during extra-time. It was the only time the Soviet Union won the event, though its striker **Oleg Salenko**, a future 1994 FIFA World Cup Golden Boot winner, took the top scorer award in 1989, with five goals. Two years later, fellow Soviet Sergei Sherbakov also finished top scorer, also with five goals, although his full international career was less successful. He played only twice for Ukraine before injuries suffered in a car accident in 1993 left him in a wheelchair.

LISBON LIONS

In 1991, **Portugal** became the first hosts to win the tournament with a team that became known as the country's "Golden Generation," featuring Luis Figo, Rui Costa, Joao Pinto, Abel Xavier and Jorge Costa. Portugal's winning squad was coached by Carlos Queiroz, who would later manage the full national side twice, with spells in charge at Real Madrid and as assistant at Manchester United in between. Its penalty shoot-out win over Brazil in the final was played at Benfica's iconic Estadio da Luz in the capital Lisbon. In 2001, Argentina became the second team to lift the trophy on home territory.

SAVIOR SAVIOLA

Javier Saviola has scored more goals in one FIFA Under-20 World Cup than any other player. He scored 11 times in seven games at the 2001 competition, as his Argentina team went on to beat 3-0 Ghana in the final, with Saviola scoring once. Saviola, born on December 11, 1981, in Buenos Aires, was playing for River Plate at the time but joined Barcelona for £15 million shortly after the finals, and later signed for the Spanish side's arch-rival Real Madrid. When Pele picked his 125 "greatest living soccer players" for FIFA in March 2004, 22-year-old Saviola was the youngest player on the list.

OSCAR WINNING

Only one player has scored a hat-trick in the final of a FIFA Under-20 World Cup: Brazilian midfielder Oscar, who hit all his team's goals in its 3-2 triumph over Portugal to claim the trophy in August 2011. He was further rewarded by making his senior Brazil debut the following month, against Argentina. They were actually Oscar's first goals of the tournament, staged in Colombia, with the Golden Shoe going to his team-mate Henrique for five goals in the preceding six matches. Henrique's goal in a 3-0 first-round victory over Austria was the 200th goal in FIFA Under-20 World Cup history.

CAPTAIN MARVELS

Two men have lifted both the FIFA Under-20 World Cup and the FIFA World Cup as captain: Brazil's Dunga (in 1983 and 1994) and Argentina's Diego Maradona (in 1979 and 1986). Many had expected Maradona to make Argentina's full squad for the 1978 FIFA World Cup but he missed out on selection. He showed his potential by being voted best player at the 1979 youth tournament in Japan.

TOURNAMENT HOSTS AND FINAL RESULTS

1977 (Host: Tunisia) USSR 2 Mexico 2 (aet: USSR win 9-8 on penalties)
1979 (Japan) Argentina 3 USSR 1
1981 (Australia) West Germany 4 Qatar 0
1983 (Mexico) Brazil 1 Argentina 0
1985 (USSR) Brazil 1 Spain 0 (aet)
1987 (Chile) Yugoslavia 1 West Germany 1 (aet: Yugoslavia win 5-4 on penalties)
1989 (Saudi Arabia) Portugal 2 Nigeria 0
1991 (Portugal) Portugal 0 Brazil 0 (aet: Portugal win 4-2 on penalties)
1993 (Australia) Brazil 2 Ghana 1
1995 (Qatar) Argentina 2 Brazil 0
1997 (Malaysia) Argentina 2 Uruguay 1
1999 (Nigeria) Spain 4 Japan 0
2001 (Argentina) Argentina 3 Ghana 0
2003 (United Arab Emirates) Brazil 1 Spain 0
2005 (Netherlands) Argentina 2 Nigeria 1
2007 (Canada) Argentina 2 Czech Republic 1
2009 (Egypt) Ghana 0 Brazil 0 (aet: Ghana win 4-3 on penalties)
2011 (Colombia) Brazil 3 Portugal 2 (aet)
2013 (Turkey) France 0, Uruguay 0 (aet: France win 4-1 on penalties)

WHAT A MESSI

Lionel Messi was the star of the show for Argentina in 2005, and not just for scoring his country's two goals in the final, both from the penalty spot. He achieved a hat-trick by not only winning the Golden Boot for top scorer and Golden Shoe for best player, but also by captaining his side to the title. This feat was emulated two years later by compatriot Sergio Aguero, who scored once in the final against the Czech Republic, before team-mate Mauro Zarate struck a late winner. Four other men have finished as both top scorer and as the tournament's best player, as voted by journalists: Brazil's Geovani in 1983, Argentina's Javier Saviola in 2001, Dominic Adiyiah of Ghana in 2009, and another Brazilian, Henrique, in 2011.

TOURNAMENT TOP SCORERS

Year	Player	Goals
1977	Guina (Brazil)	4
1979	Ramon Diaz (Argentina)	8
1981	Ralf Loose (West Germany), Roland Wohlfarth (West Germany), Taher Amer (Egypt), Mark Koussas (Argentina)	4
1983	Geovani (Brazil)	6
1985	Gerson (Brazil), Balalo (Brazil), Muller (Brazil), Alberto Garcia Aspe (Mexico), Monday Odiaka (Nigeria), Fernando Gomez (Spain), Sebastian Losada (Spain)	3
1987	Marcel Witeczek (West Germany)	7
1989	Oleg Salenko (USSR)	5
1991	Sergei Sherbakov (USSR)	5
1993	Ante Milicic (Australia), Adriano (Brazil), Gian (Brazil), Henry Zambrano (Colombia), Vicente Nieto (Mexico), Chris Faklaris (USA)	3
1995	Joseba Etxeberria (Spain)	7
1997	Adailton Martins Bolzan (Brazil)	10
1999	Mahamadou Dissa (Mali), Pablo (Spain)	5
2001	Javier Saviola (Argentina)	11
2003	Fernando Cavenaghi (Argentina), Dudu (Brazil), Daisuke Sakata (Japan), Eddie Johnson (USA)	4
2005	Lionel Messi (Argentina)	6
2007	Sergio Aguero (Argentina)	7
2009	Dominic Adiyiah (Ghana)	8
2011	Henrique (Brazil)	5
2013	Ebenezer Assifuah (Ghana)	6

BRIGHT BLUES

France won the FIFA U-20 crown for the first time when it beat Uruguay 4-1 on penalties after the second goalless tie in the final in three tournaments. Les Bleuets won despite finishing only second to favorites Spain in Group A. It then gained in confidence after a 4-1 thrashing of host nation Turkey in the second round. In Juventus midfielder Paul Pogba, France also boasted the tournament's best player, while its goalkeeper Alphonse Areola, with two spot-kick saves, was decisive in the final shootout.

FIFA U-17 WORLD CUP

First staged in China in 1985, when it was known as the FIFA Under-16 World Championship, the age limit was adjusted from 16 to 17 in 1991 and the tournament has been labeled the FIFA U-17 World Cup since 2007. The 2013 finals were staged in the United Arab Emirates when Nigeria ran out as deserved winners for a record-extending fourth time. It has also been the runner-up on three occasions.

TAKING WING

Nigeria's youth side, the "Golden Eaglets," became the first African nation to win a FIFA tournament when it triumphed at the inaugural Under-16 FIFA World Cup in 1985 (it became an Under-17 event in 1991). Its opening goal in the final against West Germany was scored by striker Jonathan Akpoborie, who would go on to play for German clubs Stuttgart and Wolfsburg.

WHOSE SHOE?

Sani Emmanuel can boast of being top scorer, while also voted best player, after starring in Nigeria's run to the 2009 final—though that last match was the only one he started. He was awarded the Golden Ball for his performances, but had to settle for the Silver Shoe prize, despite scoring five goals, the same tally as Golden Shoe winner Borja. The Spanish striker took the main award because he managed one more assist. Uruguay's Sebastian Gallegos and Switzerland's Haris Seferovic also finished the tournament with five goals apiece. Yuri Nikiforov scored a joint-best five goals for the Soviet Union at the 1987 tournament, including one in the final, as his team beat Nigeria on penalties—but FIFA awarded the Golden Shoe to Ivory Coast's Moussa Traore, who also hit five but for a lower-scoring side. The Soviet Union scored 21 goal overall, to the Ivory Coast's nine.

GOALS FLO

The first player win both the Golden Ball and the Golden Shoe at the FIFA U-17 World Cup was French striker **Florent Sinama-Pongolle**. His nine goals in 2001 set  a tournament record for one player. His tally included two hat-tricks in the opening round. Unlike Cesc Fabregas, two years later, Sinama-Pongolle ended on winning team in the final. The team goalscoring record is held by Spain, which struck 22 times on its way to third place in 1997. Sinama-Pongolle's scoring record was equaled in 2011 by Ivory Coast striker Souleymane Coulibaly. While Sinama-Pongolle played six times, the young Ivorian managed his in just four games, as team exited in the second round. Coulibaly was further rewarded, however, as he soon was transfered from Italy's Siena to English Premier League club Tottenham Hotspur.

SEOUL SURVIVOR

The final of the 2007 tournament was the first to be hosted by a former FIFA World Cup finals venue, the 68,476-capacity Seoul FIFA World Cup Stadium in South Korea's capital, which had been built for the 2002 FIFA World Cup. The game was watched by a crowd of 36,125, a tournament record. The 2007 event was the first to feature 24 teams instead of 16, and was won by Nigeria, after Spain missed all three of its spot-kicks in a penalty shoot-out.

GOOD AND BAD BOY BOJAN

Barcelona star **Bojan Krkic** quickly went from hero to villain in the final moments of Spain's semifinal victory over Ghana in 2007. He scored his team's winner with four minutes of extra-time remaining, but was then sent off for a second yellow-card offence just before the final whistle. His red card meant he was suspended for the final, which Spain lost on penalties to Nigeria.

GOLDEN HAUL

West Germany's Marcel Witeczek is the only person to finish top scorer at both a FIFA Under-16 World Championship and the Under-20 version of the event. The Polish-born striker hit eight goals at the 1985 Under-16 tournament, followed by seven more at the Under-20 championship two years later. Brazil's Adriano—a different Adriano from the one who later played for the senior side and Serie A club Internazionale—came closest to equaling the feat: he won the Golden Shoe, for top scorer, after scoring four goals at the 1991 FIFA Under-17 World Cup, then the Golden Ball, for best player, at the Under-20 event in 1993.

LITTLE ITALY

The 1991 tournament was originally scheduled to take place in Ecuador, but a cholera outbreak in the country meant it was switched to Italy instead, though games were played in much smaller venues than those used for the previous year's senior FIFA World Cup. The 1991 tournament was the first to be open to Under-17s—the first three had been known as the FIFA U-16 World Cup.

TOURNAMENT TOP SCORERS

Year	Player	Goals
1985	Marcel Witeczek (West Germany)	8
1987	Moussa Traore (Ivory Coast)	5
	Yuri Nikiforov (USSR)	5
1989	Khaled Jasem (Bahrain)	3
	Fode Camara (Guinea)	3
	Gil (Portugal)	3
	Tulipa (Portugal)	3
	Khalid Al Roaihi (Saudi Arabia)	3
1991	Adriano (Brazil)	4
1993	Wilson Oruma (Nigeria)	6
1995	Daniel Allsopp (Australia)	5
	Mohamed Al Kathiri (Oman)	5
1997	David (Spain)	7
1999	Ishmael Addo (Ghana)	7
2001	Florent Sinama-Pongolle (France)	9
2003	Carlos Hidalgo (Colombia)	5
	Manuel Curto (Portugal)	5
	Cesc Fabregas (Spain)	5
2005	Carlos Vela (Mexico)	5
2007	Macauley Chrisantus (Nigeria)	7
2009	Borja (Spain)	5
	Sani Emmanuel (Nigeria)	5
	Sebastian Gallegos (Uruguay)	5
	Haris Seferovic (Switzerland)	5
2011	Souleymane Coulibaly (Ivory Coast)	9
2013	**Valmir Berisha** (Sweden)	7

HIGH–FLYING EAGLETS

In 2013, remarkably, the teams that finished first, second and third, respectively in Group F, ended the tournament in that order. Nigeria's Golden Eaglets won in fine style to complete a memorable year—the senior team won the African Cup of Nations and qualified for the FIFA World Cup finals. The unbeaten juniors crushed Mexico 3-0 in the final. Nigeria's star forward Kelechi Iheanacho was named the best player and Dele Alampasu the top goalkeeper. Sweden, thanks in part to seven-goal top-scorer Valmir Berisha, finished third in its first-ever finals appearance.

GOMEZ AT HOME

Mexico became the first host country to lift the FIFA U-17 World Cup trophy on home soil, when it beat Uruguay 2-0 in the final in the Azteca Stadium in Mexico City in July 2011. The Golden Ball award for the tournament's best player went to Mexican winger **Julio Gomez,** who scored twice against Germany in the semifinal including a spectacular bicycle-kick for the last-minute winner. However, Gomez played only ten minutes of the final, as a substitute, after picking up an injury in the previous game.

FAB FABREGAS

Spain's Cesc Fabregas joined Florent Sinama-Pongolle as only two players to win both the Golden Shoe, for top scorer, and the Golden Ball, for best player, at a FIFA Under-17 World Cup. He took both prizes after scoring five goals at the 2003 tournament, despite losing the final to Brazil. He and team-mate David Silva would later be part of the senior Spanish team which won the 2008 and 2012 UEFA European Championships as well as the 2010 FIFA World Cup in South Africa. Fabregas, born in Arenys de Mar on May 4, 1987, left Barcelona for Arsenal a month after the 2003 tournament. After being club captain at Arsenal, Fabregas returned to Barcelona in 2011 but, three years later, moved to Chelsea.

HOSTS AND FINAL RESULTS
(Host country)

1985	(China) Nigeria 2 West Germany 0
1987	(Canada) USSR 1 Nigeria 1 (aet: USSR win 4-2 on penalties)
1989	(Scotland) Saudi Arabia 2 Scotland 2 (aet: Saudi Arabia win 5-4 on penalties)
1991	(Italy) Ghana 1 Spain 0
1993	(Japan) Nigeria 2 Ghana 1
1995	(Ecuador) Ghana 3 Brazil 2
1997	(Egypt) Brazil 2 Ghana 1
1999	(New Zealand) Brazil 0 Australia 0 (aet: Brazil win 8-7 on penalties)
2001	(Trinidad & Tobago) France 3 Nigeria 0
2003	(Finland) Brazil 1 Spain 0
2005	(Peru) Mexico 3 Brazil 0
2007	(South Korea) Nigeria 0 Spain 0 (aet: Nigeria win 3-0 on penalties)
2009	(Nigeria) Switzerland 1 Nigeria 0
2011	(Mexico) Mexico 2 Uruguay 0
2013	(United Arab Emirates) Nigeria 3 Mexico 0

FIFA CONFEDERATIONS CUP

The FIFA Confederations Cup has assumed numerous guises over the years. In 1992 and 1995, it was played in Saudi Arabia and featured a collection of continental champions. From 1997 to 2003, FIFA staged a tournament every two years. The tournament was played in its current format for the first time in Germany in 2005. It is now celebrated throughout the soccer world as the Championship of Champions.

OVERALL TOP SCORERS

1 Cuauhtemoc Blanco (Mexico)	9
= Ronaldinho (Brazil)	9
3 Fernando Torres (Spain)	8
4 Romario (Brazil)	7
= Adriano (Brazil)	7
6 Marzouk Al-Otaibi (Saudi Arabia)	6
7 Alex (Brazil)	5
= John Aloisi (Australia)	5
= Luis Fabiano (Brazil)	5
= Fred (Brazil)	5
= Vladimir Smicer (Czech Rep.)	5
= Robert Pires (France)	5

FAB'S FIVE

Brazil's victory over the United States in the 2009 final made it the first country to complete a hat-trick of FIFA Confederations Cup triumphs, following success in 1997 and 2005. But it did it the hard way, needing to come back from two goals down at half-time before winning 3-2, thanks to a late goal from captain and center-back Lucio. **Luis Fabiano**, who ended as tournament top scorer with five goals overall, struck the other two goals. His team-mate Kaka was voted best player, with Luis Fabiano second and America's Clint Dempsey third.

TOURNAMENT TOP SCORERS

1992	Gabriel Batistuta (Argentina), Bruce Murray (USA) 2
1995	Luis Garcia (Mexico) 3
1997	Romario (Brazil) 7
1999	Ronaldinho (Brazil), Cuauhtemoc Blanco (Mexico), Marzouq Al-Otaibi (Saudi Arabia) 6
2001	Shaun Murphy (Australia), Eric Carriere (France), Robert Pires (France), Patrick Vieira (France), Sylvain Wiltord (France), Takayuki Suzuki (Japan), Hwang Sun-Hong (South Korea) 2
2003	Thierry Henry (France) 4
2005	Adriano (Brazil) 5
2009	Luis Fabiano (Brazil) 5
2013	Fernando Torres (Spain) 5 Fred (Brazil) 5

FIT FOR A KING

Before being rebranded as the FIFA Confederations Cup, a tournament bringing together the world's continental champions was known as the King Fahd Cup and staged in Saudi Arabia. Copa America holders Argentina reached both finals, beating the host nation in the first in 1992—thanks to goals by Leonardo Rodriguez, Claudio Caniggia, and Diego Simeone. Only four teams contested the 1992 event, with the United States and the Ivory Coast also represented, but Germany, the world champion, and the European champion Netherlands did not take part. In 1995, a six-team version was won by European champions Denmark. The current eight-team format, with two groups and knockout semifinals, was adopted in 2005.

TON-UP SUPERSTARS

Andrea Pirlo and Diego Forlan both celebrated making their 100th international appearance at the 2013 FIFA Confederations Cup. Italy playmaker Pirlo scored the *Azzurri*'s first goal in their opening 2-1 win over Mexico in Maracana. Forlan marked his own achievement—and became the first Uruguayan to reach 100 caps—by hitting a brilliant left-footed drive which proved the decisive goal in a 2-1 victory over Nigeria.

NO STOPPING NEYMAR

The 2013 FIFA Confederations Cup crowned a memorable six months for Brazilian striker Neymar. In January he had been voted South American Footballer of the Year for the second successive year, and in June he agreed to leave Santos to take up a five-year contract with Spanish champions Barcelona. In one of his farewell appearances in Brazil, Neymar da Silva Santos Junior struck the first goal of the FIFA Confederations Cup in only the third minute of the tournament's opening game against Japan. Neymar scored in each of Brazil's group matches and then again in the defeat of Spain in the final.

HIGH-TECH INSURANCE

Goal-line technology was used at the FIFA Confederations Cup for the first time in Brazil. GoalControl, a German company, won a tender to install its system in all six venues. In fact, it was never needed to decide a goal-scoring issue, but FIFA was satisfied it functioned effectively. Howard Webb, lone English referee at the competition, hailed "the reassurance the system gives us."

BURSTING A SOUTH SEA BUBBLE

Minnows Tahiti suffered the heaviest defeat in FIFA Confederations Cup history when it crashed 10-0 to Spain in the 2013 tournament in Brazil. The South Pacific part-timers—with a squad that included an accountant, carpenter, and teacher—were not too upset, however. None of the players had ever even dreamed of playing in the legendary Maracana stadium, or against the world and European champions, and achieved both in one game. The Oceania champions also conceded a Cup-record 24 goals in its three games. Jonathan Tehau scored Tahiti's historic single goal, against Nigeria. The defeat by Spain equaled the Cup's largest single-game aggregate: in 1999, Brazil thrashed Saudi Arabia 8-2.

BRILLIANT BRAZIL

Brazil's 3-0 demolition of world and European champions Spain in the 2013 final in Maracana enhanced its historical command of the FIFA Confederations Cup. Its 12th consecutive win in the competition saw Luiz Felipe Scolari's men become the first nation to land the Cup three times in a row. Brazil scored at least three goals in each of its title match victories and is the competition's only four-times champions. Brazil, as hosts, set a standard off the pitch, too: record ticket sales generated a 16-game aggregate attendance of 804,659—an average of 50,291 per game. The 68 goals came at an average of 4.25 per game, the highest over the last six competitions.

SHARED SADNESS

The 2003 FIFA Confederations Cup was overshadowed by the tragic death of Cameroon's 28-year-old midfielder **Marc-Vivien Foe**, who collapsed on the Lyon pitch after suffering a heart attack 73 minutes into his country's semifinal win against Colombia. After Thierry Henry scored France's golden-goal winner against Cameroon in the final, he dedicated his goal to Foe, who played much of his club career in the French championship. When the trophy was presented at the Stade de France in Paris, it was jointly lifted by both teams' captains—Marcel Desailly for France and Rigobert Song for Cameroon.

CLINT MAKES AMERICA'S DAY

The United States' surprise run to the 2009 final included a shock semifinal win over Spain that ended the European champions' long unbeaten run. Heading into the game, Spain had won a record 15 international matches in a row, and shared another record with Brazil—35 successive games unbeaten. But its hopes of extending its run to 36 games were ruined by goals from striker Jozy Altidore and winger **Clint Dempsey**. The result put the Americans into the final of a FIFA men's senior competition for the first time.

FIFA CONFEDERATIONS CUP HOSTS AND FINAL RESULTS

1997	(Host country: Saudi Arabia) Brazil 6 Argentina 0
1999	(Mexico) Mexico 4 Brazil 3
2001	(South Korea and Japan) France 1 Japan 0
2003	(France) France 1 Cameroon 0
	(aet: France win on golden goal)
2005	(Germany) Brazil 4 Argentina 1
2009	(South Africa) Brazil 3 United States 2
2013	(Brazil) Brazil 3 Spain 0

FIFA CLUB WORLD CUP

As is the case with the FIFA Confederations Cup, the FIFA Club World Cup has been played in several different formats since 1960, when Real Madrid defeated Penarol. In its current guise, the competition pits the champion clubs from all six continents against each other. It has been staged on an annual basis, mostly in Japan from 2005, apart from two hostings in Abu Dhabi, and 2013 in Morocco.

CORINTHIAN SPIRIT

Brazilian club Corinthians not only succeeded Barcelona as FIFA Club World Cup champions in 2012, but also equaled the Spanish club's record as two-time winners, and with a record of six games won overall. Peruvian striker Paolo Guerrero scored the only goal of its semifinal victory over Egypt's Al-Ahly, and repeated the feat in the final against England's Chelsea. The Corinthians line-up included goalkeeper and player-of-the-tournament **Cassio**, as well as Danilo and Fabio Santos, a pair who had both won the tournament with Sao Paulo seven years earlier. Defeat for the European champions also prevented newly-appointed Chelsea coach Rafael Benitez from equaling former Barcelona boss Pep Guardiola in winning the tournament twice. Benitez had previously lifted the trophy as Internazionale coach in 2010.

WINNERS BY COUNTRY*

10 Brazil
9 Argentina, Italy
6 Uruguay, Spain
4 Germany
3 Netherlands
2 Portugal, England
1 Paraguay, Yugoslavia

*Includes Intercontinental Cup

BAYERN UBER ALLES

Bayern Munich ended 2013 in glory, celebrating its fifth trophy of the year when it defeated Raja Casablanca from the host nation Morocco by 2-0 in the final in Marrakech. Goals from Dante and **Thiago Alcantara** decided the game inside 22 minutes. This was Bayern's second trophy under new coach Pep Guardiola after the UEFA European Supercup. The previous three had been the handiwork of retirement-bound Jupp Heynckes: the German league and cup and UEFA Champions League.

SIX APPEAL

Barcelona's triumph in 2009 made it the first club to lift six different major trophies in one calendar year: the FIFA Club World Cup, the UEFA Champions League, the UEFA European Super Cup, and a Spanish hat-trick of La Liga, Copa del Rey, and Super Cup. This made its trophy cabinet one cup heavier than Liverpool's in 2001, when Gerard Houllier's men won the FA Cup, League Cup, and Charity Shield in England, and the UEFA Cup and UEFA Super Cup in Europe.

UAE O.K.

The 2009 tournament was the first of the "new" FIFA Club World Cup events to take place outside Japan—in the United Arab Emirates state of Abu Dhabi, where the tournament was also staged 12 months later. Two stadia shared the workload: the **Al Jazira Mohammed bin Zayed Stadium** and the 60,000-capacity Sheikh Zayed Stadium, the setting for the final each time. The UAE saw off rival bids from Australia and Japan to secure hosting rights for the December 2010 event. However, the competition returned to Japan in 2011 and 2012, with the final played at the Yokohama International Stadium, the venue of the 2002 FIFA World Cup final.

SWITCHING SYSTEMS

From 1960 until 1968, the Intercontinental Cup was settled, not on aggregate scores, but by using a system of two points for a win and one for a draw. This meant a third, deciding match was needed in 1961, 1963, 1964, and 1967. In three of those four years, the team with the better aggregate after two games went on to win the playoff. However, if the away goals rule had been in place to separate a tie on aggregate, Celtic would have prevailed over Argentina's Racing Club in 1967—instead, it lost the play-off 1-0. Celtic won its home leg 1-0, before losing 2-1 away. From 1980 until 2004, the annual event was a one-off match staged in Japan.

FIGURE OF EIGHT

Manchester United's 5-3 win over Gamba Osaka in the semifinal of the 2008 FIFA Club World Cup was the highest-scoring single game in the history of the competition in all its forms—bettering the 5-2 victory over Benfica by a Santos team featuring Pele in 1962. Even more amazingly, all but two of the goals in the Manchester United–Gamba game were scored in the final 16 minutes, plus stoppage-time. United was leading 2-0 with 74 minutes gone, before a burst of goals, including two by substitute Wayne Rooney—one at each end. Manchester United also became the first team to score five goals in the FIFA Club World Cup's revised format.

LONG-DISTANCE, LONG-RUNNING RIVALRY

The precursor to the modern FIFA Club World Cup was the Intercontinental Cup, also known informally as the World Club Cup and/or the Europe–South America Cup, which pitted the champions of Europe and South America against each other. Representatives of UEFA and CONMEBOL contested the event from 1960 to 2004, but now all continental federations send at least one club to an expanded Club World Cup, organized and endorsed by the world federation, FIFA. The original final, in 1960, was between Spain's Real Madrid and Uruguay's Penarol. After a goalless tie in the rain in Montevideo, Real triumphed 5-1 at its own stadium in Madrid—including three goals scored in the first eight minutes, two of them by Ferenc Puskas. The two clubs are among five sharing the record for Intercontinental Cup triumphs, with three victories apiece. The others are: Argentina's Boca Juniors, Uruguay's Nacional, and AC Milan of Italy. Milan is the only one of these clubs to add a FIFA Club World Cup to its tally, as the championship was first contested in 2000 (in Brazil) before it was swallowed up by the Intercontinental Cup and was instituted on an annual basis.

SUCCESS IN PHASES

Since FIFA introduced its expanded Club World Cup in 2000, with representatives from all the world's continental soccer confederations, Brazilian clubs have the best overall record, with inaugural champions Corinthians being one of only two multiple winners. Carlo Ancelotti's AC Milan finally broke the Brazilian stranglehold in 2007, when the trophy was lifted by club captain Paolo Maldini, who had appeared alongside Alessandro Costacurta for Milan in five Intercontinental Cup showdowns between 1989 and 2003.

AFRICAN DOUBLE

In 2010, for the first time in Intercontinental Cup or official FIFA Club World Cup history, an African team contested the final. TP Mazembe from the Democratic Republic of Congo, defeated South American champions Internacional, from Brazil, 2-0 in its semifinal. Internacional, winners in 2006, were the first former FIFA Club World Cup champions to compete for a second time. Mazembe achieved the surprise victory despite missing its star striker and captain Tresor Mputu, who was serving a one-year ban for furiously chasing a referee after a game in May 2010. Raja Casablanca, from the host nation Morocco, became the second African finalist when it finished runner-up, to Bayern Munich in 2013, losing 2-0 in the Marrakech decider.

FIFA CLUB WORLD CUP FINALS (2000–13)

2000	Corinthians (Brazil) 0
	Vasco da Gama (Brazil) 0
	(aet: Corinthians win 4-3 on penalties)
2005	Sao Paulo (Brazil) 1 Liverpool (England) 0
2006	Internacional (Brazil) 1 Barcelona (Spain) 0
2007	AC Milan (Italy) 4
	Boca Juniors (Argentina) 2
2008	Manchester United (England) 1
	LDU Quito (Ecuador) 0
2009	Barcelona (Spain) 2
	Estudiantes (Argentina) 1 (aet)
2010	Internazionale (Italy) 3
	TP Mazembe (DR Congo) 0
2011	Barcelona (Spain) 4 Santos (Brazil) 0
2012	Corinthians (Brazil) 1 Chelsea (England) 0
2013	Bayern Munich (Germany) 2
	Raja Casablanca (Morocco) 0

INTERCONTINENTAL CUP TRIUMPHS (1960–2004*)

3 wins: Real Madrid, Spain (1960, 1998, 2002); Penarol, Uruguay (1961, 1966, 1982); AC Milan, Italy (1969, 1989, 1990); Nacional, Uruguay (1971, 1980, 1988); Boca Juniors, Argentina (1977, 2000, 2003).

2 wins: Santos, Brazil (1962, 1963); Internazionale, Italy (1964, 1965); Ajax, Netherlands (1972, 1995); Independiente, Argentina (1973, 1984); Bayern Munich, West Germany/Germany (1976, 2001); Juventus, Italy (1985, 1996); Porto, Portugal (1987, 2004); Sao Paulo, Brazil (1992, 1993).

1 win: Racing Club, Argentina (1967); Estudiantes, Argentina (1968); Feyenoord, Netherlands (1970); Atletico Madrid, Spain (1974); Olimpia Asuncion, Paraguay (1979); Flamengo, Brazil (1981); Gremio, Brazil (1983); River Plate, Argentina (1986); Red Star Belgrade, Yugoslavia (1991); Velez Sarsfield, Argentina (1994); Borussia Dortmund, Germany (1997); Manchester United, England (1999).

* = not contested in 1975 and 1978

MEN'S OLYMPIC SOCCER TOURNAMENT

First played at the 1900 Olympic Games in Paris, although not recognized by FIFA as an official tournament until London 1908, the men's Olympic soccer tournament was played in strict accordance with the Games' strong amateur tradition until 1984, when pros were allowed to play. The competition is now an Under-23 event—with allowance for three over-age players—to give rising stars the chance of major tournament experience. Since World War 2, however, no Olympic champion has won the FIFA World Cup within 10 years.

CZECH OUT

The climax of the 1920 Olympic Games tournament is the only time a major international soccer final has been abandoned. Czechoslovakia's players walked off the pitch minutes before half-time, in protest at the decisions made by 65-year-old English referee John Lewis—including the dismissal of Czech player Karel Steiner. Belgium, which was 2-0 up at the time, was awarded the victory, before Spain beat the Netherlands, 3-1 in a play-off, for the silver medal.

MEN'S OLYMPIC SOCCER FINALS

1896 Not played
1900 (Paris, France)
Gold: Upton Park FC (GB) Silver: USFSA XI (France) Bronze: Universite Libre de Bruxelles (Belgium) (only two exhibition matches played)
1904 (St Louis, US)
Gold: Galt FC (Canada) Silver: Christian Brothers College (US) Bronze: St Rose Parish (US) (only five exhibition matches played)
1908 (London, England)
Great Britain 2 Denmark 0 (Bronze: Netherlands)
1912 (Stockholm, Sweden)
Great Britain 4 Denmark 2 (Bronze: Netherlands)
1916 Not played
1920 (Antwerp, Belgium) Belgium 2 Czechoslovakia 0
(Gold: Belgium, Silver: Spain, Bronze: Netherlands)
1924 (Paris, France)
Uruguay 3 Switzerland 0 (Bronze: Sweden)
1928 (Amsterdam, Netherlands)
Uruguay 1 Argentina 1; Uruguay 2 Argentina 1 (Bronze: Italy)
1932 Not played
1936 (Berlin, Germany) Italy 2 Austria 1 (aet) (Bronze: Norway)
1940 Not played
1944 Not played
1948 (London, England) Sweden 3 Yugoslavia 1 (Bronze: Denmark)
1952 (Helsinki, Finland) Hungary 2 Yugoslavia 0 (Bronze: Sweden)
1956 (Melbourne, Australia) USSR 1 Yugoslavia 0 (Bronze: Bulgaria)
1960 (Rome, Italy) Yugoslavia 3 Denmark 1 (Bronze: Hungary)
1964 (Tokyo, Japan) Hungary 2 Czechoslovakia 1 (Bronze: Germany)
1968 (Mexico City, Mexico) Hungary 4 Bulgaria 1 (Bronze: Japan)
1972 (Munich, West Germany) Poland 2 Hungary 1 (Bronze: USSR/East Germany)
1976 (Montreal, Canada) East Germany 3 Poland 1 (Bronze: USSR)
1980 (Moscow, USSR) Czechoslovakia 1 East Germany 0 (Bronze: USSR)
1984 (Los Angeles, USA) France 2 Brazil 0 (Bronze: Yugoslavia)
1988 (Seoul, South Korea) USSR 2 Brazil 1 (Bronze: West Germany)
1992 (Barcelona, Spain) Spain 3 Poland 2 (Bronze: Ghana)
1996 (Atlanta, USA) Nigeria 3 Argentina 2 (Bronze: Brazil)
2000 (Sydney, Australia) **Cameroon** 2 Spain 2
(Cameroon win 5-3 on penalties) (Bronze: Chile)
2004 (Athens, Greece) Argentina 1 Paraguay 0 (Bronze: Italy)
2008 (Beijing, China) **Argentina 1** Nigeria 0 (Bronze: Brazil)
2012 (London, England) Mexico 2 Brazil 1 (Bronze: South Korea)

BARCELONA BOUND

Future Barcelona team-mates Samuel Eto'o and Xavi scored penalties for opposing teams in 2000, when Cameroon and Spain contested the first Olympic final to be settled by a shoot-out. Ivan Amaya was the only player to miss, handing Cameroon gold.

RETROSPECTIVE MEDALS

Soccer was not played at the first modern Summer Olympic Games, in Athens in 1896, and soccer tournaments played at the 1900 and 1904 events are not officially recognized by FIFA. Medals were not handed out to the winning teams—Great Britain was represented by Upton Park FC from East London in 1900, and Galt FC of Canada won in 1904—though the International Olympic Committee has since allocated first, second, and third places to the countries taking part.

BLOC PARTY

Eastern European countries dominated the Olympic Games soccer competitions from 1948 to 1980, when professional players were officially banned from taking part. Teams comprising so-called "state amateurs" from the Eastern Bloc took 23 of the 27 medals available during those years. Only Sweden, in 1948, brought gold medals west of the Iron Curtain. Sweden also collected bronze four years later, before Denmark claimed silver in 1960 and Japan bronze in 1968.

LAPPING IT UP

Until London 2012, Uruguay had a perfect Olympic soccer record. It won gold on the first two occasions it took part (1924 and 1928). Those Games were seen as a world championship and helped prompt FIFA into organizing the first World Cup in 1930—also won by Uruguay, which included 1924 and 1928 gold medalists Jose Nasazzi, Jose Andrade and **Hector Scarone** (right) in its squad. Uruguay's 1924 champion team is thought to have pioneered the lap of honor.

LONDON CALLING

Mexico was the unexpected winner when **Wembley Stadium** became the first venue to stage two men's Olympic Games soccer finals as part of London 2012. The stadium hosted the showpiece game when England's capital held the Olympics in 1948, and London is also now the only city to stage three separate summer Games, though the soccer final back in 1908 was played at White City. **Oribe Peralta** scored both goals as Mexico—managed by Luis Tena, assistant coach to the senior team—defeated Brazil 2-1 in the 2012 final. A late reply by Hulk was little consolation for the highly-fancied South Americans—though Brazil's Leandro Damiao did end the summer as six-goal top scorer. London 2012 matches were shared with cities away the hub of the Games, including Hampden Park in Glasgow, Scotland, Old Trafford in Manchester, St James' Park in Newcastle, and the City of Coventry Stadium. A united British team competed in the Olympic finals for the first time since 1960, featuring English Premier League stars such as Ryan Giggs and Craig Bellamy.

AFRICAN AMBITION

Ghana became the first African country to win an Olympic soccer medal, picking up bronze in 1992, but Nigeria went even better four years later by claiming the continent's first Olympic soccer gold medal, thanks to Emmanuel Amunike's stoppage-time winner against Argentina. Nigeria's triumph came as a huge surprise to many, especially as its rival teams included future world stars, such as Brazil's Ronaldo and Roberto Carlos, Argentina's Hernan Crespo and Roberto Ayala, Italy's Fabio Cannavaro and Gianluigi Buffon, and France's Robert Pires and Patrick Vieira. Future FIFA World Cup or UEFA European Championship winners to have played at the Olympic Games soccer competition include France's Michel Platini and Patrick Battiston (at the Montreal Games in 1976); West Germany's Andreas Brehme and Brazil's Dunga (Los Angeles, 1984); Brazil's Taffarel, Bebeto, and Romario, and West Germany's Jurgen Klinsmann (Seoul, 1988); France's Vieira, Pires and Sylvain Wiltord, Italy's Cannavaro, Buffon, and Alessandro Nesta, and Brazil's Roberto Carlos, Rivaldo, and Ronaldo (Atlanta, 1996); Italy's Gianluca Zambrotta and Spain's Xavi, Carles Puyol, and Joan Capdevila (Sydney, 2000); and Italy's Daniele De Rossi, Andrea Pirlo, and Alberto Gilardino (Athens, 2004).

BLUE STARS FIFA
YOUTH CUP

Staged on an annual basis by Zurich club FC Blue Stars since 1939, and granted FIFA's patronage since 1991, the Blue Stars/FIFA Youth Cup tournament has become soccer's premier youth event and features many clubs from around the globe. Several of the game's greatest names—from Bobby Charlton to David Beckham—had their first taste of international soccer competition at the event.

RAISING THE BARÇA
No Spanish club took part, until Barcelona's involvement in 1988. Its team featured midfielder **Josep Guardiola** and right-back Albert Ferrer, both of whom would help Barcelona to its first European Cup triumph in 1992.

HEART OF THE BLATTER
Long before he was elected FIFA President in 1998, Sepp Blatter was a keen amateur soccer player. He played center-forward for Swiss club FC Sierre in the Blue Stars tournament in the early 1950s. He is now an honorary member of FC Blue Stars.

ABOUT SCHMID
It was third time lucky for Swiss club FC Zurich when it became the FIFA Blue Stars champion in 2012, and it followed that win by retaining the title the following year, its fifth in the competition overall. FC Zurich lost penalty shoot-outs in both the 2010 and 2011 finals, to Boca Juniors and FC Porto, respectively. But it beat Grasshopper Club of Zurich 2-0 in the 2012 final, thanks to goals from Fabio Schmid and Ali Imren. Its 2013 victory was even more emphatic as it trounced Brazilian team Botafogo 5-0 in the final. Zurich goalkeeper Thierry Urspring also saved a penalty in the 2013 final, and went on to win the "Golden Gloves" prize after not conceding a goal in all five games.

BRAZIL FORTUNE
It took until 1999 for the tournament to be won by a non-European club when Sao Paulo of Brazil edged FC Zurich on penalties. With Kaka in its squad, Sao Paulo won again in 2000 and Argentina's Boca Juniors became the third South American winners in 2010. The fourth South American champion was Atletico Paranaense in 2014.

BRAVO, GUSTAVO
Two weeks before the 2014 FIFA World Cup kicked off, Brazilians were celebrating—not back home, but in Switzerland where Atletico Paranaense marked its Blue Stars/FIFA Youth Cup debut by lifting the trophy. Samba musicians and dancers brought a carnival atmosphere to the occasion, even before the start of the final against Portugal's Benfica, watched by 15,000 spectators, including FIFA president Sepp Blatter. The game was settled in the end by a single goal by Atletico playmaker Gustavo. He was also awarded the Golden Ball for player of the tournament, while team-mate Macanhan was acclaimed as best goalkeeper. The bronze-medal game was an all-Swiss affair, with Grasshoppers beating FC Zurich on penalties.

BLUE STARS CHAMPIONSHIPS

Manchester United 18
(1954, 1957, 1959, 1960, 1961, 1962, 1965, 1966, 1968, 1969, 1975, 1976, 1978, 1979, 1981, 1982, 2004, 2005)
Grasshoppers 6
(1939, 1956, 1971, 1987, 1998, 2006)
FC Zurich 5
(1946, 1949, 2008, 2012, 2013)
Barcelona 3
(1993, 1994, 1995)
FC Young Fellows 3
(1941, 1942, 1953)
AC Milan 2
(1958, 1977)
Arsenal 2
(1963, 1964)
AS Roma 2
(1980, 2003)
FK Austria Vienna 2
(1947, 1948)
Sao Paulo 2
(1999, 2000)
Spartak Moscow 2
(1991, 1992)
Atletico Paranaense 1
(2014)
FC Basel 1
(2009)
Boca Juniors 1
(2010)
FC Porto 1
(2011)

FIFA FUTSAL WORLD CUP

Developed in South America in the 1930s, Futsal —a variant of five-a-side indoor soccer—has enjoyed a huge surge in popularity, and participation numbers, in recent years. The first FIFA Futsal World Cup was staged in the Netherlands in 1989 and has been contested on a four-yearly basis since 1992. Two teams have dominated the event: Spain (with two wins) and, above all, Brazil (five wins).

THE FIRST MANOEL

Brazilian Manoel Tobias can claim to be the FIFA Futsal World Cup's most prolific goalscorer, with 43 in 32 appearances. Tobias, born in Salgueiro on April 19, 1971, represented his country in the 1992, 1996, 2000 and 2004 tournaments—only once ending up on the losing side within normal time. He ended both the 1996 and 2000 competitions with the prizes for both best player and top scorer.

CUBAN EMBARGO

Cuba holds the record for the fewest goals scored in a single tournament. It managed only one goal in it three games at the 2000 FIFA Futsal World Cup, while conceding 20 in defeats to Iran, Argentina, and eventual champions Spain.

SAMBA SUPREMACY

Predictably for a game relying heavily on swift, deft passing and nimble footwork, Brazil has excelled at Futsal. Since FIFA inaugurated its Futsal World Cup in 1989, Brazil has won the trophy five times out of a possible seven, and it was runner-up to Spain in 2000, and third behind Spain and Italy four years later. It has ended every tournament as the top-scoring team, hitting the back of the net a record 78 times during eight games in 2000, an average of 9.3 goals per match. Its largest FIFA Futsal World Cup win was a 29-2 trouncing of Guatemala in 2000, though its best-ever scoreline—and an overall record for Futsal—came when Brazil beat East Timor 76-0 in October 2006. Strangely, its first-ever FIFA Futsal World Cup game, in the first-round group stage in 1989, ended in a 3-2 loss to Hungary.

BACK OF THE NETO

The 2012 FIFA Futsal World Cup was the largest yet, with 24 countries taking part in Thailand, four more than the 2008 tournament. Yet it was a familiar story at the climax, with Brazil and Spain contesting the final for the fourth time. The South Americans again emerged victorious, this time with a 3-2 win after extra time. Neto scored the winning goal, his second of the game, and he was also voted player of the tournament, though Russia's Eder Lima claimed the golden boot, thanks to his nine goals across the competition. The tournament also saw Falcao score his 337th goal, making him Brazil's all-time leading goalscorer in Futsal. He went on to reach the 350-goal mark in December 2013.

FIFA FUTSAL WORLD CUP FINALS (and hosts)

1989 (Hosts: Netherlands)
Brazil 2 Netherlands 1
1992 (Hong Kong) Brazil 4 United States 1
1996 (Spain) Brazil 6 Spain 4
2000 (Guatemala) Spain 4 Brazil 3
2004 (Chinese Taipei) Spain 2 Italy 1
2008 (Brazil) Brazil 2 Spain 2
(aet: Brazil win 4-3 on penalties)
2012 (Thailand) **Brazil 3 Spain 2** (aet)

NINE'S ENOUGH

Russia's Pula may have pipped Falcao to the top-scorer prize in 2008 (with 16 goals to 15), but the Brazilian, who had already won both the Golden Ball and Golden Shoe awards four years earlier, was voted player of the tournament. Pula's 16 goals across the 2008 event included nine in one game—an all-time FIFA Futsal World Cup record—as the Solomon Islands was thrashed 31-2.

FIFA BEACH SOCCER WORLD CUP

Another variant of the sport that can trace its roots to South America, beach soccer is a high-octane, all-action, made-for-TV, goal-crazy version. It is no surprise that it has enjoyed a rapid surge in popularity in recent years. First contested in 1995, at its spiritual home on Copacabana Beach in Rio de Janeiro, Brazil, the FIFA Beach Soccer World Cup became a biannual event after the 2009 tournament.

ERIC THE KING

Soccer player, actor, and wannabe poet and philosopher **Eric Cantona** coached the French team to win the 2005 FIFA Beach Soccer World Cup. It was the first tournament to be staged under the FIFA banner, having previously been known as the Beach Soccer World Championship. However, the former Manchester United striker only allowed himself limited playing time, and ended the tournament with a solitary goal to his name. It came in a 7-4 quarterfinal defeat of Spain.

MADJER FOR IT

In 2006, Angola-born Portuguese star **Madjer** set a record for goals in one tournament when he put the ball in the net 21 times, one of the five tournaments at which he has finished as the top scorer. His seven goals in one game, against Uruguay in 2009, broke the record he himself set when scoring six against Cameroon in 2006.

GOAL GLUT

The 2003 tournament was the most prolific, with an average of 9.4 goals per game—150 in total. Two years earlier had brought the lowest average—7.2 goals per game, 144 in total. The most recent tournament, in 2013, brought 243 goals at an average of 7.6 per game.

LIFE SAVING

Brazil's Paulo Sergio was voted best goalkeeper for the first four FIFA Beach Soccer World Cups but, since then, the award has gone to: Portugal's Pedro Crespo (1999), Japan's Kato (2000), France's Pascal Olmeta (2001), Thailand's Vilard Normcharoen (2002), Brazil's Robertinho (2003) and Mao (2009), Spain's Roberto (2004), Roberto Valeiro (2008), and Dona (2013), and Russia's Andrey Bukhlitsky (2011). There was no goalkeeper prize from 2005 to 2007.

RUSSIAN INVASION

The final of the 2011 FIFA Beach Soccer World Cup was the highest-scoring decider in competition history. Reigning champion Brazil lost 12-8 to a country not usually associated with the most suitable climatic conditions—Russia. It was, however, the reigning European champion and it clinched its first world title, with the help of a hat-trick in the final from Dmitry Shishin and a great game from player of the tournament Ilya Leonov. Brazil's Andre at least had the consolation of the Golden Shoe for his 14 goals.

FIFA BEACH SOCCER WORLD CUP FINALS

1995 (Host beach and city/country: Copacabana, Rio de Janeiro/Brazil) **Brazil 8 USA 1**
1996 (Copacabana) **Brazil 3 Uruguay 0**
1997 (Copacabana) **Brazil 5 Uruguay 2**
1998 (Copacabana) **Brazil 9 France 2**
1999 (Copacabana) **Brazil 5 France 2**
2000 (Marina da Gloria, Rio de Janeiro/Brazil) **Brazil 6 Peru 2**
2001 (Costa do Sauipe, Rio de Janeiro/Brazil) **Portugal 9 France 3**
2002 (Vitoria/Brazil) **Brazil 6 Portugal 5**
2003 (Copacabana) **Brazil 8 Spain 2**
2004 (Copacabana) **Brazil 6 Spain 4**
2005 (Copacabana) **France 3 Portugal 3** (France win 1-0 on penalties)
2006 (Copacabana) **Brazil 4 Uruguay 1**
2007 (Copacabana) **Brazil 8 Mexico 2**
2008 (Plage du Pardo, Marseille/France) **Brazil 5 Italy 3**
2009 (Jumeirah, Dubai/United Arab Emirates) **Brazil 10 Switzerland 5**
2011 (Ravenna/Italy) **Russia 12 Brazil 8**
2013 (Papeete, Tahiti) **Russia 5 Spain 1**

FIFA BEACH SOCCER TOP SCORERS

Year	Player	Country	Goals
1995	Zico	Brazil	12
	Alessandro Altobelli	Italy	12
1996	Alessandro Altobelli	Italy	14
1997	Junior	Brazil	11
	Venancio Ramos	Uruguay	11
1998	Junior	Brazil	14
1999	Junior	Brazil	10
	Matosas	Uruguay	10
2000	Junior	Brazil	13
2001	Alan	Portugal	10
2002	Nenem	Brazil	9
	Madjer	Portugal	9
	Nico	Uruguay	9
2003	Nenem	Brazil	15
2004	Madjer	Portugal	12
2005	Madjer	Portugal	12
2006	Madjer	Portugal	21
2007	Buru	Brazil	10
2008	Madjer	Portugal	13
2009	Dejan Stankovic	Switzerland	16
2011	Andre	Brazil	14
2013	Dmitry Shishin	Russia	11

RUIZ RULES

El Salvador's **Agustin Ruiz** became only the sixth player to score five goals in one game at a FIFA Beach Soccer World Cup, when helping his team to a nail-biting 7-6 victory over the Solomon Islands at the 2013 tournament. His overall record is 17 goals in 16 matches across four World Cups.

SOLO EFFORTS

Some 41 different countries have competed in the tournament since it began in 1995, though 11 have appeared only once so far: Australia, Belgium, Chile, Costa Rica, Denmark, England, Malaysia, Oman, Paraguay, Poland, and Turkey. Of those, England performed best, finishing third in 1995.

HOME PORT

Portugal will host its first FIFA Beach Soccer World Cup in 2015, at Canide Beach in Vila Nova de Gaia. The setting for the 2017 tournament was due to be announced by FIFA in September 2014. The 16-team format allows five qualifying spaces for Europe, three apiece for South America, Africa, and Asia, two for Central America, and one for Oceania—with the host nation always claiming one of its continent's slots.

TAHITI HIT THE HEIGHTS

Tahiti, hosts in 2013, also became the first country from Oceania ever to reach the semifinal of a FIFA tournament. It was leading eventual champion Russia, with just five minutes left of the semifinal, but conceded three quick goals to lose 5-3. It eventually finished fourth, following a 1-0 play-off penalty shoot-out loss after a 7-7 tie with Brazil. Known to local fans as the "Tiki Toa", Tahiti is coached by Switzerland's Angelo Schirinzi and enjoyed its most eye-catching upset by trouncing South American champion Argentina 6-1 in the quarterfinal.

ALONSO THE PRO

Spain's coach for its last six appearances at the tournament—including the run to the 2013 final, losing only 5-1 to Russia—was **Joaquin Alonso**. He won 18 caps for Spain's full international team, scoring once, between 1978 and 1988, and was selected for both the 1980 Olympic Games and the 1982 FIFA World Cup on home territory. The midfielder spent most of his professional career with Sporting Gijon.

SHISHIN THE MOOD

Russia's Dmitry Shishin—playing in his fifth FIFA Beach Soccer World Cup—finally won the Golden Boot when helping his team retain its title in 2013. The 27-year-old scored in every game, ending with a tally of 11, and his last-minute strike in the final edged him ahead of Brazil's ten-goal Bruno Xavier. Tournament debutant Xavier, 29, did, however, receive the award for the competition's best player. Champions Russia made it a double as it also took home the Fair Play prize.

PART 7:
WOMEN'S SOCCER

"THE FUTURE IS FEMININE" is a favorite slogan of FIFA president Sepp Blatter and his optimism for the women's game has been borne out by recent surges in participation all around the world. Up to 30 million women worldwide play soccer, with recruits more than doubling during the past decade. International women's competitions now pull in significant crowds, and their enthusiasm and support has spilled over into national league and cup competitions around the world.

Women's soccer was first organized in England, early in the last century, but it was banned by The Football Association in 1921. That led to the creation of an independent women's association with a cup competition of its own. It was also developing elsewhere, and the surge of interest eventually led, in the early 1980s, to the first formal Women's European Championships and, in 1988, to a FIFA invitational tournament in Chinese Taipei.

FIFA launched an inaugural world championship in 1991. It was won by the United States and it soon claimed primacy in women's soccer. The Americans hosted the third FIFA Women's World Cup in 1999. It saw a record attendance of 90,185 celebrate its shoot-out victory over China in the final in Pasadena. The US underlined its No. 1 status by winning the first women's soccer gold medal at the Atlanta 1996 Olympic Games, taking silver in 2000 and gold again in 2004, 2008, and 2012.

FIFA set up a world youth championship in 2002, initially for players aged Under-19, later amended to Under-20, and added an Under-17 event to the international calendar in 2008.

A professional clubs' league was launched in the USA in 2009. It attracted some of the world's finest players, including Brazil's Marta and England's Kelly Smith, but it suspended operations for the season in January 2012. England introduced its own first semi-professional women's league in April 2011. Later that year, the showpiece FIFA Women's World Cup was staged in Germany, which had dominated the preceding two tournaments. Surprise winners Japan overcame great odds to claim Asia's first FIFA world title, and demonstrated that new boundaries are still being broken.

Germany celebrates winning its sixth consecutive UEFA Women's European Championship, in Sweden in 2013. Winners in 2007, it hopes to regain the FIFA Women's World Cup in 2015, after Japan was the champion in 2011.

FIFA WOMEN'S WORLD CUP

The first FIFA Women's World Cup finals were held in China in 1991. Twelve teams, divided into three groups of four, took part, with the top two in each group, plus the two "best losers" going through to the knockout quarterfinals. The tournament was expanded to 16 teams in 1999, comprising four groups of four, with the top two in each group progressing to the quarterfinals. That is the current format, although an expansion of the tournament to 24 teams is still under consideration.

ASIA MAJORS

Japan's women became the country's first soccer team to claim a FIFA world title when it upset the odds to win the 2011 FIFA Women's World Cup, beating the favored Team USA, 3-1 on penalties after a 2-2 tie. Player of the tournament Homare Sawa had leveled the scores with just three minutes of extra-time remaining, before **Saki Kumagai** struck the winning spot-kick in the shoot-out. Japan had failed to win in the two teams' previous 25 meetings, losing 22 and tying three. The Japanese women's previous best FIFA World Cup performance had been reaching the quarterfinals in 1995. The 2011 generation's triumph was all the more moving, as it dedicated the victory to victims of the devastating tsunami that had struck Japan in March that year.

HAVELANGE'S DREAM COMES TRUE

The FIFA Women's World Cup was the brainchild of former FIFA president Joao Havelange. The tournament began as an experimental competition in 1991 and has expanded in size and importance ever since. The success of the 1999 finals in the United States was a turning point for the tournament, and it now attracts big crowds and worldwide television coverage. The US and Norway—nations in which soccer is one of the most popular girls' sports—dominated early competitions. The Americans won the inaugural competition, and again in 1999. Norway lifted the trophy in 1995, but Germany became the dominant force in the new century, winning the trophy in 2003 and retaining it in 2007. The recent emergence of challengers such as Brazil, China, and Sweden underlined the worldwide spread and appeal of the women's game.

IMMENSE DEFENSES

The 2011 FIFA Women's World Cup in Germany had the lowest goal average since the competition was first held in 1991 with an average of just 2.69 goals per game—or 86 overall. The most prolific tournament was in the US in 1999, when 123 goals—3.84 per game—were scored.

US CELEBRATE FIRST ACHIEVEMENT

Team USA's victory in the inaugural FIFA Women's World Cup in 1991 made it the first US team to win a world soccer title. The US men's best performance came when it reached the semifinal in 1930, but lost 6-1 to Argentina.

FIFA WOMEN'S WORLD CUP FINALS

Year	Venue	Winners	Runners-up	Score
1991	Ghuangzhou	USA	Norway	2-1
1995	Stockholm	Norway	Germany	2-0
1999	Los Angeles	USA	China	0-0
USA won 5-4 in penalty shoot-out				
2003	Los Angeles	Germany	Sweden	2-1 (aet)
2007	Shanghai	Germany	Brazil	2-0
2011	Frankfurt	Japan	USA	2-2 (aet)
Japan won 3-1 in penalty shoot-out				

THIRD-PLACE PLAY-OFF MATCHES

Year	Venue	Winners	Losers	Score
1991	Guangzhou	Sweden	Germany	4-0
1995	Gavle	USA	China	2-0
1999	Los Angeles	Brazil	Norway	0-0
Brazil won 5-4 in penalty shoot-out				
2003	Los Angeles	USA	Canada	3-1
2007	Shanghai	USA	Norway	4-1
2011	Sinsheim	Sweden	France	2-1

FOUR GAIN DOUBLE MEDALS

Four of the US's 1991 winners were also in the team that beat China on penalties in the 1999 final: **Mia Hamm** (left), Michelle Akers, Kristine Lilly, and Julie Foudy.

WINNERS KEEP SQUAD TOGETHER

Six Germany players appeared in its 2003 and 2007 final wins: **Kerstin Stegemann**, Birgit Prinz, Renate Lingor, Ariane Hingst, and Kerstin Garefrekes all started both games, while Martina Muller came on as a substitute both times.

TWICE AS NICE

China is the only nation to be awarded the Fair Play prize at two separate FIFA Women's World Cups. The 1999 tournament was China's best, losing in the final to hosts USA, was the finals' top scorers —with 19 goals—and it claimed the Fair Play prize. China retained the Fair Play award in 2003, but, in a major surprise, it failed to even qualify for the 2011 edition, the first time it missed out on the finals.

GERMANS SET DEFENSIVE RECORD

In 2007, Germany became the first team to make a successful defense of the FIFA Women's World Cup. It also set another record, going through the tournament, six games and 540 minutes, without conceding a single goal. As a result, Germany's goalkeeper, Nadine Angerer, passed Italy keeper Walter Zenga's record of 517 minutes unbeaten in the 1990 men's finals. The last player to score against the Germans was Sweden's **Hanna Ljungberg**, who scored in the 41st minute of the 2003 final.

LA FINALE BEATS THEM ALL

The 1999 FIFA Women's World Cup finals in the USA were the best attended of the six tournaments to date. A total of 3,687,069 spectators watched the matches, at an average of 24,913 per game. The final, between hosts US and China—at the Rose Bowl, Los Angeles on July 10—attracted 90,185 spectators, a world record for a women's match. The programme that day also included the third-place play-off between Brazil and Norway.

TOP TEAMS

Country	Winners	Runners-up	Third
Germany	2	1	-
US	2	1	3
Norway	1	1	1
Japan	1	-	-
Brazil	-	1	1
Sweden	-	1	2
China	-	1	-

TOP TEAM SCORERS

1991:	USA	25
1995:	Norway	23
1999:	China	19
2003:	Germany	25
2007:	Germany	21
2011:	USA	13

TOP ALL–TIME TEAM SCORERS

1	USA	98
2	Germany	91
3	Norway	77
4	Brazil	55
5	Sweden	54

THE FIRST GAME

The first-ever game in the FIFA Women's World Cup finals was at Guangzhou on November 16, 1991. The hosts, China, beat Norway 4-0, in front of an attendance of 65,000.

THE REGULAR EIGHT

Eight teams played in the first five FIFA Women's World Cup finals: the USA, Germany, China, Norway, Brazil, Japan, Nigeria, and Sweden.

NORWAY POST LONGEST WIN RUN

Norway, winners in 1995, holds the record for the most consecutive match-time wins in the finals—ten. Its run started with an 8-0 win over Nigeria on June 6, 1995, and continued until June 30, 1999, when it beat Sweden 3-1 in the quarterfinals. It ended when it lost 5-0 to China in the semifinal on July 4.

UNBEATEN CHINA SENT HOME

China remains the only team to go through a FIFA Women's World Cup finals without losing a game, but end without the trophy. In 1999, China won its three group games, 2-1 against Sweden, 7-0 against Ghana, and 3-1 against Australia, beat Russia 2-0 in the quarterfinals, and Norway 5-0 in the semifinals, but lost on penalties to the US in the final after a 0-0 tie. In 2011, Japan became the first team to win the Cup despite losing a first-round group game—as did its final opponents, Team USA.

FIFTEEN ON TARGET FOR NORWAY

Norway holds the record for scoring in the most consecutive FIFA Women's World Cup games—15. The run began with a 4-0 win over New Zealand on November 19, 1991, and ended with a 3-1 win over Sweden in the quarterfinals on June 30, 1999.

CHAMPIONS RUN UP 11

The biggest winning margin in the finals was **Germany**'s 11-0 rout of Argentina in Shanghai on September 10, 2007. Argentina goalkeeper Vanina Correa punched a Melanie Behringer corner into her own net after 12 minutes, Birgit Prinz and Sandra Smisek both scored hat-tricks, with Germany's other goals coming from Renate Lingor (2), Behringer, and Kerstin Garefrekes.

THE LOWEST CROWD...

The lowest attendance for any match at the finals came on June 8, 1995, when only 250 spectators watched the 3-3 draw between Canada and Nigeria at Helsingborg.

FIVE FIVE–STAR STARS

Five players have been to five different FIFA Women's World Cups. Team USA's **Kristine Lilly** was the first to achieve the feat, as part of her record 340 international appearances—she also scored 129 goals. Lilly is also the oldest scorer in FIFA Women's World Cup finals history when, aged 36 years and 62 days, she netted the last goal in a 3-0 quarterfinal win over England in September 2007. Norway goalkeeper Bente Nordby was in the 1991 squad, but did not play any games, though she did get to play in the next four tournaments. Three players joined the five-tournament honors board in 2011: Brazil's Formiga and Marta, and Germany's Birgit Prinz.

QUICKEST RED AND YELLOW

The record for the fastest red card is held by Australia's Alicia Ferguson, who was sent off in the second minute of a 3-1 defeat by China in New York on June 26, 1999. North Korea's Ri Hyang Ok received the quickest yellow card, in the first minute of its 2-1 loss to Nigeria in Los Angeles on June 20, 1999.

THE FASTEST GOAL

Sweden's Lena Videkull recorded the fastest goal in the FIFA Women's World Cup, when she scored after 30 seconds of an 8-0 rout of Japan at Foshan, China, on November 19, 1991. Canada's **Melissa Tancredi** got the second-fastest, 37 seconds into a 2-2 tie with Australia in Chengdu, China, on September 20, 2007.

PRINZ SEIZES FINALS CHANCE

In 2007, Birgit Prinz became the first player to appear in three FIFA Women's World Cup finals. She was also the youngest player to appear in a FIFA Women's World Cup final, aged 17 years and 336 days, when she started in the 2-0 defeat by Norway in 1995—and her team-mate, Sandra Smisek, was just 14 days older. The oldest player in a final was Sweden's Kristin Bengtsson, who was 33 years and 273 days when her team lost to Germany in the 2003 final.

HOT SHOT AKERS SETS THE STANDARD

US forward Michelle Akers (born in Santa Clara on February 1, 1966) holds the record for the most goals scored in a single finals tournament—ten, in 1991. She also set a record for the most goals scored in one game, with five in the US's 7-0 quarterfinal win over Taiwan at Foshan, China, on November 24, 1991. Akers scored both goals in the US's 2-1 victory in the final, including its 78th-minute winner. Judges voted her as FIFA's Women's Player of the 20th Century.

THE FASTEST SUBSTITUTIONS

The earliest substitutions in the FIFA Women's World Cup finals were both timed at six minutes. Taiwan's defender Liu Hsiu Mei was replaced by reserve goalkeeper Li Chyn Hong in its 2-0 win over Nigeria in Jiangmen, China, on November 21, 1991. Li replaced No. 1 keeper Lin Hui Fang, who had been sent off. Therese Lundin took over for the injured Hanna Ljungberg, also after six minutes, in Sweden's 2-0 win over Ghana at Chicago, USA, on June 26, 1999.

DANILOVA THE YOUNGEST SCORER

The youngest scorer at the finals was Russia's Elena Danilova. She was 16 years and 96 days when she scored her country's only goal in the quarterfinal against Germany at Portland, US, on October 2, 2003. Sadly for Russia, Germany scored seven in reply.

MORACE HITS FIRST HAT–TRICK

Carolina Morace of Italy scored the first hat-trick in finals history when she netted the last three goals in Italy's 5-0 win over Taiwan at Jiangmen China, on November 17, 1991.

NEW STARS DOMINATE THE FINALS

The FIFA Women's World Cup has been dominated by a series of great players. American forwards Michelle Akers and Carin Jennings starred in the opening tournament in 1991. Playmaker **Hege Riise** and top scorer Ann-Kristin Aarones led Norway to victory four years later. Another American great, Mia Hamm, was at the top of her game when the US triumphed for a second time in 1999. That tournament marked the emergence of the best-ever Chinese player, Sun Wen, who finished joint-top scorer and won the Player of the Tournament award. Birgit Prinz of Germany was Player of the Tournament and top scorer when Germany won for the first time in 2003. The Brazilian forward, Marta, matched that feat in 2007, though, unlike Prinz, she was on the losing side in the final. Hamm, Prinz, and Marta are the only multiple winners of FIFA Women's Player of the Year award, introduced in 2001: Hamm won in 2001 and 2002; Prinz in 2003, 2004, and 2005; Marta in 2006, 2007, 2008, 2009, and 2010; Japan captain Homare Sawa, Golden Boot and Golden Ball winner at the 2011 FIFA Women's World Cup, lifted the main trophy and was elected 2011 FIFA Women's Player of the Year. Abby Wambach of the US collected the award in 2012, succeeded by Germany's goalkeeper Nadine Angerer in 2013.

FIFA WOMEN'S WORLD CUP
PLAYER OF THE TOURNAMENT

Year	Venue	Winner
1991	China	Carin Jennings (USA)
1995	Sweden	Hege Riise (Norway)
1999	USA	Sun Wen (China)
2003	USA	Birgit Prinz (Germany)
2007	China	Marta (Brazil)
2011	Germany	Homare Sawa (Japan)

FIFA WOMEN'S WORLD CUP
FINALS TOP SCORER

1991	Michelle Akers (USA)	10
1995	Ann-Kristin Aarones (Norway)	6
1999	Sissi (Brazil)	7
2003	Birgit Prinz (Germany)	7
2007	Marta (Brazil)	7
2011	Homare Sawa (Japan)	5

ALL-TIME TOP SCORERS

1	Birgit Prinz (Germany)	14
=	Marta (Brazil)	
3	Abby Wambach (USA)	13
4	Michelle Akers (USA)	12
5	Sun Wen (China)	11
=	Bettina Wiegmann (Germany)	
7	Ann-Kristin Aarones (Norway)	10
=	Heidi Mohr (Germany)	
9	Linda Medalen (Norway)	9
=	Hege Riise (Norway)	

FIFA WOMEN'S WORLD CUP
WINNING CAPTAINS

1991	April Heinrichs (USA)
1995	Heidi Store (Norway)
1999	Carla Overbeck (USA)
2003	Bettina Wiegmann (Germany)
2007	Birgit Prinz (Germany)
2011	Homare Sawa (Japan)

MOST FINALS APPEARANCES
(BY GAMES)

30	Kristine Lilly (USA)
25	Birgit Prinz (Germany)
24	Julie Foudy (USA)
23	Joy Fawcett (USA)
	Mia Hamm (USA)
22	Bente Nordby (Norway)
	Hege Riise (Norway)
	Bettina Wiegmann (Germany)

LAST-DITCH FIRST

Japan's 2011 FIFA Women's World Cup win was bittersweet at the last for defender **Azuza Iwashimizu.** Her red card—for a foul on US forward Alex Morgan, in stoppage-time of extra-time—made her the first player to be sent off in a FIFA Women's World Cup final. Her dismissal came just minutes after Japan had tied the game at 2-2.

THE FIRST SENDING OFF

Taiwan goalkeeper Lin Hui Fang was the first player to be sent off in the FIFA Women's World Cup finals. She was red-carded after only six minutes of Taiwan's 2-0 win over Nigeria in Jiangmen, China, on November 21, 1991.

SUN RATTLES THE MEN

In 1999, Shanghai-born **Sun Wen** became the first woman player ever to be nominated for the (men's) Asian Player of the Year award, following her performances in China's run to the 1999 FIFA Women's World Cup final. Three years later, she won the Internet poll for FIFA's Women's Player of the 20th Century.

TEAM PLAYERS

Only four players have been named in the tournament all-star teams at two separate FIFA Women's World Cups: China's Wang Liping, Germany's Bettina Wiegmann, Brazil's Marta, and the USA's Shannon Boxx—despite Boxx being unfortunate enough to miss a crucial spot-kick in the 2011 final's penalty shoot-out.

MARTA'S FINAL AGONY

Brazil's Marta may have been the star of the 2007 tournament, but she was left heartbroken in the final. Germany goalkeeper Nadine Angerer saved Marta's penalty that would have tied the game, and Germany went on to win 2-0.

OLYMPIC RINGING THE CHANGES

Germany forward Birgit Prinz was the only player to score in all of the first four Olympic women's soccer finals. However, she missed out on London 2012, because Germany did not qualify. That allowed Brazil's Cristiane to push ahead as all-time top scorer, adding two to take her tally to 12. Prinz's Olympic haul of ten goals was also equaled in 2012 by Canada's Christine Sinclair.

WOMEN'S OLYMPIC FINALS

Year	Venue	Winners	Runners-up	Score
1996	Atlanta	USA	China	2-1
2000	Sydney	Norway	USA	3-2
	Norway won with a golden goal			
2004	Athens	USA	Brazil	2-1 (aet)
2008	Beijing	USA	Brazil	1-0 (aet)
2012	London	USA	Japan	2-1

THIRD-PLACE PLAY-OFFS

Year	Venue	Winners	Losers	Score
1996	Atlanta	Norway	Brazil	2-0
2000	Sydney	Germany	Brazil	2-0
2004	Athens	Germany	Sweden	1-0
2008	Beijing	Germany	Japan	2-0
2012	London	Canada	France	1-0

MEDALISTS

Country	Gold	Silver	Bronze
USA	4	1	-
Norway	1	-	1
Brazil	-	2	-
China	-	1	-
Japan	-	1	-
Germany	-	-	3
Canada	-	-	1

WOMEN'S OLYMPIC TEAM TOP SCORERS

1996:	Norway	12
2000:	USA	9
2004:	Brazil	15
2008:	USA	12
2012:	USA	16

WOMEN'S OLYMPIC INDIVIDUAL TOP SCORERS

1996:	Ann-Kristin Aarones (Norway)	
	Linda Medalen (Norway)	
	Pretinha (Brazil)	4
2000:	Sun Wen (China)	4
2004:	Cristiane (Brazil)	
	Birgit Prinz (Germany)	5
2008:	Cristiane (Brazil)	5
2012:	Christine Sinclair (Canada)	6

CRISTIANE'S TREBLE DOUBLE

Brazil's **Cristiane** is the only player to grab two Olympic Games women's soccer hat-tricks. She scored three in a 7-0 win over hosts Greece in 2004, and all three in a 3-1 win over Nigeria in Beijing four years later. Germany's Birgit Prinz, with four against China in 2004, and Canada's Christine Sinclair, a treble when losing 4-3 to the US in the London 2012 semifinal, are the only other players to register hat-tricks.

HOSTS WITH THE MOST

The FIFA Under-20 Women's World Cup is held every two years, in contrast to the four-yearly senior tournament. Since 2010, the Under-20 event that is held one year before a FIFA World Cup is hosted by the same nation. That meant 2011 FIFA Women's World Cup hosts Germany staged the FIFA Under-20s Women's World Cup a year earlier, when it became the first hosts to also win the tournament. The 2012 hosts Japan could not emulate such a feat, as Germany lost 1-0 in the final to the United States, courtesy of a goal by Kealia Ohai. It was revenge for the US as it had lost 3-0 to the Germans in a first-round group game. Japan's Kim Un-Hwa finished top scorer, on seven, while Germany's Dzsenifer Marozsan—whose father Janos Marozsan played for Hungary—was voted best player.

GERMANS CHALK UP BIGGEST WIN

Germany holds the record for the biggest win in the Olympic finals. It beat China 8-0 at Patras on August 11, 2004, with Birgit Prinz scoring four times. The Germans' other goals came from Pia Wunderlich, Renate Lingor, Conny Pohlers, and Martina Muller. Yet, in a major surprise, Germany failed to qualify for the women's soccer tournament at the 2012 Olympic Games in London. The 2011 FIFA Women's World Cup was used as UEFA's qualifiers, meaning beaten quarterfinalists Germany fell short. Semifinalists Sweden—including its most-capped player Therese Sjogran—and France, whose stars included midfielder **Louisa Necib** (right), went through to the 2012 event instead.

LATE STARTS, LATE FINISHING

Carli Lloyd scored the winning goal for Team USA, against Brazil, to win Olympic gold in 2008, and also scored both her team's goals in the London 2012 final, as the US beat Japan 2-1. Other memorable moments of the women's soccer tournament at London 2012 included Alex Morgan's winner for the USA against Canada in the semi-final—she made it 4-3, three minutes into stoppage-time at the end of extra-time, the latest goal in Olympic history. Hosts Great Britain fielded a team for the first time and although it finished top of its first round group with a perfect three wins from three, without conceding a goal, it was beaten 2-0 by Canada in the quarterfinal and thus missed out on a medal.

JAPAN'S DOUBLE JOY

Japan clinched the AFC Asian Women's Cup title for the first time in 2014, when the tournament was staged in Vietnam. Defender **Azusa Iwashimizu** not only scored the winner in extra-time stoppage-time in the semifinal against China, but also struck the only goal of the final against Australia—some solace for her red card in the 2011 FIFA Women's World Cup final. Also in 2014, Japan won the FIFA Under-17 Women's World Cup for the first time, beating Spain 2-0 in the final in Costa Rica and seeing five-goal Hina Sugita voted best player. North Korea beat the USA 2-1 in the inaugural final in New Zealand in 2008, before South Korea beat Japan on penalties following a 3-3 tie in the climax to the tournament in Trinidad and Tobago two years later. France goalkeeper Romane Bruneau was the heroine of another shoot-out in the 2012 final in Azerbaijan, decisively saving two spot-kicks after a 1-1 tie with North Korea.

US DOMINATE OLYMPIC GOLDS

The United States has dominated the Olympic soccer tournament since it was introduced at the 1996 Games in Atlanta. It has won four gold medals and a silver medal in the other tournament. Norway and China were the Americans' early challengers, with Brazil, FIFA Women's World Cup holders Germany and Japan proving its toughest rivals in the past three Olympics (2004, 2008 and 2012). The tournament has rapidly grown in popularity, attracting record crowds at the 2008 Olympic Games in Beijing. FIFA has added two worldwide competitions for younger teams, too. The FIFA U-20 Women's World Cup was staged for the first time in 2000 and the first edition of the Under-17 event followed in 2008. Once more, the US has been prominent, though it has faced a strong challenge from North Korea in recent years.

FIFA U-20 WOMEN'S WORLD CUP

FINALS

Year	Venue	Winner	Runners-up	Score
2002	Edmonton	USA	Canada	1-0 (aet)
2004	Bangkok	Germany	Chile	2-0
2006	Moscow	North Korea	China	5-0
2008	Santiago	USA	North Korea	2-1
2010	Bielefeld	Germany	Nigeria	2-0
2012	Tokyo	USA	Germany	1-0

TOP SCORERS

2002	Christine Sinclair (Canada)	10
2004	Brittany Timko (Canada)	7
2006	Ma Xiaoxu (China), Kim Song Hui (North Korea)	5
2008	Sydney Leroux (USA)	5
2010	Alexandra Popp (Germany)	10
2012	Kim Un-Hwa (Japan)	7

FIFA U-17 WOMEN'S WORLD CUP

FINALS

Year	Venue	Winner	Runners-up	Score
2008	Auckland	North Korea	USA	2-1 (aet)
2010	Port of Spain	South Korea	Japan	3-3 (aet)
	(South Korea won 5-4 on penalties)			
2012	Baku	France	North Korea	1-1 (aet)
	(France won 7-6 on penalties)			

TOP SCORERS

2008	Dzsenifer Marozsan (Germany)	6
2010	Yeo Min-Ji (South Korea)	8
2012	Ri Un-Sim (North Korea)	8

LOOK BACK IN ANGERER

Germany's 59-match unbeaten run in the UEFA Women's European Championship was ended by Norway in September 2013, which won 1-0 in a first-round group game. The Germans avenged the loss in the final, also 1-0, Anja Mittag scoring the goal, while Nadine Angerer, later voted player of the tournament, saved two penalty kicks. This was Germany's sixth straight European title, a run dating back to 1995. France captain Sandrine Soubeyrand, aged 39 years and 340 days, made her 198th international appearance and became the oldest woman to play in the finals.

KIM GRABS ONLY HAT-TRICK

North Korea's **Kim Song-Hi** netted the only hat-trick in any final of the FIFA Under-20 Women's World Cup. It came in its 5-0 win over China on September 3, 2006.

SINCLAIR HITS FIVE

Christine Sinclair of Canada and Alexandra Popp of Germany share the record for most goals scored in a single FIFA Under-20 Women's World Cup. Each struck 10, Sinclair in 2002 and Popp eight years later. Sinclair also holds the record for the most goals in one game. She netted five in Canada's 6-2 quarterfinal win over England at Edmonton on August 25, 2002. But Popp is the only player to score in all of her country's six games at a tournament. Sinclair and Popp have won both the Golden Ball for best player and Golden Shoe for top scorer. Sinclair finished the 2012 Olympics as six-goal top-scorer in the women's soccer tournament. Her tally included a hat-trick—in vain—in Canada's 4-3 semifinal defeat to the US.

APPENDIX 1: FIFA AWARDS

THE WORLD GAME enters party mode every January when FIFA hosts its annual gala to hail a range of achievements and achievers from the previous 12 months. The January 2014 Ballon d'Or event was notable for tears of emotion from both Cristiano Ronaldo, hailed as FIFA World Player of the Year, and veteran Brazilian icon Pele, who received a Prix d'Honneur in recognition of his achievement as a three-times winner of the World Cup.

The awards, in their 23rd year, underlined FIFA's global development reach. The 2013 prize-winners came from a wide range of achievement across the international, national team, and club spheres. They reached out to include Jacques Rogge, the recently-retired president of the International Olympic Committee.

One of the strengths of soccer even as a game of 11-a-side is that, when it comes to appreciation and celebration, both teams and individuals can be hailed and rewarded.

Player of the Year awards have contributed to the fabric of soccer history. One of the earliest, in England, was created in the late 1940s, while *France Football* followed up with the Ballon d'Or—its now-discontinued European Footballer of the Year award—in the mid-1950s. The first winner, of both prizes, was Stanley Matthews—later Sir Stanley Matthews—the original "Wizard of Dribble." Matthews won the award in England in 1948, and in Europe in 1956.

FIFA, in addition to its world player prize, created formal individual awards for the leading player, leading scorer and leading goalkeeper at the FIFA World Cup. Those awards are replicated at FIFA's age-group tournaments for both young male and female players.

A "perfect mix" of team and player recognition was achieved through the World XI chosen in partnership with FIFPro, the international players' union.

The 2013 FIFA/FIFpro World XI team included the three men short-listed for the 2013 FIFA Ballon d'Or: winner Cristiano Ronaldo (back row, third right), runner-up Lionel Messi (red suit), and Franck Ribery (back row, second right).

FIFA PLAYER OF THE YEAR 2013

CRISTIANO RONALDO

Cristiano Ronaldo's desire to be hailed as the FIFA World Player of the Year burst through into tears as the Real Madrid superstar finally landed the sovereign individual prize which had eluded him for the previous four years.

Ronaldo took the top prize for 2013, narrowly ahead of Barcelona's Lionel Messi as runner-up, and Bayern Munich's Franck Ribery. He had won the award once before, in 2008, since when he always had to play second or third fiddle (or, once, worse) to his nemesis from Argentina.

A ballot deadline extension—granted to the world's slow-voting national coaches and captains—happened to encompass Ronaldo's single-handed destruction of Sweden in a FIFA World Cup qualifying play-off. When the final ballots were counted, Ronaldo was a close winner. He polled 27.99 percent, followed by Messi on 24.72 percent, and Ribery on 23.36 percent.

Yet his four goals in the two-leg World Cup decider were a mere handful among the 69 he tallied in 59 games for club and country in maintaining a phenomenal striking consistency, that had eclipsed records of Madrid legends such as Alfredo Di Stefano, Ferenc Puskas, and Raul. In 2012-13, "CR7" became the first player in Real Madrid history to score 30 or more goals in three consecutive seasons, and he ended the year with six club hat-tricks to his credit. His nine goals in the 2013–14 group section of the UEFA Champions League set a new competition record for the stage. The year also saw Ronaldo equal Pauleta's record as the all-time leading marksman for the Portuguese national side, with 47 goals in 109 appearances.

As national captains both Ronaldo and Messi took part in the ballot, though neither voted for the other, or for Ribery. Ronaldo's first choice was Monaco striker Radamel Falcao, who scored 29 goals in 2013 in all competitions for Atletico Madrid, Monaco and Colombia. He picked new €100m Madrid team-mate Gareth Bale in second place, followed by former club-mate Mesut Ozil. Messi's three nominations were colleagues at Spanish champions Barcelona: Andres Iniesta, Xavi, and new arrival Neymar.

An emotional Ronaldo, joined on the award stage by son Cristiano Jnr, paid tribute to qualities of both Messi and Ribery … but dedicated his award to a Portuguese legend from another era, Eusebio, who had died two weeks earlier.

PREVIOUS WINNERS

1991 Lothar Matthaus **(Germany)**
1992 Marco van Basten **(Netherlands)**
1993 Roberto Baggio **(Italy)**
1994 Romario (Brazil)
1995 George Weah **(Liberia)**
1996 Ronaldo **(Brazil)**
1997 Ronaldo **(Brazil)**
1998 Zinedine Zidane **(France)**
1999 Rivaldo **(Brazil)**
2000 Zinedine Zidane **(France)**
2001 Luis Figo **(Portugal)**
2002 Ronaldo **(Brazil)**
2003 Zinedine Zidane **(France)**
2004 Ronaldinho **(Brazil)**
2005 Ronaldinho **(Brazil)**
2006 Fabio Cannavaro **(Italy)**
2007 Kaka **(Brazil)**
2008 Cristiano Ronaldo **(Portugal)**
2009 Lionel Messi **(Argentina)**
2010 Lionel Messi **(Argentina)**
2011 Lionel Messi **(Argentina)**
2012 Lionel Messi **(Argentina)**

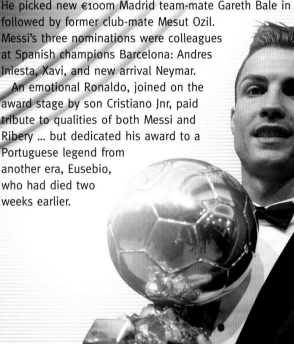

FIFA WOMEN'S PLAYER
OF THE YEAR 2013

NADINE ANGERER

Nadine Angerer became the first goalkeeper to win the FIFA Women's Player of the Year prize after a remarkable year in which her two shootout saves had edged Germany to victory over Norway, in Sweden, for a sixth consecutive UEFA European Championship.

Angerer headed an all-star German cast list at the FIFA Gala. National manager Silvia Neid took the Women's Coach of the Year honors, and the men's award went to former Bayern Munich veteran Jupp Heynckes.

The 35-year-old Angerer, formerly with 1FFC Frankfurt, before joining Brisbane Roar, took the prize on 18.85 percent ahead of 2012 winner United States forward Abby Wambach(15.02 percent), and multiple winner Marta from Brazil (14.02 percent).

Germany's European title success was the foundation for Angerer's personal triumph. She recalled: "It wasn't an easy title to win and it certainly wasn't handed to us on a plate. We had ups and downs in the tournament but we pulled ourselves through time and time again. It was a success built entirely on team spirit."

Angerer had been voted top player at Euro 2013 then hailed as UEFA's Best Women's Player in Europe. As for the crowning world award, she described herself as "a little surprised but very thankful."

She said: "First I have to thank everybody who voted for me and pay my respects to Marta and Abby, who have had an incredible year too. You never achieve success like this on your own. I have to thank my team-mates and my goalkeeping coach, Michael Fuchs, who raised me to a level that I never thought I would reach. Also I have a wonderful family who have been a great support to me over the years."

PREVIOUS WINNERS

Year	Winner	Country
2001	Mia Hamm	**(United States)**
2002	Mia Hamm	**(United States)**
2003	Birgit Prinz	**(Germany)**
2004	Birgit Prinz	**(Germany)**
2005	Birgit Prinz	**(Germany)**
2006	Marta	**(Brazil)**
2007	Marta	**(Brazil)**
2008	Marta	**(Brazil)**
2009	Marta	**(Brazil)**
2010	Marta	**(Brazil)**
2011	Homare Sawa	**(Japan)**
2012	Abby Wambach	**(United States)**

OTHER FIFA AWARDS

FIFA created its own annual awards in 1991, while Ballon d'Or partner, *France Football*, had never opened up its original European Player of the Year prize to players from clubs beyond Europe.

Hence the name of Pele, the only man to win three World Cups, did not figure in the roll of honor of either Gala host. He had played only for Santos, in Brazil, then for New York Cosmos, in the United States.

This absence was adjusted in the 2013 awards presented in the Zurich Kongresshalle in January 2014. Appropriately, in a year which would see the World Cup finals being staged in Brazil, FIFA created a Prix d'Honneur golden ball for **Edson Arantes do Nascimento**. He barely managed to hold back his own tears of emotion on receiving the award from FIFA president Sepp Blatter and from Francois Moriniere of the *L'Equipe-France Football* group.

The hour-long telecast of the gala was shown live in 180 countries, and boasted a heavy Brazilian influence, from co-presenter Fernanda Lima to the style of singer Marc Sway, and soccer guests of honor which included FIFA World Cup-winners, such as Amarildo and Cafu. But Pele was top of the Brazilian bill on even such a starry night as this.

German soccer also shone out across the awards spectrum by claiming the two Coach of the Year prizes. **Jupp Heynckes** returned from retirement to collect the men's award after guiding Bayern Munich to the treble of German league and cup plus UEFA Champions League; Silvia Neid received the women's award for a second time in four years for having masterminded Germany's UEFA European Championship triumph.

Neid finished ahead of VfL Wolfsburg's UEFA Women's Champions League-winning coach Ralf Kellermann and 2012 top coach Pia Sundhage from Sweden.

The Team of the Year as promoted by FIFPro, the international players' union, saw six of the 2012 selections return. They were: Brazil's Dani Alves, Spain's Sergio Ramos, Andres Iniesta, and Xavi, plus the inevitable Cristiano Ronaldo (Portugal), and Lionel Messi (Argentina).

Joining the latter pair in attack this time was Sweden's Zlatan Ibrahimovic, who also carried off the Puskas Award for his breathtaking bicycle kick goal in an exhibition game against England in November 2012.

Afghanistan's federation was the popular winner of the Fair Play Award for its work, despite the turmoil in the country, while Jacques Rogge of Belgium received the Presidential Award for his soccer-friendly leadership of the International Olympic Committee, before his retirement in September 2013.

FIFA Awards 2013

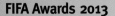

Men's Player of the Year: Cristiano Ronaldo (Portugal, Real Madrid)

Women's Player of the Year: Nadine Angerer (Germany, 1FFC Frankfurt/ Brisbane Roar)

Men's Football Coach of the Year: Jupp Heynckes (Bayern Munich)

Women's Football Coach of the Year: Silvia Neid (Germany)

FIFA Ferenc Puskas Award (outstanding goal): Zlatan Ibrahimovic ···························· (for Sweden v England)

Presidential Award: Jacques Rogge (Honorary President, International Olympic Committee)

Prix d'Honneur: Pele (Brazil)

Fair Play Award: Afghanistan Football Federation

FIFA/FIFPro Team of the Year: Manuel Neuer (Germany), Philipp Lahm (Germany), Sergio Ramos (Spain), Thiago Silva (Brazil), Dani Alves (Brazil), Andres Iniesta (Spain) Xavi (Spain), Franck Ribery (France), Lionel Messi (Argentina), Zlatan Ibrahimovic (Sweden), Cristiano Ronaldo (Portugal).

1991
Fair Play award: Real Federacion Espanola de Futbol (Spanish FA), Jorginho (Brazil)

1992
Fair Play award: Union Royale Belge des Societes de Football Association

1993
Fair Play award: Nandor Hidgekuti (Hungary)*, Football Association of Zambia
Top Team of the Year: Germany
Best Mover of the Year: Colombia
  *award presented posthumously

1994
Top Team of the Year: Brazil
Best Mover of the Year: Croatia

1995
Fair Play award: Jacques Glassmann (France)
Top Team of the Year: Brazil
Best Mover of the Year: Jamaica

1996
Fair Play award: George Weah (Liberia)
Top Team of the Year: Brazil
Best Mover of the Year: South Africa

1997
Fair Play award: Irish spectators at the FIFA World Cup preliminary match versus Belgium, Jozef Zovinec (Slovak amateur player), Julie Foudy (United States)
Top Team of the Year: Brazil
Best Mover of the Year: Yugoslavia

1998
Fair Play award: National associations of Iran, the United States and Northern Ireland
Top Team of the Year: Brazil
Best Mover of the Year: Croatia

1999
Fair Play award: New Zealand soccer community
Top Team of the Year: Brazil
Best Mover of the Year: Slovenia

2000
Fair Play award: Lucas Radebe (South Africa)
Top Team of the Year: Netherlands
Best Mover of the Year: Nigeria

2001
Presidential award Marvin Lee (Trinidad)*
Fair Play award: Paolo Di Canio (Italy)
Top Team of the Year: Honduras
Best Mover of the Year: Costa Rica
  *award presented posthumously

2002
Presidential award: Parminder Nagra (England)
Fair Play award: Soccer communities of Japan and Korea Republic
Top Team of the Year: Brazil
Best Mover of the Year: Senegal

2003
Presidential award: Iraqi soccer community
Fair Play award: Fans of Celtic FC (Scotland)
Top Team of the Year: Brazil
Best Mover of the Year: Bahrain

2004
Presidential award: Haiti
Fair Play award: Confederacao Brasileira de Futebol
Top Team of the Year: Brazil
Best Mover of the Year: China PR
Interactive World Player: Thiago Carrico de Azevedo (Brazil)

2005
Presidential award: Anders Frisk (Sweden)
Fair Play award: Soccer community of Iquitos (Peru)
Top Team of the Year: Brazil
Best Mover of the Year: Ghana
Interactive World Player: Chris Bullard (England)

2006
Presidential award: Giacinto Facchetti (Italy)*
Fair Play award: Fans of the 2006 FIFA World Cup
Top Team of the Year: Brazil
Best Mover of the Year: Italy
Interactive World Player: Andries Smit (Netherlands)
  *award presented posthumously

2007
Presidential award: Pele (Brazil)
Fair Play award: FC Barcelona (Spain)
Top Team of the Year: Argentina
Best Mover of the Year: Mozambique

2008
Presidential award: Women's soccer (presented to the United States women's team)
Fair Play award: Armenia, Turkey
Development award: Palestine
Interactive World Player: Alfonso Ramos (Spain)
Top Team of the Year: Spain
Best Mover of the Year: Spain

2009
Presidential award: Queen Rania Al Abdullah of Jordan [co-chair of 1Goal: Education for All]
Fair Play Award: Sir Bobby Robson (England)*
Development prize: Chinese Football Association

Interactive World Player: Bruce Grannec (France)
Top Team of the Year: Spain
FIFA Ferenc Puskas Award (outstanding goal): Cristiano Ronaldo, Manchester United v FC Porto
  *award presented posthumously

2010
Coach of the Year (men): Jose Mourinho (Internazionale, then Real Madrid)
Coach of the Year (women): Silvia Neid (Germany women)
FIFA Ferenc Puskas Award (outstanding goal): Hamit Altintop, Turkey v Kazakhstan
Presidential award: Archbishop Desmond Tutu, South Africa
Fair Play Award: Haiti Under-17 women's team

2011
Coach of the Year (men): Pep Guardiola (Barcelona)
Coach of the Year (women): Norio Sasaki (Japan women)
FIFA Ferenc Puskas Award (outstanding goal): Neymar, Santos v Flamengo
Presidential award: Sir Alex Ferguson, Manchester United
Fair Play award: Japan Football Association

2012
Coach of the Year (men): Vicente Del Bosque (Spain)
Coach of the Year (women): Pia Sundhage (Sweden)
FIFA Ferenc Puskas Award (outstanding goal): Miroslav Stoch, Fenerbahce v Genclerbirligi
Presidential: Franz Beckenbauer (Germany)
Fair Play award: Uzbekistan Football Federation

APPENDIX 2: FIFA/COCA-COLA WORLD RANKINGS

Germany was No. 1 when FIFA's world rankings system was calculated first and published in December 1992. It returned there in July 2014, after winning the FIFA World Cup in Brazil and deposing long-time ranking leader Spain. The system, refined after the 2006 FIFA World Cup, provides a monthly statistical insight into the rise and fall of the fortunes of both football's traditional soccer powers and aspiring minnows. The placings are computed on results in international A games and consider game status, goals scored, strength of opposition and regional balance—all based on games played over a rolling four-year phase, rather than the eight years employed until 2006. The rankings are issued each month.

Germany's 1-0 extra-time victory over Argentina in the 2014 FIFA World Cup final at the Maracana Stadium in Rio de Janeiro, Brazil, returned Joachim Low's team to the pinnacle of the world rankings.

FIFA/COCA-COLA WORLD RANKINGS 2014

The FIFA/Coca-Cola World Ranking offers a snapshot of soccer's international order, in this case as of July 2014. It took account of the FIFA World Cup which had just ended. New world champion Germany took over at the top from deposed champion Spain, which dropped to eighth, one place behind Brazil. World Cup runner-up Argentina moved up three spots to second, while the Netherlands' third-place finish propelled them 12 positions up to third position. All four losing quarterfinalists climbed dramatically: Colombia to fourth, Belgium fifth, France 10th and a highest-ever 16th for Costa Rica. Early failure was equally punished for three of the former top 10: Portugal (down to 11th), Italy (14th) and England (20th).

Costa Rica's captain **Bryan Ruiz** led by example, scoring the winning goal against Italy in a group stage victory that ensured it progressed to the round-of-16—and up to a best ever 16th in the FIFA World Rankings.

RANKINGS (as at July 2014)

Pos.	Country	Pts (+/-)
1	Germany	1724 (+1)
2	Argentina	1606 (+3)
3	Netherlands	1496 (+12)
4	Colombia	1492 (+4)
5	Belgium	1401 (+6)
6	Uruguay	1330 (+1)
7	Brazil	1241 (-4)
8	Spain	1229 (-7)
9	Switzerland	1216 (-3)
10	France	1202 (+7)
11	Portugal	1148 (-7)
12	Chile	1098 (+2)
13	Greece	1091 (-1)
14	Italy	1056 (-5)
15	United States	989 (-2)
16	Costa Rica	986 (+12)
17	Croatia	955 (+1)
18	Mexico	930 (+2)
19	Bosnia-Herzegovina	917 (+2)
20	England	911 (-10)
21	Ecuador	901 (+5)
22	Ukraine	898 (-6)
23	Russia	897 (-4)
24	Algeria	872 (-2)
25	Côte d'Ivoire	850 (-2)
26	Denmark	807 (-3)
27	Scotland	734 (0)
28	Romania	733 (+1)
29	Sweden	724 (+3)
30	Venezuela	720 (+10)
31	Serbia	717 (-1)
32	Turkey	714 (+3)
33	Panama	684 (-2)
34	Nigeria	664 (+10)
35	Czech Republic	646 (-1)
36	Egypt	645 (0)

Pos.	Country	Pts (+/-)
37	Slovenia	644 (-12)
38	Hungary	642 (+9)
38	Ghana	642 (-1)
40	Honduras	637 (-7)
41	Armenia	635 (-3)
42	Tunisia	621 (+6)
43	Austria	614 (-1)
44	Wales	606 (-3)
45	Japan	604 (+1)
46	Slovakia	588 (+3)
47	Iceland	570 (+5)
48	Paraguay	566 (+2)
49	Iran	563 (-6)
50	Montenegro	559 (+1)
51	Guinea	555 (+1)
52	Uzbekistan	523 (+7)
53	Norway	520 (+2)
53	Cameroon	520 (+3)
55	Finland	508 (+6)
56	Korea Republic	501 (+1)
57	Jordan	500 (+6)
58	Burkina Faso	495 (+2)
59	Peru	487 (-14)
60	Mali	483 (-3)
61	Poland	478 (+8)
62	Senegal	476 12)
63	Libya	471 (+1)
64	Sierra Leone	469 (-10)
65	United Arab Emirates	466 (+7)
66	South Africa	450 (-1)
67	Albania	444 (-1)
67	Israel	444 (+8)
69	Oman	443 10)
70	Rep. Ireland	440 (0)
71	Bolivia	429 (-4)
72	Bulgaria	425 (+6)

Pos.	Country	Pts (+/-)
73	Azerbaijan	410 10)
74	FYR Macedonia	406 (+6)
75	Cape Verde Is.	401 (-36)
76	Australia	397 (-14)
77	Zambia	396 (-1)
78	Saudi Arabia	384 (+12)
79	Morocco	377 (-2)
79	Angola	377 (+14)
81	Belarus	376 (+1)
82	Congo	375 (+3)
83	Jamaica	373 (-2)
84	Trinidad & Tobago	369 (-13)
85	Palestine	362 (+9)
86	Qatar	361 (+14)
87	Uganda	358 (-1)
88	Togo	357 (0)
89	Northern Ireland	356 (+1)
89	Iraq	356 (+15)
91	Benin	354 (-4)
92	Estonia	345 (+6)
93	Gabon	344 (-4)
94	China PR	342 (+9)
95	Kenya	339 13)
96	Congo DR	338 (-12)
96	Georgia	338 (0)
98	Zimbabwe	334 (+1)
99	Botswana	332 (-7)
99	Niger	332 (+13)
101	New Zealand	330 (-4)
102	Moldova	325 (-1)
103	Latvia	314 (+6)
104	Lithuania	312 (+2)
105	Bahrain	288 (+5)
106	Tanzania	287 (+7)
107	Kuwait	281 (+8)
108	Luxembourg	278 (+11)

The Netherlands, under coach **Louis van Gaal**, was unbeaten throughout at campaign at the 2014 FIFA World Cup in Brazil for the first time. Its only slips were quarter and semifinal ties against Costa Rica—after which it won the shoot-out—and Argentina, but this time it lost on penalties.

Pos.	Country	Pts (+/-)
109	Rwanda	276 (+7)
110	Ethiopia	273 (-3)
111	Equatorial Guinea	270 (-9)
112	Namibia	264 (+2)
113	Haiti	262 (-40)
114	Mozambique	257 (+4)
115	Sudan	256 (+5)
115	Liberia	256 (+1)
117	Central African Republic	253 (-12)
118	Canada	250 (-8)
119	Lebanon	249 (+6)
120	Cuba	245 (-25)
121	Malawi	234 (+1)
121	El Salvador	234 (-53)
123	Aruba	233 (-3)
124	Tajikistan	232 (+2)
125	Dominican Republic	230 (+6)
126	Burundi	222 (+2)
127	Kazakhstan	220 (-3)
128	Philippines	218 (+1)
129	Afghanistan	217 (+1)
129	Vietnam	217 (-6)
131	Lesotho	213 (+8)
131	Suriname	213 (+5)
133	Mauritania	208 (+4)
134	Guatemala	204 (-7)
135	St Vincent & Grenadines	203 (-2)
136	New Caledonia	199 (+4)
136	Guinea-Bissau	199 (-2)
138	St Lucia	195 (-1)
139	Cyprus	193 (+3)
140	Turkmenistan	183 (+3)
140	Chad	183 (-6)
142	Grenada	182 (+2)
143	Madagascar	179 (+1)
144	Kyrgyzstan	176 (+5)

Pos.	Country	Pts (+/-)
145	Maldives	171 (+2)
146	Syria	169 (-6)
147	Korea DPR	163 (-1)
148	Gambia	161 (0)
149	Antigua and Barbuda	152 (+2)
150	Malta	146 (-18)
151	Malaysia	144 (+2)
151	India	144 (+3)
153	Indonesia	141 (+4)
154	Singapore	140 (+1)
155	Guyana	136 (+1)
156	Puerto Rico	134 (+2)
157	Thailand	128 (-8)
158	St Kitts & Nevis	124 (+2)
159	Swaziland	123 (+14)
160	Myanmar	122 (-1)
161	Belize	117 (-9)
162	Hong Kong	114 (+1)
163	Bangladesh	103 (+4)
164	Nepal	102 (0)
165	Pakistan	100 (-1)
166	Montserrat	99 (0)
167	Liechtenstein	93 (-5)
167	Dominica	93 (+2)
169	Barbados	92 (+1)
170	Laos	87 (-2)
171	Tahiti	85 (-10)
172	Comoros	84 (+2)
173	Bermuda	83 (+2)
174	Guam	79 (+4)
175	Nicaragua	78 (+1)
175	Solomon Islands	78 (+5)
177	São Tomé e Príncipe	72 (-5)
178	Sri Lanka	71 (+1)
178	Chinese Taipei	71 (-2)
180	Yemen	70 (+3)

Pos.	Country	Pts (+/-)
181	Turks and Caicos Islands	66 (+26)
182	Seychelles	64 (-1)
183	Curaçao	63 (-1)
184	Faroe Islands	61 (-13)
185	Mauritius	56 (-1)
186	South Sudan	43 (-1)
187	Vanuatu	38 (+3)
188	Fiji	31 (0)
189	Mongolia	29 (-2)
190	US Virgin Islands	28 (+5)
190	Samoa	28 (-1)
192	Bahamas	26 (-6)
192	Brunei Darussalam	26 (0)
192	Timor(-Leste	26 (0)
192	Tonga	26 (0)
196	Cayman Islands	21 (0)
197	American Samoa	18 (+1)
198	Andorra	16 (+2)
199	Papua New Guinea	14 (-3)
200	Cambodia	13 (-10)
200	British Virgin Islands	13 (-2)
202	Eritrea	11 (-1)
203	Somalia	8 (-1)
204	Macau	7 (-2)
205	Djibouti	6 (-1)
206	Cook Islands	5 (-1)
207	Anguilla	1 (-1)
208	Bhutan	0 (-1)
208	San Marino	0 (-1)

INDEX

PICTURE CREDITS

The publishers would like to thank the following sources for their kind permission to reproduce the pictures in this book. The page numbers for each of the photographs are listed below, giving the page on which they appear in the book and any location indicator (C-center, T-top, B-bottom, L-left, R-right).

Action Images: /Matthew Childs: 133BR

Getty Images: 15TL; /2010 Qatar 2022: 40R; /AFP: 17BR, 25L, 38BR, 93C, 134R, 148B, 157TL, 157BL, 167B, 194BR, 199R, 206BL, 208L, 232BL; /Luis Acosta/AFP: 56BR, 156B; /Nelson Almeida/AFP: 41L; /Anadolu Agency: 32BL, 109BL, 168-169; /Odd Andersen/AFP: 22TR, 39L, 71R, 111C; /Rodrigo Arangua/AFP: 12TL, 152R; /The Asashi Shimbun: 30C; /Anthony Au-Yeung/LatinContent: 10TL; /Brian Bahr: 188BR; /Steve Bardens: 78L; /Dennis Barnard/Fox Photos: 145TL; /Scott Barbour: 170BL; /Lars Baron: 8-9, 98BL, 145B, 173BL, 218-219, 231BR; /Juan Barreto/AFP: 154T; /Farouk Batiche/AFP: 15B; /Robyn Beck/AFP: 35TR; /Sandra Behne/Bongarts: 174BL; /Fethi Belaid/AFP: 161BR; /Bentley Archive/Popperfoto: 23BR, 116C, 117BL; /Martin Bernetti/AFP: 150TR, 155BR; /Gunnar Berning/Bongarts: 31BL; /John Berry: 129BR, 245TL; /Bongarts: 21BL, 74L, 118BR; /Shaun Botterill: 32C, 34BR, 43TR, 44TR, 58T, 99BL, 166TR, 196BR; /Cris Bouroncle/AFP: 220T; /Gabriel Bouys/AFP: 71TL, 80B, 126L; /Chris Brunskill Ltd: 16TC, 20TR, 24BR, 54BL, 226TR; /Clive Brunskill: 151R; /Simon Bruty: 154BR; /Rodrigo Buendia/AFP: 141BL; /Eric Cabanis/AFP: 12R; /Jose Cabezas/AFP: 10TR; /Giuseppe Cacace/AFP: 4B, 51BR, 73T; /David Cannon: 56L, 77R, 88BR, 93BR, 112BR, 144TR, 183TR; /Nico Casamassima/AFP: 38BL; /Mario Castillo/Jam Media/LatinContent: 186BR; /Jean Catuffe: 5BC, 16TR, 26BL, 165B; /Central Press: 115BL; /Central Press/Hulton Archive: 100BR; /Andre Chaco/FotoArena/LatinContent: 37BL; /Graham Chadwick: 112TR; /Yasuyoshi Chiba/AFP: 70TL; /Stanley Chou: 241L; /Chung Sung-Jun: 15TR; /Robert Cianflone: 119T, 121L, 187BR; /Michal Cizek/AFP: 105BC; /Timothy A Clary/AFP: 191BR; /Thomas Coex/AFP: 19R; /Fabrice Coffrini/AFP: 10BR, 30BL, 34BL, 99R, 242-243; /Chris Cole: 32TR, 147BR; / Phil Cole: 95BR, 124C, 162TL, 186BL; /Vinicius Costa: 160TR; /Kevin C Cox: 4R; /Anesh Debiky/Gallo Images: 217TL; /Stephane de Sakutin/AFP: 43L, 213BR; /Carl de Souza/AFP: 27R; /Adrian Dennis/AFP: 31TR, 196TR; /Philippe Desmazes/AFP: 42TR; /Khaled Desouki/AFP: 215BL, 217C; /Dimitar Dilkoff/AFP: 90BL, 106L; /Kevork Djansezian: 189C; /Denis Doyle: 81BR, 84L; /Stephen Dunn: 164BR; /Paul Ellis/AFP: 65C; /Elsa: 46-47, 114L, 155L, 184-185; /Darren England: 12BL, 12BR; /Francisco Estrada/LatinContent: 176BR; /Evening Standard: 172; /Franck Fife/AFP: 59BR, 61TR, 61BR, 163TR, 200TR, 212TC; /Julian Finney: 87TR, 100L, 154L; /Stu Forster: 37TR, 53TL, 94C, 111BL, 130BL, 131BL, 143TL; /Stuart Franklin: 28TL, 39TR, 99T, 244BR, 245BR, 246BR; /Romeo Gacad/AFP: 96C; /Daniel Garcia/AFP: 204BR; /Lluis Gene/AFP: 75TR; /Paul Gilham: 4BR, 81TR, 85TL, 166C; /Georges Gobet/AFP: 97BR; /Sergio Goya/AFP: 204C; /Otto Greule Jr: 188TR; /Laurence Griffiths: 18T, 24L, 67TL, 80R, 94L, 114TR, 140TR, 173R, 183L, 189TR; /Alex Grimm: 4-5C, 85BR, 107TR, 223R; /Jeff Gross: 174TR, 190BR; /Gianluigi Guercia/AFP: 44BL, 69R, 214B; /Jack Guez/AFP: 14BR; /Valery Hache/AFP: 31C, 160C, 198BL; /Matthias Hangst: 143B; /Ronny Hartmann/AFP: 126TR; / Alexander Hassenstein/Bongarts: 60TR, 67R, 174L; /Haynes Archive/Popperfoto: 14TR, 101BR, 205BL; /Richard Heathcote: 165R; /Scott Heavey: 54L, 131T; /Alexander Heimann/ Bongarts: 191BL; /Marcelo Hernandez/LatinContent: 151TL; /Patrick Hertzog/AFP: 57BR, 60R, 79BR, 128TR; /Mike Hewitt: 4TR, 103BR, 106B, 149BL, 226L, 229L, 233TR, 233BL; / Antonia Hille: 136C; /Boris Horvat/AFP: 76BL, 197L; /Hulton Archive: 22BL, 30BR, 101TR; /isifa: 121BR; /Karim Jaafar/AFP: 167L, 170C, 175TN, 176L, 179BR; /Amin Mohammad Jamali: 2, 5TL, 85BL; /Alexander Joe/AFP: 215TL; /Jose Jordan/AFP: 84BR; /Jasper Juinen: 52C, 82C, 83TL, 196L; /Gorm Kallestad/AFP: 104BL; /Keystone: 56TR, 100BL, 115BR; /Keystone/Hulton Archive: 69BL, 83BL; /Saeed Khan/AFP: 10BL; /Ian Kington/AFP: 54TR; /Ross Kinnaird: 26TR; /Pedro Kirilos/LatinContent: 43R; /Glyn Kirk/AFP: 229BR; /Toshifumi Kitamura/AFP: 13C, 88T; /Joe Klamar/AFP: 95L, 105TR; /Christof Koepsel: 225C, 226BL; /Mark Kolbe: 171TL; /Patrick Kovarik/AFP: 135C; /Kirill Kudryavtsev/AFP: 43B, 114B; /LatinContent: 202-203; /David Leah: 29TL; /David Leah/Mexsport: 186TR; /Christopher Lee: 120TR, 121TR, 123C; /Bryn Lennon: 110TR; /Francisco Leong/AFP: 62TR, 115C; /Matthew Lewis: 25B, 106TR; /Alex Livesey: 11TR, 23R, 76BR, 92TR, 96TR, 103TR, 115TL, 123TL, 130C, 149R, 177BR, 201TR, 224L, 248-249; /Juan Mabromata/AFP: 89TL; /John MacDougall/AFP: 113BR; /Ian MacNicol: 5BL, 22TR; /Pierre-Philippe Marcou/AFP: 24TR, 82TL, 164TL; /Francois-Xavier Marit/AFP: 35TL, 48-49; /Clive Mason: 19BL, 64L, 87BR, 92BL, 95TR, 125C, 127BL, 165TL; /Jamie McDonald: 45, 76T, 94BR, 100TR, 110C, 122TR, 180TL, 187C, 221BR, 223BL, 251TL; /Chris McGrath: 141TR; /Miguel Medina/AFP: 57TR; /Buda Mendes: 7, 138-139; /Buda Mendes/LatinContent: 153TR, 207TR; /Philippe Merle/AFP: 157R; /Damien Meyer/AFP: 192-193, 251TR; /Douglas Miller/Keystone: 50BL; /Sandra Montanez: 239T; /Filippo Monteforte/AFP: 132C; /Dean Mouhtaropoulos: 21TR, 171TR; /Peter Muhly/AFP: 110BR, 134BL; /Marwan Naamani/AFP: 180BR; /Jonathan Nackstrand/AFP: 199L; /Hoang Dinh Nam/AFP: 178BL, 188C; /Mark Nolan: 171BR; /Jeff Pachoud/AFP: 195C; /Valerio Pennicino: 69TL; /Doug Pensinger: 52BR; /Ryan Pierse: 28B, 132BL, 182TR, 190L; /Jan Pitman/Bongarts: 36TR; /Hrvoje Polan/AFP: 90C, 92C; /Joern Pollex: 62BL, 66R, 97TL, 163C, 222C; /Popperfoto: 13BR, 21BR, 23L, 28C, 51C, 58BL, 64BR, 66BL, 67B, 72BR, 91BR, 102BL, 112L, 122C, 148L, 151BL, 175L, 178R, 179T, 181B, 189BL, 194BL, 198TR, 200B, 207BL, 208BR, 228BL; /Anne-Christine Poujoulat/AFP: 109BR; /Mike Powell: 40L; /Savo Prelevic/AFP: 137B; /Craig Prentis: 187TR; /Adam Pretty: 147TR; / Gary M Prior: 148TR; /Ben Radford: 29BR, 149C, 173T; /Roslan Rahman/AFP: 181TR; /Aizar Raldes/AFP: 156TL; /David Ramos: 244TL; /Michael Regan: 50TR, 55TR, 128B, 131BR; /Chris Ricco/Backpagepix: 217BR; /Rafa Rivas/AFP: 83R; /Miguel Rojo/AFP: 142TL, 157TR, 209TL; /Rolls Press/Popperfoto: 53B, 71B, 146TR; /Quinn Rooney: 241BC; /Clive Rose: 17TR, 22TL, 33BL, 34TL, 36BL, 52TL, 117C, 119BL, 129BL, 144BL, 152BL; /Martin Rose: 59C, 63TR, 234-235; /Martin Rose/Bongarts: 127TR, 132BR, 247; /STR/AFP: 137TR, 177TR; /Jewel Samad/ AFP: 109TR; /Mark Sandten/Bongarts: 39BR, 162BL; /Issouf Sanogo/AFP: 163BL, 167TR; /Genia Savilov/AFP: 107L; /Roberto Schmidt/AFP: 18TL; /Antonio Scorza/AFP: 153BL; /Abdelhak Senna/AFP: 216; /Lefty Shivambu/Gallo Images: 166L, 212TR, 213TR, 215C; /Torsten Silz/AFP: 25TR; /Janek Skarzynski/AFP: 201BL; /Javier Soriano/AFP: 17L, 158-159, 197BR; /Jamie Squire: 160BR, 161TL; /Michael Steele: 34TR, 91T, 122BL; /Srdjan Stevanovic: 119R; /Patrik Stollarz/AFP: 5C, 38TR, 64TR, 135BL; /Stringer/AFP: 127BR; /Graham Stuart/AFP: 116TR; / Henri Szwarc/Bongarts: 195B; /Bob Thomas: 36C, 42B, 44BR, 65R, 68TR, 70BL, 70BR, 86TR, 97R, 102TR, 103C, 103BL, 107BR, 108TR, 110BL, 150BL, 116L, 130TR, 130BR, 142BR, 143C, 146BL, 153BR, 161TR, 175BR; /Bob Thomas/Popperfoto: 11B, 38TC, 66TL, 84TR, 136BL, 145TR; /Mark Thompson: 104TR, 212BR; /John Thys/AFP: 88BR, 89R, 135R; /Omar Torres/AFP: 176TR, 209BR; /Pedro Ugarte/AFP: 27B; /VI Images: 75TL, 78B, 79T; /Robert van den Brugge/AFP: 86BL; /Manus van Dyk/Gallo Images: 214L; /Claudio Villa: 73BL, 136BR; /Claudio Villa/Grazia Neri: 72TR; /Friedemann Vogel: 236C; /Nigel Waldon: 105BL; /Ian Walton: 77BL, 82B, 190TR, 210-211, 215R; /Koji Watanabe: 228TR

Press Association Images: 118TR, 142R, 206BR, 229TR; /ABACA Press: 19TL; /AP: 20BL; /Matthew Ashton: 147C, 171C, 182BL, 191TR, 238BR; /Greg Baker/AP: 237BL; /Jon Buckle: 239BR; /Roberto Candia/AP: 237TL; /Barry Coombs: 98TR; /Malcolm Croft: 13TL; /Claudio Cruz/AP: 224C; /DPA: 16BL, 60L, 65TL, 75B, 170TR; /Adam Davy: 236B; /Sean Dempsey: 63BR; /Paulo Duarte/AP: 108L, 108C; /Denis Farrell/AP: 40B; /Dominic Favre/AP: 124BR; /Gouhier-Hahn-Orban/ABACA: 124TR; /Michel Gouverneur/Reporter: 222BL; /Jae C Hong/AP: 183B; /Intime Sports/AP: 98C; /Silvia Izquierdo/AP: 232L, 232R; /Julie Jacobson/AP: 238TL, 241BR; /Lee Jin-Man/AP: 238TR; /Ross Kinnaird: 207C; /Tony Marshall: 21TL, 72L, 77TL, 126BL, 146TL, 205TR, 221TL, 224TR, 225TR, 230; /Cathal McNaughton: 50C; /Phil O'Brien: 68BL; /Panoramic: 222R; /Eraldo Peres/AP: 231BL; /Natacha Pisarenko/AP: 208C; /Nick Potts: 57BL; /Duncan Raban: 144BR; /Peter Robinson: 33TR, 63L, 73BR, 74TR, 102C, 116BR, 118L, 120BL, 129TR, 140L, 220BL, 220BR; /S&G and Barratts: 30TR, 51T, 53TR, 55B, 108BR, 111BR; /SMG: 117TR; /Ariel Schalit/AP: 162R; /Murad Sezer/AP: 61C; /Matthias Schrader/AP: 240BR; /Sven Simon: 146BR; /Neal Simpson: 89BL, 91BL, 113TR, 125BR, 206T; /Michael Sohn/AP: 240TR; /Jon Super/AP: 227, 237TR; /Topham Picturepoint: 123BL, 134TL, 140B; /John Walton: 133TR, 143TR; /Witters: 35B

Every effort has been made to acknowledge correctly and contact the source and/or copyright holder of each picture and Carlton Books Limited apologizes for any unintentional errors or omissions that will be corrected in future editions of this book.

ABOUT THE AUTHOR

Keir Radnedge has been covering soccer for more than 40 years. He has written countless books on the subject, from tournament guides to comprehensive encyclopedias, aimed at all ages. His journalism career included the *Daily Mail* for 20 years, as well as the *Guardian* and other national newspapers and magazines in the UK and abroad. He is a former editor of *World Soccer*, generally recognized as the premier English-language magazine on global soccer. In addition to his writing, Keir has been a regular analyst for BBC radio and television, Sky Sports and the American cable news channel CNN. He also edited a tournament newspaper at the FIFA World Cup tournaments of 1982, 1986, and 1990. He has also scripted video reviews of numerous international soccer tournaments. He is also the London-based editor of SportsFeatures.com, the soccer and Olympic news website.